Rescued by

A+ CERTIFICATION

EXAM PREPARATION

Kris Jamsa, PhD, MBA

THOMSON

DELMAR LEARNING ™

Australia • Canada • Mexico • Singapore • Spain • United Kingdom • United States

OnWord Press

Rescued by A+ Certification Exam Preparation
by Kris Jamsa

Business Unit Director:
Alar Elken

Channel Manager:
Fair Huntoon

Technical Editor:
Phillip Schmauder

Executive Editor:
Sandy Clark

Marketing Coordinator:
Brian McGrath

Editorial Assistant:
Jennifer M. Luck

Senior Acquisitions Editor:
Gregory L. Clayton

Executive Production Manager:
Mary Ellen Black

Art/Design Coordinator:
David Arsenault

Senior Development Editor:
Michelle Ruelos Cannistraci

Production Manager:
Larry Main

Cover Design:
Design Graphx

Executive Marketing Manager:
Maura Theriault

Senior Project Editor:
Christopher Chien

Full Production Services:
Liz Kingslien

ISBN 0-7668-5007-2

NOTICE TO THE READER

TABLE OF CONTENTS

LESSON 4

Installing, Removing, and Troubleshooting Software

LESSON 5

Getting a Handle on Kilo, Mega, Giga, and Tera)

LESSON 6

Understanding the PC Startup Process

LESSON 7

Inside the System Unit

LESSON 8

Understanding Device Drivers

LESSON 9

Working with Cards and Chips

LESSON 10

Taking a Closer Look at Common Cables and Ports

LESSON 11

Working with the Keyboard and Mouse

LESSON 12

Locating a Lost File

LESSON 13

Restarting Windows and Ending Hung Programs

LESSON 14

Cleaning and Maintaining Your PC

LESSON 15

Protecting a System from Viruses

LESSON 16

Understanding the PC BIOS

LESSON 17

Taking a Closer Look at the Windows Control Panel

LESSON 22

Understanding the CPU

LESSON 23

Understanding Random-Access Memory (RAM)

LESSON 24

Making Sense of PC Memory Technologies

LESSON 25

Understanding Virtual Memory

LESSON 26

Configuring the PC's CMOS Settings

LESSON 27

Understanding PC Bus Types

LESSON 28

Understanding Interrupts and I/O Port Addresses

LESSON 29

Understanding Direct Memory Access (DMA)

LESSON 30

Connecting Devices to a SCSI Adapter

LESSON 31

Using a Universal Serial Bus (USB)

LESSON 32

Using FireWire and InfraRed Devices

LESSON 33

Taking Advantage of Plug-and-Play Devices

LESSON 34

Taking Advantage of PCMCIA Cards

LESSON 35

Introduction to Networking

LESSON 36

Understanding the ISO/OSI Network Model

LESSON 37

Understanding Network Technologies

LESSON 38

Getting Started with TCP/IP High-Speed Internet Connections

LESSON 39

Configuring a TCP/IP Network

LESSON 40

Using a Notebook Computer

LESSON 41

Supporting Handheld Personal Digital Assistants

LESSON 42

Understanding How Disks Store Data

LESSON 43

Using ScanDisk to Locate and Correct Disk Errors

LESSON 49

Performing Monitor Operations

LESSON 50

Taking a Closer Look at Video Operations

LESSON 51

Understanding PC Printer Operations

LESSON 52

Taking a Closer Look at Laser Printer Operations

Find Answers to Your A+ Certification Questions on the Web

To help you better prepare for the A+ Certification exam, each of this book's lessons ends with review questions that examine key concepts you must know. You can find the answers to each of the questions at the *Rescued by A+ Certification* Web site, which you can access through *www.onwordpress.com*.

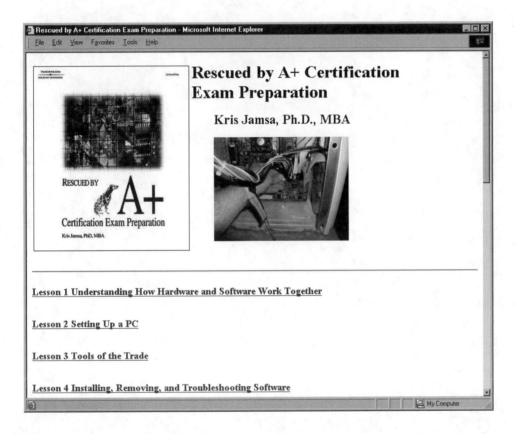

Figure 1 Find answers to the end of lesson questions at the *Rescued by A+ Certification* Web site.

Dedication

To Sandie,

For your friendship, support, and positive thoughts.

Lesson 1

Understanding How Hardware and Software Work Together

As you prepare for the A+ Certification Exam, you will improve your knowledge and understanding of key system components by understanding the individual roles that hardware and software play in the component's operation. In addition, as you troubleshoot problems, you will find that you will save considerable time and effort in resolving the problem by first determining whether the problem is hardware based or software based.

Throughout this book's lessons, you will examine specific hardware devices and key software in detail. This lesson's purpose is to help you start evaluating the PC and its devices in terms of the hardware itself and the software that allows the device to perform its task.

F A C T S

- Hardware consists of the PC's components that you can see and touch. The keyboard, mouse, monitor, printer, and system unit are hardware components. Within the system unit, the motherboard and the chips it houses are also hardware.

- Software is another term for computer programs. A computer program is simply a list of instructions the CPU executes to perform a specific task.

- Programmers create programs by using a programming language to specify the instructions the CPU must perform to accomplish a specific task.

- Programs reside on disk within files that use the *.exe* (for executable) or *.com* (for command) file extensions.

- The PC works in terms of ones and zeros. Within the PC, the electronic components can use the value 1 to represent the presence of a signal on a wire and the value 0 to represent the signal's absence.

- An executable program file (a file with the *.exe* or *.com* extension) contains the ones and zeros that represent the instructions the CPU is to execute to accomplish a task.

- Users frequently categorize software as either application or system software.

- Application software consists of the programs you run to perform a specific operation, such as a word processor, e-mail program, Web browser, or drawing program.

- System software corresponds to software that runs behind the scenes, such as the Windows operating system that oversees the PC's resource use or the network software that a Web browser or e-mail program use to access the Internet.

- The operating system (Windows) is the first program the PC runs. After the operating system is running, the user can use the operating system to run other programs.

- The operating system's two primary roles are to let the user run programs and to let the user store and retrieve information that resides within files on disk.

3

FACTS

- Users often describe the operating system as the PC's resource manager.

- As programs run, they will often take advantage of library files that contain instructions the CPU can execute to perform a specific operation, such as displaying text and graphics on the screen, accessing information from a network, or printing a document's contents. Users refer to the library files as dynamic link library files or simply DLL files.

- When you install new software, the installation programs may overwrite one or more DLL files on your disk with a newer version of the library. Unfortunately, the newer version of the DLL file may not be compatible with your existing programs, which causes one or more programs to stop working. As you troubleshoot system errors, you must pay close attention to the version numbers of the DLL files the system is running.

Hardware Consists of Components You Can Touch

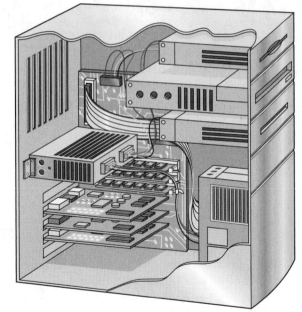

Hardware consists of the PC's physical components, such as the keyboard, mouse, monitor, system unit, and printer, as shown in Figure 1.1. In addition, you should categorize the cables that connect a printer, network card, or other device to the PC as hardware. Many users describe hardware as the PC components you can physically touch. Within the PC's system unit, the cards and chips, such as the motherboard, the CPU, and the PC's random access memory (RAM) are also hardware.

Figure 1.1 Examples of PC hardware.

Software Consists of Computer Programs

Software is simply another term for computer programs. A computer program is simply a list of instructions the CPU executes to accomplish a specific task. A word processor, Web browser, and even Windows itself are software programs.

Programmers create programs using a programming language such as Visual Basic, C++, or Java. There are literally thousands of programming languages. However, most programmers use only a few key programming languages.

In general, to create a program, a programmer specifies the instructions the CPU must perform to accomplish a specific task. A programming language lets the programmer specify the instructions in a human-readable form. The following statements, for example, show the C++ statements a programmer would write to display the message "Hello A+ World" on the screen display:

```
void main (void)
{
   cout << "Hello A+ World";
}
```

Although you may not understand the program statements (unless you are a C++ programmer), you can at least read the statements. Years ago (in the late 1940s and 1950s), programmers had to write programs using the ones and zeros the computer understood. To specify the previous program using ones and zeros, the programmer might have to use a combination of 500 or more ones and zeros. If the programmer inadvertently transposed a one and zero, the program would not work. As you can imagine, writing and later troubleshooting programs based on ones and zeros was very difficult and quite time consuming. Programming languages provide programmers with a much easier way to specify program instructions.

Computers work in terms of ones and zeros. You can think of the PC's low-level circuitry as consisting of switches that either allow or deny the presence of a signal on a wire. The PC can represent the signal's presence or absence using the values 1 and 0. Users often refer to computer operations as binary operations. The binary number system presents values using ones and zeros.

After a programmer uses a programming language to create a program, the programmer then uses a special program called a compiler to convert the instructions from the programming language that the programmer understands into the ones and zeros the CPU understands. The compiler stores the program's ones and zeros in a file that uses the *.exe* (for executable) file extension.

Before the CPU can execute (run) a program, the program's instructions and data must reside within the PC's RAM. When you run Microsoft Word, for example, Windows will load the contents of the file *Winword.exe* into RAM. Then, the CPU will begin to execute the program's instructions.

Understanding How Hardware and Software Work Together

As you use your PC, the hardware components actually perform the bulk of the work. The monitor, for example, displays images. The printer prints documents. The keyboard and mouse respond to user operations. Without hardware, there would be no reason for software.

That said, hardware would be of little use without the software (the instructions) telling the hardware what operations to perform.

Categorizing Software

Users often categorize software as application or system software. Application software consists of the programs you run to accomplish a specific task, such as using a word processor to create a document or a Web browser to surf the World Wide Web. Examples of application software include:

- An e-mail program you use to send and receive messages
- A database program you use to store and retrieve data
- A computer-based game
- A photo-editing program you use to manipulate images
- An accounting or tax program

System software consists of programs such as the operating system that exist to perform key operations other programs require in order to operate. Before your PC can use a hardware device such as a modem or network interface card, your system must have special software installed called a device driver that lets programs interact with the device. Examples of system software include:

- The Windows operating system
- Device driver software
- Security software that limits network access

Understanding the Role of the Operating System

Each time the PC starts, the first program the PC runs is the operating system (normally Windows). After the operating system is up and running, users can then run other programs, such as their e-mail software, word processor, and Web browser.

In general, the operating system exists to let users run programs and save and retrieve information from files on disk. You can think of the operating system as the PC's resource manager. The operating system oversees, for example, which programs can use a device and when, how much memory a program can use, the locations on disk where a program stores data, and so on. Within the Windows operating system, a user can run several programs at the same time. The operating system resolves conflicts that may occur, such as when a program tries to send data to the printer and the printer is already in use by other application.

Behind the scenes, the operating system provides special software called device drivers that provide the instructions the CPU executes in order to interact with a device. Each device on your system requires a unique device driver. Without the device-driver software, programs could not use a device. Lesson 6, "Understanding Device Drivers," examines device-driver operations in detail. After you install a new hardware device, you must load the corresponding device-driver software on to your system before you can use the device.

Most users think of Windows as simply one large program. As it turns out, Windows consists of hundreds of programs, most of which run behind the scenes. Using the System Information utility, you can, as shown in Figure 1.2, list the programs your PC is currently running by performing these steps:

1. Select the Start menu Programs option and choose Accessories. Windows will display the Accessories submenu.
2. Within the Accessories submenu, select the System Tools option and choose System Information. Windows will run the System Information utility.

3. Within the System Information utility, click on the plus sign that precedes the Software Environment. The System Information utility will display a branch of options.

4. Within the option branch, select the Running Tasks entry. The System Information utility will list the programs your system is currently running, as shown in Figure 1.2.

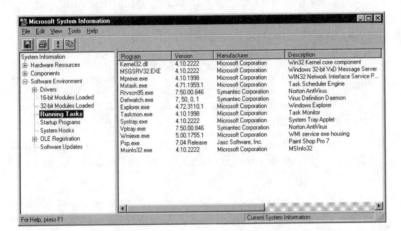

Figure 1.2 Displaying a list of programs a PC is currently running.

Understanding How Windows Uses DLL Files

The program files (*.exe* files) that reside on your disk contain the binary instructions the CPU executes to accomplish a specific task. In addition to the *.exe* file, most Windows-based programs make extensive use of special library files that users refer to as dynamic link library or more simply DLL files. As you might guess, the dynamic link libraries reside in files with the *.dll* extension.

In general, a DLL file contains instructions that correspond to specific operations. One DLL file might contain instructions that let a program interact with a network. A second DLL file may contain instructions that let a program display text and graphics within a window on the screen. Yet another DLL file may provide instructions a program can use to send a document to the printer.

By taking advantage of the instructions that reside in DLL files, programmers eliminate their need to write the instructions for these difficult operations.

When you install Windows, the installation process may place a thousand or more DLL files onto your hard drive. Each of these DLL files contains instructions that correspond to a specific task. When you install new software on a PC, there may be times when the installation replaces an existing DLL file within a newer version. Unfortunately, the newer DLL file is not always compatible with your older programs. As a result, programs that previously ran before you performed the installation may stop running.

In some cases, when you install a new hardware device, the Setup program that installs the device's drivers may also update one or more DLL files on your system. Should you encounter errors following the installation, you would first believe the device's hardware might be to blame. However, the cause of the error may be the device's software.

Throughout this book's lessons, you will examine tools you can use to detect and troubleshoot DLL-based errors. To better understand the number of DLL files your system is using, you can view the loaded DLL files within the System Information utility, as shown in Figure 1.3, by performing these steps:

1. Select the Start menu Programs option and choose Accessories. Windows will display the Accessories submenu.

2. Within the Accessories submenu, select the System Tools option and choose System Information. Windows will run the System Information utility.

3. Within the System Information utility, click on the plus sign that precedes the Software Environment list. The System Information utility will display a branch of options.

4. Within the option branch, select 16-bit Loaded Modules or 32-bit Loaded Modules if you are using Windows 98 or Loaded Modules under Windows 2000. The System Information utility will list the DLL files your system is currently running, as shown in Figure 1.3.

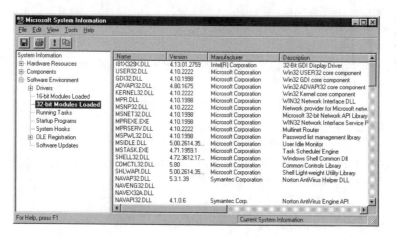

Figure 1.3 Viewing specifics about the DLL files Windows is currently using.

Firmware—the Gray Line Between Hardware and Software

As you have learned, hardware consists of chips, cards, cables, covers, and the other items you can touch. In contrast, software consists of program instructions the CPU executes.

Within the PC, however, you will encounter some chips, such as the BIOS chip which oversees the PC startup operations and power on self-test, that contain built-in instructions the CPU executes. Based on the previous definitions, the fact that the BIOS resides on a chip would make it hardware. Similarly, because the chip contains program instructions, one could argue that the chip is software.

Users frequently refer to chips that contain program instructions as firmware.

Revisiting the Distinction Between Hardware and Software

As you troubleshoot user systems, you must first determine if the cause of an error is hardware or software related. Then, you can proceed accordingly to resolve the error.

If you work in an office that contains many PCs, identifying an error as hardware based may be as easy as removing a suspect card from one system and replacing it with a card from another. If the second card works, the first card is bad.

As you will learn, detecting software errors can be more challenging. Fortunately, throughout this book's lessons you will examine many tools you can use to detect software errors.

EXAM REVIEW

CERTIFICATION

① _____ is the term that describes the PC's physical components, such as the keyboard, monitor, and mouse.

② _____ is another term for computer programs.

③ A computer program is a list of _____ the CPU executes to perform a specific task.

④ DLL is an acronym for _____.

⑤ True or False
DLL files contain instructions programs can use to accomplish a specific task.

⑥ Users categorize software as either _____ or _____ software.

⑦ Which of the following are examples of application programs:

- ☐ Word processor
- ☐ Spreadsheet program
- ☐ Web browser
- ☐ TCP/IP network software
- ☐ Windows
- ☐ PC-based video games

Setting Up a PC

Whether you manage hundreds of PCs within an office or simply your own home PC, you will eventually need to set up the PC, either because you have purchased a new system or because you must move your existing system.

This lesson examines the steps you must perform to set up a PC. To reduce the number of technical support calls to which their staff must respond, most PC manufacturers have gone to great lengths to simplify the setup process. Today, most cables are color coded to match the corresponding port on the back of the PC system unit.

Finally, this lesson will examine several steps you can perform to troubleshoot common setup problems.

F A C T S

✛ Ideally, before you set up your PC, you should select a workspace that is well lit and that provides you with ample space to place your working documents.

✛ As you position your PC system unit, make sure you provide adequate space for venting the hot air your PC generates. Do not place your system unit close to a wall or desk in a way that prevents the system unit fan from dispensing the hot air the PC's electronics create.

✛ If you work in a dry environment, you may need to introduce a source of humidity into your office or use a special carpet spray to reduce the risk of electrostatic discharge (a static shock) that can damage your PC's sensitive electronic components.

✛ To reduce the possibility of an electrical spike damaging your PC, monitor, or other key components, you should plug your hardware devices into a surge suppressor.

✛ To simplify the PC setup process, most PCs either color code ports and their matching cables or place small icons next to ports that correspond to the device you should connect to that port.

Selecting the Proper Work Area

Although it may seem quite obvious, the selection of a proper work area will impact your PC use on a daily basis. Ideally, you should select a workspace that satisfies the following conditions:

• A well-lit area that makes it easy for you to view not only your computer monitor, but also the documents that you place on your desk.

• An area that provides adequate space for your working documents (print outs) and reference materials (books and magazines).

• An area that lets you align your monitor with respect to a window to reduce glare.

• An area that provides sufficient space between your PC and your desk or wall, so that the fans on the back on the PC system unit can vent the heat generated by the PC's electronic components.

Depending on the location of electrical plugs, phone jacks, and network connections, you may have to place cables across your floor. To reduce the risk of someone tripping on or damaging the cables, you should place the cables within a plastic cable cover.

Although you may not be able to control some environmental factors, such as heat or cold in a warehouse, you should keep in mind that temperature extremes may cause the PC to experience intermittent errors that are very difficult to troubleshoot. Also, environments that are dry pose a greater risk of static electricity. Often, in a very dry environment, users will place a humidifier or plants the into room to increase humidity. Further, they might use an antistatic spray on the carpet to reduce electrostatic shocks.

Start with a Surge Suppressor

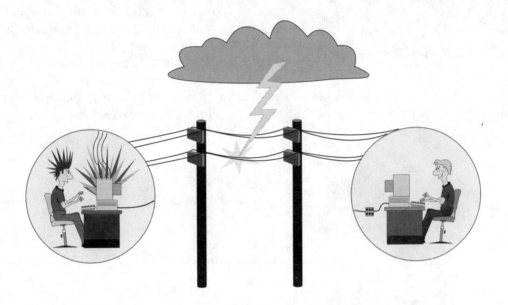

When you set up a PC, you should first start by attaching the PC's power cords to a surge suppressor similar to that shown in Figure 2.1. By using a surge suppressor, you reduce the risk of a power spike (which may be caused by lightning or a problem with a local electrical substation) from damaging your PC and its sensitive electronic components.

Do not yet connect the power cords to the PC, monitor, or printer. You will first connect devices such as your printer, mouse, keyboard, and speakers to your PC before you plug in and power on your system.

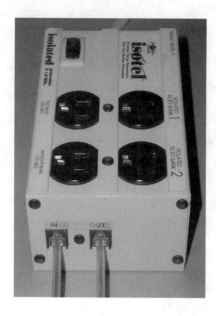

Figure 2.1 Plug your PC and other devices into a surge suppressor to reduce the risk of damage from an electrical spike.

NOTE: *As you shop for a surge suppressor, do not confuse a power strip that lets you plug multiple devices into a single outlet with a surge suppressor that provides protection from electrical spikes. A power strip provides no such protection.*

Connecting Your Mouse and Keyboard

In Lesson 11, "Working with the Keyboard and Mouse," you will learn that depending on their keyboard and mouse types, users can connect the devices to the PC in a variety of ways. Most users, however, connect the mouse and keyboard using a 6-pin DIN connector, as shown in Figure 2.2. Because the mouse and keyboard use similar connectors, most PC's color code the ports and cables or place a small keyboard or mouse icon next to the corresponding port.

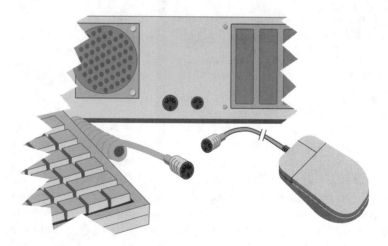

Figure 2.2 Most users connect a mouse and keyboard using 6-pin DIN connectors.

To reduce wrist strain, many users will place a small pad in front of their keyboard. Further, some users find that a track ball creates less strain on their wrist than a traditional mouse.

Connecting the Monitor

As shown in Figure 2.3, a monitor normally attaches to a 15-pin connector that corresponds to the video card that resides within the PC system unit. After you connect the monitor to the PC, you can plug in the monitor's power cord.

After you power on your PC and monitor for the first time, you may need to align the image the monitor displays by moving the image up or down or right to left. As you will learn in Lesson 49, "Performing Monitor Operations," you can use the buttons that appear on the front of the monitor to adjust the image alignment and brightness.

Figure 2.3 Connect the monitor's 15-pin male connector to the matching port on the back of the PC system unit.

Your monitor's position can impact your comfort while you work at your PC and how your neck, shoulders, and back will feel after you spend hours in front of the PC. Ideally, as shown in Figure 2.4, you should position your monitor so that the top of the monitor is slightly below your eyes.

Figure 2.4 To reduce neck and eye strain, users often place their monitor so that the top of the monitor is slightly below the height of their eyes.

Connecting Your Printer

Depending on your printer type, how you connect your printer to your PC may differ. To start, all printers support a parallel connection that uses a cable with a 25-pin connector to connect the printer to the PC. As shown in Figure 2.5, you should attach the cable's 25-pin male connector to the PC and the "Centronix" connector to the printer.

Figure 2.5 Parallel printers use a cable that has a 25-pin male connector at one end and Centronix at the other end.

In addition to supporting a parallel-port interface, many newer laser printers provide a network connector that you can use to attach the printer directly to the network. Even if you do not plan on sharing the printer (which might be the case for a home PC), an advantage of connecting a printer directly to the network is speed. A standard parallel port supports a data transfer rate of 150KBs, whereas most networks support speeds of 10Mbs to 100Mbs.

In Lesson 10, "Taking a Closer Look at Common Cables and Ports," you will learn that most PCs provide an extended capabilities port (ECP) or enhanced parallel port (EPP) that supports bi-directional communication and high data rates of up to 2MBs. After you connect the printer to the PC, you must plug in the printer's power cord.

Connecting Speakers to the PC

Today, most PCs ship with speakers that you can use to play back voice, sounds, and music. In addition, most PCs come with a microphone you can use to record sounds. Depending on your sound card type, the number of ports that appear on the card may differ. Normally, as shown in Figure 2.6, sound cards support three ports, one for speakers, one for an external audio input, and one for a microphone.

Figure 2.6 Most sound cards provide ports you can use to connect speakers, a microphone, and an external audio device.

As shown in Figure 2.7, some sound cards and speakers provide a volume control knob. Take time to examine your sound card and speakers. If either contains a volume control knob and you have problems adjusting the volume in Windows to a level that you desire, you may first need to establish a base-level volume using the volume control knobs knobs, which you can later fine-tune using the Windows volume controls.

Figure 2.7 Many sound cards and speakers provide volume control knobs.

Connecting a Modem

Today users connect PCs to various modem types that include traditional dial-up modems, such as that shown in Figure 2.8, and high-speed DSL and cable modems. If you use a dial-up modem, make sure you insert the phone-jack cable into the modem port labeled Line. If you want to use the phone jack with a phone when the modem is not in use, connect the phone to the modem port labeled Phone.

Figure 2.8 Connecting a phone cable to a dial-up modem.

If you are using a DSL or cable modem, the modem will connect to either a network interface card or universal serial bus.

Connecting Your PC to a Network

Because of the complexity of network operations, this book presents five different lessons that examine specific network operations. That said, depending on your network type, the way you connect your PC to a network may vary. Fortunately, in an office environment, the network administrator will normally connect your PC to the network for you. The most common network connection uses an RJ-45 adapter, as shown in Figure 2.9. The RJ-45 connector contains 8 wires and looks like a large version of a standard phone plug. If you use a cable modem or DSL modem to connect your PC to a high-speed Internet connection, you will likely use an RJ-45 cable to connect the modem to a network interface card that resides inside your PC.

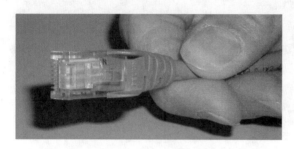

Figure 2.9 Most users connect their PC to a network hub using an RJ-45 connector.

Extending a Cable

Depending on your workspace, there may be times when a cable you use to connect your printer, mouse, keyboard, monitor, or other device to your PC does not quite reach the device location you desire. Normally, you can purchase an extension cable that extends a cable by six feet or more. By using cable extensions, you can position devices in the locations that best suit your needs.

Plugging in the PC

The last step you should perform when you set up a PC is to plug in the PC system unit. By plugging in the system unit last, you ensure that you do not attach a device to a system unit that is powered on, which could damage either the PC or the device.

Before you plug in the PC, make sure that you left sufficient space between the PC and your desk or wall, into which the PC can vent the heat its electronic components generate. Finally, you are ready to plug in and power on your printer, monitor, and PC system unit.

If you are starting a PC for the first time, the PC may begin the Windows installation. Most PC manufacturers preload Windows on the PC's hard drive, so that after you power on your PC for the first time, you can complete the installation process by customizing various Windows settings to best suit your needs.

Troubleshooting the PC Setup

Throughout this book, you will examine specific steps you can follow to troubleshoot various PC components. This section will examine a few common setup problems.

You do not hear the PC's fan whir—After you power on your PC, should immediately hear the whir of the fan that resides inside the PC power supply. If your PC does not start and you do not hear the fan whir, double check your power cords and power plug. If you are using a surge suppressor, make sure the suppressor is powered on and that the suppressor has not thrown an internal breaker which you must reset.

The monitor does not display text or graphics—Normally, after you power on your PC, your monitor will display text messages that describe your PC manufacturer, BIOS type, RAM, and so on. Eventually, the PC should display the Windows graphical user interface. If your monitor does not display text or graphics, check the monitor's power cord and cable connection. In any event, do not open your monitor case. As you will learn in Lesson 49, the monitor contains a high-voltage capacitor that can produce an electrical shock sufficient to kill you.

The monitor displays a message about a keyboard error—Most PCs will not start without a keyboard attached to the system unit. If, during the system startup, your monitor displays an error message about a keyboard error, double check the cable that connects your keyboard to the system unit. Also, make sure you do not have a book or another object that is inadvertently depressing a keyboard key.

Your mouse pointer does not move as you move your mouse—After Windows displays its graphical user interface, your monitor should move the mouse pointer across the screen as you move the mouse across your desktop. If your mouse pointer does not move, double check the cable that connects the mouse to the system unit. Because of its simple electronics, a mouse seldom fails. However, if you have a second identical mouse available, you may want see if your system will respond to the second mouse. Before you attach the second mouse, shut down and power off your system.

Your PC does not generate sounds—If your PC does not generate sounds, either for music, voice, or standard Windows sounds, first use the Control Panel Sounds icon to make sure that Windows does not have sounds muted. Then, check your sound card or speakers to see if there is a volume control knob you may need to adjust. Finally, double check your cable connectors to ensure that you have the speakers connected to the correct port.

Your printer does not print—Before you can send jobs to a printer, your system must have a device driver installed for the printer. Using the printer's Properties dialog box, try sending a test page to the printer. Double check the cable that connects your printer to the system unit. If you are using a network connection, make sure that your network software is functioning properly. Also, you may need to enable the printer's support of network operations using the menu that appears on the front of the printer.

Your modem cannot establish a dial-up connection—Troubleshooting modem operations can be challenging. If your PC cannot establish a modem connection, make sure that you have connected the cable from the wall outlet to the modem port labeled Line (as opposed to the port labeled Phone). You may want to unplug the modem and then use a standard phone to make sure that the phone jack is working properly.

Your PC does not see computers in the network—If you connect your PC to a local-area network and you cannot see other PCs or printers within the Network Neighborhood folder, first double check the cable that connects your PC's network interface card to the network. Then, you may need to configure the PC's network settings as discussed in Lesson 39, "Configuring a TCP/IP Network."

EXAM REVIEW

1. **True or False**
   To prevent a power spike from damaging your PC components, you should plug your hardware devices into a power strip.

2. **True or False**
   If you work in a humid environment, your PC and its sensitive electronic components are at a high risk of damage from electrostatic discharge.

3. **True or False**
   You can use an extension cable to extend the cable length of most devices you attach to your PC.

4. If you do not hear the PC fan whir when you power on your PC, you should first check _____.

5. **True or False**
   The monitor contains a capacitor that maintains a potentially fatal voltage, even after it has been unplugged and powered off for an extended period of time. To avoid electrocution, users should not open the monitor case.

Lesson 3

Tools of the Trade

If you are like many PC technicians, you probably own a variety of screwdrivers, wire-crimping devices, and anti-static bags. Unfortunately, when you need the tools, you may not have them, or worse yet, you may not remember where you left them.

As you troubleshoot systems, having the correct tools available for the task at hand can save you a considerable amount of time and frustration. This lesson examines several key items you should have in your PC toolkit.

F · A · C · T · S

- To reduce the risk of electrostatic discharge (ESD) damaging your PC's sensitive electronic components, you should wear an electrostatic wristband that provides grounding for you against static shocks when you work inside the PC unit .

- To prevent a potentially fatal electric shock, you should NOT wear an electrostatic wristband when you work with the PC's power supply or when you work inside a monitor's case.

- To minimize the chance of losing screws that you remove while working on a PC, try storing them in a plastic pill container or Ziploc baggie.

- To reduce the risk of electrostatic discharge damaging a hardware card that you remove from your PC, you should store the card in a static-free bag.

- To remove dust that accumulates on PC components, you should use an aerosol blower.

- Some household screwdrivers magnetize the tip to hold a screw in place. You should not use such screwdrivers when you work on your PC. The magnet can damage information stored on a disk.

- To remove and place jumpers on a hardware card, you should use needle-nose pliers.

- You should carry bootable floppy disks for the operating systems your company uses. Should a computer fail to start from its hard drive, you may be able to boot the computer using the floppy drive. Then, you can run diagnostic programs on the computer to determine the cause of the error.

- As you troubleshoot system problems or install new hardware on a PC, you should record, in detail, the steps you perform as well as the original values for any settings you may change.

- Because the location of a PC can sometimes make viewing chip labels and card settings difficult, make sure to carry a small flashlight in your toolkit to use to illuminate items inside the PC case.

Using an Electrostatic Wristband to Reduce the Risk of Electrostatic Discharge

Electro-static discharge is a technical term for a "shock" created by static electricity. A typical electrostatic discharge can produce up to 2,000 volts. It requires only 50 volts to damage your PC's sensitive electronics. To reduce the risk of electrostatic discharge, you show wear an electrostatic wristband, as shown in Figure 3.1, when you work inside your PC's system unit. The wristband routes static electricity away from your PC's electronics to a grounding source. Some wristbands attach to the PC chassis while others attach to an antistatic pad.

Figure 3.1 Using an electrostatic wristband to reduce the risk of electrostatic discharge damaging PC components.

NOTE: *Never use an electrostatic wristband when you work with the PC's power supply or when you work within the monitor case. The power supply and monitor contain a large capacitor that can store sufficient power to kill you, even when the device is turned off and unplugged. If you wear an electrostatic wristband while you work on these two devices, you run the risk of the capacitor discharging its voltage down the wristband to you.*

Keeping Track of Screws and System Settings

In the past, to open most system units, users had to remove several screws that held the unit cover in place. Then, to install new hardware, the user likely had to remove screws that held an old card or an expansion-slot cover in place. To reduce the chance of misplacing screws, you should place the screws that you remove while you work into one or more plastic pill containers or Ziploc baggies.

Further, as you install hardware, there may be times when you change one or more switch settings on a card or jumper settings. Before you make such changes, you should record the original settings so you can recall and restore the settings should your new settings fail to work.

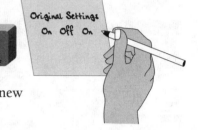

Selecting the Correct Screwdriver Types

To perform most PC upgrade and maintenance operations, you simply need medium-sized flathead and Phillips screwdrivers. In addition, you may want to purchase a star driver that users sometime refer to as a "trox," that you may need to use to remove the screws that hold a disk drive in place.

NOTE: *As you choose your screwdriver set, make sure you do not select a magnetic screwdriver (which magnetizes the tip of the screw driver to hold screws in place). The magnet within such a screwdriver can damage information stored on your PC's disk.*

Using Needle-Nose Pliers to Change Jumper Settings

Lesson 9, "Working with Hardware Boards and Chips," examines switches and jumpers that card manufacturers place on cards to let you change various settings. Older cards, for example, often used jumper switches to let the user select the card's interrupt request. A jumper is essentially a switch. When the jumper is in place, current can flow through the jumper from one wire to another. When the jumper is not in place, current cannot flow. The easiest way to remove or place a jumper onto its corresponding pins, is to use a pair of needle-nose pliers, as shown in Figure 3.2.

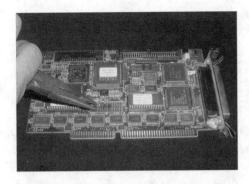

Figure 3.2 Using needle-nose pliers to remove or place a jumper on a hardware card.

In addition to adding needle-nose pliers to your toolkit, you should also include a set of tweezers that you can use to pick up a screw or jumper pin that you drop inside the system unit. Also, you should place a small flashlight in your toolkit to illuminate items in a dark system unit.

Storing Hardware Cards in Antistatic Bags

As you perform PC upgrades, you will often replace one hardware card with another. You might, for example, replace a 10Mbs network card with a faster 100Mbs card. In Lesson 9 you will learn that to remove a card from an expansion slot, you may need to gently rock the card. After you remove the card, you should place the card into an antistatic bag, similar to that shown in Figure 3.3. By placing the card in the antistatic bag, you reduce the risk of an electrostatic discharge from damaging the card's components.

Figure 3.3 Storing a hardware card in an antistatic bag.

Using a Multimeter to Test PC Components

As you troubleshoot PC hardware and cable problems, you can often determine if a card or cable is working properly by measuring voltage, current, or resistance using a multimeter similar to that shown in Figure 3.4. A multimeter is a device that lets you measure multiple items. In the past, technicians often used one device to measure voltage and possibly a second device to measure resistance.

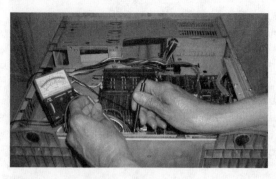

Figure 3.4 Using a multimeter to troubleshoot a PC device.

Using a Chip Extractor

Only a few years ago, technicians often replaced chips on the motherboard as well as other hardware cards. To remove the chips, technicians often used special tools called chip extractors. In general, there are two types of chip extractors. The first is a tweezer-like device that has hooks you can place underneath each end of the chip. The second type of chip extractor looks similar to a metal hypodermic needle that contains a small metal plunger you press to extract the chip.

Today, the chips that are most frequently replaced are the CPU and memory chips (which are very small cards that slide into a memory slot). Most PC manufacturers, therefore, make the CPU and memory chips quite easy to remove and replace.

When to Use Wire Strippers and Wire Crimpers

Many network professionals state that a network's cabling can consume 10 to 15 percent of the total cost of a network. To reduce costs, many technicians create their own network cables using wire strippers and crimpers. In addition, many technicians enjoy creating their own printer cables. If you find that a user's printer or network cable is not working, replace the cable to get the user up and running quickly. You can always fix the broken cable later, when you have the time. When a user's system is down, replacing the cable is the cost-effective alternative.

Avoid Using a Soldering Iron

Years ago, technicians made extensive use of soldering irons to repair broken pins on a hardware card and, in some cases, to change the processing that a card performs. For most technicians, a soldering iron provides a quick way to turn a small computer problem into a big problem. You should be able to troubleshoot and correct virtually all PC problems without the use of a soldering iron.

Keep Bootable Floppy Disks in Your Toolkit

Lesson 6, "Understanding the PC Startup Process," examines the steps the PC performs each time you start your system. If a PC fails to start the operating system from the hard disk, you should try to start the system using bootable floppy disks. Then, after the system starts, you can examine the user's hard disk (using a program such as *Scandisk*) and run diagnostic programs that may help you pinpoint the problem cause.

Depending on the operating system the user is running, the number of startup floppy disks will vary, as will the steps you must perform to create the disks. To create a startup disk for Windows 98, perform these steps:

1. Select the Start menu Settings option and choose Control Panel. Windows will open the Control Panel window.
2. Within the Control Panel, double-click on the Add/Remove Programs icon. Windows will display the Add/Remove Programs dialog box.
3. Within the Add/Remove Programs dialog box, select the Startup Disk tab. Windows will display the Startup Disk sheet, as shown in Figure 3.5.
4. Within the Startup Disk sheet, click on the Create Disk button. Windows, in turn, will start a software program (that users refer to as a Wizard) that will walk you through the steps of creating the disk.

Figure 3.5 Using the Windows 98 Startup Disk sheet to create a bootable floppy disk.

To create a set of bootable floppy disks for Windows 2000, perform these steps:

1. Place the CD-ROM you used to install Windows into your CD-ROM drive.
2. Select the Start menu Run option. Windows will display the Run dialog box.
3. Within the Run dialog box Open field, type *x:\bootdisk\makeboot a:* replacing the letter *x* with the drive letter that corresponds to your CD-ROM drive. Windows, in turn, will run the makeboot program that will guide you through the process of creating the disks.

NOTE: *In addition to placing bootable floppy disks in their toolkit, many technicians also place a disk that contains hardware diagnostic programs which can be used to troubleshoot the cause of the error as well as a disk that contains virus-detection software.*

Selecting a Fire Extinguisher

If you work in an office, you should have one or more fire extinguishers readily available that can suppress an electrical fire as well as fire from paper. As you shop for a fire extinguisher, look for a type C extinguisher that can put out an electrical fire (a type ABC extinguisher will also work). As listed in Table 3.1, a fire extinguisher's type specifies the type of fires for which the extinguisher is well suited.

Type	Fire
A	Paper and wood
B	Flammable liquids
C	Electrical
D	Flammable metals
ABC	Multipurpose

Table 3.1 A fire extinguisher's type specifies the types of fires for which the extinguisher is well suited.

EXAM REVIEW

1. To reduce the risk of electrostatic discharge from damaging PC components, you should wear a _____ when you work within the PC system unit.

2. When a user cannot start the operating system from a PC's hard drive, you should boot the system using _____ and then run diagnostics programs to determine the cause of the error.

3. True or False
   You should use a screwdriver with a magnetic tip to simplify many upgrade operations because the screwdriver will hold the screw readily in place.

4. You should never wear an electrostatic wristband when you work on _____ or _____ because the devices contain capacitors that can store a powerful voltage even when the device is powered off and unplugged.

5. To protect hardware cards that you are not currently using from electrostatic discharge, you should place the cards into an _____.

6. Before you change jumpers or switches on any hardware, you should first _____.

7. A _____ is a device you can use to measure voltages, currents, and resistance.

Installing, Removing, and Troubleshooting Software

As you maintain and troubleshoot user systems, there will be times when you must install a new program or special software called a device driver before the user can use a hardware device. Or, there may be times when, because a user's system has stopped functioning properly or because the user's disk space is very low, that you must remove one or more programs.

This lesson examines the steps you must perform to install and remove programs within Windows. In addition, the lesson will examine steps you can perform to resolve software conflicts. Finally, you will learn ways to collect key information about your system that you can provide to a company's technical support staff, should you be unable to resolve an error yourself.

F A C T S

- Most Windows-based programs provide an installation program named Setup that you can use to install the software onto the user's hard disk and which lets you configure various program settings.

- Often, when users insert the CD-ROM disc that contains a new program, Windows will automatically run the software's installation program. Behind the scenes, when you insert a CD-ROM disc, Windows examines the disc for a file named *autorun.inf*. If the file exists, Windows uses the file's contents to automatically run the specified setup program.

- When a user's system is running low on disk space, you may want to remove one or more programs that the user is no longer running.

- Using the Control Panel Add/Remove Programs icon, you can install new software, remove existing software from your system (either to resolve a conflict or to free up disk space), and you can add and remove various Windows components, such as the Windows Notepad accessory.

- Many Windows-based programs make extensive use of special library files that contain program instructions that perform specific tasks. The program might use one library file to perform network operations and a second to display video.

- When the program must perform the operations a library file implements, the program will locate the library's file on disk and load the instructions the library contains into memory for execution. Programmers refer to such library files as dynamic link libraries. The dynamic link library file uses the *.dll* file extension.

- When you install a new program, there may be times when a program's installation process overwrites a DLL file on your disk that is in use by other programs. Normally, to prevent errors that occur due to an incompatible DLL file, the installation program will not overwrite a newer version of a DLL file with an older version.

- Windows makes extensive use of DLL files. Using the System Information utility, you can view the DLL files that Windows is currently using (that Windows has loaded within RAM).

- Over time, it is possible that a key Windows system DLL file may become corrupt and introduce errors that cause various operations to fail. Using the System File Checker utility, you can examine Windows 98 files for DLL files that have changed since the Windows installation and which may be corrupt. Likewise, within Windows 2000, a system administrator can run the *sfc* command to verify key system files.

Installing a New Software Program

Often, when you insert the CD-ROM disc that contains a new program, Windows will automatically run an installation program that resides on the CD-ROM in order to install the program on your hard drive. If Windows does not automatically run the installation program, you must locate and run the program yourself from the CD-ROM.

Normally, the documentation that accompanies your new software will provide you with step-by-step instructions that you must perform to install the software. That said, the steps you must perform to install most Windows programs is the same, as follows:

1. Insert the CD-ROM disc that contains the new software.
2. Within Windows, select the Start menu Run option. Windows, in turn, will display the Run dialog box.
3. Within the Run dialog box, select the Browse button. Windows will display the Browse dialog box that you can use to locate the installation program on the CD-ROM. Most applications name the installation program *Setup.exe*. After you run the Setup program, the software will normally walk you through the installation process.

Using *Autorun.inf* to Launch Programs

Often, when you insert a CD-ROM disc, Windows will automatically run a program that resides on the disc, such as an installation program. As it turns out, each time you insert a CD-ROM or floppy disk, Windows examines the disk for a file named *Autorun.inf*. If Windows locates the file, Windows will examine and process the entries contained in the file. Within the file, one of the entries will direct Windows to run a specific program.

In addition to launching an application program using the Run dialog box, you can also install software using the Control Panel Add/Remove Programs icon. When you select the icon within Windows 98, your screen will display the Add/Remove Programs dialog box, as shown in Figure 4.1.

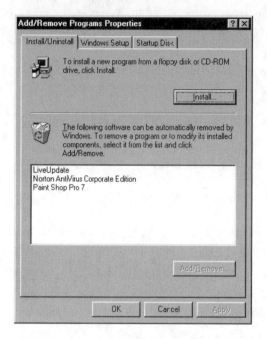

Figure 4.1 The Windows 98 Add/Remove Programs dialog box.

To install a software program using the Add/Remove Programs dialog box, perform these steps:

1. Select the Start menu Settings option and choose Control Panel. Windows will display the Control Panel window.

2. Within the Control Panel, double-click on the Add/Remove Programs icon. Windows will display the Add/Remove Programs dialog box as previously shown in Figure 4.1.

3. Within the Add/Remove Programs dialog box, click on the Install button. Windows will start a software wizard that will direct you to insert the floppy or CD-ROM. Windows will then examine the disk for an installation program. If Windows locates the installation program, Windows will run it. Otherwise, Windows will display a dialog box that contains a Browse button that you can select to search the disk for the installation program.

Likewise, to use the Add/Remove Programs entry within Windows 2000, perform these steps:

1. Select the Start menu Settings option and choose Control Panel. Windows will display the Control Panel window.

2. Within the Control Panel, double-click on the Add/Remove Programs icon. Windows will display the Add/Remove Programs dialog box.

3. Within the Add/Remove Programs dialog box, click on the Add New Programs button. Windows will change the Add/Remove Programs dialog box as shown in Figure 4.2.

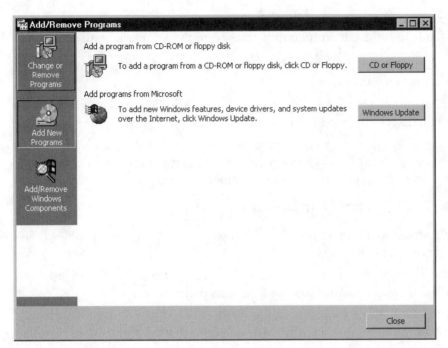

**Figure 4.2
Using the
Windows
2000
Add/Remove
Programs
dialog box.**

4. Insert the CD-ROM that contains the software that you want to install and then click on the CD or Floppy button that appears within the Add/Remove Programs dialog box. Windows, in turn, will examine the CD-ROM for an installation program. If Windows locates the installation program, Windows will load and run the program which should walk you through the installation process.

Removing a Program

Years ago, within the MS-DOS environment, to remove a program from your disk users simply deleted the folder or folders that contained the program files.

Within the Windows environment, in contrast, removing a program requires that you not only delete the program files, but also that you remove any library files the program's installation placed on your hard disk, as well as program entries within the Registry database (a special Windows database that applications can use to place configuration information).

Just as most Windows-based programs provide a Setup program you can run to install the program, most provide a program you can run to "uninstall" the application.

Using the Control Panel Add/Remove Program icon, you can easily run an application's uninstall program. To uninstall a program within Windows 98, perform these steps:

1. Select the Start menu Settings option and choose Control Panel. Windows will display the Control Panel window.

2. Within the Control Panel, double-click on the Add/Remove Programs icon. Windows will display the Add/Remove Programs dialog box.

3. Within the Add/Remove Programs dialog box, click on the program you want to remove and then select the Add/Remove button. Windows will display a dialog box prompting you to confirm that you want to remove the program. Select Yes.

Likewise, to uninstall a program within Windows 2000, perform these steps:

1. Select the Start menu Settings option and choose Control Panel. Windows will display the Control Panel window.

2. Within the Control Panel, double-click on the Add/Remove Programs icon. Windows will display the Add/Remove Programs dialog box.

3. Within the Add/Remove Programs dialog box, click on the Change or Remove Programs button. Windows, in turn, will display a list of applications you can remove.

4. Within the application list, click on the application you want to remove and then click the Change/Remove button. Windows, in turn, will launch the application's uninstall program to remove the application.

Adding or Removing Windows Components

To make better use of your disk space, the Windows installation program does not install all of the software components that reside on the installation CD-ROM. Using the Control Panel Add/Remove Programs icon, you can install one or more components as your needs require. To install a Windows component, you must have the Windows CD-ROM.

If a user finds that a specific component is never used, you can free up disk space on the user's disk by removing the component. To add or remove a Windows component within Windows 98, perform these steps:

1. Select the Start menu Settings option and choose Control Panel. Windows will display the Control Panel window.

2. Within the Control Panel, double-click on the Add/Remove Programs icon. Windows will display the Add/Remove Programs dialog box.

3. Within the Add/Remove Programs dialog box, select the Windows Setup tab. Windows will display the Windows Setup sheet that you can use to add or remove Windows components.

4. Within the component list, place a checkmark in the checkbox that appears next to the component you want to install, or remove the checkmark for items you want to remove from your system. Some of the components will let you individually select specific component programs. To install or remove specific programs, select the component you desire and then click your mouse on the Details button. Windows, in turn, will display a list of the individual programs, each preceded by a checkmark that you can use to add or remove the item.

5. After you select the components you desire, click on the OK button. Windows will add and remove the items you specified.

Likewise, to add or remove a Windows component within Windows 2000, perform these steps:

1. Select the Start menu Settings option and choose Control Panel. Windows will display the Control Panel window.

2. Within the Control Panel, double-click on the Add/Remove Programs icon. Windows will display the Add/Remove Programs dialog box.

3. Within the Add/Remove Programs dialog box, click on the Add/Remove Windows Components button. Windows, in turn, will display a list of components you can add or remove.

4. Within the component list, place a checkmark in the checkbox that appears next to the component you want to install, or remove the checkmark for items you want to remove from your system. Some of the components will let you individually select specific component programs. To install or remove specific programs, select the component you desire and then click on the Details button. Windows, in turn, will display a list of the individual programs, each preceded by a checkmark that you can use to add or remove the item.

5. After you select the components you desire, click on the Next button. Windows will add and remove the items you specified.

Understanding DLL Files

Most Windows-based programs use a file with the *.exe* extension to store the program's executable instructions. Microsoft Word, for example, uses a program file named *WinWord.exe*. Likewise, Microsoft Excel uses a program file named *Excel.exe*.

In addition, most programs use one or more library files that provide instructions the CPU executes to perform a specific task. A program might, for example, use the instructions that reside in one library to interact with a modem and instructions that reside in a different library to display graphics images. Windows libraries normally reside in files with the *.dll* file extension. The letters DLL are an acronym for dynamic link library.

DLL files are so named because when a program needs the library's instructions, the program locates the library on disk and loads the library into memory so the CPU can execute the corresponding instructions. Programmers refer to a program's use of such libraries as "dynamic linking" because the program locates and loads the library on the fly (as the program first executes).

Within the Windows environment, programs often share the same DLL files. By sharing library files, programs reduce the amount of disk space they would otherwise consume if each program had to have its own private copy of the library. Further, because only one copy of the library file exists, it becomes easier in the future to update applications when a library changes because you (actually an installation program) must only update one file as opposed to multiple copies of the file.

When you install a new software program, there may be times when the application's installation program overwrites an existing DLL file with a newer version. Unfortunately, due to a programming error or other incompatibility, the new DLL file does not work with your existing software. As a result, your new program may run, but your older programs may not.

Users commonly refer to such DLL file conflicts as "DLL hell." When such conflicts occur, you can remove the new application so that your older programs can run, or you may need to try to find an update for the older program that works with the new version of the DLL file.

Viewing Specifics About DLL Files

As you troubleshoot software installations, you should make note of the DLL files your system is currently using (the DLL files Windows has loaded into memory). To view specifics about the DLL files, such as the version number and file size, you can use the System Information utility, as shown in Figure 4.3.

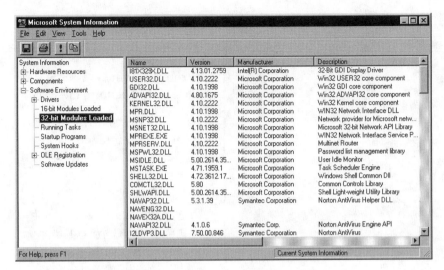

Figure 4.3 Viewing DLL specifics within the System Information utility.

To display the DLL specifics using the System Information utility, perform these steps:

1. Select the Start menu Programs option and choose Accessories. Windows will display the Accessories submenu.

2. Within the Accessories submenu, select System Tools and choose System Information. Windows will display the System Information utility.

3. Within the System Information utility, click on the plus sign that precedes the Software Environment entry and then click on the 16-bit Modules Loaded or the 32-bit Modules Loaded entry (under Windows 2000, you will click the Loaded Modules entry).

Verifying Key Windows DLL Files

If programs on a user's system simply stop working, the problem may be that a DLL file has become corrupt. Often, the easiest way to resolve the problem is simply to reinstall the program that no longer runs. Unfortunately, there may be times when the corrupt DLL file is not an application file, but rather a key Windows file. If you are using Windows 98, you can use the System File Checker shown in Figure 4.4 to examine the Windows DLL files to ensure the files are correct.

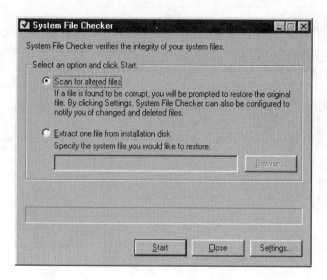

Figure 4.4 Using the System File Checker to examine Windows 98 DLL files.

To run the Windows 98 System File Checker, perform these steps:

1. Select the Start menu Programs option and choose Accessories. Windows will display the Accessories submenu.

2. Within the Accessories submenu, select System Tools and choose System Information. Windows will display the System Information utility.

3. Within the System Information utility, select the Tools menu and choose System File Checker.

If you are a Windows 2000 system administrator, you can run the System File Checker from a command-line prompt as shown here:

```
C:\> SFC /scannow   <Enter>
```

Obtaining Key System Settings

Before you call a company's technical support staff for assistance in resolving a software error, you should take a minute to print a copy of your system's key settings, such as the operating system version number, BIOS version, and processor type. To display your key system settings, perform these steps:

1. Select the Start menu Programs option and choose Accessories. Windows will display the Accessories submenu.

2. Within the Accessories submenu, select System Tools and choose System Information. Windows will display the System Information utility.

3. Within the System Information utility, click on the System Summary entry. The System Information utility will display your system settings as shown in Figure 4.5.

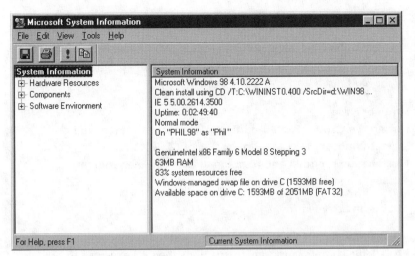

Figure 4.5 Using the System Information utility to display key system settings.

Downloading and Installing Program Updates

Often, software companies will post updates (which programmers refer to as "software patches") on their Web site that you can download and install on your system to bring your program up to date. As a rule, you should only download program patches from reputable sites, such as the software manufacturer's Web site. Because programs you download from across the Web can contain computer viruses, you should not download and install software from sites you do not know.

To make it easy for you to update various Windows components, the Start menu provides a Windows Update option that you can select to the Microsoft Web site. After you connect to the site, you can run software that resides on the site that will examine your system for components that are out of date. The software will then create links you can select to download and install various updates.

A+ CERTIFICATION

EXAM REVIEW

① Most Windows-based programs provide an installation program named _____ that you can run to load the program onto your hard disk.

② True or False
Using the Control Panel Add/Remove Programs option, you can direct Windows to scan a floppy disc or CD-ROM for an installation program and to automatically run the program should one exist.

③ DLL is an acronym for _____.

④ True or False
A DLL file contains program instructions the CPU executes to perform a specific task.

⑤ Using the Control Panel Add/Remove Programs option, you can (select all that apply):

☐ Install a new program
☐ Remove an existing program
☐ Add or remove Windows components
☐ Verify your system's DLL files

⑥ To quickly check the Microsoft Web site for updates to Windows and various Windows components you should _____.

Getting a Handle on Kilo, Mega, Giga, and Tera)

When users discuss computer speeds, they frequently refer to a processor's (the CPU's) speed in terms of megahertz (MHz) or gigahertz (GHz), such as a 733MHz or 1.2GHz system. Likewise, users express the amount of random access memory (RAM) a PC contains in terms of megabytes (MB) and a hard disk's storage capacity in terms of megabytes or gigabytes (GB).

In contrast, when users discuss modem and network speeds, the discussion changes from bytes to bits. A dial-up modem, for example, may transfer data at 28.8 kilobits (Kb) per second (note the use of the lowercase b to represent bits as opposed to the uppercase B to represent bytes). Likewise, a fast Ethernet-based network might transfer data at 100 megabits (Mb) per second.

This lesson examines bits and bytes as well as the meaning of the terms kilo, mega, giga, and tera. You will also examine the terms that users use to express PC device speeds. Lastly, you will examine the binary, octal, and hexadecimal numbering systems.

F A C T S

+ The term bit stands for binary digit. A binary digit can store either the value 0 or 1.

+ Within a PC, hardware devices use a bit to represent the presence or absence of an electronic signal. The value 1 would typically indicate a signal is present, whereas the value 0 would indicate the signal is absent.

+ The PC and its hardware components represent all information using combinations of ones and zeros.

+ Computers often group binary digits into groups of eight to create a byte of data. One byte corresponds to 8 bits.

+ Users express the PC's storage capacity in terms of bytes.

+ To simplify the expression of large sizes, users use the prefixes kilo, mega, giga, and tera.

+ With respect to file and disk sizes, the term kilo stands for 1,024. A file whose size is one kilobyte contains 1,024 bytes. Likewise, a file that is two kilobytes in size contains 2,048 bytes.

+ Users abbreviate the term kilobyte as KB. When you do not require an exact size, you can generalize the term KB as meaning 1,000. A 64KB file contains roughly 64,000 bytes. If you must be exact, the file would contain 64 x 1,024 bytes or 65,536 bytes.

+ With respect to file and disk sizes, the term mega stands for 1,048,576. A file whose size is one megabyte contains 1,048,576 bytes.

+ Users abbreviate the term megabyte as MB. When you do not require an exact size, you can generalize the term MB as meaning 1,000,000. A 500MB disk can store roughly 500,000,000 bytes. If you must be exact, the disk would contain 500 x 1,048,576 bytes or 524,288,000 bytes.

+ With respect to file and disk sizes, the term giga stands for 1,073,741,824. A file whose size is one gigabyte contains 1,073,741,824 bytes.

+ Users abbreviate the term gigabyte as GB. When you do not require an exact size, you can generalize the term GB as meaning 1,000,000,000. A 20GB disk can store roughly 20,000,000,000 bytes. If you must be exact, the disk would contain 20 x 1,073,741,824 bytes or 21,474,836,480 bytes.

+ With respect to file and disk sizes, the term tera stands for 1,099,511,627,776. A disk whose size is one terabyte contains 1,099,511,627,776 bytes.

+ Users abbreviate the term terabyte as TB. When you do not require an exact size, you can generalize the term TB as meaning 1,000,000,000,000. A 5TB disk can store roughly 5,000,000,000,000 bytes. If you must be exact, the disk would contain 5 x 1,099,511,627,776 bytes or 5,497,558,138,880 bytes.

+ When you examine computer values expressed in terms of KB, MB, GB, or TB, understand that that uppercase B normally corresponds to bytes, whereas the lowercase b corresponds to bits. A 56Kbs modem, for example, can send or receive 56K bits per second (not bytes).

+ Within the CPU, a very fast clock synchronizes the operations the PC performs. The speed of the clock determines the CPU's speed. In general, each time the clock ticks, the CPU can execute an instruction.

+ Users use the term hertz to describe the number of times per second an operation occurs. A clock that ticks 10 times per second, for example, operates at 10 hertz. Users abbreviate the term hertz as Hz. A clock that ticks one million times per second operates at one million hertz or 1MHz.

+ A 533MHz CPU contains a clock that ticks 533 million times per second. Likewise, a PC that uses a 2GHz CPU contains a clock that ticks two billion times per second. Knowing that a CPU can execute one instruction per clock tick, a 2GHz CPU can execute two billion instructions per second.

+ Binary is the base-2 numbering system. A binary digit can represent a 1 or a 0.

+ Octal is the base-8 numbering system. Octal values let programmers group binary digits into sets of three. An octal digit can represent a number in the range 0 to 7.

+ Decimal is the base-10 numbering system. The numbers we use to count and to perform arithmetic operations are decimal numbers. A decimal digit can store a number in the range 0 to 9.

+ Hexadecimal is the base-16 numbering system. Hexadecimal values let programmers and hardware designers group binary digits into sets of four. A hexadecimal digit can represent values in the range 0 to 15 using the numbers 0-9 and the letters A-F. When you examine PC memory addresses and I/O port addresses, you will find that Windows represents the addresses using hexadecimal.

Making Sense of Bits and Bytes

Within the PC, operations occur based on the presence or absence of electronic signals. At a specific time, a signal is either on (present) or off (absent) across a specific wire. The PC represents the signal's two-state value using a binary digit, which can hold the value 0 or 1. Users frequently refer to a single binary digit as a bit and multiple binary digits as bits. In addition to using binary digits to represent a signal's state, the PC also uses binary digits to represent information such as a numeric value or the characters that make up a name.

Most operations a PC performs require a considerable number of bits. As you examine various PC hardware, you will find devices and cables expressed in terms of bits. One electrical bus (set of wires) within the PC may transfer 8 bits of data at a time, making the bus an 8-bit bus. A second 64-bit bus might transfer 64 bits of data at a time.

Many PC operations use 8 bits at a time. Users refer to a group of 8 bits as a byte. In general, you can think of one byte as a single character of data. To store the message "Hello" which contains 5 characters would require 5 bytes.

When users express a file's size, or their PC's RAM or hard-disk capacity, the user will always express the size in terms of bytes.

Expressing Large Files and Disk Sizes

To simplify the expression of large file sizes or large disk capacities, users frequently use the terms kilo, mega, giga, and recently tera to express thousands, millions, billions, and trillions of bytes. A 500 megabyte hard drive, for example, can store roughly 500 million bytes.

Users frequently abbreviate the terms kilobytes, megabytes, gigabytes, and terabytes using KB, MB, GB, and TB. (Note the use of the uppercase B to represent bytes.) As you examine hardware descriptions, you may encounter abbreviations such as Kb, Mb, and Gb that use the lowercase b to indicate bits (remember that a byte contains 8 bits). A device that transfers data at 10MBs (10 megabytes per second) would transfer data much faster (8 times faster to be exact) than a device that transfers data at 10Mbs (10 megabits per second). As you examine PC speeds, you must pay attention to the use of the lower and uppercase B.

Earlier in this lesson, you learned you can think of KB as roughly 1,000 bytes, MB as roughly 1,000,000 bytes and so on. To be exact, a KB contains 1,024 bytes. Likewise, a MB contains 1,048,576 bytes. Table 5.1 briefly summarizes the abbreviations KB, MB, GB, and TB.

Abbreviation	Description	Exact Value	General Description
KB	Kilobyte	1,024 bytes	1 thousand bytes
MB	Megabyte	1,048,576 bytes	1 million bytes
GB	Gigabyte	1,073,741,824 bytes	1 billion bytes
TB	Terabyte	1,099,511,627,776 bytes	1 trillion bytes

Table 5.1 Descriptions of the terms KB, MB, GB, and TB.

Making Sense of PC Speeds

Within the PC, millions of operations occur per second. Users refer to the number of times an event occurs per second in terms of hertz (Hz). For example, in Lesson 49, "Performing Monitor Operations," you will learn that to display an image, many monitors refresh (essentially redisplay) the entire screen 75 times per second. Using the term hertz, you would describe the monitor's refresh rate as 75 hertz (or 75Hz).

Within the CPU is a very fast clock that, depending on the processor's type, ticks several hundred million to more than a billion times per second. Each time the CPU's clock ticks, the CPU can execute an instruction.

A 733-megahertz processor, which you would abbreviate as 733MHz, contains a clock that ticks 733 million times per second. Likewise, a 2-gigahertz (2GHz) CPU contains a close that ticks two billion times per second, which means the CPU can execute two billion instructions per second!

Understanding Data Transmission Speeds

Throughout this book, you will examine the speed at which many devices communicate. Users often use the term *bandwidth* to describe the amount of data a device can transmit over a specific interval of time. Normally, users express data throughput in terms of bits per second.

A 56Kbs modem, for example, can send and receive data at a throughput rate of roughly 56,000 bits per second. Likewise, a 100Mbs Ethernet network transmits data at 100 megabits per second.

By keeping in mind that users normally express data transmission speeds in terms of bits per second, you will reduce your chance of misinterpreting 100Mbs in terms of bytes as opposed to bits per second.

Making Sense of Number Systems

When people work with numbers, they use decimal (base-10) numbers. A decimal digit can represent a value in the range 0 through 9. To represent the value 10, you must use two decimal digits (one that contains the value 1 and one that contains 0). Two decimal digits can represent values in the range 0 to 99. To represent the value 100, you would need to use three decimal digits.

Internally, the PC performs its operations based on the presence or absence of electronic signals. Using a binary digit, the PC can represent whether a signal is on or off by storing the value 1 or 0. Binary is the base-2 numbering system. The PC represents all data using one or more binary digits. To represent the values 0 to 15, for example, the PC would use the following binary digits:

Decimal Value	Binary Representation	Decimal Value	Binary Representation
0	0000	8	1000
1	0001	9	1001
2	0010	10	1010
3	0011	11	1011
4	0100	12	1100
5	0101	13	1101
6	0110	14	1110
7	0111	15	1111

In a similar way, to represent the values 65,530 to 65,535, the PC would use the following binary digits:

Decimal Value	Binary Representation
65,530	1111111111111010
65,531	1111111111111011
65,532	1111111111111100
65,533	1111111111111101
65,534	1111111111111110
65,535	1111111111111111

As you can imagine, working with long sequences of binary digits can be quite error prone for programmers and hardware designers. By simply transposing two binary digits, the programmer or designer will introduce errors that are difficult and time consuming to detect and correct. To simplify the process of representing and manipulating data, programmers and hardware designers often work in terms of the octal and hexadecimal number systems.

The octal (base-8) number system lets you group binary digits into groups of three, which results in each octal digit storing a value in the range 0 to 7. For example, to represent the binary digits 10110011 using octal, you could group the digits as shown in Figure 5.1.

10 110 011

Figure 5.1 Grouping binary digits into sets of three to form an octal value.

In a similar way, the hexadecimal (base-16) number system lets you group binary digits into sets of four. Hexadecimal digits use the numbers 0-9 and the letters A-F to represent values in the range 0 to 15 as shown here:

Decimal Value	Hexadecimal Representation	Decimal Value	Hexadecimal Representation
0	0	8	8
1	1	9	9
2	2	10	A
3	3	11	B
4	4	12	C
5	5	13	D
6	6	14	E
7	7	15	F

To represent the binary value 10110011 using hexadecimal, you would group the digits as shown in Figure 5.2.

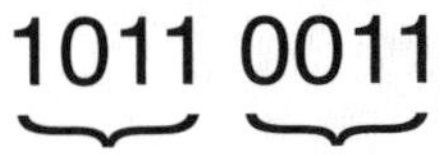

1011 0011

Figure 5.2 Grouping binary digits into sets of four to form a hexadecimal value.

As you examine memory addresses and I/O port addresses in later lessons of this book, you will find that Windows frequently expresses address values using hexadecimal. Figure 5.3, for example, illustrates I/O port addresses within the System Information utility. As you can see, the program displays each port address using hexadecimal digits.

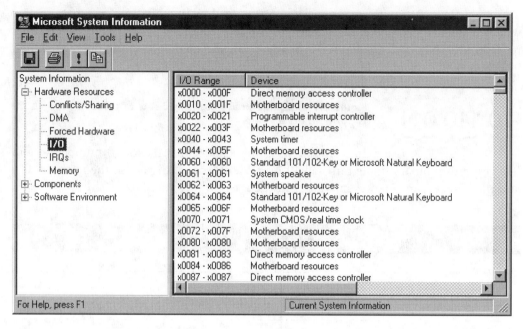

Figure 5.3 Many Windows applications express addresses using hexadecimal digits.

A number system lets you represent a value in a specific way. You can represent the same value using binary, octal, decimal or hexadecimal. Depending on the operations a programmer or hardware designer is performing, the individual will select the number system that best meets those needs.

CERTIFICATION

① Internally, the PC can represent the presence or absence of a signal using _____.

② True or False
Binary, the base-2 numbering system, can represent only the values 0 or 1.

③ Computers often group binary digits into groups of eight bits to form a _____.

④ _____ is a term used to describe an object's size.

⑤ How do the values 100MB and 100Mb differ?

⑥ A 50GB disk can store roughly _____ bytes.

⑦ _____ is a term used to describe operations per second.

⑧ A 500MHz CPU can execute roughly _____ instructions per second.

⑨ Data transmission operations normally express speeds in terms of _____ not _____.

⑩ Rather than work with long sequences of binary digits, programmers and hardware designers often group binary digits into sets of three to create an _____ value or sets of four to create a _____ value.

⑪ Many Windows-based programs express memory addresses and I/O port addresses using _____, the base-16 number system.

⑫ A hexadecimal digit can represent a value in the range 0 to 15 using the numbers _____ and the letters _____.

Understanding the PC Startup Process

Each time the PC starts, it performs the same steps to load the operating system. If a user's system will not start, you must begin your troubleshooting by determining the stage in the startup process at which the PC is failing. Then you can look for the specific cause of the error.

This lesson focuses on the steps the PC's hardware performs during the startup process. Depending on the operating system the system is running, the files loaded during the startup process will differ. After Windows is up and running, Windows will automatically run programs that reside in the Startup folder, as well as programs that contain an entry in the Registry that directs Windows to run the program. Many systems run programs that users do not require. By allowing the programs to run, users increase the already time-consuming startup process and they let the programs consume resources that other programs might put to better use.

F A C T S

- When you power on a PC, you should immediately hear the PC's fan start to whir. If you do not hear the fan and the PC does not start, you should examine the PC's power source.

- Before you proclaim that the PC's power supply has failed, double check the wall outlet to ensure that it is providing electricity, then check the PC's power cable to ensure it is properly connected, and, if you are using a surge suppressor, make sure the suppressor is powered on and that it has not tripped an internal breaker that you must reset.

- When the PC first starts, the PC BIOS, a special chip that resides on the motherboard, will perform a special power on self-test (POST) that examines the PC's key hardware components to verify they are in working order.

- If the power on self-test encounters an error, the PC may display an error message that briefly describes the error. Then, the PC may generate a series of beeps users refer to as beep codes that you can decode to determine the cause of the error.

- The PC's beep codes are BIOS dependent. Typically, you will hear a series of long and short beeps. You can look up the meaning of the beeps on the BIOS manufacturer's Web site. The AMI BIOS, for example, generates two short beeps when a memory parity error occurs within the PC's first 64KB of RAM.

- During the startup process, the BIOS relies on configuration information that the PC stores in a special battery-powered memory users refer to as the CMOS settings. Within the CMOS settings, the PC stores such information as the disk drive type, the boot device order, as well as information regarding the PC's RAM and cache use.

- The CMOS memory is unique in that it requires minimal voltage to maintain the information it stores. When the PC is not powered on, the PC uses a small 5V (or less) battery to power the CMOS memory.

- Over time, the battery that powers the CMOS memory will fail and the system settings contained in the CMOS will be lost. When the BIOS cannot locate the system settings within the CMOS, the BIOS will display a message stating that the PC's settings are invalid. You must then replace the CMOS battery and use a special program called the CMOS Setup to restore the previous settings.

- Within the CMOS settings is an entry that tells the BIOS what disk drive order it should search to find a bootable disk. Using the drive-order entry, you can direct the PC to boot first from your hard drive, floppy disk drive, or CD-ROM drive based on your preference and needs.

➕ After the BIOS determines the boot disk, it will read a special disk sector, called the operating system's boot sector, into the PC's random access memory. The boot sector contains instructions the CPU can execute to begin loading the operating system from disk into RAM.

➕ If the BIOS does not find a bootable disk, the BIOS will display an error message stating that the operating system was not found.

➕ After the operating system begins to load itself into RAM, the files and programs the operating system loads will differ.

➕ After Windows successfully loads, Windows will automatically run programs based on entries within the Registry, Startup folder, and *win.ini*. Often, Windows will run programs the user does not require.

➕ To help you troubleshoot system startup operations, you can direct Windows to log various startup operations, such as whether or not it is able to successfully load specific device drivers. Windows 98 places the log file information within the root directory Bootlog.txt file. Windows 2000 places the log within the *\Winnt\Wtbtlog.txt* file.

Powering On the PC

When you power on the PC, the first positive indication you will receive that the PC is working is the whir of the power-supply's fan. If you do not hear the fan, you quite likely have a power problem. Fortunately, the PC's power supply rarely fails, which means the problem is likely the wall outlet, a loose power cable, or an internal breaker within a surge suppressor that you must reset.

If the PC has power, the PC will first transfer control to a special chip called the BIOS. The BIOS, in turn, contains instructions that test to make sure the PC is in working order. Eventually, if all goes well, the BIOS will start the process that loads the operating system.

Performing the BIOS-Based Power On Self-Test

As discussed, before the PC loads the operating system, the BIOS performs a special hardware test that users refer to as the power on self-test (POST). During the POST, the BIOS examines key hardware, such as the CPU, RAM, keyboard, and so on.

If the POST encounters an error, the PC may display a message on the screen that briefly describes the error. Then the PC may generate a series of long and short beeps that you can decode to determine more information about the error. These beeps, which users refer to as beep codes, are BIOS-dependent. The AMI BIOS, for example, will generate six short beeps to indicate a keyboard error.

Because the list of errors the POST can encounter is quite long, so too is the list of the corresponding beep codes. After you determine your BIOS type, as discussed in Lesson 16, "Understanding the PC BIOS," you can look up the beep code meanings on the BIOS manufacturer's Web site.

Using CMOS Settings

To let you customize settings for key devices, the PC provides a special memory that users commonly refer to as the system's CMOS settings. Within the CMOS memory, the system maintains such information as:

- The disk drive order the BIOS will search to locate the operating system
- Specifics about the hard drive's geometry (track and sector layout)
- Settings to fine-tune the PC's power management capabilities
- Device settings for legacy devices that support plug-and-play operations
- RAM and cache settings
- Processor and bus speeds

In Lesson 26, "Configuring the PC's CMOS Settings," you will examine the CMOS settings in detail. You will also learn how to use a special program called the CMOS Setup to view and change entries.

CMOS is an acronym for complementary metal oxide semiconductor. In general, CMOS is a material with which chip designers can use to build chips. What makes CMOS memory unique is that it requires minimal voltage to maintain its contents. When the PC is not powered on, the CMOS memory uses a small 5V battery to power the memory.

Because the battery provides the CMOS memory with constant power, the PC can retain its key settings after you power off the PC.

Over time, the CMOS battery (like all batteries) will fail and the CMOS memory will lose its contents. When the BIOS cannot locate CMOS entries following a battery failure, the BIOS will display a message similar to the following on your screen.

```
Invalid settings — Run Setup
```

At that time, you must replace the CMOS battery and restore the previous system settings using a special program built into the BIOS called the CMOS Setup.

BEYOND A+ CERTIFICATION

Directing the PC to Perform a Fast Startup

Each time the PC starts, the BIOS performs its power on self-test which ensures the PC is in working order. Most users will find that the PC will successfully execute its self-test for years without ever encountering a problem. To speed up the slow PC startup process, many CMOS setup programs provide a Fast Boot option that lets users direct the BIOS to skip many of the startup tests (such as a complete examination of the PC's RAM).

If a user begins to experience intermittent errors that you find hard to detect, make sure the PC is not performing a fast boot operation due to a CMOS entry. By forcing the PC to complete the full power on self-test, you may encounter errors that help you determine the source of the intermittent problems the user was encountering.

Determining the Boot Device

When the PC starts, the BIOS does not know, nor does it care, which operating system the PC is running. The steps the BIOS performs to load the operating system are the same if the PC is running MS-DOS or Windows 2000.

To start, the BIOS will examine the CMOS entries to determine the disk drive order it should search to find the operating system. After the BIOS locates the boot disk, the BIOS will read the operating system's boot sector from the disk into RAM. The boot sector contains instructions the CPU will execute to begin the process of loading the operating system.

If the BIOS encounters a disk that does not contain the operating system, such as a floppy disk that a user left in drive A, the BIOS will display a message similar to the following that states that the disk is not a valid system disk:

```
Invalid system disk
Press any key to continue
```

Managing the Programs Windows Runs Each Time Your System Starts

After Windows completes its startup process, Windows will automatically run a number of programs the user may or may not require. Windows runs programs following the startup process based on entries that reside in the following locations:

• Program files that reside in the Startup folder

• Entries in the Registry that launch a program

• Entries within the *win.ini* file

Some of the programs Windows runs each time the system starts perform a key service, such a virus detection program. Other programs may correspond to hardware devices a user is not longer using, such as software that monitors a scanner. By directing Windows to no longer run specific programs, you may reduce the amount of time your system startup requires because Windows will no longer have to load and start the program, and you may free up resources the program is consuming (such as RAM) that may be better used by the programs you need.

To better understand the programs Windows automatically runs each time your system starts, restart your system and then use the System Information utility to show the programs the system is currently running, as shown in Figure 6.1.

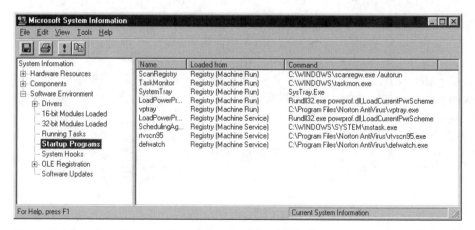

Figure 6.1 Viewing programs currently running within the System Information utility.

By examining the Loaded from field within the System Information utility's output, you can determine if the program was started because of an entry within the Startup folder, Registry, or *win.ini* file. To view running programs within the System Information utility, perform these steps:

1. Select the Start menu Programs option and choose Accessories. Windows will display the Accessories submenu.

2. Within the Accessories submenu, select System Tools and choose System Information. Windows will display the System Information utility.

3. Within the System Information utility, click on the plus sign that precedes the Software Environment entry and then click on the Startup Programs entry.

Controlling the Programs Windows Automatically Starts

As discussed, by directing Windows not to automatically run specific programs each time the system starts, you may let your computer start faster and you may recapture resources that programs you don't use were unnecessarily consuming. An easy way to control which programs Windows runs each time your system starts is to use the Startup sheet that appears within the System Configuration Utility, as shown in Figure 6.2. Within the Startup sheet, you can disable a program's automatic execution by removing the checkmark from the checkbox that precedes the program entry. You can run the System Configuration Utility from the Tools menu within the System Information utility.

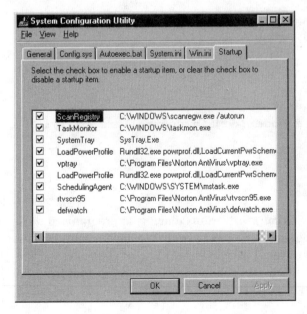

Figure 6.2 Using the System Configuration Utility, you can control which programs Windows automatically runs each time your system starts.

Starting a PC in Safe Mode

If your system fails to start Windows successfully, you may be able to direct Windows to start using a "scaled down" safe mode which you can then use to troubleshoot the startup process.

When you start Windows in "safe mode," Windows will not process the contents of the Registry database. As a result, Windows will not automatically run programs based on Registry entries. In addition, because it does not process the Registry, Windows may not load many different device drivers (one of which may be causing the error that prevents Windows from starting). Finally, Windows will disable network operations.

To start Windows within Safe mode, you must press the Ctrl key as the BIOS performs the PC's power on self-test (many systems also support the F8 function key). If you are using Windows 98, your screen will display a menu similar to the following that you can use to select Safe mode:

```
Microsoft Windows 98 Startup Menu
=============================================
     1. Normal
     2. Logged (BOOTLOG.TXT)
     3. Safe mode
     4. Step-by-step confirmation
     5. Command prompt only
     6. Safe mode command prompt
```

If you are using Windows 2000, your screen will display the Windows 2000 Advanced Options menu as shown here:

```
Windows 2000 Advanced Options Menu
Please select an option:

   Safe Mode
   Safe Mode with Networking
   Safe Mode with Command Prompt

   Enable Boot Logging
   Enable VGA Mode
   Last Known Good Configuration
   Domain Services Restore Mode (domain controllers only)
   Debugging Mode

   Boot Normally
   Return to OS Choice Menu
```

After Windows starts in Safe mode, you can run various diagnostic programs and use utilities such as the Device Manager to examine your system for device conflicts. You can also use the boot log files to determine if Windows is failing to start due to a specific device driver file. If you find Windows 9x is experiencing a driver problem, you may be able to use the Automatic Skip Driver Agent discussed in Lesson 8, "Understanding Device Drivers."

Taking Advantage of Boot Log Files

Depending on the operating system the PC is running, the files used by the operating system during the startup process will differ. After Windows is up and running, Windows may run a variety of programs based on entries as discussed next. In some cases, Windows may encounter an error processing a specific file (such as a device driver) that causes the startup process to fail.

If you are using Windows 9x, you can view the contents of a root directory file named *Bootlog.txt* that contains entries you can view to ensure Windows successfully loaded various device drivers. To direct Windows 98 to log startup operations, you must enable boot logging from the startup menu discussed previously in this lesson.

If you are using Windows 2000, you can enable boot-logging operations by pressing the F8 function key during the Windows startup process. Windows 2000, in turn, will display the Windows 2000 Advanced Options menu which you can use to enable logging. Windows 2000 will place the entries within the *\Winnt\Ntbtlog.txt* file.

EXAM REVIEW

CERTIFICATION

① If, after you power on a PC, you do not hear the PC's fan whir, you should check the _____, _____, and _____.

② POST is an acronym for _____.

③ If the POST encounters errors, the BIOS will generate audible beeps that correspond to the error. Users refer to the beeps as _____.

④ Following the power on self-test, the BIOS uses several key system settings that reside within a special battery-powered memory called the _____.

⑤ True or False
The BIOS begins the operating system startup processing by loading the boot sector into RAM.

⑥ Each time Windows starts, Windows will automatically run programs based on entries within the following (check all that apply):

☐ Registry
☐ Startup folder
☐ *BootStart.ini*
☐ *Win.ini*
☐ AutoRun folder

⑦ If Windows fails to start, you can direct Windows to boot in a "scaled-down" version called _____ which you can use to troubleshoot the system.

⑧ To display a menu of Windows startup options, you should press the _____ key as the BIOS performs the power on self-test.

⑨ To help you detect device driver errors, Windows logs various startup operations. Windows 98 stores the startup log within the _____ file. Likewise, Windows 2000 uses the _____ file.

Inside the System Unit

Throughout this book's lessons, you will work with various hardware components such as RAM, disk drives, the CMOS battery, and more, which you must open the PC system unit to work on. In each case, the corresponding lesson will provide you with the step-by-step instructions you should follow to perform the operations you require.

This lesson will provide you with an overview of the items you will encounter with the system unit. By the time you finish this lesson, you will be able to quickly locate and identify key components, such as the CPU, RAM, expansion slots, power cables, and so on.

FACTS

➕ The system unit houses the PC's key electronic components.

➕ Before you remove the system unit cover, you should shut down Windows and power off and unplug your PC.

➕ As you remove and later attach the system unit cover, you should take care to not damage or unplug the ribbon cables that connect your disk drives to the motherboard.

➕ To reduce the risk of an electrostatic shock damaging the PC's sensitive electronic components, you should wear an antistatic wristband when you work inside the system unit.

➕ The motherboard is home to the CPU, BIOS, RAM, and key buses.

➕ The CPU is normally the largest chip on the motherboard.

➕ Depending on the CPU and motherboard type, the CPU will use an edge or socket connector to connect to the motherboard.

➕ As it operates, the CPU generates heat due to the billions of electronic signals it generates per second. To help the CPU disseminate the heat, many systems attach a metal heat sink or fan to the CPU.

➕ The PC's random access memory (RAM) is comprised of one or more chips that reside within special slots on the motherboard.

➕ The power supply is the largest component in the system unit. You should never open the power supply itself. The power supply contains a capacitor that holds sufficient voltage to kill you.

➕ The power supply converts the wall outlet's high voltage alternating current (AC) into low voltage direct current (DC), which the PC's components require.

➕ The power supply provides small power cables that connect to the motherboard and to any devices (such as a hard drive) that you might install in the system unit.

➕ Most system units provide two or more drive bays into which you can place a floppy drive, hard drive, or CD-ROM drive. After you install a drive into a bay, you must connect the drive to the motherboard (or to a disk controller) using a ribbon cable, and you must power the device using one of the power supply's small power cables.

➕ To expand the PC's capabilities, users install hardware cards, such as a network interface card or modem in expansion slots that reside on the motherboard.

Preparing to Open the System Unit

Before you open a PC's system unit, you should always first shut down Windows and then power off and unplug your PC. Although it is normally possible to open the system unit while the PC is powered on, doing so puts you and the PC's sensitive electronic components at risk (some PCs will not let you open the system unit if the power cord is plugged in). Unless you have a specific reason to do so (perhaps you are troubleshooting a potential heat-related problem), you should never remove the system unit cover while the PC is powered on.

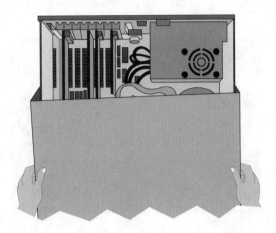

As discussed in Lesson 3, "Tools of the Trade," you should normally wear an antistatic wristband when you work inside the PC. The wristband provides a constant source of "ground" to which electricity will travel that reduces the risk of an electrostatic shock from damaging one or more electronic components.

The only time you should not wear an antistatic wristband is when you work with the PC's power supply. The power supply contains a capacitor that holds a charge with sufficient voltage to kill you. Should you replace a power supply, for example, you would not want the power supply to inadvertently discharge the capacitor's voltage across the wristband to you.

Finally, before you open the system unit, make sure you have sufficient work space available to place the cards and hardware devices that you will install or remove from the PC.

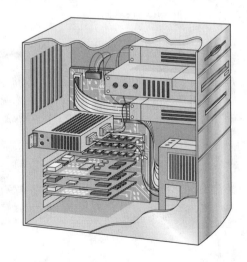

Opening the System Unit

Depending on your PC type, how you will remove the system unit cover may vary. Years ago, users had to remove several screws that held the cover in place. Today, most PCs provide latches you depress to release the cover for removal.

As you remove the system unit cover, do so slowly and with caution to ensure that you do not inadvertently damage or unplug one of the ribbon cables that connect your disk drives to the motherboard, as shown in Figure 7.1.

Figure 7.1 Remove and replace the system unit cover with care so you do not damage or unplug the ribbon cables inside the PC.

Taking a First Look Inside the System Unit

Regardless of the PC's manufacturer, such as Dell, Gateway, or another third party, the components you will find within the PC's system unit will be the same. Figure 7.2 illustrates the layout of a typical system unit. In general, the PC system unit is the home of the following components:

- The motherboard that houses key components such as the CPU, BIOS, and RAM
- Floppy disk, hard disk, and CD-ROM drives
- The power supply that converts the 110V alternating current (AC) into a suitable (low-voltage) direct current (DC) that the PC's sensitive electronic components require
- Expansion slots into which you can insert hardware cards, such as a modem or network interface card, which extend the PC's capabilities
- The small battery that powers the PC's CMOS memory that maintains the system's configuration settings

Figure 7.2 Viewing PC components inside the system unit.

Taking a Closer Look at the PC Motherboard

Within the system unit, the motherboard houses the PC's key electronic components, such as the CPU, RAM, the BIOS, as well as expansion slots. Figure 7.3 illustrates the layout of a typical PC motherboard.

Figure 7.3 The motherboard houses the PC's key electronic components.

Lesson 20, "Understanding the Central Processing Unit (CPU)," examines the central processing unit (CPU), the chip that performs the majority of the PC's processing. When you run a program, the CPU executes the instructions that direct the PC how to accomplish the program's specific task. Normally, the CPU will be the largest chip on the motherboard. Depending on the CPU's type, the CPU may use an edge connector or a socket connector (that provides receptacles for specific pins), as shown in Figure 7.4.

Figure 7.4 CPUs connect to the motherboard using either an edge or slot connector based on the CPU and motherboard types.

To execute a program's instructions, the CPU processes billions of electronic signals per second. As the signals travel through the CPU, they generate heat. Depending on the CPU's design, it may, as shown in Figure 7.5, use a metal heat sink or a fan to help the CPU disperse the heat it generates.

Figure 7.5 CPUs often use a metal heat sink or a fan to disperse the heat it generates.

Before the CPU can execute a program, the program's instructions and data must reside in the PC's random access memory (RAM). As you will learn in Lesson 23, "Understanding Random Access Memory (RAM)," the PC's RAM resides on the motherboard within chips you insert in several small slots, as shown in Figure 7.6.

Figure 7.6 The PC's RAM chips reside in small slots on the motherboard.

Understanding Motherboard Form Factors

Users refer to the size and shape of the motherboard as the motherboard's form factor. If you must replace a motherboard, for example, you must choose a motherboard that will fit inside your PC. The ATX motherboard is the most common motherboard form factor. An ATX motherboard is 12.0 x 9.6 inches. Table 7.1 briefly describes several of the most common motherboard form factors.

Form Factor	Dimensions
ATX	12.0 x 9.6 inches
Flex ATX	9.0 x 5.5 inches
Mini ATX	12.2 x 8.2 inches
Micro ATX	9.6 x 9.6 inches

Table 7.1 Common motherboard form factors.

Understanding the Power Supply

Inside the system unit, the power supply is the largest component. The power supply's purpose is to convert the 110V alternating current (AC) available at a wall outlet into a much lower voltage direct current (DC). As the power supply converts the high voltage alternating current to low voltage direct current, the power supply generates considerable heat. To dissipate the heat, the power supply uses a small fan to vent the hot air out the back of the PC, as shown in Figure 7.7.

Figure 7.7 The power supply uses a built-in fan to vent the heat it generates.

When you power on a PC, one of the first sounds you should hear is that of the power supply's fan starting to whir. If you do not hear the fan, you should first check the outlet into which you have plugged the power supply to ensure the outlet is working. Power supplies rarely fail. If the plug is working, ensure that the cable you have plugged into the PC is properly connected. If the fan still does not whir, you will need to replace the power supply as discussed in Lesson 21, "Power Supplies, Surge Suppressors, and UPS."

NOTE: *The power supply contains a capacitor that holds a charge with sufficient voltage to kill you. To prevent a potentially fatal shock, you should never open a power supply. The power supply can retain the charge even after it has been powered off and unplugged for an extended period of time (months or more).*

If you examine the power supply, you will find that it provides several small electrical cables, as shown in Figure 7.8, which you can use to power devices you install inside the PC. Normally, two of the cables will connect to the motherboard (to power the CPU, RAM, and the other motherboard components). As you install devices such as a hard drive or CD-ROM drive within the system unit, you will use one of the small cables to power the device.

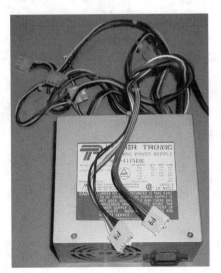

Figure 7.8 The power supply provides several cables you can use to power devices within the system unit.

Locating Your Disk Drives

As shown in Figure 7.9, your floppy disk, hard drive, and CD-ROM drive reside within the system unit. Normally the system unit will contain several drive bays (holders) into which you can insert the drive. If you examine each drive, you will find that the drive has a power cable and a ribbon cable. The drive uses the ribbon cable to transfer data to and from the motherboard buses.

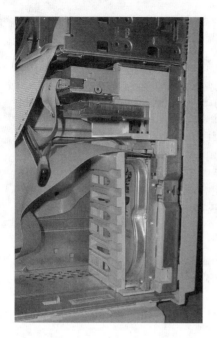

Figure 7.9 The floppy, hard disk, and CD-ROM drives reside in drive bays within the system unit.

Because smoke or dust can easily damage the hard drive's precise mechanical components, the drive is enclosed within a sealed case. Never open a hard drive's case. In so doing, you would likely damage the drive and the magnetic surface the drive uses to record data. The dust particles in an office space are much larger than the distances that separate the drive's read/write head from the disk's recording surface.

Although you may be able to view the working components within a floppy disk drive or CD-ROM drive, you should never look into an operational CD-ROM drive. The drive uses a small laser to read data on the surface of the CD. Should you look into the laser, you may permanently damage your eye.

Understanding the PC's Expansion Slots

Throughout this book's lessons, you will learn ways you can expand your PC's capabilities by installing a hardware card, such as a modem, network interface card, or SCSI adapter into one of the expansion slots that reside on the PC motherboard.

Depending on the motherboard type, the number and type of expansion slots will differ. Lesson 27, "Understanding Buses," examines the various expansion slot types in detail.

In general, to install a card into an expansion slot, you will first remove the metal slot cover that appears on the back of the system unit. Then, as shown in Figure 7.10, you will gently insert the card into the expansion slot. Then, using the screw that previously held the slot cover in place, you should secure the card.

Figure 7.10 Inserting and securing a card into a PC expansion slot.

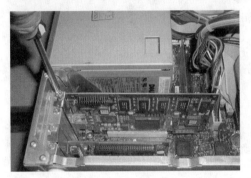

Cleaning the System Unit and Closing the System Unit Cover

Over time, depending on your work environment, your PC system unit may accumulate dust. As a general rule, you should not open the system unit simply to clean it. As you clean the PC's sensitive electronic components, you may likely damage a key chip or connector.

That said, should you open the PC unit to install a device or card and find that the system unit is quite dusty, you should use an aerosol blower as shown in Figure 7.11 to blow the dust from the system unit. Do not place the aerosol blower near the motherboard and the chips it contains. The cold air the blower generates can damage sensitive chips.

Finally, when you close the system unit cover, do so with care so you do not inadvertently damage or unplug a ribbon cable that connects a disk drive to the motherboard.

Figure 7.11 Use an aerosol blower to remove dust from inside the system unit.

Replacing the Motherboard

Because the motherboard contains the PC's key electronic components, most users are quite intimidated by the prospect of having to replace a failed motherboard. Because you may have to remove your disk drives or other devices before you can gain access to the motherboard, the process of replacing the motherboard can be time consuming.

After you shut down and power off your PC, you should wear an antistatic wristband as you begin to work with the motherboard. You should have a clean, well-lit location where you can safely place any components you remove. As you work, you should keep a list of the cables you remove and their orientation, so you can later check off the cables after you install the new motherboard.

In addition to attaching power and ribbon cables, you will need to move your CPU from your old motherboard to your new board (when you purchase a new motherboard, it will not come with a CPU). In addition, provided your old RAM is compatible with your motherboard, you will need to move your RAM chips as well.

EXAM REVIEW

1. The largest component within the PC system unit is the _____.

2. The largest chip on the motherboard is typically the _____.

3. True or False
   The PC's RAM resides on chips you insert into slots on the motherboard.

4. The power supply's purpose is to convert _____ into _____.

5. True or False
   A CD-ROM drive contains a laser that could potentially damage your eye should you look into the drive as it reads a CD's contents.

6. To expand the PC's capabilities, you can insert a hardware card into an _____ that resides on the motherboard.

7. True or False
   The power supply provides small power cables you can use to power devices external to the PC.

Understanding
Device Drivers

To communicate with a device such as a printer, modem, mouse, or network interface card, the operating system uses special software called a device driver. When you install Windows, the setup program installs device driver software for common devices. Later, when you purchase a new hardware device, you must install the corresponding device driver before Windows can use the device.

Often, a device manufacturer will update device driver software, either to correct program errors (bugs), to improve performance, or to add new capabilities. Using the Windows Device Manager, you can easily check for and install such updates.

This lesson examines device driver operations in detail. You will learn how to determine when Windows is unable to use the current device driver, how to determine the driver's version information, and how to check for and install driver updates.

F A C T S

- A device driver is special software that the operating system uses to communicate with a device. Before you can use a device, you must install the device driver software.

- When you purchase a hardware device, the device will normally come with a CD-ROM or floppy disk that contains the device driver software.

- The steps you must perform to install a device driver may differ. In some cases, you will run a special setup program to install the driver. Other times, when Windows recognizes the new hardware device, Windows will display a dialog box that prompts you to insert the CD-ROM or disk that contains the driver. The documentation that accompanies your hardware device will tell you the steps you must perform.

- Using the Windows System Information utility, you can display a list of the device drivers installed on your system as well as information regarding the driver's version number.

- The Windows Device Manager lets you view specifics about a device driver, and in some cases, you can use the Device Manager to check for and to install an update to the driver that exists on the Microsoft Windows Update Web site.

- Most device manufacturers make their device drivers available for downloading from the World Wide Web.

- Each time Windows starts, Windows must load the device driver software for each of the hardware devices installed on your PC. There may be times, perhaps due to a corrupt file, when Windows cannot successfully load a device driver.

- By directing Windows to log its startup operations, you can determine which drivers Windows successfully loaded as well as drivers that Windows was unable to load. Windows 98 places its startup log within the root directory file *Bootlog.txt*. Likewise, Windows 2000 uses the *Winnt\Wtbtlog.txt* file. Using the WordPad accessory, you can view the log file's contents.

- Depending on the error Windows encounters while trying to load a device driver, there may be times when the error prevents Windows itself from starting. In such cases, you can direct Windows to start in Safe mode, which is a scaled-down version of the operating system that you can use to perform your troubleshooting operations.

Operating Systems Use Device Drivers to Interact with Hardware Devices

In general, operating systems such as Windows exist to let users run programs and store and retrieve information on disk. Behind the scenes, the operating system sits between the applications that users run and the computer hardware. To communicate with specific hardware devices, an operating system relies on special software called a device driver.

When you print a document, for example, Windows does not have to know the specifics about your printer. Instead, Windows interacts with the printer's device driver software, telling the driver the data that Windows wants the printer to print. The device driver, in turn, interacts with the printer, perhaps sending the printer special values that direct it to print the document in landscape mode, high resolution, and so on.

By relying on the device driver to interact with the hardware device, Windows does not have to understand the "ins and outs" of the thousands of printers that exist today. Each hardware device has a device driver that sits between Windows and the device.

As new devices become available, the only change that Windows requires before it can interact with the device is that the user install a device driver specific to the device.

Installing a Device Driver

When you purchase a device, such as a new modem, network interface card, or video card, you will receive a CD-ROM (or possibly a floppy disk) that contains the device driver software you must install before Windows can interact with the device.

In some cases, using the CD-ROM, you must run a special setup program that will install the device driver on your system. Other times, Windows will recognize that you have installed new hardware and will display a dialog box similar to that shown in Figure 8.1 that prompts you to insert the CD-ROM or floppy disk that accompanied the device. After Windows installs the device driver, you must restart your system before Windows will begin to use the driver to interact with the device.

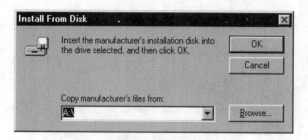

Figure 8.1 After Windows identifies a new hardware device, Windows may prompt you to insert a CD-ROM or floppy disk that contains the corresponding device driver software.

Viewing the Device Drivers Installed on Your System

Behind the scenes, Windows uses a myriad of device drivers. To view a list of the drivers installed on your system, run the System Information utility as shown in Figure 8.2.

Name	Version	Manufacturer	Description
KERNEL	4.10.1998	Microsoft Corporation	Windows Kernel core component
SYSTEM	4.10.1998	Microsoft Corporation	Windows System Driver core component
KEYBOARD	4.10.2222	Microsoft Corporation	Windows Keyboard Driver
MOUSE	9.01.0.000	Microsoft Corporation	Microsoft Pointing Device Driver
DISPLAY	4.13.01.2759	Intel(R) Corporation	Intel Graphics Driver
DIBENG	4.10.1998	Microsoft Corporation	Windows 98 DIB Engine
SOUND	4.10.1998	Microsoft Corporation	Windows Sound Driver core component
COMM	4.10.1998	Microsoft Corporation	Windows COMM Driver
GDI	4.10.2222	Microsoft Corporation	Windows Graphics Device Interface core co...
USER	4.10.2222	Microsoft Corporation	Windows User-interface core component
DDEML	4.10.1998	Microsoft Corporation	DDE Management library
MSPLUS	4.40.500	Microsoft Corporation	Cool stuff for Windows
MSGSRV32	4.10.2222	Microsoft Corporation	Windows 32-bit VxD Message Server
MMSYSTEM	4.03.1998	Microsoft Corporation	System APIs for Multimedia
POWER	4.10.1998	Microsoft Corporation	Advanced Power Management driver
LZEXPAND	4.00.429	Microsoft Corporation	LZExpand Libraries
VER	4.10.1998	Microsoft Corporation	Version Checking and File Installation Libraries
SHELL	4.10.1998	Microsoft Corporation	Windows Shell library
COMMCTRL	4.10.1998	Microsoft Corporation	Custom Controls Library
SYSTHUNK	4.10.1998	Microsoft Corporation	Windows System Thunk Library
OLECLI	1.20.000	Microsoft Corporation	Object Linking and Embedding Client Library
OLESVR	1.10.000	Microsoft Corporation	Object Linking and Embedding Server Library
SYSDM	4.10.2222	Microsoft Corporation	System Control Panel Applet
SETUPX	4.10.2222	Microsoft Corporation	Windows Setup Functions
SETUP4	4.10.1998	Microsoft Corporation	Windows Setup Functions
COMMDLG	4.00.950	Microsoft Corporation	Common Dialogs libraries
PIFMGR	4.10.2222	Microsoft Corporation	Program Information File (PIF) Management S...
TOOLHELP	4.10.1998	Microsoft Corporation	Windows Debug/Tool helper library

Figure 8.2 Using the System Information utility, you can view a list of drivers installed on your system.

To view your system's device drivers using the System Information utility, perform these steps:

1. Select the Start menu Programs option and choose Accessories. Windows will display the Accessories submenu.

2. Within the Accessories submenu, select System Tools and choose System Information. Windows, in turn, will display the System Information utility.

3. Within the System Information utility, click on the plus sign that precedes the Software Environment entry. If you are using Windows 2000, click on the Drivers entry. If you are using Windows 98, click on the 16-bit Modules Loaded entry or the 32-bit Modules Loaded entry.

Within Windows 98, the 16-bit modules correspond to older device drivers, from Windows 3.x, that Windows still uses. The 32-bit modules correspond to newer device drivers. Under Windows 2000, all device drivers are 32-bit drivers. In addition, within Windows 98, you will find a Drivers entry that you can expand to display a list of Kernel drivers (key drivers that are built into Windows itself) as well as MS-DOS-based and user-mode drivers.

As you examine the drivers your system is using, you may encounter drivers for devices you are no longer using. By removing those drivers from your system, you can free up resources such as RAM and disk space for other uses. In Lesson 18, "Using the Windows Device Manager," you will learn how to remove a device driver that you no longer require.

Troubleshooting a Device Driver Problem

Each time Windows starts up, it must load the device drivers for each of the devices installed or connected to your system. If, after you install a device driver and restart your system, Windows does not see a specific device, the problem may be that Windows failed to successfully load the device driver.

As discussed in Lesson 6, "Understanding the PC Startup Process," you can direct Windows to log its startup operations to a file. Then, by using the WordPad accessory program to view the file's contents, as shown in Figure 8.3, you can determine if Windows successfully loaded the driver.

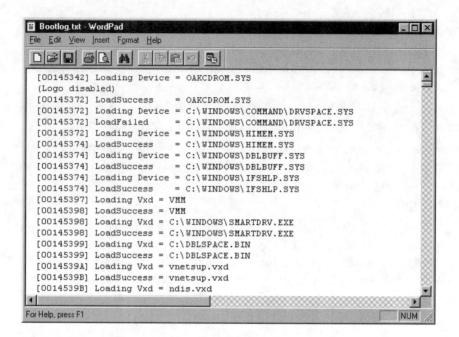

Figure 8.3 Viewing the Windows startup log file to determine if Windows successfully loaded a device driver.

If Windows did not successfully install the driver, you may need to reinstall the device driver software because the file that contains the driver may have become corrupt. If, after you reinstall the driver and restart your system, Windows still fails to successfully load the driver, you should look on the device manufacturer's Web site for an update to the driver software.

Using the Windows Device Manager to Identify Device Driver Errors

In Lesson 18, "Using the Windows Device Manager," you will examine a special program called the Device Manager that you can use to view specifics about the devices on your system, such as device driver information as well as each device's resource use (interrupt request lines and I/O ports). As you will learn in this lesson, you can also use the Device Manager to detect device driver problems and to check for and to install device driver updates.

When the Device Manager determines that Windows is unable to use a device due to a device driver error, the Device Manager will precede the device's entry with a yellow circle that contains a black exclamation mark, as shown in Figure 8.4.

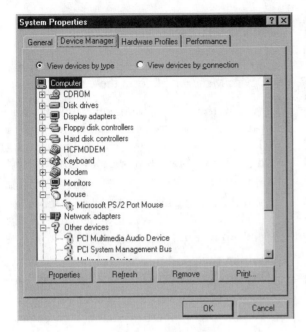

Figure 8.4 The Device Manager indicates device driver problems by preceding a device entry with a yellow circle that contains a black exclamation mark.

To run the Device Manager under Windows 98, perform these steps:

1. Select the Start menu Settings option and choose Control Panel. Windows will display the Control Panel window.

2. In the Control Panel, double-click on the System icon. Windows will display the System Properties dialog box.

3. Within the System Properties dialog box, select the Device Manager tab.

If you are using Windows 2000, you display the Device Manager by performing these steps:

1. Select the Start menu Settings option and choose Control Panel. Windows will display the Control Panel window.

2. Within the Control Panel, double-click on the System icon. Windows will display the System Properties dialog box.

3. Within the System Properties dialog box, select the Hardware tab. Windows will display the Hardware sheet.

4. Within the Hardware sheet, click the Device Manager button.

The Device Manager organizes the devices on your system using a treelike structure. To display specific devices within a device branch, click on the plus sign that precedes the device-type entry. The Device Manager will expand the list of corresponding devices.

Viewing Specifics about a Device Driver

If you encounter errors while trying to use a device, the device manufacturer's technical support staff may ask you to provide them with specifics about the device driver, such as its version number. In addition, the technical support staff may want to know which resources (IRQ and I/O port settings) the device may be using. Using the Windows Device Manager, you can view specifics about a device driver as shown in Figure 8.5.

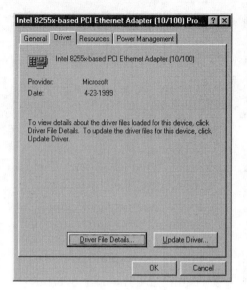

Figure 8.5 Using the Device Manager to view specifics about a device driver.

To view specifics about a device driver within the Device Manager, perform these steps:

1. Within the Device Manager, click on the plus sign that precedes the device type. The Device Manager will expand the device type branch to display entries for specific devices.

2. Within the device list, right-click on the device you desire. Windows will display a pop-up menu.

3. Within the pop-up menu, select Properties. Windows will display the device's Properties dialog box.

4. Within the Properties dialog box, select the Driver tab.

Upgrading a Device Driver

If you encounter an error while trying to use a device or if Windows fails to successfully load a device driver, you should determine if a newer version of the device driver exists on the manufacturer's Web site that you can download and install. Device manufacturers periodically update device drivers to correct programming errors (bugs), to improve performance, or to add new functionality.

If a device is working properly, you may not want to install a driver upgrade simply because a new driver is available. It is possible that the upgrade, due to an unforeseen incompatibility with your other software, may introduce an error that prevents the device from working.

That said, some device manufacturers make it easy for you to check for and install an upgrade using the Windows Device Manager by placing an Update Driver button on the Driver sheet that appears within the device's Properties dialog box, as shown in Figure 8.6. When you select the Update Driver button, Windows display a list of locations (floppy, CD-ROM, a specific disk location, as well as the Internet) that you can direct Windows to search for a new device driver. By selecting the Microsoft Windows Update option, you direct Windows to examine the Web site for a new version of the device driver software. If the software exists, you will have the opportunity to download and install it.

Figure 8.6 Using the Device Manager to update a device driver.

Using Safe Mode to Recover from a Driver Error

If you install a device driver and Windows later fails to start, you should start your system in "Safe mode" as discussed in Lesson 6. When you direct Windows to start in Safe mode, Windows will not process the Registry's contents, will only load the device drivers it needs to get up and running, and will not enable network support. After Windows starts in Safe mode, you can begin troubleshooting the cause of the error.

Directing Windows 98 to Skip a Device Driver's Loading

If you are using Windows 98 and you find (by viewing the *Bootlog.txt* file) that Windows is not successfully loading a device driver, you can use the Automatic Skip Driver Agent shown in Figure 8.7 to direct Windows not to load a specific device driver the next time the system starts. By directing Windows to skip a driver in this way, you may be able to start Windows in Normal mode so you can troubleshoot the error and replace the driver.

Figure 8.7 Using the Automatic Skip Driver Agent to direct Windows not to load a driver.

Device Drivers and MS-DOS

Installing a device driver within Windows is a relatively easy task. You normally run a setup program that installs the driver or you respond to a dialog box that prompts you to insert the CD-ROM that contains the driver and then Windows does the rest.

In contrast, to install a device driver within the MS-DOS operating system, users had to edit the root directory file *config.sys* and place a DEVICE= entry within the file that specified the directory path to the device driver file. Within the MS-DOS environment, most device driver files used the *.sys* file extension. The following entry illustrates the use of the DEVICE= entry within *config.sys*. After you edited the *config.sys* file, you had to restart MS-DOS before the operating system would use the device driver.

```
DEVICE=C:\mouse\mouse.sys
```

EXAM REVIEW

CERTIFICATION

① To communicate with hardware devices, operating systems use special software called _____.

② True or False
Each time Windows starts, Windows logs information about the device drivers it successfully loaded within the *drivers.txt* file.

③ Using the _____ program, you can view a list of the device drivers Windows is currently running.

④ By removing a device driver for a device Windows is no longer using, you can free up resources such as _____ and _____.

⑤ A user's hard drive fails and you must reinstall Windows. During the installation process, Windows identifies a new hardware device and prompts you to insert a CD-ROM that contains the driver, which you do not have. How can you get the missing device driver?

⑥ Within the MS-DOS environment, users installed device drivers by placing a _____ entry within the *config.sys* file.

⑦ If Windows is unable to recognize a device or encounters an error with the device's driver, the Device Manager will indicate the error by _____.

Lesson 9

Working with Cards and Chips

Within the PC system unit, you will find a myriad of hardware cards and chips. In general, regardless of the function the card or chip provides, the steps you must perform to remove or replace the card or chip will be the same.

Throughout this book's lessons, you will learn about a wide range of hardware cards. With the exception of the CPU and RAM, you will normally not have to work with chips. That said, however, should you install the CPU or RAM incorrectly, your system will not operate. By following the recommendations this lesson provides, you will reduce your risk of damaging a card or chip's sensitive electronics.

F A C T S

+ When users install a card or chip, the greatest risk to the card or chip is an electrostatic shock. To reduce the risk of static discharge, always wear an antistatic wristband when you work with cards or chips.

+ Never remove or insert a card or chip while the system unit is plugged in. The power supply provides constant power to the motherboard that could damage a card or chip.

+ After you remove a card or chip, you should store the card or chip inside an antistatic bag.

+ To remove or insert a card, you may need to gently rock the card in the expansion slot.

+ Before you install a hardware card, make sure the socket is free from dust and that cards connectors are free from dust and smudges.

+ To clean a card's connector, use a Q-Tip with rubbing alcohol or a pencil eraser.

Preparing to Work with a Card or Chip

If you follow the guidelines this lesson presents, the greatest risk to your cards and chips will be electrostatic shock. To reduce the risk of static damaging a card or chip, you should always wear an antistatic wristband similar to that shown in Figure 9.1 whenever you work with cards or chips. The wristband provides a constant source of ground to which electrons will travel.

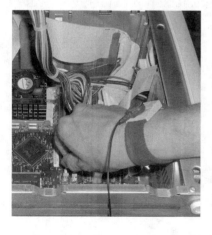

Figure 9.1 To protect your cards and chips, wear an anti-static wristband.

Next, never insert a card or chip while the PC is plugged in. As it turns out, even after you power off your PC, the power supply provides power to the motherboard. If you examine the motherboard after you power off your system, you may find an illuminated LED on either the motherboard or an expansion slot. The power supply provides continual power to the motherboard so that the PC can awaken itself at a specific time (based on a CMOS setting) or upon an incoming modem or network connection.

If you are going to insert or remove a card or chip, first unplug your system.

Use an Antistatic Bag to Store Cards and Chips

If you remove a card from your PC, you should place the card into an antistatic bag, as shown in Figure 9.2. Similarly, if you remove a chip from your system, you should also place the chip inside an antistatic bag. Further, if the chip has pins which may be easily bent or broken, you may want to gently press the pins into a small piece of styrofoam.

Figure 9.2 Always place cards or chips that you remove from your PC into an antistatic bag.

Removing a Card or Chip

To remove a hardware card, you will normally need to first unscrew and remove a small screw that holds the card in place within the expansion slot. In some cases, you may need to rock the card gently to free the card from the socket.

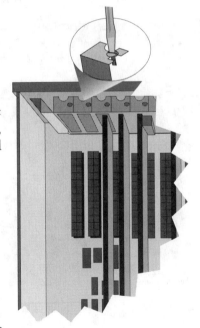

Depending on the type of chip you are removing, the steps you must perform may differ. Some chips use a zero insertion force (ZIF) connector that contains a small lever you can open or close to release or secure the chip into place within the socket. Other chips may

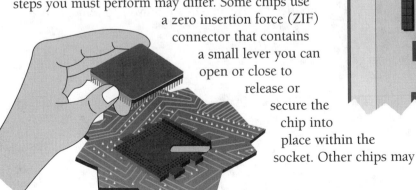

require that you use a small chip extractor to remove the chip.

If you do not have a chip extractor, you may be able to bend a small screwdriver in a way that lets you slide the edge of the driver under the chip so that you can gently pry the chip from the socket. Again, after you remove the card or chip, you should place it into an antistatic bag.

Inserting a Card or Chip

When you insert a hardware card, connectors within the expansion slot make an electrical contact with connectors on the card itself. If either connectors are smudged or dirty, the card and socket may fail to make a proper connection that prevents the card from working.

Before you insert a card into an expansion slot, you may want to use an aerosol blower to remove any dust that may have accumulated in the slot, as shown in Figure 9.3.

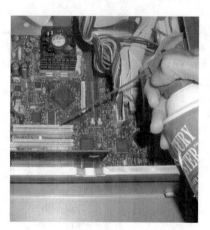

Figure 9.3 Use an aerosol blower to clean dust from expansion slots.

Next, examine the card's connectors. If the connectors are dirty or smudged, use a Q-Tip and rubbing alcohol to clean the connectors. Some users will use a pencil eraser to gently clean the connectors. Should particles of the eraser accumulate on the connector, use an aerosol blower to remove them.

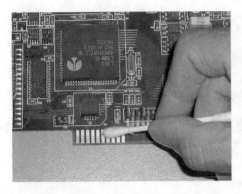 

Figure 9.4 Remove any dust or smudges from a card's connectors before you insert the card.

After you clean the socket and the card's connectors, gently slide the card into the socket. Again, you may need to gently rock the card into place. After the card is fitted into the socket, secure the card into place with the small screw that connects the card to the system unit.

If you are inserting a chip, make sure you align the chip in the correct orientation, so that pin one on the chip corresponds to pin one on the socket. Then, gently press the chip into the socket, making sure that each of the pins slides into place and that you do not have a misaligned pin that will prevent a card from working.

Troubleshooting After You Move a PC

If your PC stops working after you move the PC from one location to another, it is quite possible that a card or chip has come free from its socket. Users refer to this phenomenon as chip or card creeping. Open your system and examine each of your cards and chips. Make sure you are wearing an antistatic wristband. Then, gently push each card and chip securely into place.

EXAM REVIEW

A+ CERTIFICATION

1. When you install cards or chips, the greatest source of damage to the chip or card is _____.

2. Users refer to a card or chip's ability to work itself free from a slot or socket as _____.

3. ZIF is an acronym for _____.

4. To clean a card's connectors, you can use _____ or _____.

Taking a Closer Look at Common Cables and Ports

Throughout this book, we will examine ways that users can connect a myriad of devices to a PC. As you examine specific lessons, you will learn the advantages of each technique, such as speed, ease of configuration, or hot swapping. Further, you will learn to determine which connection type is well suited for various devices.

To get you up and running, this lesson examines the common PC ports and the cables you use to connect devices to the ports. Although many users are readily familiar with connecting devices to the common PC ports, few users know specifics about the ports, such as their speeds. This lesson will provide you with key facts you should know as you prepare for the A+ Certification exam.

F A C T S

- A port is a connector on the PC to which a user can connect an external device.

- Users describe ports and cables in terms of the number of pins the connector contains as well as the connector's gender.

- A male port or cable is a connector that contains pins that protrude from the connector. In contrast, a female connector contains receptacles into which you can plug a male connector.

- On the back of the PC system unit, you will find several common ports: mouse, keyboard, video, parallel, serial, and a Universal Serial Bus (USB).

- Users connect a mouse and keyboard using a small round six-pin mini-DIN connector. DIN is an acronym for Deutsche Industry Norm—a German standards group.

- If a device such as a mouse, keyboard, monitor, or printer does not reach your PC, you can normally use an extension to increase the cable's length.

- The most widely used network connector is the RJ-45, which looks like a large version of a standard phone plug.

- Depending on a network's technology, such an Ethernet or token-ring network, the network interface card that connects a PC to the network will differ, as well as the port on the card to which the user connects the network cable. Today, network interface cards commonly use RJ-45, BNC, and USB-based connections.

- A parallel port uses a 25-pin female connector. Users use parallel ports to connect a printer directly to a PC.

- Parallel printer cables use two different connector types. The end of the cable that connects to the PC uses a 25-pin male connector. The end of the printer cable that connects to the printer uses a special Centronix connector.

- All parallel ports are not created equal. Older PCs used standard parallel ports that support only output operations. In contrast, newer PCs often use extended capabilities ports (ECP) or enhanced parallel ports (EPP) that support bi-directional communication and high data rates. Using the bi-directional port, a printer can provide status information (such as a paper jam) to the PC. In addition, users can connect a wide range of devices to the port, such as a scanner, hard drive, and so on.

- Parallel ports transfer 8 bits of data at the same time over 8 data wires within the parallel cable.

F A C T S

- All PCs come with at least one serial port. The serial port may use a 9-pin or 25-pin male connector. Most serial devices use only 9 wires. If a PC contains a 9-pin port and a device uses a 25-pin connector, you can use an adapter to convert the 9-pin port to a 25-pin port, or the 25-pin cable to a 9-pin cable.

- For years, PC users made extensive use of serial ports to connect devices such as a mouse, modem, or even a printer. Today, however, few newer devices use the serial port due to the port's slow speed.

- Serial devices transfer one bit of data a time, over a single data wire within the serial cable. Within the serial port (and within serial devices) is a special chip called a UART that oversees the sending and receiving of bits across the data wire.

- VGA video cards normally use a 15-pin female connector to which you can connect a monitor.

- Most PCs provide two Universal Serial Bus (USB) ports to which users can connect a wide range of devices. The USB is unique in that when you connect a device to the bus, you do not have to worry about IRQs and I/O port settings—the bus does not use them. In addition, the bus supports hot swapping which means you can add or remove a device without having to first shut down the system.

- You can connect up to 127 devices to a USB by using hubs that provide multiple device ports and by connecting a device to another that provides a USB port.

Understanding PC Ports

A PC *port* is simply a connector into which you plug a cable in order to attach a device to the PC. A PC's ports reside at the back of the PC system unit, as shown in Figure 10.1. Depending on the PC's configuration, the number and type of ports the PC provides may differ. Most PCs provide a parallel port to which you can connect a printer, a serial port to which you can

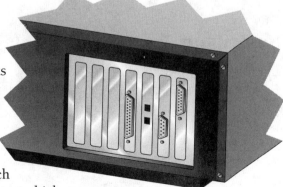

connect a modem, mouse, or other slower device, a video port to which you connect the monitor, a network port, and a Universal Serial Bus (USB) port to which you can attach (using hubs and ports on a USB-based device) up to 127 devices.

Figure 10.1 PC ports exist to let users connect external devices to the PC.

To expand a PC's capabilities, users insert hardware adapter cards (such as a SCSI or FireWire) into one of the PC's expansion slots that reside on the motherboard. The adapter card the user installs in the PC may provide one or more ports to which the user can attach a device.

If you are using a notebook PC, you will normally find the ports on the back of the PC, often behind a small cover that you open to reveal the ports, as shown in Figure 10.2. Most notebook PCs provide the same ports as a desktop PC. In addition, as discussed in Lesson 34, "Taking Advantage of PCMCIA Cards," many notebook PC users insert cards into the PC's PCMCIA slots that extend the PC's capabilities by providing support for a modem, network, or other interface.

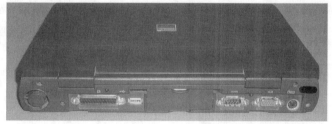

Figure 10.2 Notebook PC's provide ports identical to those you will find on a desktop PC.

Describing Ports and Cables

Users frequently describe ports and cables as either male or female based on the connector type. A male connector has pins, as shown in Figure 10.3. In contrast, a female connector has receptacles into which the pins can be inserted, as shown in Figure 10.4.

Figure 10.3 Male connectors have visible pins.

Figure 10.4 Female connectors have receptacles into which a male connector's pins are inserted.

Users further describe connectors based on the number of pins the connector contains. The parallel port on the back of the PC, for example, uses a 25-pin female connector. Likewise, the PC's serial port will use either a 9-pin or 25-pin male connector.

Connecting a Mouse and Keyboard

In Lesson 11, "Working with the Keyboard and Mouse," you will examine keyboard and mouse operations in detail. As you will learn, today, most keyboards and mice use a small 6-pin mini-DIN connector as shown in Figure 10.5. DIN is an acronym for Deutsche Industry Norm—a standards committee. Because the keyboard and mouse connectors are identical, most PCs place a small icon (an image of either a keyboard or mouse) next to the corresponding connector, or the PC color codes the cables and ports.

Figure 10.5 Connecting a keyboard and mouse to a PC.

Depending on the size of your desk and the location of your PC, there may be times when your mouse or keyboard cannot connect to the PC due the device's short (normally six foot) cable length. In such cases, you can use an extension cable to increase the length of the cable by six. Normally, you will not encounter any errors by using a keyboard or mouse cable of 12 feet or less. If you increase the cable a greater distance, you may encounter intermittent errors due to the timing of the signals that travel across the cable.

Connecting a PC to a Network

Because of the explosive growth of computer networks, first within businesses and today within homes, many PCs now ship with a network interface card. As you will learn in Lesson 37, "Taking a Closer Look at Network Technologies," the most common network port type is the RJ-45 connector. As shown in Figure 10.6, the RJ-45 plug and cable look similar to, but is larger than, a standard phone plug.

**Figure 10.6
Most network interface cards use an RJ-45 connector.**

Depending on the type of network to which you are connecting a PC, the type of network interface card (and hence the port type) will vary. Some newer wireless networks, for example, let users connect a small wireless transmitter/receiver to a Universal Serial Bus. Likewise, as shown in Figure 10.7, some bus-topology networks connect PCs to the network using a BNC connector.

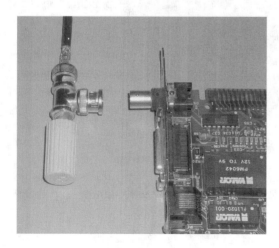

Figure 10.7 Many bus-topology networks connect PCs using a BNC connector.

As you will learn in Lesson 37, network interface cards differ based on the network's technology (such as Ethernet or token ring), as well as by speed.

Connecting a Printer

Today, most high-speed laser printers let you connect the printer directly to the PC or to a network cable (to simplify printer sharing and to increase performance). To connect a printer directly to a PC, users normally attach the printer to the PC's parallel port. As shown in Figure 10.8, the parallel port uses a 25-pin female connector.

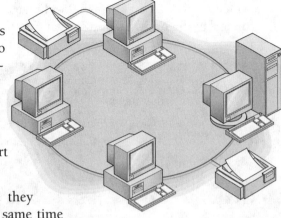

Parallel ports are so named because they transmit 8 bits of data (a byte) at the same time over 8 different data wires within the parallel cable. In contrast, a serial port, as discussed in the next section, transmits one byte of data at a time over a single data wire. Because the parallel port can transfer 8 bits at a time, the parallel port is much faster than the serial port.

Figure 10.8 Parallel ports use a 25-pin female connector.

Today, PCs normally have one parallel port. Unfortunately, all parallel ports are not created equal. Older PCs used a standard parallel port for output operations only that transferred data at speeds up to 150KBs. Newer PCs normally use an extended capabilities port (ECP) or an enhanced parallel port (EPP) to support high-speed bi-directional communication—meaning, the port can output data to a device and the device can send data back to the port. A printer, for example, might send status information back to the PC that tells the PC that the printer is out of paper. To take advantage of a bi-directional port, you must use a special bi-directional parallel cable. In addition to supporting printer operations, users can use the bi-directional ports to connect devices such as Zip disks, modems, and more.

The enhanced parallel port (EPP) was introduced in the early 1990s. By fine-tuning the interactions the parallel port and a device had to perform to exchange data, the EPP improved data throughput to 2MBs. Soon after the EPP's release, Microsoft and Hewlett-Packard released the extended capabilities port (ECP) that achieved similar data throughput rates by taking advantage of direct memory access (DMA) operations.

The parallel cable you use to connect a printer to the PC is unique in that the end of the cable you connect to the PC uses a 25-pin male connector, whereas the end of the cable you connect to the printer uses a special Centronix connector, as shown in Figure 10.9.

Figure 10.9 The parallel printer cable uses a 25-pin male connector (left) to attach to the PC and a Centronix connector (right) to attach to the printer.

Connecting Devices to the Serial Port

Years ago, users made extensive use of the PC's serial port to attach modems, mice, joysticks, and even printers to the PC. Today, PCs normally ship with one serial port, which may use a 9-pin or 25-pin male connector, as shown in Figure 10.10. Do not confuse the 25-pin serial port with the 25-pin parallel port. The ports are different. The serial port uses a male connector whereas the parallel port uses a female connector. Users refer to the serial port connectors as DB25 or DB9 connectors based on whether the port is a 25-pin or 9-pin connector.

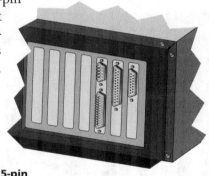

Figure 10.10 Serial ports use a 9-pin or 25-pin male connector.

Serial devices normally only use 9 wires or less. As such, the 25-pin port and the 9-pin port are functionally equivalent. In fact, if your PC has a 9-pin serial port and a device uses a 25-pin serial cable (or vice versa), you can buy a converter that changes the port or cable from a 9-pin to 25-pin cable or vice versa.

The serial port is so named because it transmits data one bit at a time over a single wire. To transmit a byte of data, for example, the serial port must send each of the bits, one at a time, across the wire in a serial fashion. In contrast, the parallel port sends 8 bits of data at the same time across 8 wires.

Within a serial port, a special chip called a Universal Asynchronous Receiver Transmitter (UART) is responsible for taking a byte of data and breaking it into the individual bits for transmission across the cable. At the other end of the cable, a UART within the device receiving the data packages the individual bits back into a byte. In general, a UART is a chip (users commonly refer to the UART based on its chip type as a 15500 or 16550) that oversees the sending and receiving of data through the serial port.

Connecting the Monitor

Lesson 49, "Performing Monitor Operations," and Lesson 50, "Taking a Closer Look at PC Video Operations," examine the monitor and PC video cards in detail. Over the years, the number of pins used by the cable that connects the monitor to the video adapter has changed. The original IBM PC and its monochrome display adapter, for example, used a 9-pin connector. The color graphics adapter (CGA) and the enhanced graphics adapter (EGA) also used a 9-pin connector. Today, the VGA adapter uses 15 pins, as shown in Figure 10.11.

Figure 10.11 The VGA adapter provides a 15-pin female connector.

Connecting Devices to the Universal Serial Bus

Over the past few years, the Universal Serial Bus (USB) has emerged as one of the simplest ways to connect a myriad of devices to the PC. Lesson 31, "Using a Universal Serial Bus (USB)," examines the USB in detail.

In general, by using the USB, you can connect devices to the PC such as a USB-based mouse, keyboard, modem, network interface card, and more. As shown in Figure 10.12, most PCs come with two USB ports. If you require more than two USB-based devices at the same time, you can connect a hub to the port to which you can connect multiple devices. Further, some USB devices provide a port to which you can attach another USB device. By combining hubs and device-to-device connections, you can attach up to 127 devices to the USB.

Figure 10.12 The Universal Serial Bus provides a port for a small rectangular connector.

The devices that you connect to the USB share the bus's bandwidth. Further, many of the smaller devices you connect to the USB (such as a mouse) will receive the power the device needs to operate from the bus itself.

The USB is very simple to use—you simply attach a device. As you will learn in Lesson 31, you do not have to specify IRQ and I/O port settings for USB-based devices, the bus and the devices do not use them. Further, the USB lets you hot swap devices, meaning, you can connect or remove a device without having to first shut down your system.

EXAM REVIEW

CERTIFICATION

① Users refer to port and cable connectors by the number of _____ in the cable's connector and the connector's _____.

② True or False
A male connector has pins that protrude from the connector.

③ The keyboard and mouse each use a small 6-pin connector that users commonly refer to as a _____ connector.

④ The most common network port is the _____, which resembles a large version of a standard telephone plug.

⑤ True or False
The parallel port uses a 25-pin male connector.

⑥ True or False
An enhanced capabilities parallel port (ECP) uses a special 36-pin connector.

⑦ Serial ports use either a _____-pin or _____-pin male connector.

⑧ True or False
Using a special adapter, you can attach a 9-pin serial cable to a 25-pin serial port (or vice versa).

⑨ Identify the following ports:

A.

_____

B.

_____

C.

_____

D.

_____

⑩ Because of its ease of use, users connect devices to a bus called the _____ or USB.

⑪ VGA monitors normally connect to a _____-pin female connector.

⑫ The serial port uses a special chip called the UART to oversee the transmission of individual data bits. UART is an acronym for _____.

⑬ Newer PCs support _____ parallel ports that support output and input operations.

⑭ To connect a printer to a parallel port, you use a cable that contains a 25-pin male connector and a special connector called a _____ that connects to the printer.

⑮ Using a Universal Serial Bus (USB), you can connect up to _____ devices to a PC.

Lesson 11

Working with the Keyboard and Mouse

With respect to actual "hands on" user operations, the keyboard and mouse get more use than any other PC components. Although the keyboard and mouse are mechanical devices with moving parts, both devices are amazingly reliable.

Admittedly, you may have to periodically clean the keyboard to remove dust (or pizza crumbs). In Lesson 14, "Cleaning and Maintaining Your PC," you will examine the steps you must perform to clean the keyboard and mouse. In this lesson, you will examine ways you can connect a keyboard or mouse to a PC, as well as software techniques you can perform to improve your keyboard and mouse responsiveness.

F A C T S

- Because of the characters that appear on the top-left row of the keyboard keys, users frequently refer to the keyboard's layout as a QWERTY layout.

- Users normally connect keyboards to a PC using a 6-pin mini-DIN connector. However, USB- and IR-based keyboards do exist.

- Users normally connect a mouse to the PC using a 6-pin mini-DIN connector. However, USB- and serial-port-based connectors, as well as IR-based connectors, exist.

- To communicate with the PC, the keyboard and mouse send signals across wires within the cable that connects the device to the PC.

- Within the keyboard and mouse are electronics (a controller) that generate the electronic signals the device sends to the PC.

- Each time you press a keyboard key, the keyboard controller sends a special value to the PC called a scancode that the PC uses to determine the key you pressed.

- Using the Control Panel Keyboard icon, you can improve the keyboard's responsiveness by changing the repeat delay and repeat rate settings.

- Using the Control Panel Mouse icon, you can increase or decrease the speed at which the mouse pointer moves across the screen and you can fine-tune the system's responsiveness to double-click operations.

Understanding Keyboard and Mouse Electronics

Like all devices, the keyboard and mouse communicate with the PC by exchanging electronic signals. Each time you press a keyboard key or move your mouse across your desk, the device sends signals to the PC.

The keyboard and mouse each contain electronics (one or more chips) that technicians refer to as the *controller*. To operate, the controller requires power that it receives from the PC via the cable that connects the device to the system unit. Figure 11.1 illustrates the keyboard electronics that exist beneath your keyboard keys.

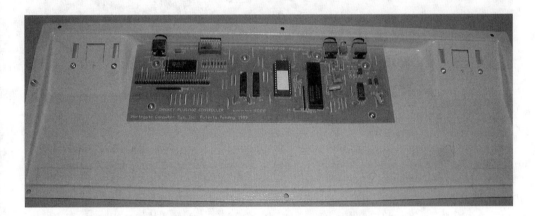

Figure 11.1 The keyboard electronics reside beneath the keypad.

When you power on the PC, the BIOS-based power on self-test (POST) interacts with the keyboard controller to verify the keyboard is working. If the keyboard controller does not respond to the test's queries, the system will display an error message and the PC will likely not start. As a result, you normally cannot start a PC that does not have a keyboard connected. Some CMOS setup programs, as discussed in Lesson 26, "Configuring the PC's CMOS Settings," will let you direct the PC to start despite the fact that no keyboard is attached. The ability to start a PC that does not have a keyboard is convenient when you have servers to which you do not want to attach a keyboard in order to increase security.

Taking a Closer Look at Keyboard Connectors

Years ago, users connected keyboards to a PC using a large 5-pin connector called a DIN (Deutsch Industry Norm) connector. Today, most keyboards use a small 6-pin mini-DIN connector. Over the past few years, USB-based keyboards have also emerged. Figure 11.2 illustrates the various common keyboard connectors.

Figure 11.2 Connecting a keyboard using a 5-pin DIN, 6-pin mini-DIN, and a USB connector.

Some PCs also support InfraRed (IR) keyboard connections. In fact, if you must work on a crowded desk and you want to get rid of your keyboard cable, you can purchase an IR-based keyboard that communicates with a small receiver that you connect to a USB port or to a hardware card installed in one of your PC's expansion slots. To operate successfully, the IR-based keyboard must have a clear line of site to the IR receiver.

Understanding Keyboard Scancodes

When you press a key on your keyboard, the keyboard controller sends a signal to the PC that indicates the key you selected. When you press the A key, for example, the controller does not send the letter A to the PC, but rather, a special value that users refer to as a scancode. Each key on the keyboard has a unique scancode value. By using scancodes, as

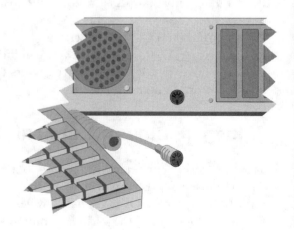

opposed to characters, PCs (Windows actually) can more easily support international keyboard layouts.

Within the United States, most users work with QWERTY-based keyboards which are so named because the top row of keys corresponds to the letters Q, W, E, R, T, and Y, as shown in Figure 11.3. Outside of the United States, a keyboard's layout may use an entirely different set of characters. In either case, the keyboard controller passes a scancode to the PC to indicate the key pressed. Most users and programmers can ignore the fact that the keyboard controller sends scancodes to the PC. However, technicians who are preparing for the A+ Certification exam should understand the term scancode.

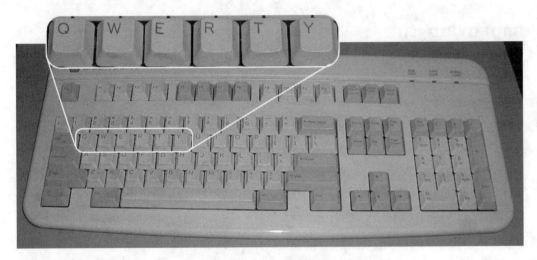

Figure 11.3 Users commonly refer to keyboards as QWERTY keyboards.

Taking a Closer Look at Mouse Connectors

Years ago, users normally connected a mouse to the PC's 9-pin serial port. Today, most users connect the mouse to the PC using a small 6-pin mini-DIN connector. Further, many newer mouse devices support USB connections as well. Figure 11.4 illustrates the common mouse connections. In addition, some PCs also support IR-based mice.

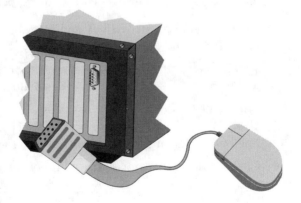

Figure 11.4 Connecting a mouse using a 9-pin serial port, a 6-pin mini-DIN, and a USB connector.

Improving the Keyboard's Responsiveness

As you know, when you hold down a keyboard key, the keyboard will repeat the keystroke. If you spend considerable time editing documents, you may want to improve your keyboard's responsiveness by decreasing the amount of time the keyboard controller waits before it begins to repeat a key. Users refer to the delay interval as the *repeat delay*. In addition, you can change the controller's *repeat rate* that controls how fast the keyboard will repeat the keystroke when you hold down a key.

To fine-tune your keyboard's responsiveness, perform these steps:

1. Select the Start menu Settings option and choose Control Panel. Windows will display the Control Panel.

2. Within the Control Panel, double-click on the Keyboard icon. Windows, in turn, will display the Keyboard Properties dialog box, as shown in Figure 11.5.

3. Within the Keyboard Properties dialog box, use the top slider to assign a short Repeat delay. Then, use the bottom slider to select a fast Repeat rate. You can test your setting by clicking in the white text box and then holding down a key.

4. Choose OK to put your settings into effect.

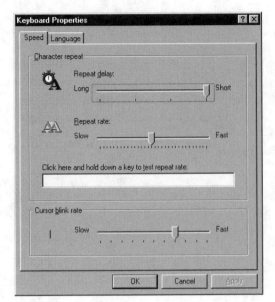

Figure 11.5 The Keyboard Properties dialog box.

Improving the Mouse's Responsiveness

As you know, when you move your mouse across the desk, Windows will move the mouse pointer across your screen. Depending on a user's mouse proficiency, you may want to speed up or slow down the rate at which the mouse pointer moves as the mouse moves. Also, as you know, many operations within Windows require that the user double-click the mouse on an object. To simplify the double-click process, you can shorten or lengthen the interval of time within which the user can double-click the mouse. One user, for example, may want to double-click on an object quite rapidly, while another may require more time between the click operations.

To fine-tune your mouse responsiveness, perform these steps:

1. Select the Start menu Settings option and choose Control Panel. Windows will display the Control Panel.

2. Within the Control Panel, double-click on the Mouse icon. Windows, in turn, will display the Mouse Properties dialog box, as shown in Figure 11.6.

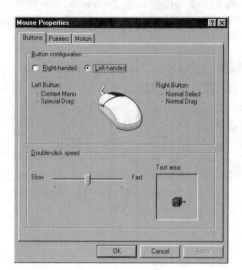

Figure 11.6 The Mouse Properties dialog box.

Depending on your mouse type and the software you are running, the Mouse Properties dialog box that Windows displays may differ. As such, the exact steps you must perform to fine-tune your mouse's responsiveness may vary slightly.

EXAM REVIEW

1. Users commonly connect keyboards to PCs using connectors that include: _____, _____, and _____.

2. True or False
   Users commonly refer to the organization of keys on the keyboard as QWERTY.

3. Users commonly connect a mouse to a PC using connectors that include _____, _____, and _____.

4. True or False
   In the past, if a system did not have a keyboard attached, the system would not start.

5. When you press a keyboard key, the keyboard controller passes a special value to the PC called a _____.

6. To improve a keyboard's responsiveness, you can change the keyboard's _____ that controls how long the keyboard controller waits when you hold down a key before it starts repeating the key and the keyboard's _____ that controls how fast the keyboard controller will repeat the keystroke.

7. To improve a mouse's responsiveness, you can change the _____ and the _____.

Locating a Lost File

Although the A+ Certification exam may not ask specifics about it, one of the most common help-desk calls technicians receive is that a user has lost a file. The user may have been editing the file before he or she left for lunch, or the user may have made a few changes to the file yesterday before he or she left for the day. In either case, the file is now gone and somehow, the user thinks that the misplaced file is your fault.

In this lesson you will learn several simple steps you can perform to quickly locate a misplaced file or e-mail message on a user's disk. To start, you will learn how to quickly locate a recently-used file within an application. Then, you will learn how to use the Windows Find File dialog box to search a disk for a file by name or based on the file's contents. You will also learn how to search a disk for files the user has created or changed during a specific time frame, such as since the previous day, week, month, and so on. Finally, you will learn how to use the Find File dialog box to locate large files on the user's disk that you may be able to delete in order to free up disk space.

F A C T S

+ Many Windows-based programs track a user's most recently used files and make those files readily available from the File menu.

+ In Windows, you can often access the user's most recently used files from the Documents menu.

+ Often, users inadvertently delete files they still need. As you search a user's disk for a missing file, you should open the Recycle Bin folder to determine if the user previously deleted the file.

+ The Windows Find File dialog box lets you search for a file by name, contents, or by the date the user last used the file.

+ You can configure many software programs, such as a word processor, to automatically create a backup copy of the file's original contents before the program saves the changes the user has made to the file. This backup copy of the file can be used later if the user decides not to keep those changes.

+ Many users fail to save their work on a regular basis. To prevent a user from losing hours of work, you should configure programs that support an "autosave" feature to save changes to documents at specific time intervals, such as every five to ten minutes.

Using an Application's File Menu to Locate Recently Used Files

When users are first learning to organize files within folders on their disk, the users will frequently misplace files. Fortunately, most Windows-based programs, such as Word and Excel, track a user's most recently used files and place each file's name within the File menu, as shown in Figure 12.1. If a user cannot locate a file, first determine which program the user was running to create the file, and then start that program to see if the file is listed in the File menu.

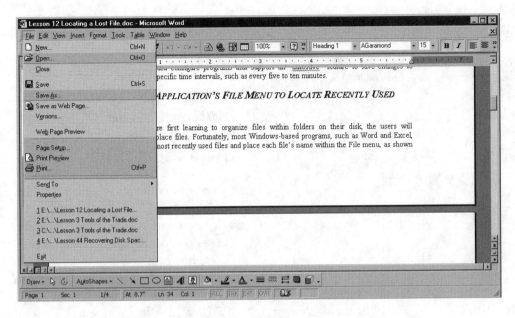

Figure 12.1 Locating recently used files within an application's File menu.

Using the Windows Document Window to Locate a Lost File

If a user cannot locate a file using an application's File menu, it is possible that you may locate the file in the Window's Documents menu, as shown in Figure 12.2. To display the Documents menu, select the Start menu Documents option. The Documents window will normally track the user's 15 most recently used documents.

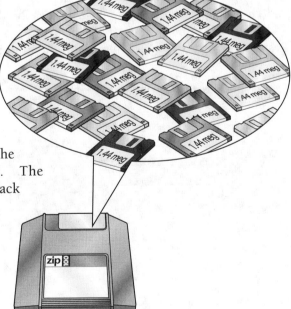

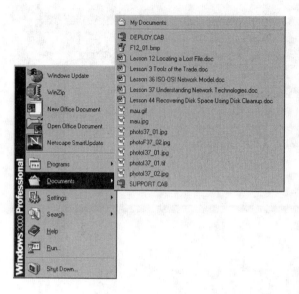

Figure 12.2 Using the Windows Documents menu to locate a recently used file.

Using the Windows Find File Dialog Box to Locate a Missing File

Using an application's File menu or the Windows Documents menu provides you with a quick way to locate a user's recently used files. Many times, however, a user cannot locate a file that he or she has not used for several weeks or months. In such cases, the Windows Find File dialog box, shown in Figure 12.3, lets you search a user's disk for files with a specific name, files that contain specific text, or files created during a specific time frame, such as the files the user created or changed in the last six months. Depending on whether you are using Windows 98 or Windows 2000, the steps to perform a search will differ. In Window 98, select the Start menu Find option and choose Files and Folders. In Windows 2000, select the Start menu Search option and then choose For Files or Folders. Windows 2000, in turn, will display the Search Results dialog box, which is similar to the Find File dialog box shown in Figure 12.3.

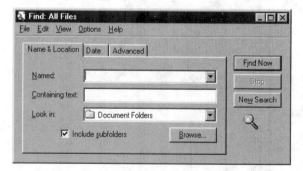

Figure 12.3 Using the Find File dialog box to locate a file by name, content, or creation date.

To use the Find File dialog box to locate a file by name, perform these steps:

1. Within the Named field, type in the file's name. You can use the asterisk (*) and question mark (?) wildcard characters within the filename.

2. Using the Look in field pull-down list, select the disk drive you want to search.

3. To search all the folders on the disk for the file, make sure the Include subfolders checkbox has a checkmark.

4. Select Find Now. Windows, in turn, will search your disk for the corresponding file. As Windows locates matching files, Windows will display directory information about the files within a Window, as shown in Figure 12.4. Within the window, you can normally double-click on an entry to open the file within its corresponding application. You can also view the file's directory path within the window so that you can later use it to open the file within an Open dialog box.

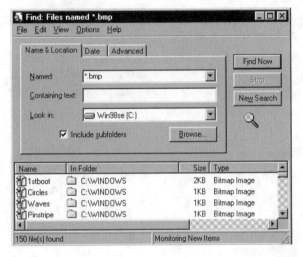

Figure 12.4 Viewing files that match the search criteria.

Often, a user will not recall the name that was assigned to a file, but will remember information about the contents of the file, such as an individual's or company's name that appears within the document. In such cases, you can use the Find File dialog box's Containing text field to search your disk for files that contain specific text.

If you are unable to locate a file by name or by searching for specific contents, you can use the Find File dialog box to locate files the user has created within a specific time frame, such as the previous day, week, month, or since a given date. To search a disk for files created or changed during a given time frame, select the Find File dialog box Date tab. Windows, in turn, will display the Date sheet, as shown in Figure 12.5, where you can type the time frame you desire.

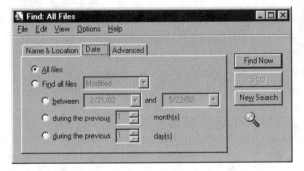

Figure 12.5 Searching a disk for files created or changed during a specific time frame.

Locating Files That Consume a Large Amount of Disk Space

In Lesson 44, "Cleaning Up a Disk," you will learn ways to free up space on a disk that is being used by temporary or previously deleted files. If you perform the operations Lesson 44 presents and you find a user still does not have sufficient disk space, you can use the Find File dialog box to locate files that are consuming large amounts of disk space. You might, for example, search a user's disk for files larger than 5MB.

To search a user's disk for large files, select the Find File dialog box Advanced tab. Windows, in turn, will display the Advanced sheet, as shown in Figure 12.6. Within the Size is pull-down list, select the At least option. Then, within the Size field, type in the file size you desire. The field specifies the file size in KB. So, to search for a 5MB file, you would type in 5000.

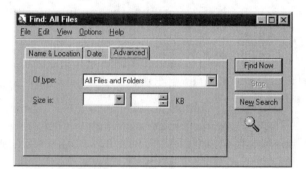

Figure 12.6 Using the Find File dialog box to locate large files on your disk.

Locating a Lost E-Mail Message

Just as users often misplace files, users who send and receive large amounts of e-mail frequently have problems locating a specific e-mail message. Many e-mail programs provide a Find dialog box you can use to search a user's messages for a message from a specific user or a message that contains specific text. For example, if the user is running Microsoft Outlook, you can use the Advanced Find dialog box, shown in Figure 12.7, that provides several options a user can select to search his or her messages for specific text. To search messages for specific text within Outlook, select the Tools menu Find option. Outlook will display a window you can use to search for text. To use the Advanced Find dialog box, click the Advanced Find button that appears in the window.

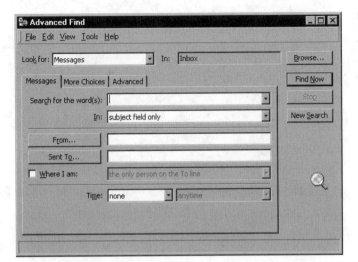

Figure 12.7 Searching e-mail messages for specific text within Microsoft Outlook.

EXAM REVIEW

① The three most common ways to locate a file on a user's disk are: _____, _____, and _____.

② If a user cannot remember the name of a file on his or her disk, but knows that it was created within the past seven days, what steps would you perform to locate the file?

③ Your boss suspects a user is visiting "improper" Web sites using a company computer to view images. How can you use the Find File dialog box to confirm the boss' suspicions?

④ A user is complaining that he or she has little disk space. List the steps you would perform to find large files (bigger than 10MB) that may be consuming the user's disk space.

Lesson 13

Restarting Windows and Ending Hung Programs

For years, computer users have argued over when and how often users should restart their systems. In many offices, users never turn off their systems. In other offices, users shut down their system at the end of each day and then turn on their systems the following morning.

The advantage of restarting Windows once a day is that the system regains use of any resources (normally RAM) that it may have lost because a program ended (perhaps due to a programming error) before the program could release the resource back to Windows. The primary disadvantage of restarting a system is that Windows takes a considerable amount of time to start.

In this lesson, you will learn how to monitor a system's resources to determine when a user should restart his or her system. You will also learn ways to speed up the start-up process.

F A C T S

- When programs run, Windows allocates resources to the program, the most common of which is RAM.

- If a program crashes (due to a programming error), the program may fail to give back resources it has allocated from Windows. Such resources will remain unavailable until the user restarts his or her system.

- Over time, Windows may run low on resources because programs have failed to return resources they previously allocated to Windows. Users refer to such losses of resources as memory leaks.

- As the resources available to Windows decreases, so too will the system's performance.

- Using the Windows Resource Monitor program, you can monitor your system's available resources. When the resources become low, you should restart your system.

- When a Windows-based program hangs (stops responding), you can often direct Windows to end the program by pressing the Ctrl-Alt-Del keyboard combination. When you press Ctrl-Alt-Del within Windows 98, your system will display the Close Program dialog box, where you can select the program you want to end.

- When you press Ctrl-Alt-Del within Windows 2000, your system will display the Windows Security dialog box. If you select the Task Manager button, Windows will display the Task Manager window, which contains a list of your system's active programs. To end a program, right-click on the program's entry and then choose End Task from the pop-up menu that Windows displays. In addition, you can select the program from the list (by clicking on the program entry) and then clicking the End Task button.

- Many newer PCs contain a CMOS setup entry that you can use to power on your system at a specific time. You might use the setting to automatically turn on the office computers each morning at 7:00.

- Each time Windows starts, it runs a myriad of programs, many of which operate behind the scenes. Oftentimes, users do not need or use many of these programs. By directing Windows not to automatically run specific programs upon startup, you free up the resources the programs were consuming and you speed up the system startup process.

Determining When to Restart Your System

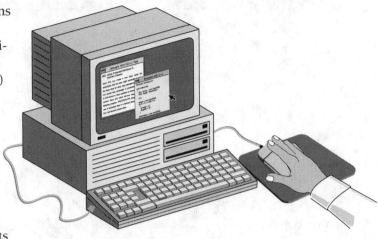

The longer Windows runs without restarting, the more likely it will experience a loss of resources (most importantly RAM) due to programs that allocate resources and then fail to return the resources to Windows after the program ends. In some cases, a program may hang (stop responding) before it can give back its resources to Windows. In other cases, programming errors (bugs) within the program code may cause the program not to give back the resources.

As a general rule, most users should restart their system once a day to maintain adequate resources for use by Windows.

BEYOND A+ CERTIFICATION

Directing a PC to Automatically Power Itself On

Lesson 26, "Using the CMOS Settings," will examine the PC CMOS and its system configuration settings in detail. Within the CMOS setup of many newer PCs, you will find an "autostart" option similar to that shown in Figure 13.1 that you can use to specify a time each day at which the PC will automatically power itself on.

If you have PCs within an office, for example, you might use the CMOS setting to start the PCs automatically each morning at 7:30, so that users find their PCs up and running when they enter the office at 8:00. By automatically starting the PCs in this way, users will not have to wait the minute or two it takes the PC to start and load Windows. At the end of the day, the user can simply shutdown their systems.

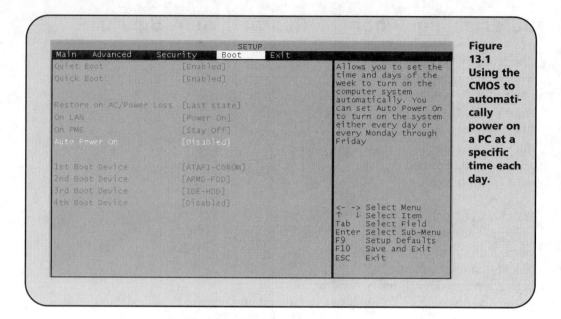

Figure 13.1 Using the CMOS to automatically power on a PC at a specific time each day.

Monitoring Windows Resources

If a system's resources become very low, Windows or a program you are running may display a message stating that the system does not have enough available resources for it to complete the operation. In some cases, the message may direct you to end other programs to free up resources. Normally, however, after the message appears, you will need to restart your system soon.

Often, the first indication that a system is low on resources is that operations begin to slow down. A program or document, for example, may take longer to load. Sometimes, you may begin to hear more disk activity as Windows tries to temporarily move programs from RAM to disk to free up resources.

To help you monitor your system's available resources, Windows provides programs such as the Resource Meter shown in Figure 13.2 that displays information regarding your system's available resources.

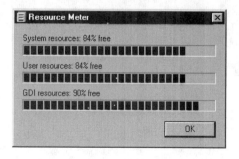

Figure 13.2 Using the Resource Meter to monitor available system resources.

If you are using Windows 9x, you can also use the Windows System Monitor to monitor your system's resource use as shown in Figure 13.3. To start the System Monitor, perform these steps:

1. Select Start menu Programs options and choose Accessories. Windows, in turn, will display the Accessories menu.

2. Within the Accessories menu, select System Tools and choose System Monitor. Windows will open the System Monitor window.

Within the System Monitor, you can use the Edit menu to add items you want to chart and to stop tracking a specific item. When you select Edit menu Add Item, for example, the System Monitor will display the Add Item dialog box you can use to select the item you want to monitor. When you select an item within the Add Item dialog box, the System Monitor will display a list of subitems you can select. Within the subitem list, you can select one item, or you can select multiple items by holding down the Ctrl key as you click on each item (you can also hold down the Shift key to select a group of successive items). After you select the items you want to track, choose OK.

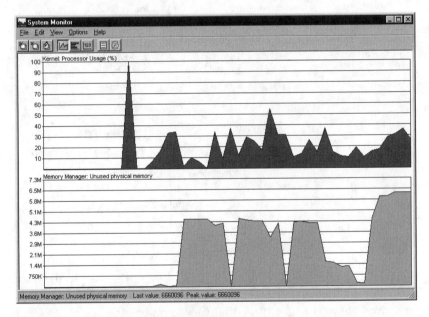

Figure 13.3 Using the System Monitor to examine your system.

If you are using Windows 2000, you can use the Microsoft Management Console Performance Monitor program to monitor your system performance. The Performance Monitor is an application, which users refer to as a "snap in" that runs within the Microsoft Management Console.

The Microsoft Management Console (MMC) is a tool you can use, much like a shell, to launch programs that you use to "manage" your system. As you work with Windows 2000, you may encounter many different programs that you can "snap into" the Microsoft Management Console. As it turns out, Windows 2000 includes the Performance Monitor within the MMC for you. Figure 13.4 illustrates the use of the

Performance Monitor within Windows 2000. To run the Performance Monitor in Windows 2000, perform these steps:

1. Select Start menu Settings option and choose Control Panel. Windows 2000 will display the Control Panel window.

2. Within the Control Panel, double-click on the Administrative Tools icon. Windows, in turn, will open the Administrative Tools window.

3. Within the Administrative Tools window, double-click on the Performance icon. Windows will open the Performance Monitor.

4. Within the Performance Monitor toolbar, click on the plus sign (+) icon. Windows will open the Add Counters dialog box.

5. Within the Add Counters dialog box, use the Performance Object pull-down list to select the item you want to monitor.

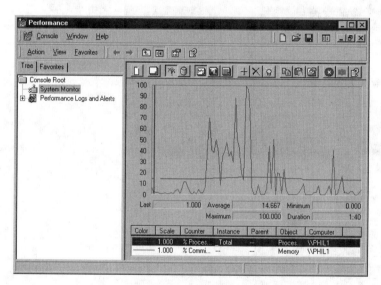

Figure 13.4 Using the Microsoft Management Console Performance Monitor to monitor system performance.

Determining the Problem Application

Often, when a system is experiencing a significant loss of resources, a specific program is the culprit. To help the user determine which program is consuming resources, have the user run either the Resource Meter or the System Monitor. Then ask the user to note how the amount of available memory and other resources change as he or she starts and stops programs throughout the day. Because most users run a relatively small number of programs, tracking the resource use should be quite straightforward. If you find that a program fails to give back resources, you should determine the program's version number (which you can normally display by selecting the Help menu About option) and then contact the manufacturer's technical support group.

Ending a Hung Program

When a program stops responding to a user's mouse and keyboard operations (meaning the program is hung), you can often direct Windows to end the program. If you are using Windows 9x, you can direct Windows to end the program by performing these steps:

1. Press the Ctrl-Alt-Del keyboard combination. Windows, in turn, will display the Close Program dialog box, as shown in Figure 13.5.

2. Within the Close Program dialog box, highlight the program you want to end and then select the End Task option.

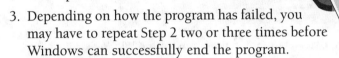

3. Depending on how the program has failed, you may have to repeat Step 2 two or three times before Windows can successfully end the program.

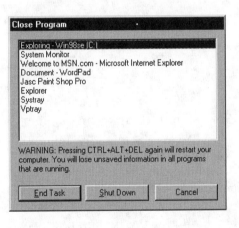

Figure 13.5 Using the Close Program dialog box to end a program in Windows 98.

Likewise, if you are using Windows 2000, you can direct Windows to end a program by performing the following steps:

1. Press the Ctrl-Alt-Del keyboard combination. Windows, in turn, will display the Windows Security dialog box.

2. Within the Windows Security dialog box, select Task Manager. Windows, in turn, will open the Task Manager window, as shown in Figure 13.6, that lists the programs your system is currently running.

3. Within the Task Manager window, right-click on the program you want to end. Windows will display a pop-up menu.

4. Within the pop-up menu, select the End Task option.

Figure 13.6 Using the Task Manager to view running programs within Windows 2000.

Speeding Up the System Startup Process

If you ask users to list the programs their system is running, most users will respond with a list including Windows, my e-mail program, my browser, and Microsoft Word. Behind the scenes, however, the user's PC could be running as many as one hundred programs. One program, for example, might manage a user's printer operations, another may monitor the system's modem or network connection, and another may monitor the system for viruses. Unfortunately, some of the programs that are running in the background may exist to manage hardware you no longer have connected to your system, or to assist programs you no longer run.

To display a list of the programs that Windows is running behind the scenes, you can use the System Information utility, as shown in Figure 13.7.

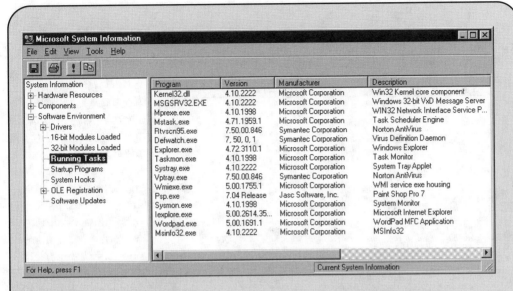

Figure 13.7 Using the System Information utility to view programs running within the system.

To view active programs using the System Information utility, perform these steps:

1. Select the Start menu Programs options and choose Accessories. Windows, in turn, will display the Accessories submenu.

2. Within the Accessories submenu, select System Tools and then choose System Information. Windows will open the System Information utility's window.

3. Within the System Information utility window, click on the plus sign (+) that precedes the Software Environment entry. The System Information utility will expand the entry to display additional subentries.

4. In the subentry list, select Running Tasks.

If you are using Windows 2000, you can view the programs your system is running from within the Task Manager, as shown in Figure 13.8. To view programs using the Windows 2000 Task Manager, press the Ctrl-Alt-Del keyboard combination. Windows 2000, in turn, will display the Windows Security dialog box. Within the dialog box, click on the Task Manager button. Next, to display all the programs your system is running, select the Processes Tab.

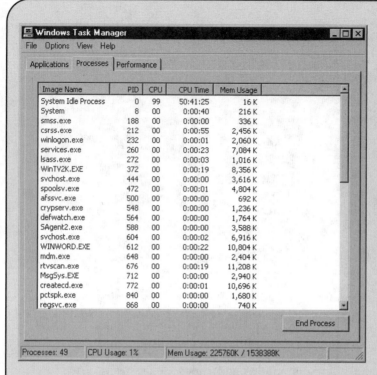

Figure 13.8 Using the Windows 2000 Task Manager to view the programs the system is running.

Often, a user will not require some of the programs the system is running. Some of the background programs, for example, may manage hardware devices that are no longer connected to the user's computer. Or, one or more the programs may exist to support applications the user no longer runs.

By directing Windows not to start such programs, you will free up resources used by these programs, and you can decrease the amount of the time windows requires to start because Windows no longer must load the programs.

Windows will load programs when it starts because of entries that appear in one of the following locations:

- An entry for the program appears in the Windows Startup folder.

- A RUN= entry for the program appears in the WIN.INI file.

- An entry within the Windows registry is launching the program.

Within the System Information utility, you can determine, as shown in Figure 13.9, where each program was launched from by selecting the Startup Programs subentry within the Software Environment branch.

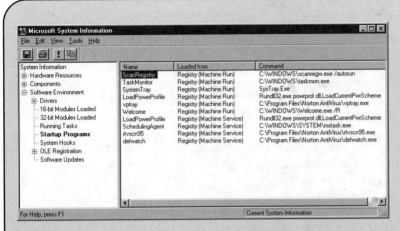

Figure 13.9 Using the System Information utility to determine the location that is launching programs Windows runs each time the system starts.

If you determine that your system does not require one or more programs Windows is launching each time your system starts, you can quickly disable the program from running by using the System Configuration Utility by performing these steps:

1. Within the System Information utility, select the Tools menu and choose System Configuration Utility. Windows, in turn, will run the System Configuration Utility program.

2. Within the System Configuration Utility window, click on the Startup tab. Windows, in turn, will display the Startup sheet, as shown in Figure 13.10, that you can use to enable or disable programs from automatically running each time Windows starts. To enable a program's execution, place a checkmark in the checkbox that precedes the program you want to run. To disable the program's execution, remove the checkmark.

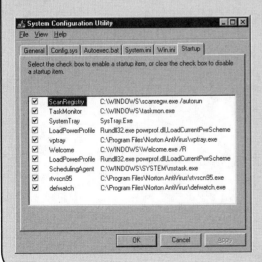

Figure 13.10 Using the System Configuration Utility to enable or disable programs from running each time Windows start.

EXAM REVIEW

A+ CERTIFICATION

1. Users refer to programs that fail to return memory to Windows after the program ends as a _____.

2. To monitor Windows resources, you can run programs such as _____ or _____.

3. True or False
The Windows task bar that normally appears at the bottom of a user's screen contains icons for every program Windows is currently running.

4. During the Windows startup process, Windows will automatically run programs based on entries you can find within the _____, _____, or _____.

5. True or False
Using the Windows Startup Programs icon within the Control Panel, you can specify which programs Windows should run and not run during the startup process.

6. To end a hung program in Windows 98, you _____. To end a hung program in Windows 2000, you _____.

7. True or False
To recover lost resources, users, as a general rule, should restart their system daily.

Cleaning and Maintaining Your PC

Depending on a PC's work environment, the amount of cleaning you must perform to maintain the PC will differ. In a dust-free office, for example, you may only have to periodically clean the monitor's display screen. In contrast, in a warehouse, the PC, monitor, keyboard, printer, and mouse can accumulate a significant amount of dust.

Likewise, if you are using a laser or ink-jet printer, you will eventually need to change your printer's toner or ink-jet cartridge at which time, you should normally take a few minutes to clean your printer.

When you take the A+ Certification exam, you can expect questions regarding how to properly discard PC batteries, toner cartridges, cleaning solvents, and even monitors that you no longer plan to use.

F A C T S

+ To avoid electrical shock that may injure you or damage your hardware, you should always power off and unplug your PC equipment before you clean it.

+ As your PC and monitor operate, each generates a substantial amount of heat that the device must vent. Make sure that users provide ample space between their PC and a desk or wall into which the PC fan can vent the hot air that is generated by the PC's electronic components. Also make sure that users do not obstruct a monitor's vents by placing books, magazines, or papers on top of the monitor.

+ The PC provides power to chips that reside within the keyboard and mouse. To reduce potential damage to the device, shut down the system and unplug the mouse or keyboard before you clean them.

+ To clean dust from a monitor's display screen, first try using a lint-free cloth, such as a cloth you would use to clean eyeglasses. Before you clean the monitor, power the monitor off. The monitor's screen can attract static electricity that can damage your PC's sensitive electronics.

+ As the PC operates, its fan can accumulate dust that decreases the fan's effectiveness. To clean the fan, you should use an aerosol blower.

+ If you keep the PC fan clean and your workspace dust free, you will normally not need to clean inside the PC's system unit. In fact, by opening the PC system unit and trying to remove dust, you may damage your PC's sensitive electronic components.

+ Before installing a new hardware card into an expansion slot on a dusty motherboard, you should use an aerosol blower to remove any dust that may have accumulated in the slot. In addition, you can use the blower to remove dust that may reside on the card's connector. If the card's connector contains smudges, you may want to use a pencil eraser to clean the connector.

+ After you remove a card from an expansion slot, you should place the card into an antistatic bag, and you should replace the metal slot cover over the slot's opening on the back of the system unit.

+ To clean the outside of the system or monitor, power off and unplug the device and then use a damp cloth and possibly a little rubbing alcohol.

+ To clean a mouse, disconnect it from the system unit and then remove the cover from underneath the mouse that holds the mouse ball in place. Remove the ball and use an aerosol blower to remove any dust or lint that has collected inside the mouse. You may need to use a Q-tip and rubbing alcohol to clean the mouse rollers.

F A C T S

- To clean a keyboard, first disconnect the keyboard from the system unit. Often, you can use an aerosol blower to clean dust and crumbs from within the keyboard. You can use a damp cloth to clean the surface of the keyboard keys.

- Under normal conditions, you should not have to clean your disk's floppy drives. If you work in a very dusty environment, you may be able to clean the floppy drive using an aerosol blower. Never open your PC's hard drive.

- Many ink-jet printers support special "cleaning sheets" that you can put through the printer that will clean the printer heads.

- Never simply throw away a used toner cartridge, ink-jet cartridge, battery, cleaning solvents, or a monitor (which may contain lead, making the monitor a hazardous material). Instead, follow closely the instructions on the object's box for specifics on properly discarding the object.

- If you have questions regarding the proper way to discard an item, visit the National Recycling Coalition Electronics Recycling Initiative on the Web at *www.nrc-recycle.org/resources/electronics/managing.htm.*

Maintaining Proper Ventilation

As the PC operates, its electronics generate a substantial amount of heat. To avoid damage to its sensitive electronic components, the PC must vent the hot air. If you examine the back of your system unit, you will find one fan that vents the power supply and possibly a second fan that vents the motherboard, as shown in Figure 14.1.

Often, because of limited space, users will slide their PC system units up next to a wall or the back of the user's desk. In so doing, the PC will not have sufficient space for venting the hot air it produces.

Figure 14.1 The PC system unit provides one or more fans to vent the heat produced by the PC components.

Similarly, if you examine the top of your monitor, as shown in Figure 14.2, you will find that the monitor's case provides openings through which the monitor can vent the hot air its electronics produce as they display images on the monitor's screen. Many users cover the monitor vents with books, magazines, papers, and other items. If the monitor cannot properly vent, the heat the monitor produces may damage the monitor's electronics or possibly become a fire hazard.

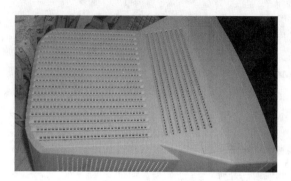

Figure 14.2 Make sure users do not block the vents that appear at the top of a monitor's case by placing objects on top of the monitor.

Cleaning Your Monitor

As you will learn in Lesson 49, "Performing Monitor Operations," to display an image, a monitor uses electron guns that heat red, green, and blue phosphors that correspond to pixels on the display. The electrons the monitor fires against the screen phosphors often produce a static electricity on the face of the screen, which causes the display screen to attract dust.

You can clean the monitor's display with a soft lint-free cloth, similar to one which you would use to clean your glasses, as shown in Figure 14.3. Before you clean the screen, you should power the monitor off (and ideally unplug the monitor) to reduce the possibility of electrostatic discharge that may damage your PC's electronic components.

If your screen contains fingerprints or other smudges, you may want to dampen a cloth using a little rubbing alcohol (which will evaporate quickly). You can also use the damp cloth to clean the monitor case. If the monitor's vents have accumulated dust, you can use an aerosol blower to clean the vents.

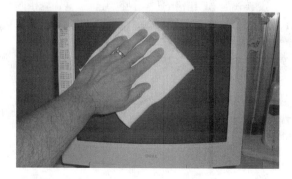

Figure 14.3 Use a soft cloth to clean your monitor's screen display.

NOTE: *Although the A+ Certification exam may ask you questions regarding operations you can perform within your monitor's case, as a rule, you should not open your monitor's case. The monitor, like the PC's power supply, contains a capacitor that can maintain a sufficient voltage (even after the monitor has been powered off and unplugged for an extended period of time) to kill you.*

Cleaning Your Mouse

If you find that a user's mouse pointer moves awkwardly across the screen (meaning the pointer's motion is not smooth with respect to the movement of the mouse on the desk), the user's mouse likely needs cleaning. The mouse receives power for its electronic circuits from the PC. Before you clean the mouse, you should disconnect the mouse from the system unit.

Next, turn over the mouse and remove the cover that holds the mouse ball in place. Often, using an aerosol blower, as shown in Figure 14.4, you can remove lint and dust that have accumulated inside the mouse. In some cases, the rollers within the mouse that respond to the movement of the mouse ball, will build up lint that you must remove using tweezers or a Q-tip dampened lightly with rubbing alcohol.

Figure 14.4 Using an aerosol blower to clean a mouse.

Cleaning Your Keyboard

Because the keyboard has more human contact than any other PC component, it will often need cleaning to remove smudges as well as dust and crumbs. Like the mouse, the PC provides power to the keyboard's electronics. Before you clean your keyboard, you should unplug it from the system unit. Should you ever inadvertently spill a drink onto the keyboard, you should immediately disconnect the keyboard from the PC. Users have reported various successes in cleaning a keyboard upon which the user spilled a soda by using a damp cloth. Some allow the soda to dry on its own (which will likely leave a sticky residue that later becomes a magnet for dust). Others will warn that cleaning the keyboard with hard water can leave mineral deposits that can damage the keyboard's electronics. Personally, I'll take my chances with a soft cloth and rubbing alcohol.

To clean the keyboard and its keys, you can use a cloth that you dampen slightly (again, I often use rubbing alcohol because it evaporates quickly). To clean crumbs and other items from the keyboard itself, many users will purchase a small static-free vacuum. If you keep the vacuum away from your PC components, you can also attach a small straw to a standard vacuum that you then use to clean the keyboard as shown in Figure 14.5. The straw's small size creates sufficient suction to clean most of the keyboard and prevents you from vacuuming up a keyboard key.

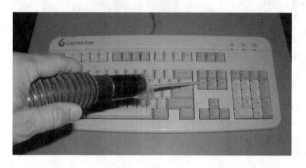

Figure 14.5 Attaching a straw to a vacuum hose to clean a keyboard.

If you find that a key on the keyboard begins to stick, you can normally use a screwdriver to gently remove the key so you can clean the key's spring. In some cases, to clean the keyboard, you may need to remove the cover (which is held in place by a few screws) and expose the keyboard electronics, as shown in Figure 14.6. After you remove the keyboard cover, you can often use an aerosol blower to remove dust and other objects inside the keyboard.

Figure 14.6 Removing a keyboard's cover to simplify cleaning.

Cleaning Your System Unit

Normally, you should not have to clean your system unit. If you want to remove smudges that appear on the outside of the system unit case, you should use a damp cloth and possibly some rubbing alcohol. Other than that, you should simply ensure that the system unit fan is not accumulating dust (you can use an aerosol blower to remove dust on the fan) and that the system unit cover is closed securely to reduce the amount of dust that can enter the chassis.

Unless you work in a very dusty environment, you should not have a need to clean inside the system unit. If, when you install a hardware card into an expansion slot inside your PC, you find that the system unit is filled with dust, you may use an aerosol blower to remove the dust. Do not, however, place the blower near the motherboard or other electronic components. The very cold air the blower produces can damage a chip's sensitive electronics.

Cleaning Cards and Expansion Slots

If, before you install a card (such as a modem or network card) into a PC expansion slot you find that the motherboard contains considerable dust, you should use an aerosol blower to remove any dust that may have accumulated within the slot, as shown in Figure 14.7.

Figure 14.7 Using an aerosol blower to clean an expansion slot.

Also, before you insert the card, you should examine the card's edges (the gold connectors you will slide into the expansion slot) for smudges that may prevent the card from conducting an electronic signal. To remove the smudge, gently rub the connector with a rubber pencil eraser, as shown in Figure 14.8, (the rubber does not conduct electricity and does not pose an electrostatic risk) to remove the smudge. Then, if necessary use an aerosol blower to remove any eraser flakes that accumulated on the connector.

Figure 14.8 Using a rubber eraser to clean a card's connector and an aerosol blower to remove any eraser flakes from on the card.

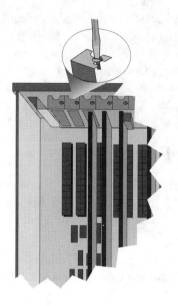

If you remove a hardware card from an expansion slot, make sure you replace the expansion metal slot cover to reduce the amount of dust that can enter the system unit.

Cleaning a CD-ROM Drive and Disc

As a general rule, you should not need to clean a CD-ROM (or DVD) drive. Periodically, a drive may accumulate dust that prevents the drive from reading a disc (which you can normally clean using an aerosol blower). Normally, when a drive cannot read a CD-ROM or DVD disc, the cause of the problem is a smudge or scratch on the disc itself. To clean a smudge from a disc, you can use a soft lint-free dust. When you clean the CD-ROM or DVD, you should wipe from the center out and not in a circular pattern.

Maintaining a Laser Printer

As you will learn in Lesson 53, "Taking a Closer Look at Laser Printer Operations," to print a page, a laser printer fuses toner (ink) to the page. Over time, the toner cartridge within the laser printer will run low on toner. Often, to extend a toner cartridge's life, and to print a few more pages, you can remove the cartridge and gently shake it from left to right in order to spread out the toner in the cartridge. Eventually, however, you must replace the empty cartridge.

Before you replace the toner cartridge, you should power off and unplug the printer. Then, you may want to let the printer sit for a period of time to cool off. To "fuse" the toner to a sheet of paper, the printer components create considerable amount of heat. To avoid burning yourself as you change the toner cartridge and clean the printer, you should provide time for the printer to cool off.

After you remove the toner cartridge, you may want to attach a small straw to a vacuum hose so you can vacuum up toner that may have spilled from the cartridge as well as dust that has accumulated from the sheets of paper that have moved through the printer, as shown in Figure 14.9.

Figure 14.9 When you change a laser printer's toner cartridge, you should take time to clean dust and lint from inside the printer.

NOTE: *Do not throw the empty toner cartridge in the trash. Instead, you should recycle it. Many new laser printer cartridges come with a prepaid shipping label you can use to return your old cartridge for recycling.*

Maintaining an Ink-Jet Printer

Just as you must eventually replace the laser printer's toner cartridge, the same is true for ink-jet printer cartridges. Depending on your printer type, the exact steps you must perform to change an ink cartridge may differ.

An ink-jet printer essentially sprays ink from a cartridge onto a page through several very small nozzle-like openings. Over time, it is possible for ink to accumulate on these nozzles, causing one of the jets to clog so that no ink passes through it or for accumulated ink to smear the paper, creating small smudges or streaks. When such accumulations occur, you must clean the jets.

To simplify the cleaning process, many ink-jet printers support a special cleaning paper that you feed through the printer. The cleaning paper is slightly porous and it scrapes the ink accumulations free from the jets and collects any ink that may have deposited itself inside the printer. If you do not have cleaning paper available, you may be able to use several Q-tips dampened with rubbing alcohol to clean the jets, as shown in Figure 14.10.

Figure 14.10 Using a Q-tip and rubbing alcohol to remove accumulated ink from an ink-jet cartridge.

Disposing of PC Components

Many PC components are hazardous materials, which means you simply cannot throw them in the trash. Items that fall into the hazardous material category include:

- Empty laser toner cartridges and ink-jet cartridges
- Notebook computer batteries

- Monitors (they may contain lead)
- Chemical solvents and aerosol cans

Normally, when you purchase a new toner cartridge (and possibly an ink-jet cartridge), you will receive instructions on how to dispose of the cartridge. Many manufacturers will suggest that you return your old cartridge to the manufacturer's recycling center. Users refer to the disposal instruction sheet as a Material Data Safety Sheet (MSDS). If you must dispose of a PC component and you do not have specific instructions from a manufacture on the proper steps to follow, you can likely find a related MSDS for the item on the Web, either at the manufacturer's Web site or at a site such as *www.ilpi.com/msds*. You may also call your local county government to find out if they provide a recycling facility for computer components at which you can discard your objects.

The A+ Certification exam will contain questions regarding the proper way to dispose of various computer components.

EXAM REVIEW

1. **True or False**
   Before you clean PC components, you should power off and unplug your PC.

2. **Monitors eliminate the heat their electronics generate through** _____.

3. **True or False**
   When you throw away a laser printer cartridge, you should place the cartridge in a box or bag to prevent toner from spilling.

4. **True or False**
   To clean most PC components, you should use an aerosol blower.

5. **MSDS is an acronym for** _____.

6. **True or False**
   An MSDS provides instructions on how you should properly dispose of a material.

7. **True or False**
   If ScanDisk repeatedly reports errors on your hard drive, you should use an aerosol blower to clean drive's surface.

Protecting a System from Viruses

One of the first responsibilities you should take on when you begin to manage PCs is to ensure that each PC is running virus detection software on a regular basis and that the company has a virus policy that clearly states each employee's responsibilities for protecting his or her PC from viruses. The policy should explicitly state the "do's and don'ts" employees should follow to reduce the risk and impact of a computer virus.

According to Computer Economics of Carlsbad, CA, viruses cost companies over $17 billion in the year 2000, up from $12 billion in 1999.

That said, in over twenty years of working with PCs, I have only experienced one computer virus—the famed Nimda virus that attacked Windows 2000 servers in 2001.

I'm often amused by the number of times computer viruses receive the blame for problems that MIS personnel do not know how to solve. I have heard viruses blamed for printer errors, unknown Web addresses, and slow network operations. When an MIS staffer cannot tell you exactly which virus attacked the system, you should interpret the statement "A virus was the problem, so I reinstalled Windows" as meaning "I don't have a clue what the problem was so I am blaming a virus."

This lesson not only examines the steps you should perform to reduce the risk of viruses, it also shows you how to determine which specific virus may have attacked a system.

F A C T S

+ A computer virus is a program written by a malicious programmer to damage the information you store on your PC.

+ There are a lot of things called viruses with nondestructive payloads. Meaning the viruses infect, but do not damage, a system.

+ Normally, a computer virus travels from one PC to another by attaching itself to files (meaning, the virus infects the files) that users exchange.

+ A virus, like all programs, must reside within the PC's RAM before the CPU can execute its instructions.

+ Some viruses, referred to as "Trojan Horse" viruses, attach themselves to other programs. When a user later runs the program, the virus is unknowingly loaded into the PC's RAM.

+ Ideally, to reduce the risk of computer viruses, you should not run programs that you receive from other users on disk or via e-mail or programs that you download from the Internet.

+ Computer viruses can also attach themselves to documents, such as a Word or Excel document. When you later open the document, the virus will load itself into memory.

+ Malicious users often send document-based viruses via e-mail.

+ To protect yourself against document-based viruses, you must use virus detection software. You should never open a document that you receive from another user on disk or via e-mail without first scanning the document for viruses.

+ Should you download programs from across the Net, only download such programs from reputable companies. Then, use a virus detection program to scan the program file for viruses before you run the program.

Understanding Computer Viruses

A virus is a computer program written by a malicious programmer, normally with the intent of damaging the information that resides on your disk. The Symantec Corporation, who tracks viruses, estimates that there are 61,000 existing viruses, with more than ten new viruses appearing each day.

How a virus behaves depends on the instructions the programmer who wrote the virus specifies. One virus, for example, might delete all the files on your disk. Another may simply display a message such as "Boom" and then restart your system. Yet another may send an e-mail message from you to everyone in your address book that suggests they visit a new pornography site.

Before a program can run, the program must reside within the computer's random access memory (RAM). A computer virus program is no exception. As you might suspect, few users would knowingly run a virus program. Instead, most viruses disguise themselves as a different program, or the viruses attach themselves to programs that you run on a regular basis.

A malicious user, for example, might send a program to users in an e-mail message that contains a message such as "Try this new 3D graphics computer game." The unknowing recipients, in turn, may run the program expecting to see a video game, but instead, they encounter a virus.

Again, depending on the instructions the programmer included within the virus, a virus may immediately perform its malicious operations, or the virus may wait twenty-four hours, a week, or longer before it attacks the system. Assume, for example, the virus programmer actually creates a simple video game that contains a virus. If the game runs for thirty days before it attacks a system, it is possible that users who receive the game may send it to their friends, which helps the virus move from one system to another. Users refer to viruses that present themselves as an innocent program as "Trojan Horse" viruses.

Often, after a virus program is running, the virus may attach itself to other programs on the user's disk. In this way, the virus ensures that the user will load the virus into RAM at a future date when the user runs one of the other programs. Further, some viruses, which users refer to as boot-sector viruses, attach themselves to the boot sector that loads the operating system into RAM each time the system starts. By attaching itself to the boot sector, the virus makes sure that it too is loaded into RAM during the system startup.

Do Not Run Programs You Download from the Internet or Receive from Unknown Users

Users often infect their PCs with a virus by running a program that they download from the Internet or that they receive from another user on a floppy disk. If you are serious about protecting your system from viruses, you will never run such programs.

Understanding Document-Based Viruses

For many years, if you did not download and run programs from the Internet, or run programs that were given to you by another user, you essentially eliminated your chance of encountering a computer virus. By opening a document, such as a Word document or an Excel spreadsheet, you could not infect your system with a virus.

Unfortunately, times have changed.

Today, viruses can take advantage of the macro-programming capabilities provided by programs such as Word and Excel that let users automate tasks. A user might, for example, create a Word macro that searches a document for state abbreviations (such as CA and AZ) and then replaces the abbreviations with the corresponding state name. In other words, the macro is somewhat like a computer program.

Unfortunately, a malicious programmer can create a macro (a list of instructions similar to a program) that the programmer attaches to a document. Later, when a user opens the document, the macro-virus executes. Again, depending on the instructions the programmer specifies, the operations a macro-based virus performs will differ. To make matters worse, most users configure Word and Excel so that when they open a document that contains such a macro, Word or Excel automatically loads the macro into RAM and executes the instructions it contains.

The good news is that most virus-detection software can identify such document-based macros. To reduce your risk of viruses, you should never open a document file that you have not first scanned using your virus protection software. In addition, within programs that support macros, such as Word and Excel, you can disable the program's automatic macro execution. In this way, when you first open a document, Word or Excel won't run a potentially damaging macro.

Protecting PCs Against Computer Viruses

The first step you should take to reduce the risk of a computer virus is to install and use antivirus software. Across the Web, many companies sell antivirus software. Two of the best-known and most commonly used antivirus programs are Norton AntiVirus and McAfee VirusScan. If you are not currently running antivirus software, you should download and install a trial version of Norton AntiVirus from the Symantec Web site at *www.symantec.com* or McAfee VirusScan trial version from *www.mcafee.com*.

Normally, you can run antivirus software in one of two ways. First, when another user gives you a disk or file, you can run your virus protection software and direct it to scan the file for viruses. Second, you direct antivirus program to run continuously, so that the software scans each file you plan to open, run, save, and so on. By running the virus protection software continuously, you increase your chances of detecting a virus in files that you download from across the Net.

When the antivirus software detects a virus on your system, the software will normally ask you how you want it to proceed. Most virus protection software, for example, can delete the file or possibly remove the virus from the program. Figure 15.1, for example, shows the Norton AntiVirus software scanning files on a disk.

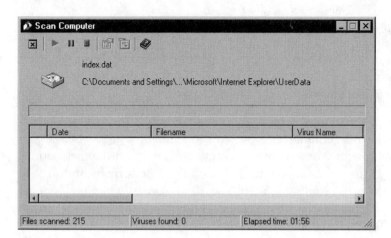

Rules to Reduce Your Risk of a Computer Virus

To reduce your chance of infecting your PC with a virus, perform these steps:

1. Install antivirus software and use the software to examine every file you receive from other users, regardless of whether the file came on disk or via an e-mail message.

2. Do not open or copy files from a floppy disk or Zip disk until your antivirus software examines the disk for viruses.

3. Do not run programs sent to you by users across the Internet or given to you on floppy disk. If you receive a program attached to an e-mail message, delete the message and program immediately.

4. If you must download programs (such as a device driver) from across the Internet, only download programs from reputable well-known companies, such as Microsoft, Netscape, and Symantec. Then, before you run the programs you download, use your antivirus software to scan the program files for viruses.

5. Do not open documents that you receive as files attached to e-mail messages without first scanning the document files for viruses.

Learning Virus Specifics

If you suspect you may have been infected by a virus, you can find out details about most viruses (such as how the virus attacks a system and more importantly, the steps you must perform to remove the virus) by visiting the Symantec Virus Encyclopedia Web site at *www.symantec.com*, as shown in Figure 15.2. The site provides details on tens of thousands of viruses. In addition, the site can tell you whether or not an e-mail message you received regarding a virus is true or a hoax. In general, any e-mail message that you receive that warns of a virus and tells you to notify everyone in your address book immediately is likely a hoax. The Department of Energy Computer Incident Advisory Capability (CIAC) tracks hoaxes at *http://hoaxbusters.ciac.org*.

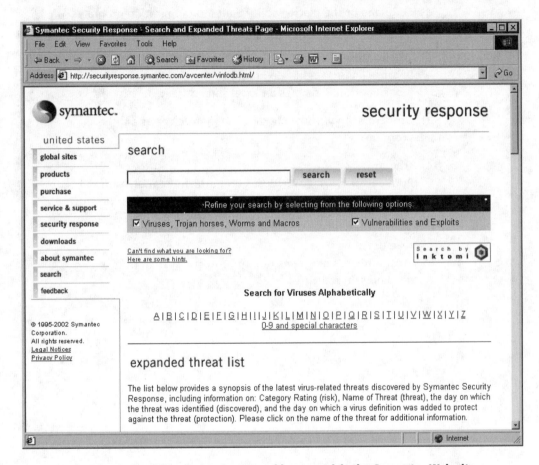

Figure 15.2 To learn specifics about viruses and hoaxes, visit the Symantec Web site.

① **True or False**

Malicious programmers create viruses using a programming language or the macro facility built into application programs such as Word and Excel.

② **True or False**

Because a virus requires a program, you cannot get a virus from a document file, such as an Excel spreadsheet.

③ Users refer to viruses that disguise themselves as another program as _____.

④ **True or False**

Boot-sector viruses are viruses that attach themselves to the disk's boot sector so that the operating system loads the virus into memory each time the system starts.

⑤ **True or False**

Most antivirus programs cannot protect a system from a document-based virus.

Understanding the PC BIOS

Within the PC, the CPU executes the instructions in each program you run. To support the CPU, the PC provides a special chip called the BIOS (pronounced "bye-ose") that provides the PC's Basic Input Output System. The BIOS supports the PC by providing six key operations: implements the system startup and power on self-test, provides the CMOS setup program, provides support for plug-and-play devices, provides power management support for key devices, and provides instructions that the operating system can use to perform input and output to various devices.

Normally, users can ignore the BIOS. However, there may be times when a newer device requires a specific BIOS version. In such cases, you must upgrade the BIOS before you can use the device. In the past, users upgraded the BIOS by replacing the BIOS chips on the motherboard. Today, most BIOS chips are software upgradeable, which means you can run a special program called a BIOS upgrade to change the instructions the BIOS chip provides.

F · A C T S

+ BIOS is an acronym that stands for Basic Input Output System.

+ The BIOS is a chip that resides on the PC motherboard.

+ The BIOS provides six key capabilities:
  - Performs the PC's power on self-test
  - Initiates the operating system startup
  - Provides a CMOS setup program used to view and configure key system settings
  - Supports plug-and-play devices
  - Supports the PC's power management capabilities
  - Provides instructions that the operating system can use to interact with various hardware devices

+ When you first power on your PC, the BIOS executes the PC's power on self-test that examines key hardware components to ensure the PC is in working order.

+ If the power on self-test encounters errors, the BIOS may display a message describing the error and then sound a series of long and short beeps you can use to determine the cause of the error. The meaning of the beeps, which users refer to as beep codes, are BIOS-dependent.

+ After the BIOS successfully completes its power on self-test, the BIOS loads the operating system's boot (startup) sector from disk into RAM. The boot sector contains the instructions the PC executes to load the operating system.

+ The BIOS provides support for a special PC memory area called the CMOS that contains low-level hardware settings for key devices (such as your CPU, RAM, and disk drives). The BIOS also provides a special CMOS setup program used to view and change settings within the CMOS.

+ The BIOS provides support for plug-and-play operations by letting you reserve hardware settings (interrupt request and I/O ports) for older non-plug-and-play devices (which users refer to as legacy devices) within the CMOS entries.

+ The BIOS provides support for the PC's power management capabilities that let the PC spin down a hard drive that is not in use or power off the monitor after a period of inactivity.

+ The MS-DOS operating system made extensive use of BIOS-based instructions to interact with devices. Today, most operating systems do not use the BIOS instructions to communicate with devices. Instead, the operating systems rely on device driver software.

F A C T S

+ Periodically, a new hardware device will require a specific BIOS version. To determine your BIOS version, you can use the Windows System Information utility.

+ In the past, to upgrade the BIOS, users had to replace the BIOS chips that reside on the motherboard. Today, most BIOS chips use the flash-memory technology that you can upgrade by running a special software program (a BIOS upgrade program) that you can download from your PC manufacturer's Web site.

Understanding the PC BIOS

Years ago the MS-DOS operating system made extensive use of the BIOS to perform input and output operations. Today, however, newer operating systems such as Windows 2000 do not use the BIOS at all after the system completes its POST and starts the operating system's boot process. Instead, to perform the operations that BIOS performed within MS-DOS, such as video and disk operations, operating systems simply provide their own program instructions.

Today, the BIOS exists to start the PC's boot process, to provide the user with a way to access CMOS settings, to assist in the PC's power management capabilities, and to provide operating system support for plug-and-play devices.

The BIOS Resides on the Motherboard

The BIOS is a chip that resides on the PC motherboard, as shown in Figure 16.1. In older PCs, the BIOS consisted of two chips, which users referred to as the *odd* and *even* BIOS chips. To upgrade the BIOS, users replaced the BIOS chips. Today, most systems have a single flash-based BIOS chip which users can upgrade by running a special software program.

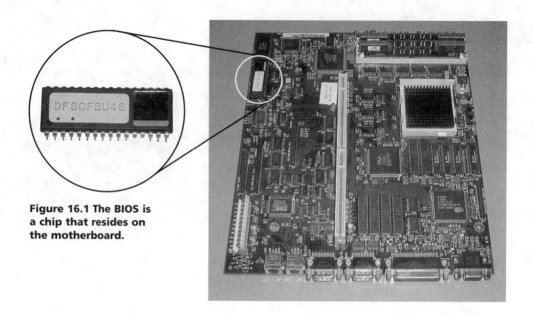

Figure 16.1 The BIOS is a chip that resides on the motherboard.

Understanding the Power On Self-Test (POST)

As discussed in Lesson 8, "Understanding the PC Startup Process," you learned that when you turn on your PC, the BIOS initiates the PC's power on self-test (POST). During the test, the BIOS examines key hardware devices (such as the CPU, CMOS battery, keyboard, RAM, and so on) to ensure your PC hardware is in working order. Depending on your PC's BIOS type, the specific tests the BIOS performs and the order the BIOS performs the tests may vary. You can determine the specific tests your BIOS performs by viewing BIOS specifics that can normally be found at your BIOS manufacturer's Web site.

If the power on self-test encounters an error that will prevent your PC from functioning properly, the BIOS will normally display an error message that describes the error and sound a series of beeps that correspond to the error. Users refer to these beeps as the BIOS *beep codes*.

Each BIOS has its own set of codes, the meaning of which are specific to the BIOS. The BIOS may generate short and long beeps as well, much like Morse code. For example, if the AMI BIOS encounters a CPU error, the BIOS will sound five short beeps. Normally, you can locate your BIOS beep codes on the Web simply by entering your BIOS chip type followed by the key words "beep codes", in a search engine.

Viewing Post Codes Using a POST Analyzer Card

When the BIOS encounters errors during the PC's power on self-test, the BIOS will normally sound one or more beep codes that you can interpret to determine the cause of the error. To help you troubleshoot the error, the BIOS will place a numeric code within I/O port 80H that corresponds to the current test the POST was performing when the error occurred. By examining the numeric code, you can determine the specific test that caused the PC to fail. Depending on the BIOS chip, the meaning of the status code value may differ.

To view the numeric error code, you can install a special card called a *POST analyzer* card into the PC and then restart the PC. The card will display a numeric code (or a series of lights you can interpret to determine the code). Because the POST analyzer cards are not inexpensive, you might only use such a card if you must troubleshoot POST errors on a regular basis. Most POST analyzer cards will also provide diagnostic software you can run to better troubleshoot the error.

Understanding the BIOS Role in the System Startup Process

After the BIOS successfully completes the power on self-test, the BIOS is ready to begin the process of loading the operating system. To begin, the BIOS will search the CMOS entries to determine the disk drives that it should search for a bootable system disk. If the CMOS does not provide a search order, the BIOS will first examine drive A for a bootable disk followed by drive C.

If the BIOS locates a disk, the BIOS will then read the operating system's boot sector from the disk into RAM. The boot sector contains instructions the PC will execute to continue the process of loading the operating system. If the disk is not a bootable disk, the BIOS will display an error message similar to the following:

```
Non-System disk or disk error
```

This error message commonly occurs when a user forgets to remove a floppy disk from drive A.

Understanding the Plug-and-Play BIOS

As you will learn in Lesson 33, "Making Sense of Plug-and-Play Devices," hardware upgrades have become much easier for users to perform thanks to plug-and-play devices. In the past, before a user installed a new hardware device, the user had to determine the resources, such as interrupt request (IRQ) and I/O port settings, other devices were using and then manually configure new cards using jumpers and switches to select resources that were not in use. In contrast, when you install a plug-and-play hardware card into the PC, the device identifies itself to the system and tells the other devices its resource requirements. The other devices then tell the new device which resources are available and the device can then automatically configure itself.

In addition, a plug-and-play BIOS also provides support for older legacy devices that do not support plug-and-play operations by letting the CMOS setup programs reserve IRQ and I/O port addresses for legacy cards. The CMOS stores this information within a CMOS memory location that users refer to as the Extended System Configuration Data (ESCD). When a new plug-and-play device asks devices in the system which resources are available, the plug-and-play BIOS essentially "speaks up" for the legacy devices, telling the new device about the settings that are reserved for the older device's use.

To support plug-and-play operations, a PC must have a plug-and-play BIOS chip and must be running an operating system, such as Windows, that supports plug-and-play operations. BIOS chips that were manufactured in the last five years should provide plug-and-play support.

Understanding the BIOS Power Management Capabilities

To better conserve energy, most PCs now provide support for power management that you can use to reduce the PC's power consumption. Using the power management capabilities, you can, for example, direct Windows to power off a monitor and to spin down a hard drive after a period of no user activity.

Support for the PC's power management begins with the BIOS. When hardware manufacturers first provided power management capabilities, they included special instructions within the BIOS called the PC Advanced Power Management (APM) capabilities. In general, the APM defines a hardware-independent interface which an operating system could use to interact with devices in order to reduce power consumption and to increase a notebook PC's battery life. Unfortunately, because most of the power management capabilities resided within the BIOS, the operating system could not fully leverage its knowledge of the user's current level of activity.

Today, most operating systems have built upon the BIOS power management capabilities, to introduce support for the Advanced Configuration and Power Interface (ACPI) specification. The ACPI specification provides operating systems with a standardized access to the PC's power management capabilities. The ACPI specification defines a set of routines that programs can use to interact with the PC's power management capabilities, some of which the operating system implements and some of which correspond to the BIOS-based APM capabilities.

Understanding the BIOS Role in Input/Output Operations

The acronym BIOS stands for Basic Input Output System. Years ago, a key role of the BIOS was to provide instructions which the operating system (MS-DOS) could use to interact with disk drives, the video display, keyboard, printer, and more in order to perform input and output operations.

Today, most operating systems provide their own instructions to interact with devices or the operating systems rely on the device driver software. As such, the role of the BIOS for input and output operations is much less important than it once was.

Viewing Your PC's BIOS Type and Version

Normally, each time your system starts, your monitor will briefly display information about your BIOS, such as the chip manufacturer and version number. In addition, if you enter the CMOS setup program, as discussed in Lesson 26, "Using the PC's CMOS Settings," you can display specifics about your BIOS, as shown in Figure 16.2.

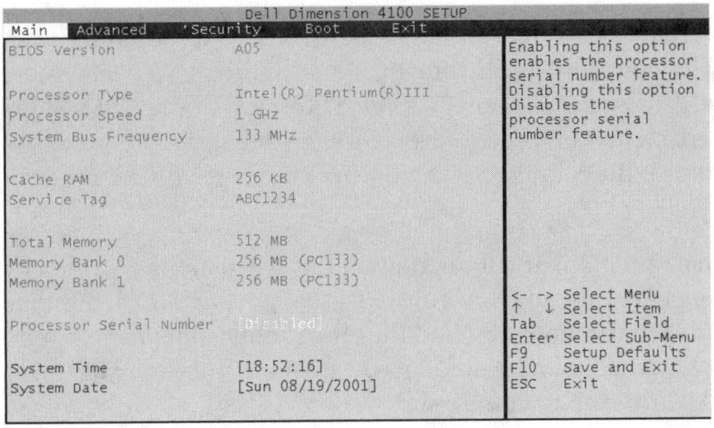

Figure 16.2 Using a CMOS setup program to display BIOS information.

In addition, using the System Information utility you can display BIOS information, as shown in Figure 16.3, by performing these steps:

1. Select the Start menu Programs option, and choose Accessories. Windows will display the Accessories submenu.

2. Within the Accessories submenu, select the System Tools option, and choose System Information. Windows will run the Microsoft System Information utility.

3. Within the System Information utility, click on the plus sign (+) that precedes Components. The System Information utility will expand its list of components.

4. Within the system component list, click on the System entry. The System Information utility will display its list of system components.

5. Within the System Component list, click on the Advanced radio button and then scroll through the list to locate the motherboard BIOS entry.

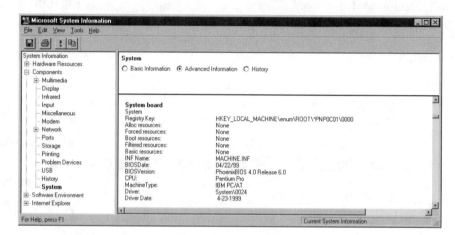

Figure 16.3 Using the System Information utility to display BIOS specifics.

Upgrading Your PC BIOS

Today, most PCs have a flash BIOS that you can upgrade by running a special software program which you normally download from your PC manufacturer's Web site. Most users will never have a need to upgrade their PC's BIOS. In fact, to prevent a BIOS upgrade from introducing errors that prevent your PC or hardware devices from working, you should only perform a BIOS upgrade when a new hardware device requires new BIOS support.

When you run a BIOS upgrade program, it will reprogram the instructions provided by the BIOS chip. The BIOS upgrade program you run must match your BIOS chip type as well as your motherboard. You can normally find the correct BIOS upgrade program at your PC manufacturer's Web site. If, you cannot get an upgrade from your PC manufacturer, look to your BIOS chip manufacturer's site.

Again, before you upgrade your flash BIOS, make sure that the BIOS upgrade program is compatible with your motherboard. If the upgrade program is not compatible with your system, your system may not start following the upgrade.

Download the BIOS upgrade program and place it on a bootable floppy disk (you can create bootable floppy disks using the Control Panel Add/Remove Programs entry). You should also download a copy of the program file that corresponds to your current BIOS and place it on the bootable floppy disk as well, to simplify the steps you must perform to recover your system's current settings should the BIOS upgrade fail. Each BIOS version will reside in a file whose name corresponds in some way to the version number. You can place the upgrade and current BIOS files on the same floppy disk.

Next, restart your system, booting from the floppy. When the operating system displays its command-line prompt, type in the program's filename to run the upgrade program. After the upgrade completes, remove the floppy disk and restart your system.

Should the BIOS upgrade introduce an error that prevents your system from starting, you will need to restore the previous BIOS by running the BIOS upgrade program that corresponds to your previous BIOS.

EXAM REVIEW

A+ CERTIFICATION

① True or False

The BIOS is special software built into the Windows operating system.

② The BIOS performs which of the following tasks (check all that apply):

☐ Performs the POST
☐ Provides a CMOS setup program
☐ Provides support for USB devices
☐ Provides power management support
☐ Begins the process of loading the operating system from disk into RAM

③ To upgrade most newer BIOS chips you:

☐ Replace the BIOS chips on the motherboard
☐ Run a special BIOS upgrade program
☐ You cannot upgrade the BIOS

④ POST is an acronym for _____.

⑤ If the BIOS encounters errors during the POST, the BIOS will display a message and possibly sound a series of long and short beeps that users refer to as _____.

⑥ The BIOS supports plug-and-play operations by
_____.

⑦ To view information about the BIOS, such as the BIOS version number, you can use the:

☐ Windows Device Manager
☐ Control Panel BIOS icon
☐ System Information utility
☐ Windows System Monitor

Taking a Closer Look at the Windows Control Panel

Within Windows, a special folder named the Control Panel provides icons you can select to access settings for a wide range of hardware devices. Throughout this book's lessons, you will use the Control Panel icons to launch the Device Manager, to add or remove software, to configure modem, network, and printer settings, and much more.

As you prepare for the A+ Certification exam, you should make sure that you can readily identify the Control Panel icons and the operations each provides.

This lesson provides you with a summary overview of the Control Panel icons. Depending on the software you have installed on your system, your Control Panel folder may contain more entries than those this lesson presents. Throughout this book, you will use the majority of the Control Panel entries as you examine specific hardware devices. This lesson examines the Control Panel entries that are not discussed in other lessons.

F A C T S

◆ The Accessibility icon lets you access settings you can use to fine-tune operations for users who have special vision, hearing, or mobility needs.

◆ The Add New Hardware icon launches the Windows Add New Hardware Wizard which walks you through the steps you must perform to install the device driver software that Windows needs before it can communicate with a new device.

◆ The Add/Remove Programs icon displays the Add/Remove Programs Properties dialog box that you can use to install and remove application programs as well as Windows components (such as Accessory programs). In addition, the dialog box lets you create startup floppy disks that you can use to boot your system in the event of a hard-disk error.

◆ The Date/Time icon displays the Date/Time Properties dialog box that you can use to change your system's date and time. In addition, you can use the dialog box to change your system's current time zone.

◆ The Display icon opens the Display Properties dialog box that you can use customize your screen settings. Most importantly, the Display Properties dialog box lets you control your screen resolution and the number of colors Windows supports. In addition, the dialog box lets you assign a background image to the Windows desktop, select and customize a screen saver, or customize the colors that Windows uses to display menus, title bars, and other screen objects.

◆ The Fonts icon displays the Fonts folder that lets you view the fonts installed on your system. Within the Fonts folder, you can install or remove fonts and view or print a font's character set.

◆ The Game Controllers icon lets configure and test game-controller hardware devices.

◆ The Internet Options icon displays the Internet Properties dialog box that you can use to customize a user's Internet settings (such as the user's default Web site that the browser will display each time the user starts the browser or various security options). In addition, you can use the dialog box to remove cookies, temporary files, and programs that your browser may have downloaded from across the Web. Finally, you can use the dialog box to clear the history of sites you visit that the browser maintains as you surf the Web.

◆ The Keyboard icon displays the Keyboard Properties dialog that you can use to fine-tune the keyboard's responsiveness and which you can use to install international keyboard layouts, such as a Spanish or German key layout.

+ The Modems icon displays the Modem Properties dialog box that you can use to add or remove a modem or change a modem's properties. In addition, the dialog box lets you change the settings the modem uses to place a call, such as your area code information or the numbers you must press to "dial out" of a building. If you do not have any modems installed, selecting the Modems icon will launch the New Modem Wizard.

+ The Mouse icon displays the Mouse Properties dialog box. Depending on the mouse (and mouse driver) you are using, the Mouse Properties dialog box's contents may differ. In general, the Mouse Properties dialog box lets you fine-tune the mouse's responsiveness and customize the mouse pointer that appears on the screen display.

+ The Multimedia icon displays the Multimedia Properties dialog box that you can use to customize settings for sound cards, video playback, MIDI music interfaces, audio CD playback, as well as your speaker volume. In addition, the dialog box lets you configure advanced settings such as the compression software (which users refer to as a codec) that various multimedia devices use to reduce the amount of data the device must send or receive.

+ The Network icon displays the Network dialog box that you can use to configure network settings such as your TCP/IP settings that network programs use to determine the gateway to the Internet within a local area network, as well as server information that specifies how the PC receives its Internet Protocol (IP) address. In addition, the dialog box lets you enable or disable file and printer sharing.

+ The Passwords icon displays the Passwords Properties dialog box which lets Windows 98 users change the password used to log into the system. In addition, users can use the setting to enable or disable remote system management.

+ The Power Management icon displays the Power Management Properties dialog box that you can use to select and configure the PC's power management scheme. Using the Power Management Properties dialog box, you can, for example, direct the PC to spin down the hard drive and to turn off the monitor after 10 minutes of inactivity.

+ The Printers icon displays the Printers folder that contains icons for each printer installed on your system or any that are available to the system from across a network. In addition, the folder contains the Add Printer icon you can use to install device driver software for a new local or network printer.

F A C T S

✦ The Regional Settings icon displays the Regional Settings Properties dialog box that you can use to select the currency, number, and date and time settings for a specific region (country).

✦ The Sounds icon displays the Sounds Properties dialog box that you can use to customize the sounds Windows plays when a specific event occurs.

✦ The System icon displays the System Properties dialog box that you can use to display the Device Manager, which lets you view information about device conflicts as well as device resource settings. The System Properties dialog box also lets you configure hardware profiles that let you customize device settings for various user-defined profiles. You might, for example, create a profile named AtWork that contains network and printer information about devices that are available when you connect your PC to the local area network at your office. Then, you might also create a profile named AtHome that contains information about devices you have at home.

✦ The System Properties dialog box Performance sheet provides buttons that you can use to fine-tune file system, video, and virtual memory settings.

✦ The Telephony icon lets you configure settings that correspond to dial-up connections, such as the numbers the modem must dial to access an outside line, the user's area code, and so on.

✦ Within Windows 98, the Users icon launches a Wizard you can use to create a profile for a new user who will be sharing the PC with others. The profile will contain user-specific data such as a user's screen colors, Desktop image, and e-mail settings.

Accessing the Windows Control Panel

Throughout this book's lessons, you will make extensive use of entries within the Windows Control Panel, shown in Figure 17.1. To open the Control Panel window, select the Start menu Settings option and choose Control Panel. Depending on the programs you have installed and your Windows version (such as 2000 or 9x), the icons that appear in the Control Panel may differ.

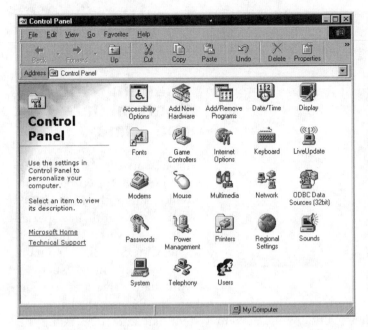

Figure 17.1 Entries within the Windows Control Panel.

Using the Control Panel Accessibility Icon to Simplify Key Operations

The Windows graphical user interface has become such a key role in our lives, that most of us now take keyboard and mouse operations for granted. To simplify such operations for users with special vision, hearing, or mobility needs, Windows provides the Accessibility Properties dialog box, shown in Figure 17.2. Using the sheets that appear within the dialog box, users can fine-tune keyboard, mouse, display and sound settings.

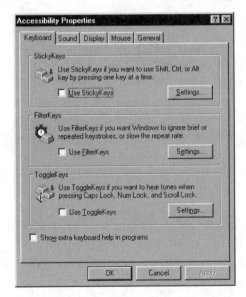

Figure 17.2 The Accessibility Properties dialog box.

For example, a user who is unable to press two keys at a time can use the dialog box to fine-tune sticky-key operations which let the user simulate key combinations, such as Alt-PrtSc.

Using the Windows 2000 Administrator Tools

If you manage PCs running Windows 2000, many of the lessons this book presents will direct you to perform operations using one of the tools contained in the Administrative Tools dialog box, shown in Figure 17.3. To use the tools, you must be logged into the PC as the System Administrator.

Figure 17.3 The Windows 2000 Administrative Tools dialog box.

Changing the System Date and Time

In Lesson 26, "Configuring the PC CMOS Settings," you will examine the PC's CMOS entries that reside in a special battery-powered memory. The CMOS settings contain key system entries such as your hard drive type, system startup options, and so on. When the PC is not powered on, the PC uses the battery to power its real-time clock that maintains the current system date and time. Using the Date/Time Properties dialog box shown in Figure 17.4, you can set your system's current date and time. You can also use the dialog box to select your current time zone.

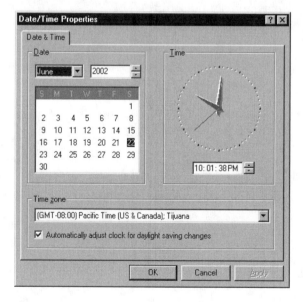

Figure 17.4 The Date/Time Properties dialog box.

Managing Your System's Fonts

A font defines a typeface that controls how text appears on a page or screen display. By assigning different fonts to text within a document, you can draw the user's attention to specific sections of the text. Today, with the wide-spread use of Microsoft Word, most users make extensive use of fonts and font attributes, such as bolding and italics. Using the Fonts dialog box, shown in Figure 17.5, you can display a list of the fonts that reside on your system.

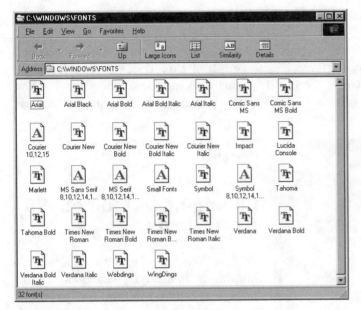

Figure 17.5 The Fonts dialog box.

To preview how a font will appear within a document, simply double-click on the font's icon within with the Fonts dialog box. Windows, in turn, will display a window similar to that shown in Figure 17.6 that presents a sample of the font's use.

Figure 17.6 Previewing a font within Windows.

If you work on documents with other users, there may be times when another user will send a font for use in the document that does not reside on your system. Using the Fonts dialog box, you can install on the font by performing these steps:

1. Within the Fonts dialog box, select the File menu Install New Font option. Windows, in turn, will display the Add Fonts dialog box.

2. Within the Add Fonts dialog box, select the disk drive and folder that contains the font file you want to install. Then, select the font file. Choose OK. Windows will install the font onto your system.

Fine-Tuning a Game Controller

If you attach a game controller, such as a joystick, to a PC, you can use the Game Controller dialog box shown in Figure 17.7 to add, configure, test, and troubleshoot a myriad of controllers. The Game Controller dialog box supports controllers ranging from a simple joystick to a controller with a steering wheel and brake and gas pedals.

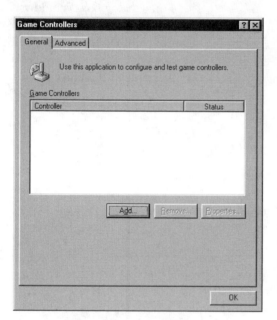

Figure 17.7 The Game Controller dialog box.

Managing Windows 98 Passwords

Within Windows 98, the Passwords Properties dialog box, shown in Figure 17.8, lets a user change the password used to log into the system. In addition, using the dialog box, a user can enable or disable remote system management, which lets a system administrator manage the system's files and settings from across a network.

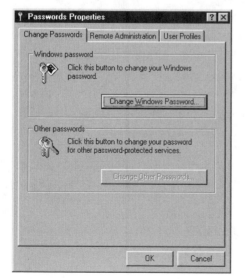

Figure 17.8 The Passwords Properties dialog box.

NOTE: *To change a password within Windows 2000, a user should press the Ctrl-Alt-Del keyboard combination. Windows 2000, in turn, will display the Windows Security dialog box, within which the user can select the Change Passwords button to display the Change Password dialog box.*

Managing a PC's Regional Settings

Around the world, different countries use different formats to present currency amounts, dates and times, and so on. If you travel from one country to another or if you must create documents using a different language (and hence you must use the country's formatting settings and keyboard template), you can direct Windows to use the country's settings within the Regional Settings dialog box as shown in Figure 17.9. Users who must support multiple country settings can direct Windows to provide support for the corresponding countries and then press a specific keyboard combination to switch between the regional settings as they require. Before you can create documents using a different character set, such as the Japanese or German character sets, you must first install the character set you desire.

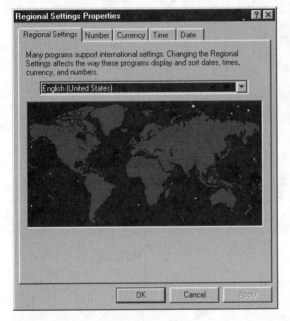

Figure 17.9 The Regional Settings dialog box.

Managing Users

In many offices, users share the same PC. If the PC is running Windows 2000 and each user logs into the system using a different username, one user cannot access files created by another, unless the user who created the file grants the second user with access to the files.

In contrast, Windows 9x does not provide such security. The users who log into a Windows 9x system can access all the files on the system, regardless of who created the files. Windows 98, however, does let users customize various system settings, such as screen colors, Desktop images, and e-mail settings (which gives semiprivate e-mail to each user). Windows 9x refers to customizable system settings as user profiles. Each time a user logs into a Windows 9x system, Windows uses the settings the user has saved in his or her profile. Using the Control Panel Users icon, you can add a new user, delete a user, change passwords, and so on.

In a similar way, within Windows 2000, a system administrator can control which users can log into the system (or change user settings, such as the user's password) using the Control Panel Users and Passwords icon.

Settings Your PC's Telephony Options

If you use a dial-up connection to access the Internet, you can use the Dialing Properties dialog box shown in Figure 17.10 to control call waiting, to specify your area code, to define the access code the modem must dial to reach an outside line, and so on. If you travel with a notebook PC and you have trouble establishing a dial-up connection, the problem may be a setting within the Telephony/Dialing Properties dialog box.

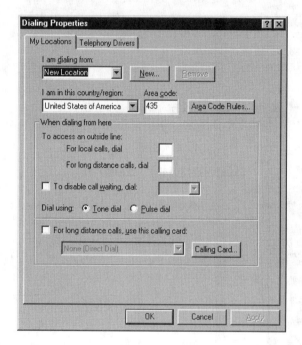

Figure 17.10 The Dialing Properties dialog box.

① A user complains that the screen is difficult to read. To make the screen's contents easier to read, you enable a high-contrast display using the Control Panel _____ icon.

② True or False
Using the Windows Regional Settings option, you can direct Windows-based programs to display documents created in languages such as Chinese.

③ A user tells you that a document received as an e-mail attachment does not match a hard copy of the document's contents. The document, which uses the Garamond font, looks fine on your system. To resolve the problem, you

_____.

④ In Windows 2000, you are unable to access tools in the Administrative Tools dialog box. The most likely cause of the problem is _____.

Lesson 18

Using the Windows Device Manager

Several of the lessons this book presents discuss the steps you must perform to install different hardware devices. If a device supports plug-and-play operations, the installation process will be much easier. That said, there will be times when you will encounter a conflict between devices (actually the resources such as an IRQ or I/O port that the devices are using) that prevents one or both of the devices from working.

To help you resolve device conflicts, Windows provides a special program called the Device Manager. Using the Device Manager, you can quickly identify device conflicts, as well as devices that Windows is unable to access (normally because of a device driver problem).

F A C T S

✦ To help you resolve hardware conflicts, Windows provides the Device Manager.

✦ To run the Device Manager, you select the Control Panel System icon. Then, depending on whether you are running Windows 98 or Windows 2000, the steps you must perform to display the Device Manager will differ slightly.

✦ The Device Manager groups hardware devices in a treelike fashion. To expand a branch of the tree in order to display more information about a device, click on the plus sign that precedes the device entry.

✦ If a hardware conflict prevents Windows from using a device, the Device Manager will precede one or both of the conflicting devices with a red X, indicating that Windows has disabled and will not use the device.

✦ If Windows believes a device is missing or Windows does not recognize a device due to a device driver problem, the Device Manager will precede the device with a yellow circle that contains a black exclamation mark (!).

✦ If a user overrides the settings for a plug-and-play device, the Device Manager will precede the device entry with a blue uppercase I.

✦ If Windows has an unknown device (a device that Windows does not recognize and for which Windows cannot select a device driver), the Device Manager will precede the device with a question mark (?).

✦ Using the Device Manager, you can view and in some cases change a device's resource settings.

✦ Within the Device Manager, you can check for and install a device driver update from the Microsoft Windows Update Web site on the Internet.

✦ Using the Device Manager, you can remove the software (the device driver) for a device that you are no longer using. By removing the device driver software, you free up resources for other uses. In addition, if you believe a device driver may be corrupt, you can remove the current driver and then reinstall the driver.

✦ Within the Device Manager, you can print a summary of the devices on your system which includes the device's resource use (IRQ and I/O port settings) as well as the device's driver version number.

Reviewing Device Conflicts

Each hardware device you install in your PC must have unique resources that the device uses to interact with the CPU. The two most common resources are the interrupt request (IRQ) line and I/O ports.

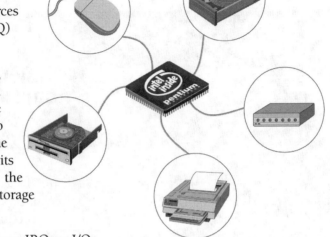

As you will learn in Lesson 28, "Understanding Interrupts and I/O Port Addresses," a device uses its interrupt request line to signal the CPU that it needs the CPU to perform processing on its behalf. To exchange data with the CPU, the device uses special storage locations called I/O ports.

If two devices try to use the same IRQ or I/O port, one or both of the devices will not work. Lesson 28 discusses the steps you must perform to assign unique settings to each device.

As you will learn in the next section, using the Windows Device Manager, you can often determine which devices are conflicting. To display the Device Manager within Windows 98, perform these steps:

1. Select the Start menu Settings option and choose Control Panel. Windows will display the Control Panel window.

2. Within the Control Panel, double-click on the System icon. Windows will display the System Properties dialog box.

3. Within the System Properties dialog box, select the Device Manager tab.

If you are using Windows 2000, you display the Device Manager by performing these steps:

1. Select the Start menu Settings option and choose Control Panel. Windows will display the Control Panel window.

2. Within the Control Panel, double-click on the System icon. Windows will display the System Properties dialog box.

3. Within the System Properties dialog box, select the Hardware tab. Windows will display the Hardware sheet.

4. Within the Hardware sheet, click the Device Manager button.

The Device Manager organizes the devices on your system using a treelike structure. To display specific devices within a device branch, click on the plus sign that precedes the device-type entry. The Device Manager will expand the list of devices as shown in Figure 18.1.

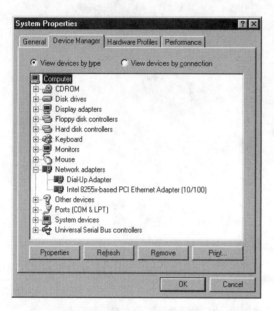

Figure 18.1 Expanding device-type branches within the Device Manager.

Viewing Device Conflicts

When two devices try to use the same resource (an IRQ setting or I/O port), a device conflict occurs and one or both of the devices will not work. In some cases, Windows may disable one or both of the conflicting devices. When the Device Manager recognizes that Windows has disabled a device, the Device Manager will precede the device entry with a red X, as shown in Figure 18.2.

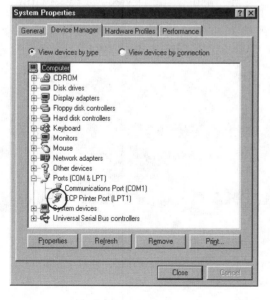

Figure 18.2 The Device Manager precedes disabled devices using a red X.

If you encounter a device entry preceded with a red X, view and possibly change the device's resource use as discussed later in this lesson. After you are sure the device's resources do not conflict with another device, right-click on the device entry. Windows will display a pop-up menu. If you are using Windows 2000, you can then select the Enable option. If you are using Windows 98, select the Properties option. Windows 98, in turn, will display the device's Properties dialog box, within which you can select the Enable button.

In addition to resource conflicts preventing Windows from using a device, there may be times when Windows encounters an error with the device's driver software. In such cases, the Device Manager will precede the entry with a yellow circle that contains a black exclamation mark (!), as shown in Figure 18.3.

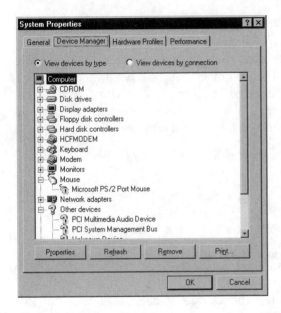

Figure 18.3 The Device Manager indicates device driver problems by preceding an entry with a yellow circle that contains a black exclamation mark.

If you encounter the yellow circle and exclamation mark before a device entry, reinstall the device driver and restart your system. If the error persists, you may need to try a different device driver. Often, you can find a driver update at the device manufacturer's Web site. In addition, you can also direct the Device Manager to search the Microsoft Windows Update site for a new driver as discussed later in this lesson.

If Windows simply cannot recognize a device, and as such, Windows does not know which driver to use, the Device Manager will precede the unknown device's entry with a question mark.

NOTE: *When Windows ME cannot find the correct driver for a device, but can use a compatible driver, the Device Manager will precede the device entry with a green question mark.*

Finally, there may be times when a user must override a device's plug-and-play settings. In such cases, the Device Manager will precede the device entry with a blue uppercase I.

Printing the Device Manager Settings

As you troubleshoot device conflicts, it is often convenient to know specifics about each device installed in the system. Using the Device Manager, you can print system and device specifics, such as each device's IRQ, I/O port, and driver version number, by selecting the Print button in Windows 98 or the View menu Print option in Windows 2000.

The Device Manager, in turn, will display a Print dialog box within which you can select the report type you desire.

Checking for Device Driver Updates

If the Device Manager displays a yellow circle that contains a black exclamation mark, Windows either cannot recognize the device or Windows is having problems with the device driver. Should you encounter the yellow circle and exclamation mark before a device entry, first ensure that the device is properly connected to the PC and that the device card is properly inserted in an expansion slot. Then, if the error persists after you restart your system, you can use the Device Manager to view specifics about the device's driver software by performing these steps:

1. Within the Device Manager, right-click on the device entry. Windows will display the device's Properties dialog box.

2. Within the Properties dialog box, click on the Driver tab. The Device Manager will display the device driver specifics, as shown in Figure 18.4.

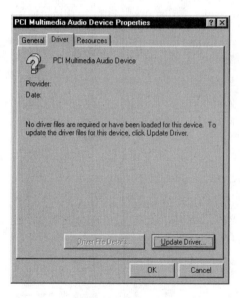

Figure 18.4 Displaying device driver specifics within the Device Manager.

Using the Device Manager, you can quickly check the Microsoft Windows Update Web site for an update to a driver and optionally install the driver by selecting the Update Driver button. Windows, in turn, will start a Wizard that will walk you through the steps of looking for and installing a new driver.

Disabling a Device

As you work, there may be times when you will want to disable a device. For example, if you use a notebook PC at work and at home, you may have different hardware devices available for use depending on your location. At your office, you may connect your notebook to a local area network. When you are at home, you may want to disable the notebook's network card.

Using the Device Manager, you can disable a device in Windows 98 by performing these steps:

1. Within the Device Manager, right-click on the device entry. Windows will display the device's Properties dialog box.

2. Within the Properties dialog box, click on the checkbox labeled Disable in this hardware profile, placing a checkmark in the box.

3. To later enable the device, you simply remove the checkmark.

If you are using Windows 2000, you can disable a device by right-clicking on the device entry and then selecting Disable from the pop-up menu. To later enable the device, you simply select Enable from the pop-up menu.

Often, to simplify the process of enabling and disabling devices, users take advantage of hardware profiles. In the previous scenario, the notebook PC user might create one hardware profile named Work and one named Home. Within the Work hardware profile, the user would enable the network card. Within the Home hardware profile, the user would disable the card. Each time the user started the system, Windows would display a dialog box prompting the user to select the hardware profile that is desired. Windows would then enable and disable devices based on the profile's settings.

To create a hardware profile in Windows 98, perform these steps:

1. Within the System Properties dialog box, select the Hardware Profiles tab. Windows will display the Hardware Profiles sheet.

2. Within the Hardware Profiles sheet, click on the Copy button. Windows will display the Copy Profile dialog box.

3. Within the Copy Profile dialog box, type in the name of the profile you want to create and then choose OK.

4. Close the System Properties dialog box and restart your system. Windows will display a dialog box within which you can select the profile you desire. After you select the profile, use the Device Manager to enable or disable the devices you desire within that profile.

To create a hardware profile in Windows 2000, perform these steps:

1. Within the System Properties dialog box, select the Hardware tab. Windows will display the Hardware sheet.

2. Within the Hardware sheet, click on the Hardware Profiles button. Windows will display the Hardware Profiles dialog box.

3. Within the Hardware Profiles dialog box, click on the Copy button. Windows will display the Copy Profile dialog box.

4. Within the Copy Profile dialog box, type in the name of the profile you want to create and then choose OK.

5. Close the System Properties dialog box and restart your system. Windows will display a dialog box within which you can select the profile you desire. After you select the profile, use the Device Manager to enable or disable the devices you desire within that profile.

Removing Device Driver Software

If you are no longer using a device that still appears in the Device Manager's device list, you can direct the Device Manager to remove the device's driver software from your system. By removing the device in this way, you remove the driver files from your disk, which frees up disk space.

To direct the Device Manager to remove a device in Windows 98, click on the device entry and then choose the Remove button. To remove a device using the Device Manager in Windows 2000, right-click on the device entry and then choose Uninstall from the pop-up menu Windows displays.

Directing the Device Manager to Search for a New Device

If a device does not appear in the Device Manager's device list, you can direct the Device Manager to search your system for a new hardware device. In Windows 98, select the Device Manager Refresh button. In Windows 2000, select the entry that corresponds to the PC (normally the topmost entry in the device list) and then select the Action menu Scan for hardware changes option.

If the Device Manager still does not display the device, reinstall the device driver and restart your system.

Managing a Device's Resource Settings

Each device you install in a PC must have unique settings for an interrupt request (IRQ) line, as well as unique I/O port settings. In addition, some devices require unique direct-memory access (DMA) settings. Using the Device Manager, you can view a device's current resource use by performing these steps:

1. Within the Device Manager, right-click on the device entry. Windows will display a pop-up menu.

2. Within the pop-up menu, select Properties. Windows will display the Properties dialog box.

3. Within the Properties dialog box, select the Resources tab. Windows will display the Resources sheet as shown in Figure 18.5.

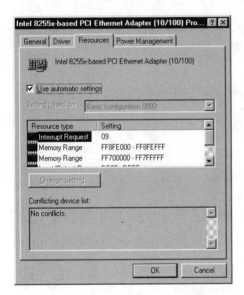

Figure 18.5 Viewing a device's resource use within the Device Manager.

In some cases you can use the Device Manager to change a device's resource settings by clicking on the setting you desire (such as the IRQ setting) and then selecting the Change Settings button.

EXAM REVIEW

① Within the Device Manager, a red X before a device entry indicates _____.

② If a user manually overrides a plug-and-play device's resource settings, the Device Manager will precede the device entry with a _____.

③ True or False
A yellow circle with a black exclamation mark before a device indicates that the device has begun to operate.

④ To view a device's driver specifics within the Device Manager, you _____.

⑤ True or False
Using the Device Manager, you can quickly search the Microsoft Windows Update Web site for a update to a device driver.

Lesson 19

Automating Tasks on a User's System

Throughout this book, you will examine operations users should perform on a regular basis, such as scanning a user's disk for errors, freeing up disk space by removing temporary files, or defragmenting a disk to improve performance. Rather than relying on the user to perform these operations on a consistent basis, you should use the Windows Task Scheduler to direct Windows to perform the operations at specific intervals. You might, for example, use the Task Scheduler to defragment a user's hard disk each Friday evening at 6:00, after the user leaves the office for the week. Or, you might use the Task Scheduler to scan the user's hard disk for viruses every day during the lunch hour.

This lesson examines ways you can use the Task Scheduler to automate key operations you need users to perform on a regular basis. Admittedly, the A+ Certification exam may not ask you questions specifically related to the Windows Schedule Task Wizard. However, by knowing how to schedule operations within Windows, you can much more effectively manage user systems.

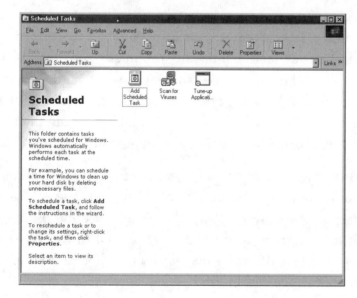

F A C T S

+ Using the Schedule Task Wizard, you can select a program and schedule it to run at specific times.

+ By scheduling operations such as ScanDisk, disk defragmentation, or virus detection to occur at fixed intervals, you can simplify the task of managing user systems.

+ The Schedule Task Wizard makes it easy for you to direct Windows to run a specific program daily, weekly, monthly, each time a system starts, or at a specific date in the future.

Scheduling a Task

In general, regardless of the program you want Windows to schedule to run on a regular basis, the steps you must perform will be the same. Because most users should defragment their hard disk on a regular basis, the following steps will show you how to schedule the Windows 98 Disk Defragmenter utility.

Figure 19.1 Viewing the list of programs Windows has scheduled to run.

To begin, select the Start menu Programs option and choose Accessories. Windows, in turn, will display the Accessories submenu. Within the Accessories submenu, select System Tools and choose Scheduled Tasks. Windows will display the Scheduled Tasks window, as shown in Figure 19.1.

Within the Scheduled Tasks window, you can view specifics about each program your system has scheduled to run, such as the last time your system ran the program and the next time Windows is set to run the program. You can also change a scheduled program's settings, remove a scheduled program, or schedule a new task.

To schedule the Disk Defragmentation program to run weekly, perform these steps:

1. Within the Schedule Task window, double-click on the Add Scheduled Task entry. Windows, in turn, will start the Scheduled Task Wizard.

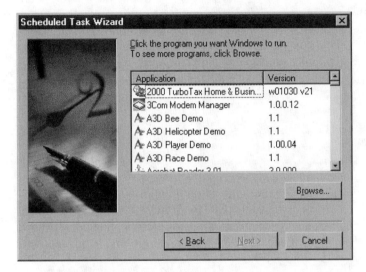

Figure 19.2 Selecting the program you want to schedule.

2. Within the Scheduled Task Wizard window, click the Next button. The Wizard, in turn, will display a dialog box similar to that shown in Figure 19.2 that lists the programs on your system that you can schedule.

3. Within the list of programs, select the Disk Defragmenter and then click the Next button. The Wizard, in turn, will display a dialog box that lets you specify how often you want the program to run, as shown in Figure 19.3.

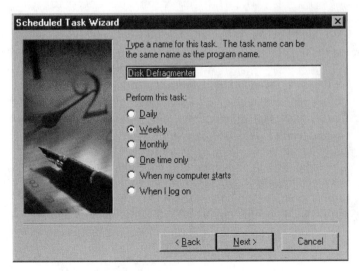

Figure 19.3 Specifying the frequency at which you want a scheduled program to run.

4. Within the dialog box, select the Weekly option to run the Disk Defrag-menter once a week and then click the Next button. The Wizard, in turn, will display a dialog box similar to that shown in Figure 19.4 that lets you specify the program's start time and day.

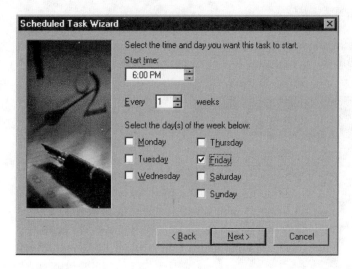

Figure 19.4 Selecting a scheduled program's start day and time.

5. Within the dialog box, select the day and time you desire and then click Next. The Wizard, in turn, will display a dialog box stating that it has scheduled your task. Select Finish. The Scheduled Task window will now display an entry for the Disk Defragmenter.

Should you later decide to remove a scheduled task, simply right-click on the entry for that program listed in the Scheduled Task window. Windows, in turn, will display a pop-up menu. From that menu, select Delete.

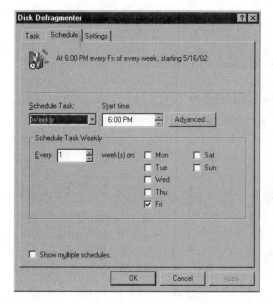

Figure 19.5 Changing a scheduled task's settings.

If you decide to change a program's schedule, right-click on the entry for that program listed in the Scheduled Task window and then choose the pop-up menu Properties option. Windows, in turn, will display the Properties dialog box where you can select the Schedule tab similar to that shown in Figure 19.5, which you can use to change the date, time, or frequency that the application runs. If the PC is not running when the date or time of a scheduled task occurs, Windows will ignore the "past due" event the next time the system starts.

Taking Advantage of Advanced Scheduling Options

If you schedule tasks on a regular basis, there may be times when you need greater control over a program's processing. For example, you may want to limit the amount of time a scheduled program can run, or you may only want the program to run when the PC appears to be idle (not in use by other applications).

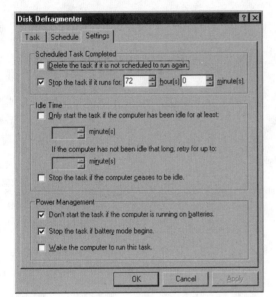

Figure 19.6 Using the Settings sheet to fine-tune a scheduled task's processing.

To fine-tune a scheduled task's settings, you should use the Settings sheet as shown in Figure 19.6. To display a task's Settings sheet, right-click on the entry for that program listed in the Scheduled Tasks window and then choose the pop-up menu Properties option. Windows, in turn, will display a dialog box where you can select the Settings tab to display the Settings sheet.

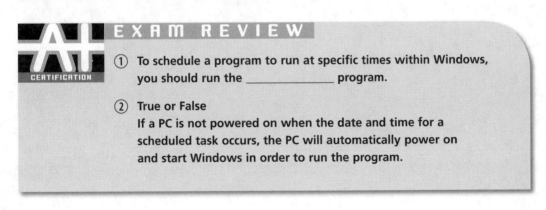

EXAM REVIEW

① To schedule a program to run at specific times within Windows, you should run the _____ program.

② True or False
If a PC is not powered on when the date and time for a scheduled task occurs, the PC will automatically power on and start Windows in order to run the program.

Understanding the Windows Registry

Within Windows, as well as most Windows-based programs, you can configure a wide range of settings, from screen colors to default file locations. When you customize various Windows and application settings, Windows normally stores the settings in a special database called the Registry.

Years ago, Windows and Windows-based programs would store settings in individual files that used the *.ini* file extension (ini for initialization). Each time you started a program that used an *.ini* file, the program would open the file and use its contents to configure the corresponding settings.

The Windows Registry essentially consolidates the various *.ini* files into one database. When a program starts, the program can retrieve its settings from the Registry.

As you troubleshoot hardware problems, there may be times when you must view (or change) specific values in the Registry. This lessons examines the steps you should follow to perform such operations.

FACTS

- The Registry is a database that Windows and Windows-based programs use to store key settings.

- When a program runs, the program can retrieve its configuration information from the Registry. Each time Windows starts, Windows uses entries in the Registry to configure key settings.

- The Registry contains settings without which Windows or some of your programs could not run. Each time you start your system, Windows uses the Registry database. If Windows does not encounter any errors within the Registry, Windows will make a backup copy of the Registry's contents. Should you later encounter an error after you change a program or Windows setting, you can restore the backup copy of the Registry.

- Windows 98 places the Registry files *system.dat* and *user.dat* in the Windows folder. Windows 98 places backup copies of the Registry in cab files (compressed files) in the *Windows\sysbckup* folder.

- Windows 98 maintains up to five backup copies of the Registry. Windows names the files *RBxxx.cab*, where the *xxx* corresponds to the backup number. The backup file contains four files: *system.dat, user.dat, win.ini,* and *system.ini*.

- Windows 2000 stores the Registry within the several files that reside in the *\Winnt\System32\config* folder and the *\Documents* and *Settings\Username* folders.

- Unlike Windows 98 that automatically backs up the Registry contents each time your system starts successfully, Windows 2000 does not. To backup the Registry under Windows 2000, you must use the Backup facility.

- As you troubleshoot hardware and software, there may be times when you must change, delete, or create an entry within the Registry. Windows provides a utility called RegEdit that you can use to view and change entries within the Registry database. If you are using Windows 2000, you can also use the RegEdt32 program that offers capabilities beyond those of RegEdit.

- Using the RegEdit utility, you can also validate and back up the Registry's contents.

- The Registry database organizes entries using a tree-like structure much like a directory tree on a disk that contains levels of related information. In Windows 98, the Registry uses six primary branches, beneath which Windows and Windows-based programs organize entries.

- The HKEY_CLASSES_ROOT entry contains entries that Windows uses to associate a file extension with a specific application.

Understanding the Registry Database

For years, Windows and Windows-based programs made extensive use of configuration files with the *.ini* extension to store key settings. When a user, for example, changed the image that appears on the Windows desktop, or the colors of various items, Windows would store the user's selections within an *.ini* file (such as *win.ini* or *system.ini*). Each time the user started Windows, Windows would read and apply each of the entries within its configuration files. In a similar way, many Windows-based applications would store user settings within specific *.ini* files.

With the Windows 95 release, Windows changed from storing system settings within *.ini* files to using a special database called the Registry. Today, Windows and Windows-based programs make extensive use of the Registry.

Should the Registry database become corrupt, it is possible that Windows or one or more of your Windows-based programs will not run. Fortunately, as you will learn in this lesson, to prevent such problems, Windows maintains several backup copies of the Registry database.

Understanding the Registry Database Files

In Windows 98, the Registry resides within two files: *system.dat* and *user.dat*. Windows 98 places the Registry files within the Windows folder. The *system.dat* file contains information about the local machine and the software it contains. The *user.dat* file contains user-specific information for applications as well as the machine.

In contrast, Windows 2000 stores the Registry within files that reside in Windows the *\Winnt\System32\config* folder. Within the folder, you will find files with various extensions. Files without extensions contain the actual data for a root node—which users refer to as hives.

Editing the Registry Database May Corrupt Your System

When you perform various troubleshooting operations, there may be times when a technical support specialist will direct you to edit (change) or delete an entry from within the Registry. Because the Registry contains entries that Windows requires to start, you should edit the Registry with great care. Should you assign an incorrect value to a Registry entry, it is possible that your system may not start.

Using the Registry Editor

To let you view, change, and delete entries within the Registry, Windows provides a special program called the Registry Editor. To run the Registry Editor, perform these steps:

1. Select the Start menu Run option. Windows will display the Run dialog box.

2. Within the Run dialog box, type RegEdit if you are running Windows 9x and RegEdt32 if you are running Windows 2000. Windows, in turn, will run the Registry Editor, as shown in Figure 20.1.

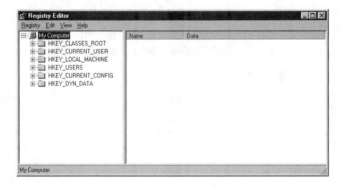

Figure 20.1 Using the Registry Editor to view, change, or delete an entry from the Registry database.

Understanding the Registry Branches

As discussed, Windows and Windows-based programs make extensive use of the Registry to store key settings. Depending on the applications you are using, your Registry database may hold tens of thousands of entries. To better organize its entries, the Registry uses a treelike structure (much like a directory tree) to group related information.

Within the Registry Editor, if you click on the plus sign that precedes a branch, the Registry Editor will expand the branch, as shown in Figure 20.2.

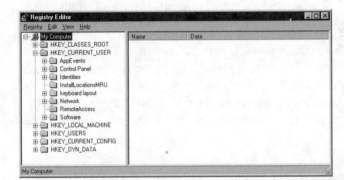

Figure 20.2 Expanding branches within the Registry Editor.

Using its various branches, the Registry will group data by application, hardware device type, user, and so on. Table 20.1 briefly describes the information you will find beneath the Registry's primary branches.

Branch	Contents
HKEY_CLASSES_ROOT	Contains entries Windows uses to associate a file extension with a specific application.
HKEY_CURRENT_CONFIG	Contains settings for the current hardware.
HKEY_CURRENT_USER	Contains settings specific to the user who is currently logged into the system.
HKEY_DYN_DATA branch	Contains a copy of Registry entries Windows has copied into the system cache to improve performance.
HKEY_LOCAL_MACHINE	Contains information about the system's hardware and software settings.
HKEY_USERS	Contains information about the users who can log into the system.

Table 20.1 Branches within the Registry database.

Given that the Registry database may contain tens of thousands of entries, locating a specific entry within the database by opening various branches and sub-branches could become quite time consuming. Fortunately, the Registry Editor provides a Edit menu Find option that you can select to display the Find dialog box shown in Figure 20.3.

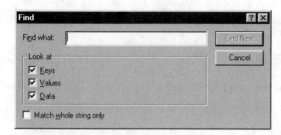

Figure 20.3 Using the Find dialog box to locate a Registry entry.

Editing a Registry Database Entry

Because an incorrect entry within the Registry database can prevent a program or Windows itself from working, you should never change the value of a Registry entry that you do not fully understand. Further, before you change an entry, you should write down the entry's original setting, in case you later need to restore the value.

After you locate an entry within the Registry, select the Edit menu Modify option to change the entry's value. The Registry Editor, in turn, will display a dialog box you can use to change the entry. Depending on the type of value (string, binary, and so on), the contents of the dialog box that the Registry Editor displays will differ. Figure 20.4 illustrates a dialog box within which you can change the value of an entry that stores a character string value.

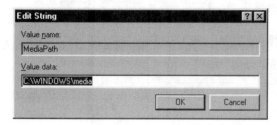

Figure 20.4 Changing the value of an entry within the Registry database.

Printing the Contents of the Registry Database

One way to fully understand how Windows and Windows-based programs use the Registry is simply to examine the Registry's contents. To do so, you may simply want to print one or more of the Registry branches. To print a specific branch within the Registry, click on the branch you desire and then select the Registry menu Print option. The Registry Editor, in turn, will display a dialog box you can use to print the selected branch or the entire Registry's contents.

Backing Up the Registry Database

Under Windows 9x, Windows will automatically make a backup copy of the Registry's current contents each time your system starts successfully. Windows will place the backup copy in a "cab" file (a compressed file) that resides within the *Windows\sysbckup* folder. By default, Windows will maintain five backup copies of the Registry. Windows will name the files that contain the backups *RCxxx.cab*, where *xxx* corresponds to the number of the backup.

Should Windows 9x encounter a Registry error as it tries to start, Windows will try each of the backup files in succession. Should you have to restore a Windows 9x backup of the Registry, perform these steps:

1. Close your current applications.

2. Select the Start menu Shutdown option. Windows will display the Shutdown System dialog box.

3. Within the Shutdown System dialog box, select the Restart In MS-DOS Mode option. Windows, in turn, will restart your system, displaying a command-line prompt.

4. At the command-line prompt, type *scanreg/restore* and press Enter.

Windows 2000, in contrast, does not automatically back up the Registry. Instead, you must use the Emergency Disk Repair (ERD) settings within the Windows Backup utility to direct Backup to copy the Registry files to the *\winnt\repair* folder each time you perform a backup operation. To restore a backup copy of the Registry, you must use the Backup utility.

Backing Up the Windows 9x Registry

By default, each time you successfully start a Windows 9x system, Windows will make a backup copy of the Registry's current contents. Using the Registry Checker utility shown in Figure 20.5, you can manually validate and then back up the Registry's current contents.

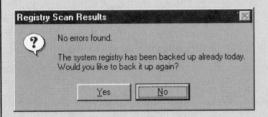

Figure 20.5 Using the Registry Checker to validate and back up the Windows 9x Registry database.

To run the Registry Checker, perform these steps:

1. Select the Start menu Programs option and choose Accessories. Windows will display the Accessories dialog box.

2. Within the Accessories dialog box, select System Tools and choose System Information. Windows will display the System Information utility.

3. Within the System Information utility, select the Tools menu Registry Checker option.

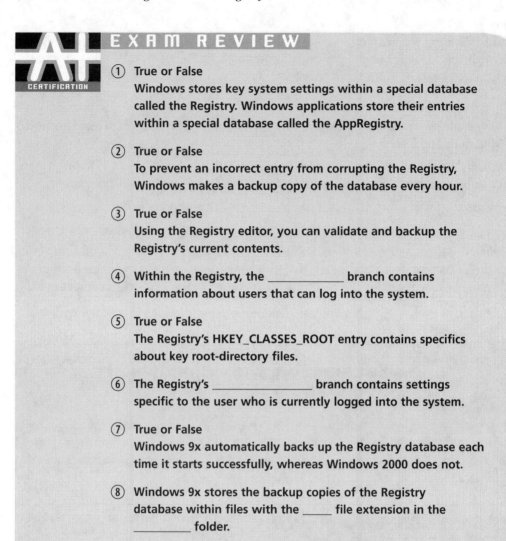

EXAM REVIEW

① True or False
Windows stores key system settings within a special database called the Registry. Windows applications store their entries within a special database called the AppRegistry.

② True or False
To prevent an incorrect entry from corrupting the Registry, Windows makes a backup copy of the database every hour.

③ True or False
Using the Registry editor, you can validate and backup the Registry's current contents.

④ Within the Registry, the _____ branch contains information about users that can log into the system.

⑤ True or False
The Registry's HKEY_CLASSES_ROOT entry contains specifics about key root-directory files.

⑥ The Registry's _____ branch contains settings specific to the user who is currently logged into the system.

⑦ True or False
Windows 9x automatically backs up the Registry database each time it starts successfully, whereas Windows 2000 does not.

⑧ Windows 9x stores the backup copies of the Registry database within files with the _____ file extension in the _____ folder.

⑨ Using the _____ utility, you can back up the Windows 2000 Registry.

Lesson 21

Power Supplies, Surge Suppressors, and Uninterruptible Power Supplies (UPS)

P Cs use electronic devices that operate by exchanging electronic signals. When you plug in a PC, you actually plug in the PC's power supply. The power supply converts the wall outlet's high-voltage alternating current (AC) into the low-voltage direct current (DC) which the PC's sensitive electronic components require.

This lesson examines the PC power supply. By the time you finish this lesson, you will understand terms such as watts, volts, and amps. In addition, you will examine "green" energy efficient devices and ways you can use Windows to fine-tune the power use of these devices. Finally, you will examine a notebook PC's use of batteries.

FACTS

- Within the PC system unit, the PC's electronic components communicate by exchanging electrical signals.

- When you plug in a PC, you actually plug in the PC's power supply.

- The power supply converts the wall outlet's high-voltage alternating current (AC) into a low-voltage direct current (DC) that the PC's sensitive components require.

- Current corresponds to the flow of electrons across a wire. The wall outlet's alternating current is so named because the current changes direction 60 times per second. The PC's direct current, in contrast, only moves in one direction.

- As the PC converts high-voltage AC to low-voltage DC, the power supply generates heat. The power supply uses a small fan to vent the heat.

- To protect your devices from electrical spikes, you should plug the devices into a surge suppressor or uninterruptible power supply (UPS).

- A UPS protects your PC from a temporary power loss by providing battery-based power. Depending on the type of UPS and the amount of power your devices are consuming, the amount of time you receive from the battery will vary.

- Energy-efficient "green" devices have the ability to reduce their power consumption by switching to a "sleep mode" when the device is not in use.

Making Sense of Watts, Volts, and Amps

The PC is an electronic device that requires power to operate. Power, which users measure in terms of watts, corresponds to the amount of voltage and current available at a specific location.

In the United States, a wall outlet provides electricity at 110 volts (110V). In Europe, wall outlets provide electricity at 220V. Think of voltage as being the difference in charge between two poles. A 9V battery, for example, has a 9-volt difference between its positive and negative poles.

Current is a measure of the flow of energy across a wire. Users measure current in terms of amperes (amps). When you place a wire between a battery's positive and negative poles, the battery's negatively charged electronics will move toward the positive charge. The electron's movement across the wire creates a current.

A wall outlet provides an alternating current (AC) that moves in one direction for a brief instant of time and then changes to the opposite direction. In the United States, the alternating current changes direction 60 times per second. To change the current's direction, the power company switches the charge at each end of the power cable so that the electrons reverse and move toward the positive charge. None of the appliances in your home, such as a lamp, hair dryer, or your television, care that the current changes direction. The devices simply require the flow of current.

In contrast, the PC's electronics require a direct current (DC) that flows in only one direction. Inside the PC system unit, the power supply performs two key tasks. First, the power supply converts the wall outlet's high voltage to a more suitable low voltage (PC devices use 3V to 12V). Second, the power supply converts the wall outlet's alternating current into a direct current.

The power supply's purpose is to provide power to various electronic components within the system unit. If you shop for a power supply, you will find that power supplies differ by the number of watts of power they provide. Today, most PCs use a 300- to 400-watt power supply. Table 21.1 describes the amount of power various PC components require.

Component	Power Requirements
Accelerated Graphics Port (AGP)	25W
CD-ROM drive	25W
EISA bus	40W
Floppy drive	5W
Hard drive	15W
ISA card	5W
Motherboard	30W
Network interface card	5W
PCI card	5W
SCSI controller	10W
Sound card	10W

Table 21.1 Power requirements for common PC components.

Taking a Closer Look at the Power Supply

If you examine the power supply, as shown in Figure 21.1, you will see that it has several small cables you can use to provide power to system unit devices. Normally, the power supply will label two connectors as P8 and P9. These two connectors power the motherboard. If you are using an ATX power supply, it will use only one larger connector to power the motherboard. If you examine the disk drives inside your system unit, you will find power supply cables that connect to and which power each drive.

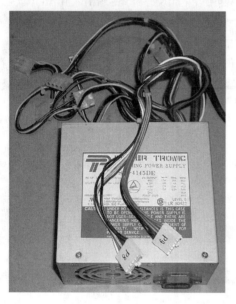

Figure 21.1 The power supply provides cables that you use to power the system unit devices.

Most users will not use all the available power supply cables. If, however, you install several drives within your system unit and you run out of power cables, you can use a cable splitter to convert one plug into two.

Each time you power on your system, the first sound you should hear is the whir of the power supply's fan. If you do not hear the fan and your system fails to start, you should first check your power cables, plugs, and power outlet. Power supplies rarely fail.

Never open a power supply. The power supply contains a capacitor that retains sufficient power to kill you—even after the power supply has been unplugged and powered off for an extended time (even many months). In addition, do not wear an antistatic wristband when you work on the power supply. Should the power supply discharge the voltage within its capacitor, you would not want the wristband to provide an electrical path to you.

As the power supply reduces the high-voltage alternating current to low-voltage direct current, the power supply can generate considerable heat. At the back of the power supply, you will find a fan that it uses to vent the heat. As you position your PC, make sure you provide ample space between your PC and a desk or wall, in order to efficiently vent that heat. Over time, the fan may accumulate dust. To clean the fan, use an aerosol blower, as shown in Figure 21.2.

Figure 21.2 To eliminate dust from the power supply fan, use an aerosol blower.

Using a Surge Suppressor or Uninterruptible Power Supply (UPS)

Rather than plugging your PC, monitor, printer, and other devices into a wall outlet, you should instead plug those power cords into a surge suppressor similar to that shown in Figure 21.3. A surge suppressor reduces the risk of a power spike from damaging your PC and its sensitive electronic components. Do not confuse a power strip that lets you plug multiple devices into a single outlet with a surge suppressor that provides protection from electrical spikes. A power strip provides no protection from power spikes.

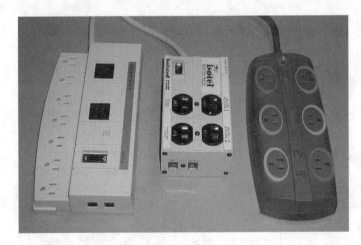

Figure 21.3 Plug devices into a surge suppressor to protect the devices from electrical spikes.

An uninterruptible power supply (UPS) is similar to a surge suppressor in that it provides your devices with protection from electrical spikes. In addition, an UPS can provide you with several minutes of power from a battery in the event of a power failure. Should the power fail, the UPS will switch to its built-in battery. Using the roughly 15 minutes of battery power, you can save your current work and then shut down your PC. Figure 21.4 shows a typical UPS.

Figure 21.4 Use a UPS to protect your system from a temporary power loss.

Understanding "Green" (Energy Efficient) Devices

To conserve electricity, most PCs, monitors, and printers can switch to a "sleep mode" when the device is not in use, which reduces the device's power consumption by as much as 70 percent. Later, when the user returns to work, the device will "wake up." Because such devices are "environmentally friendly," users refer to them as "green" devices. Often, such devices will display the Energy Star logo on their case.

Using the Windows Power Management Options dialog box, shown in Figure 21.5, you can control your PC, monitor, and disk drive's power settings. To display the dialog box, perform these steps:

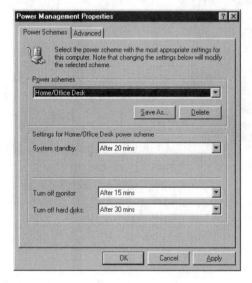

1. Select the Start menu Settings option and choose Control Panel. Windows will open the Control Panel window.

2. Within the Control Panel, double-click on the Power Management icon (if you are using Windows 2000, double-click the Power Options icon).

Figure 21.5 Using the Power Management Options dialog box, you can configure device power settings.

If you find that you cannot set power settings for your PC, it is possible that someone may have disabled the PC's power management support using an entry within the PC's CMOS settings. Using the CMOS Setup program, you can enable the PC's power management.

Automatically Powering on Your PC

When you power off your PC, the power supply actually continues to provide power to the motherboard. Using an entry within your PC's CMOS settings, you can direct the PC to awaken and power itself on at a specific time.

In an office, for example, you might use the power-on setting to turn on PCs at 7:30 each morning. That way, when the users arrive in the office at 8:00, they will find their PCs up and running.

Taking a Look at Power Management Details

For years, the PC BIOS provided most of the PC's power management capabilities. Users referred to the BIOS-based power settings as the PC's Advanced Power Management (APM) capabilities. The APM provided a set of hardware-independent services that the operating system could use to control the PC's power settings.

Today, operating systems, such as Windows, have expanded upon the APM capabilities to implement the Advanced Configuration and Power Interface (ACPI). The ACPI is an open-industry specification that attempts to standardize PC power management.

To enable a PC's ACPI settings, you can normally use an entry in the CMOS settings, as shown in Figure 21.6.

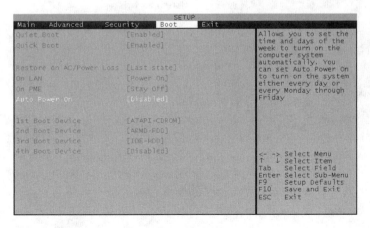

Figure 21.6 Using the CMOS setup program to enable or disable a PC's power management support.

Power and Notebook PCs

A notebook PC does not have a large power supply similar to that which you would find in a desktop PC. Instead, the notebook PC's power adapter, as shown in Figure 21.7, converts the wall outlet's high-voltage alternating current into low-voltage direct current.

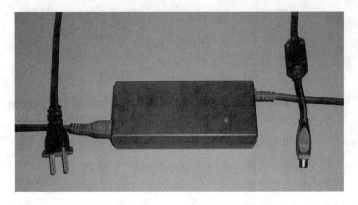

Figure 21.7 A notebook PC's power adapter provides the same functions as a power supply.

As you know, a notebook PC can operate on battery power when the PC is not plugged into a power outlet. Depending on the notebook PC's type (CPU type, screen size, and so on) and how you use the device (number of disk operations and so on), the length of battery life will vary.

Older notebook PCs used heavy nickel cadmium (NiCad) batteries which were not very efficient. Next, nickel metal hydride (NiMH) batteries improved upon the battery's ability to recharge. Today, most notebook PCs use lithium ion (Li-Ion) batteries. The Li-Ion batteries contain built-in circuitry that prevents the battery from being over or under charged. Figure 21.8 shows a typical Li-Ion battery.

Figure 21.8 Today, most notebook PCs use lithium ion (Li-Ion) batteries such as this.

EXAM REVIEW

① AC is an acronym for _____. Likewise, DC is an acronym for _____.

② True or False
Power is a term that describes the flow of energy across a wire.

③ Wall outlets provide high-voltage _____ current.

④ The PC's electronic components require low-voltage _____ current.

⑤ To protect devices from electrical spikes, you should plug your devices into a _____ or _____.

⑥ UPS is an acronym for _____.

⑦ The power supply provides two main functions: _____ and _____.

⑧ APM is an acronym for _____.

⑨ ACPI is an acronym for _____.

⑩ True or False
Operating systems extend the ACPI specification by providing support for APM.

⑪ Most notebook PCs use _____ batteries.

Understanding the CPU

Within the system unit, the vast majority of the processing the PC performs occurs in the central processing unit (CPU). Many users refer to the CPU as the computer's electronic brain. The CPU's sole purpose is to execute program instructions.

Inside the CPU is a very fast clock that, depending on the CPU's type, ticks several hundred million to over a billion times per second. The number of times the clock ticks defines the CPU's speed. The clock inside a 2GHz CPU, for example, ticks two billion times per second. In general, each time the clock ticks, the CPU executes a program instruction. A 2GHz CPU, therefore, can execute two billion instructions per second.

This lesson examines the key CPU attributes. You will learn how to determine your PC's CPU type and speed. You will briefly examine the CPU's power use, number of transistors, and use of cache memory.

F A C T S

A+ Certification Facts

+ The central processing unit (CPU) is the PC's "work horse," performing the vast amount of the processing that occurs within the PC.

+ The CPU's sole purpose is to execute program instructions.

+ Inside the CPU is a built-in clock that controls the operations the CPU performs. The number of the times the clock ticks per second determines the CPU's speed.

+ Each time the CPU's clock ticks, the CPU executes a program instruction. (Some instructions may take two clock ticks to complete and in some cases, the CPU can perform more than one instruction in a clock tick. In general, however, you can assume one instruction per clock tick.)

+ Depending on the CPU's type, the CPU will connect to the motherboard using either a socket or single-edge connector.

+ Although the Intel Pentium is the best-known CPU, other manufacturers such as AMD and Via create CPUs for PCs.

+ Within the CPU are millions of electronic switches called transistors.

+ The CPU, like all motherboard chips, requires power to operate. Depending on the CPU's type, the amount of power the CPU consumes will range from 1V to 5V.

Identifying the CPU on the Motherboard

The CPU is a single chip that resides on the motherboard. As shown in Figure 22.1, the CPU is normally the largest motherboard chip.

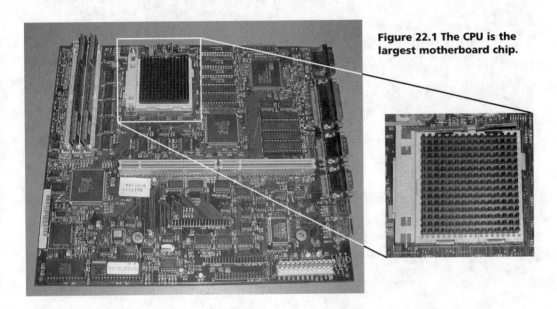

Figure 22.1 The CPU is the largest motherboard chip.

Depending on the CPU's chip design, the CPU may have pins that you plug into matching sockets or the CPU may use a single-edge connector (SEC). Figure 22.2 illustrates the two CPU types.

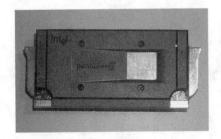

Figure 22.2 CPUs either plug into a socket-based connection or single-edge slot.

As the CPU executes instructions, it generates billions of electronic signals per second. As the signals travel through the CPU, they generate heat. Often, to prevent the CPU from overheating, which can lead to intermittent errors that are very difficult to troubleshoot, many PC manufacturers will attach either a fan or a heat sink to the CPU, as shown in Figure 22.3. A heat sink provides a surface area across which the chip can dissipate heat.

Figure 22.3 To dissipate heat generated by the CPU's electronic signals, you can attach a fan or heat sink to the CPU chip.

What's in a Name?

Because of Intel's worldwide marketing efforts, users frequently use the terms "Pentium" and "CPU" interchangeably. Pentium, however, is simply a brand name for Intel's line of CPUs. The original Pentium processor emerged in 1993. Since that time, Intel has released the Pentium II, III, and IV.

Intel is not the only CPU manufacturer. Many PCs use CPUs designed by companies such as AMD and Via.

Making Sense of Transistors

To execute program instructions, the CPU makes use of millions of very small electronic switches—transistors. The term integrated circuit (IC) describes the millions of electronic paths that reside within a chip. Table 22.1 lists the number of transistors that exist within each Pentium CPU type.

Pentium Type	Transistors
I	3,100,000
I MMX	4,500,000
II	7,500,000
III	28,000,000
IV	55,000,000

Table 22.1 The number of transistors in various Pentium processor types.

Making Sense of CPU Speeds

Inside a CPU, a very fast clock drives the CPU's operations. The number of times the clock ticks per second determines the CPU's speed. A 733MHz CPU, for example, contains a clock that ticks 733 million times per second. Likewise, a 1GHz CPU has a clock that ticks one billion times per second.

The CPU exists to execute program instructions. In general, each time the CPU's clock ticks, the CPU executes an instruction. A 733MHz CPU, therefore, executes 733 million instructions per second.

Taking a Quick Look at the CPU's Power Consumption

The CPU, like each of the PC's electronic components, requires power to operate. Like all chips on the motherboard, the CPU requires direct current (DC). Depending on the CPU's type, the amount of voltage the CPU requires may vary slightly. Table 22.2 lists the power requirements of various CPU types.

Socket Type	Power Requirements
4	5V
5	3.3V
7	2.5V to 3.3V
8	3.3V
370	1.0V to 2.1V
423	1.0V to 1.85V
478	1.0V to 1.85V

Table 22.2 Power requirements for various CPU socket types.

Understanding the CPU's Relationship with RAM

Before the CPU can execute a program, the program's instructions and data must reside within the PC's random access memory (RAM). When the CPU requires the next program instruction or a specific data value, the PC must retrieve the instruction or data from RAM. After the PC retrieves the item from RAM, the PC transfers the item to the CPU using the system bus.

To improve performance by reducing the number of times the CPU must request items from RAM, CPUs have a built-in high-speed memory within which the CPU can store items it commonly uses (such as a set of specific program instructions or data). Users refer to the high-speed memory as the CPU's L1 cache memory. Most CPUs provide about 32KB of L1 cache memory.

When the CPU requires an instruction or data, the CPU first checks to see if the item resides within its cache memory. If so, the CPU can quickly retrieve the item. Otherwise, the PC must retrieve the item from RAM, which is a much slower operation.

Viewing Your PC's CPU Type

Normally, when a PC starts, the startup program will briefly display a message that contains information about the CPU, such as its manufacturer and speed. Within Windows, you can use the System Information utility, as shown in Figure 22.4 to display information about the CPU, by performing these steps:

1. Select the Start menu Programs option and choose Accessories. Windows will display the Accessories submenu.

2. Within the Accessories submenu, select System Tools and choose System Information. Windows will display the System Information utility, the opening screen of which will contain the CPU specifics.

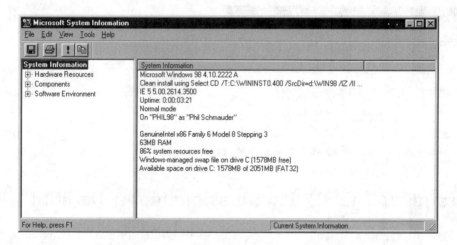

Figure 22.4 Using the System Information utility to display CPU specifics.

Replacing a CPU

If you are replacing a CPU with an identical CPU, the steps you must perform are quite straightforward:

1. Shut down, power off, and unplug your PC.

2. Ground yourself by touching your desk or another object. Ideally, you should wear an antistatic wristband.

3. Gently open and remove the system unit cover.

4. Locate and remove the existing CPU from the motherboard.

5. Gently insert the new CPU into the motherboard slot.

6. Gently replace the system unit cover.

7. Plug in and power on your PC.

To make it easier for you to remove the CPU chip from the motherboard, many CPU sockets provide a small lever (called a zero-force insertion socket) that you can lift to gently release the CPU from the socket. Later, to secure the chip within the socket, you close the lever.

If you are upgrading to a faster CPU, you must first ensure that the new CPU is compatible with your existing motherboard. To operate properly, the CPU operates hand-in-hand with several key motherboard chips that designers refer to as a "chip set." Besides the CPU, a typical chip set might include memory and bus controllers. When you upgrade your CPU, the new CPU must be compatible with the motherboard's chip set.

A Quick Word on Floating-Point Processors

A floating-point processor is a special chip designed to quickly perform arithmetic operations that use floating-point numbers (such as 3.1459). Prior to the Pentium CPU, most of the CPUs within the IBM PC and compatibles did not support floating-point operations. Instead, many users would install a second chip, called a math coprocessor or floating-point processor. In the case of the 8088 CPU, the math coprocessor was named the 8087. Likewise, for the 286, 386, and 486 processors, the math coprocessors were named the 287, 387, and 487 (some later 486 processors finally integrated floating-point operations into the CPU itself). Today, the Pentium and compatible CPUs provide support for floating-point operations, eliminating the need for the coprocessor.

Understanding CPU Overclocking

The CPU contains a fast built-in clock that controls the CPU's operations. The number of times the clock ticks determines the CPU's speed. To ensure compatibility with other chips that reside on the motherboard, PC manufacturers often slow down the CPU's internal clock. In other words, the CPU may not be running to its full potential.

Many PCs provide users (technically astute users) with the ability to speed up the CPU's clock. Users refer to this process as overclocking. Depending on the PC's type, the user might use a CMOS setting to speed up the clock or the user may set jumpers or switches that appear on the motherboard.

In general, the overclocking process requires a little "trial and error" testing. A user may simply speed up the CPU clocks and then watch to see if the PC still operates. If the PC encounters problems, the user simply restores the PC to its previous speed.

The problem with overclocking the CPU is that increasing the clock speed increases the number of signals the CPU generates, which, in turn, increases heat. Often, users must attach a fan or heat sink to the overclocked CPU to help dissipate the heat.

Although overclocking the CPU sounds quite straightforward, the process can damage or destroy chips. Most users can find many easier ways to increase their system performance other than overclocking the CPU.

EXAM REVIEW

1. The CPU's sole purpose is to _____.

2. In general, an 800MHz CPU can execute _____ instructions per second.

3. True or False
   The CPU is the largest chip on the motherboard.

4. To prevent the CPU from overheating, users often attach a _____ or _____ to the CPU chip.

5. The CPU consists of millions of tiny electronic switches called _____.

6. To improve performance, the CPU uses a very fast built-in memory that users refer to as the _____.

7. Before the CPU can execute a program's instruction or retrieve a program's data, the instructions or data must reside in _____.

Lesson 23

Understanding Random-Access Memory (RAM)

Before a program can run, the program's instructions and data must reside within the computer's random-access memory (RAM). In general, RAM provides your PC's short-term storage. Unlike a hard drive that stores data magnetically (creating long-term storage that does not require continual power), RAM chips are electronic devices that require constant power. When you turn off your PC, the contents of RAM are lost.

Over the years, RAM chips have evolved to support faster access and higher storage capacities. This lesson examines the various memory technologies that have emerged and the way the PC combines different memory types to balance performance and cost.

This lesson will present a myriad of acronyms such as SIMM, DIMM, RIMM, SRAM, DRAM, WRAM and so on. Unfortunately, you will need to understand each as you prepare for the A+ Certification Exam.

F A C T S

✚ Random access memory (RAM) is so named because the amount of time the PC requires to store or retrieve data (the access time) from the memory chip is the same for each of the storage locations within the chip. In other words, if you retrieve data from random locations in memory, the access time for each retrieval would be the same. In contrast, the access time for data on a hard drive varies based on the data's track and sector location.

✚ Before the CPU can run a program, the program's instructions and data must reside in RAM.

✚ Your PC's RAM consists of one or more chips that reside on the motherboard.

✚ Most RAM chips actually consist of several smaller chips that store the data. Users often refer to the larger RAM chips as a module or package.

✚ The three most common RAM packages include SIMM, DIMM, and RIMM chips. Your PC's documentation will specify the type of RAM package your PC requires.

✚ SIMM (Single In-line Memory Module) chips normally use a 72-pin connector.

✚ DIMM (Dual In-line Memory Module) chips normally use a 168-pin connector.

✚ RIMM (Rambus In-line Memory Module) chips normally use a 184-pin connector.

✚ When you install RAM chips in your PC, you must "fill a memory bank" which, depending on your RAM type and your PC's system bus size, may require that you install more than one chip at a time.

✚ The PC uses a system bus (set of wires) to transfer data between the CPU and RAM. Depending on the PC's type, the PC will use either a 32-bit or 64-bit data bus. RIMM chips use a data channel that is only 16 bits wide. RIMM chips can have 1, 2, or 4 channels, meaning, the chip can transfer anywhere from 16 to 64 bits.

✚ SIMM chips typically transfer 32 bits of data at a time whereas DIMM chips transfer 64 bits.

✚ To "fill a memory bank" you must install the number of chips required to match the chip's data size to the PC's data bus size. For example, if your PC uses a 64-bit data bus in a PC that supports SIMM chips, you would need to install two 32-bit SIMM chips. In contrast, if the PC used DIMM chips, you could fill the bank using one 64-bit DIMM chip.

✚ RIMM chips are unique in that if a memory slot on the motherboard does not contain a memory chip, you must place a special continuity chip within the slot. You cannot leave a RIMM slot empty.

Making Sense of Memory Chips

Your PC's RAM, like the CPU and other key components, resides on the motherboard, as shown in Figure 23.1. Depending on the type of RAM chip your PC is using and the amount of RAM the PC contains, the number of RAM chips on the motherboard will vary.

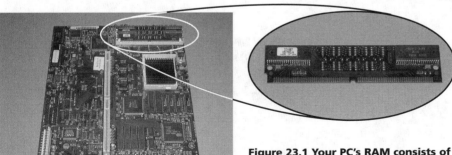

Figure 23.1 Your PC's RAM consists of one or more chips on the motherboard.

If you take a close look at the RAM chip, you will find that it actually consists of several smaller memory chips. Because the RAM chip houses smaller chips in this way, users often refer to the chips as a memory package or memory module.

Depending on the RAM chip's electronics (the chip's packaging), the chip is normally categorized as either a Single In-line Memory Module (SIMM), Dual In-line Memory Module (DIMM), or more recently, a Rambus In-line Memory Module (RIMM).

When you purchase more RAM for your PC, you must know whether your PC uses SIMM, DIMM, or RIMM chips. To determine which chip type your PC uses, you must refer to the your PC documentation. You cannot intermix the chips.

SIMM, DIMM, and RIMM chips essentially house other memory chips. Older SIMM chips, for example, provided 256KB of storage by using eight smaller 32KB chips. Depending on the type of memory the chip houses, the amount of data the memory package can store will differ.

SIMM, DIMM, and RIMM chips look very similar. You may be able to determine a memory chip's type by examining the chip's connectors. Today, most SIMMs use 72-pin connectors, most DIMMs use 168-pin connectors, and RIMM chips use 184-pin connectors. Figure 23.2 shows, from left to right, a SIMM, DIMM, and RIMM chip.

The 72-pin SIMM can transfer 32 bits of a data at one time. In contrast, the DIMM chips can transfer 64 bits of data at one time. RIMM chips, depending on the chip's channel use, can transfer 16, 32, 48, or 64 bits at one time.

Figure 23.2 SIMM, DIMM, and RIMM memory chips.

Matching Memory Chips to Memory Banks

Depending on the motherboard's design, the number of memory slots and the type of chip (SIMM, DIMM, or RIMM) the slots support will differ. Adding RAM to a PC is more difficult than simply inserting a RAM chip. Depending on your motherboard's design, you may have several rules you must follow when you install memory chips.

To begin, behind the scenes, the CPU sends and receives data to and from RAM over a data bus. In older systems, the data bus was 32-bits wide. Newer systems use a 64-bit data bus. Likewise, RAM chips can be 32-bit or 64-bit chips.

Users often refer to the memory slots on the motherboard as *memory banks*. In general, a memory bank corresponds to a group of sockets that provides enough data bits to match the number of data bits in the system bus. If, for example, the PC uses a 64-bit system bus and you are using 32-bit memory chips, you would need to place two 32-bit chips into consecutive memory slots to provide the 64 bits the bus requires. If you only install one 32-bit chip, you would not fill the bank and the PC would not use the memory.

As you have learned, a 72-pin SIMM chip supports 32 data bits. Likewise, DIMM and RIMM chips support 64 data bits. To fill a bank, you must match the number of data bits the chip supports to the system bus size. That said, all SIMM, DIMM, or RIMM chips are not created equal. You might, for example, have a 16MB SIMM chip and a 32MB SIMM chip. Both chips transfer data 32-bits at a time. One chip can simply store more data than the other. Similarly, one SIMM chip may be faster than another. The size and speed differences can also occur with DIMM and RIMM chips.

Depending on your motherboard, when you fill a memory bank, you may have to use the same size memory chips. In other words, you could not place a 16MB chip in the first slot and a 32MB chip in the second. In addition, the motherboard may require that the chips you place in a bank be the same speed.

Normally, you can place different size memory chips in different banks. Meaning, you could place two 32MB chips in the first two slots (to fill one bank) and then place two 16MB chips in the next two slots. Before you shop for memory, you must determine any restrictions your motherboard may place on the memory banks.

Often, within your system's CMOS settings, you can view your PC's memory bank use, as shown in Figure 23.3.

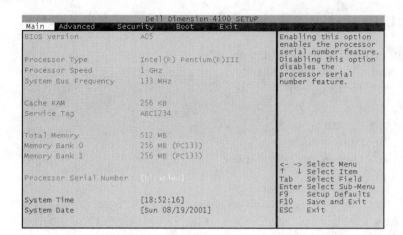

Figure 23.3 Displaying memory bank use within a CMOS setup program.

Understanding Dynamic Random-Access Memory (DRAM)

As you will learn, PCs use a variety of memory types, each of which is well suited for different uses. Because is it inexpensive, supports high-density storage, and is relatively fast, dynamic random-access memory (DRAM) is the most widely used memory type. A memory chip's storage density controls how much data the chip can store in a small area. Because the DRAM chips require only one transistor and one capacitor to store a bit, a single DRAM chip can store large amounts of data. Most PCs use DRAM chips for the system's main memory.

Within the DRAM chip, a capacitor stores a bit's current value (either a one or a zero). Because a capacitor can only sustain a charge for a finite period of time, the DRAM chip must continually refresh each capacitor's value. To maintain data values, the memory chip normally refreshes capacitors at a frequency of 66MHz.

To refresh a capacitor's value, the memory controller must read the capacitor's current value by draining the capacitor's current voltage across the transistor. Then, the memory controller restores the value back into the capacitor. Because the memory controller must continually refresh the chip's capacitors, DRAM chips are slower than other memory technologies.

Similarly, each time the CPU requests data stored in DRAM, the memory controller retrieves the data values by reading (draining and restoring) the corresponding capacitor settings. Because the memory controller must drain the capacitor each time it reads the capacitor's value, users refer to the process as a *destructive read*.

Because DRAM chips require only a capacitor and a transistor, the chips are quite simple to create and therefore less expensive than other technologies, a key factor in the chip's widespread use. Further, because of the chip's high density, DRAM chips can store large amounts of data. Because DRAM chips require the memory controller to continually refresh the chip's capacitors, DRAM chips are slower than other memory types. Also, because DRAM chips require a destructive read operation, the memory controller cannot read the DRAM chip's contents as fast as other memory types.

Understanding Static Random–Access Memory (SRAM)

Static random-access memory (SRAM) chips are so named because the SRAM chips do not lose their contents over time (as does a DRAM chip which requires capacitor refreshing). In addition, unlike the DRAM chip, the SRAM chip does not require a destructive read operation, which means the memory controller can read the chip's contents much faster. For example, a DRAM memory access typically takes 60 to 70 nanoseconds, whereas a SRAM memory access may take 10 nanoseconds or less!

The SRAM technology is more complex than the simple DRAM chip, which reduces the chip's storage density. In contrast to the single capacitor and transistor used by the DRAM chip to store a bit of data, the SRAM chip uses several transistors per bit. As a result, a SRAM chip cannot store as much data as a similarly sized DRAM chip could. Because of their fast memory access speeds, SRAM chips are well suited for use as cache memory.

Understanding Memory Technologies

To improve performance, memory chip designers continually work on ways to reduce memory access times (the length of time it takes the memory controllers to retrieve a value that resides in RAM). Over the decade, chip designers have focused on reducing the access time for subsequent memory operations. Meaning, when the CPU retrieves a range of values from memory, the first memory reference may require slightly more time than the retrievals for nearby data. By reducing the retrieval time for the subsequent memory locations, the PC improves the overall access times.

PC memory chips store information using a table format—meaning, you can visualize memory locations as consisting of row and column locations. To retrieve the value than resides at a specific memory address, the memory controller must first locate the row that contains the value. Then, the memory controller must locate the column position within the row where the value begins.

The following sections examine memory technologies that have emerged over the past years. In most cases, the technologies reduce access time for subsequent memory locations by remembering the row position of the previous value. By eliminating the need for the memory controller to determine the row location, the memory technologies can shave nanoseconds off memory access times.

Understanding Fast Page Mode (FPM) Memory

To retrieve information from memory, the memory controller must first locate the data within the memory chip. By reducing the length of time its takes a controller to find the data, chip designers can reduce the overall memory access time. During the late 1980s, fast page mode (FPM) memory reduced memory access times by letting the memory chip remember the row location of the previous memory operation.

Assume, for example, that it normally takes the memory controller 15 nanoseconds to locate data within the memory chip. Because programs typically reference memory locations that are close to one another, the memory controller may be able to eliminate the need to look up the row position for each memory operation. As a result, the first reference for a block of data may require 60 nanoseconds because of the 15-nanosecond row-lookup operation. Because the memory controller would not have to look up the row position for subsequent memory references that are close to the previous reference, the memory controller would reduce the memory access time to 45 nanoseconds.

Behind the scenes, fast page mode memory divides memory into fixed-size pages, which might range from 512 bytes to 4KB. Each page uses the same row location within the memory chip. By tracking page references, the memory chip can reduce the access time for subsequent memory references.

Understanding Extended Data Out (EDO) Memory

During the mid-1990s, Pentium processors switched from the fast page mode (FPM) memory technology to extended data out (EDO) memory. To locate data within a memory chip, the memory controller first locates the row that contains the data. Then, within that row, the controller must determine the column location at which the data begins.

EDO memory chips improved performance by reducing access time of subsequent memory references by reducing the chip's column lookup time. This was done by performing subsequent lookup operations while the memory chip is outputting data for the previous request.

Understanding Synchronous Dynamic Random-Access Memory (SDRAM)

Throughout the 1990s, the speeds of memory chips continued to improve. However, the PC's performance with respect to memory access was still limited because the memory chips operated at speeds different from the system bus. By the late 1990s, synchronous dynamic random-access memory (SDRAM) chips improved system performance by synchronizing memory operations with the system bus.

Normally, because SDRAM chips operate at the system bus speed, you will find SDRAM chip speeds specified in megahertz. To determine the cycle time of an SDRAM chip, simply divide 1 by the corresponding speed. For example, an SDRAM chip running at 100MHz has an access time of 10 nanoseconds.

To drive faster memory operations, memory manufacturers have released double data rate SDRAM chips (DDR SDRAM) that improve performance by transferring data two times during a single clock cycle. In addition, enhanced SDRAM (ESDRAM) chips improve performance using a built-in cache.

Understanding RAMBUS Memory

Earlier in this lesson, we discussed RIMM chips that use a 184-pin connector to transfer 16 data bits at a time across the data channel. The RIMM chips can use up to four data channels, which means the chip can transfer between 16 and 64 bits at a time. RIMM chips correspond to Rambus memory that manufacturers released in 1999. Rambus memory improves system performance by using a special high-speed bus to transfer the data between RAM and the CPU. Using the special bus, the Rambus memory transfers 16 bits of data at speeds of 800MHz.

Rambus memory uses a special memory chip called a RIMM (Rambus in-line memory module). A unique aspect of the RIMM bus is that each RIMM slot must contain either a RIMM chip or a special continuity module that completes the bus.

Understanding Video RAM (VRAM)

To display an image, the video card holds the image's pixel colors within RAM chips that reside on the video card. To improve video performance, video cards use a special dual mode chip that supports simultaneous read and write operations. By exploiting dual mode operations, the video controller can update the video memory's contents, while the card's digital-to-analog converter reads the memory contents in order to send the image to the monitor for display.

Understanding Windows Accelerator Card RAM (WRAM)

Windows RAM (WRAM) is a memory technology similar to video RAM but which operates much faster because it works with larger blocks of data. The memory was developed in the mid-1980s by Samsung specifically for use by Windows accelerator cards. In addition to being faster than traditional VRAM, Windows RAM is also less expensive. WRAM chips normally provide a 25 percent performance improvement over VRAM chips.

Summarizing Memory Technologies

This lesson has presented several different memory technologies. Often, the A+ Certification exam may present a question that corresponds to the speeds of various memory technologies. Table 23.1 briefly summarizes the memory technologies this lesson presents.

Technology	Time Frame	Access Time
Fast Page Mode (FPM)	1987	50ns
Extended Data Out (EDO)	1995	50ns
Synchronous Dynamic RAM (SDRAM)	1997	66MHz (PC66 SDRAM)
SDRAM	1998	100MHz (PC100 SDRAM)
RAMBUS Dynamic RAM (RDRAM)	1999	800MHz (16-bit)
SDRAM	1999	133MHz (PC133 SRAM)
Double Data Rate Synchronous Dynamic RAM (DDR SDRAM)	2000	266MHz

Table 23.1 Understanding PC memory technologies.

NOTE: *To determine the memory access times for technologies expressed in terms of megahertz (MHz), simply divide 1 by the technology's speed. For example, a 133MHz SDRAM chip has an access time of 1/133,000,000 or 7.5 nanoseconds.*

Upgrading Your System Memory

After you decide to upgrade your system's RAM, you should visit your PC manufacturer's Web site to determine the specific RAM types you should choose. To begin, you must determine if your system uses SIMM, DIMM, or RIMM chips. Then, you must determine your memory bank size and if your motherboard has specific requirements regarding the size and speed of chips you can place in each memory bank.

Whether you are installing the SIMM, DIMM, or RIMM chips, the steps you will perform to install the memory are quite similar:

1. Shut down, power off, and unplug your system.

2. Gently remove your chassis cover.

3. Before you touch any of your PC's electronic components, make sure you ground yourself by first touching your desk or an object other than your PC. Ideally, wear a grounded wristband as you perform your memory installation.

4. If you are replacing or moving any memory chips, gently remove the chip(s) from its memory slot. To remove a chip, you must gently push back the edge connectors that hold the chip in place.

5. Gently insert your new memory chip into the memory slot. If you are inserting a SIMM chip, you may need to slightly angle the chip in order to slide the chip into place. Note that the edge connectors that hold the SIMM chip in place are very fragile. If you break a connector, you may not be able to use the memory slot (and possibly slots beyond that slot).

6. If you are inserting a DIMM or RIMM chip, make sure you close the edge connectors that hold the chip in place. Also, if you are installing a RIMM chip, make sure that you place a continuity RIMM in each unused slot.

7. Gently replace your system's chassis cover. Plug in and power on your system. As your system starts, the power-on self-test should display a count of your system's memory, which includes your newly added memory.

Normally, after you power on your PC after installing new memory, your system will automatically detect and use the new memory. An older system, however, will require that you update the PC's CMOS settings to specify the amount of memory each memory bank contains.

Understanding the PC's Storage Layers

As you know, the PC uses disks to store information from one PC session to the next, or for long periods of time ranging from months to years. To store information, the disk drive magnetizes data onto the disk's surface. Because the disk stores information magnetically, the disk does not require constant power in order to maintain the data it contains. Because the disk drive maintains data after you power off the PC, users often refer to disk drives as a *nonvolatile* storage device. In contrast, the PC's RAM is a volatile storage device, which means that the RAM loses its contents when power is lost. Within the PC, a disk drive provides long-term storage. Unfortunately, because disk drives are mechanical devices, they are much slower than the PC's electronic RAM.

To improve performance and to ensure that the PC remains affordable, the PC uses a variety of storage devices that range from standard RAM and disk drives to cache memory and registers within the CPU. To better understand how the PC uses each storage technology, you should consider the technology's speed, cost, volatility and storage capacity. Figure 23.4 illustrates the common levels of storage devices within the PC, from the fastest (registers within the CPU) to the slowest (mechanical disk drives).

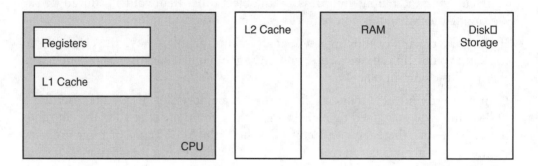

Figure 23.4 The PC uses a variety of storage technologies.

Random access memory can differ in speed and cost. As you might guess, the fastest RAM chips are also the most expensive. As a tradeoff between cost and speed, the PC normally uses a small amount of expensive high-speed memory as a special storage location called a cache. Each time the CPU needs data or an instruction, the CPU first examines the contents of the cache memory. If the CPU finds the data or instruction within the cache, the CPU can quickly retrieve the item. If the data or instruction is not in the cache, the CPU must retrieve the item from the slower (and less expensive) memory.

Many PCs take the cache concept one step further by placing very high-speed cache storage locations within the CPU itself. Users refer to this "on board" cache memory as the L1 cache. Then, the PC places a second slightly slower and slightly less expensive cache memory on the motherboard, which users refer to as the L2 cache.

When the CPU needs an instruction or data, the CPU first looks for the item in the L1 cache. If the CPU does not find the item within the L1 cache, the CPU then looks in the L2 cache. If the L2 cache does not contain the item, the CPU must then retrieve the item from the PC's RAM.

EXAM REVIEW

① RAM is an acronym for _____.

② True or False
RAM is so named because the CPU can store data and instructions in random locations.

③ DRAM is an acronym for _____.

④ True or False
Because it was very expensive, few PCs use DRAM chips today.

⑤ True or False
Because RAM chips lose their contents when you power off the PC, users refer to the chips as being nonvolatile.

⑥ To fill a memory bank for a PC using a 64-bit bus, you would have to use _____ SIMM chips or _____ DIMM chips.

⑦ True or False
DIMM chips are unique in that you must fill unused memory slots with a special continuity chip.

⑧ To improve performance, most CPUs use an onboard cache (that resides within the CPU chip itself) that users refer to as the _____ cache and possibly a second cache (which may or may not reside in the CPU) that users refer to as the _____ cache.

⑨ True or False
Because cache memory is inexpensive, most PCs make extensive use of large caches.

⑩ Order the following memory technologies according to their speed:

☐ FPO
☐ DDR SDRAM
☐ WRAM
☐ EDO
☐ RDRAM
☐ SDRAM

Making Sense of PC Memory Technologies

O ver the years, the PC has used several different memory technologies that combine hardware and software schemes to increase the amount of memory the PC could access. Although these memory technologies existed for the MS-DOS environment, you will encounter discussion about each as well as related questions on the A+ Certification exam.

The original IBM PC supported 640KB of conventional memory, within which the MS-DOS operating system stored programs and data. The PC reserved the memory region between 640KB and 1MB for use by the video display and other hardware devices. As the amount of data used by the programs increased, Lotus, Intel, and Microsoft created a new memory technology based on the Expanded Memory Specification (EMS) that let programs access data by swapping the data from a special memory card to a region in the PC's reserved memory. Although the swapping process allowed programs to access larger amounts of data, the constant swapping of data introduced overhead that slowed system performance.

With the advent of the IBM PC AT, a new memory technology called extended memory let MS-DOS programs store and retrieve data from memory locations beyond 1MB without having to swap data. This lesson examines conventional, expanded, and extended memory in detail. You will also learn techniques the MS-DOS operating system let users perform to maximize PC memory use.

F A C T S

- The original IBM PC could access 1MB of RAM. Users referred to the PC's first 640KB memory as conventional memory and the memory region between 640KB and 1MB as reserved memory.

- The MS-DOS operating system stored programs and data in the first 640KB of the PC's memory—the PC's conventional memory.

- The PC reserved the memory region between 640KB and 1MB for use by the video card, the BIOS, and other hardware devices.

- To let MS-DOS-based programs access more data (primarily large spreadsheets), Lotus, Intel, and Microsoft defined the expanded memory specification (EMS, which users also referred to as LIM-EMS to include the initials of the companies that defined the specification).

- The expanded memory specification defined the use of software and a special memory card (EMS memory) to let programs swap data from the card into a region within the PC's reserved memory. By allowing programs to swap data from the card into the reserved-memory region, expanded memory let programs access data beyond the PC's conventional memory.

- Not all programs supported the use of expanded memory. Those programs that did could use expanded memory to store and retrieve data that did not reside in conventional memory. Programs could only use expanded memory to store data. Program instructions could not reside in expanded memory.

- To access data stored on the expanded memory card, the EMS-based software would move data between the expanded memory card and a 64KB region within the PC's reserved memory. Depending on how the program accessed data on the expanded memory card, the swapping of data between the card and the PC's reserved memory could introduce substantial overhead that slowed system performance.

F A C T S

- To use expanded memory, the MS-DOS operating system had to install a device driver (whose filename was normally dependent on the memory card manufacturer) using a DEVICE= entry within the *CONFIG.SYS* file.

- The IBM PC AT introduced extended memory that let MS-DOS programs access data beyond 1MB without having to first move the data (as was required with expanded memory).

- To use extended memory, the MS-DOS operating system had to install the *HIMEM.SYS* device driver using a DEVICE= entry within the *CONFIG.SYS* file.

- Many MS-DOS programs did not take advantage of extended memory. Most MS-DOS users used extended memory for a disk cache or RAM drive.

- MS-DOS users sometimes refer to the reserved-memory area between 640KB and 1MB as the upper-memory area. Beginning with MS-DOS version 5, users could install device drivers and other memory-resident programs within the upper-memory area to free up conventional memory for other program use.

- To load a device driver into the upper-memory area, MS-DOS users used the DEVICEHIGH= entry within the *CONFIG.SYS* file. To load a memory-resident program into the upper-memory area, MS-DOS users used the LOADHIGH command.

- Users refer to the first 64KB memory region above 1MB as the high-memory area. Beginning with MS-DOS version 5, users could direct MS-DOS to load itself into the high-memory area to free up conventional memory for program use. To direct MS-DOS to load itself into the high-memory area, users placed a DOS=HIGH entry within the *CONFIG.SYS* file.

- To view a PC's memory use (conventional, expanded, and extended), you can use the MS-DOS MEM command.

Understanding Conventional Memory

The original IBM PC, released in 1981, supported 1MB of random access memory. Users referred to the first 640KB of the PC's RAM as conventional memory. The MS-DOS operating system would place the programs (and their data) that users ran (as well as its own software) within conventional memory. MS-DOS-based programs always ran within the 640KB conventional-memory program space. If a program could not fit within the 640KB memory region, MS-DOS could not run the program.

The PC reserved the 384KB above conventional memory for use by the video display and other hardware devices.

As programs needed to work with larger amounts of data, PC manufacturers first developed the expanded specification that let MS-DOS-based programs access data that resided on a special memory card, giving programs the ability to store and retrieve data beyond the PC's conventional memory.

Understanding Expanded Memory

As discussed, the original IBM PC supported only 1MB of memory. As spreadsheet programs (at the time Lotus 1-2-3) began to support large amounts of data, the programs quickly consumed the PC's available memory. To provide the PC with more memory, hardware developers came up with *expanded memory*, a way to trick the PC into using memory beyond 1MB.

Lotus, Intel, and Microsoft actually designed EMS for the original IBM PC. Using special EMS-memory cards and EMS device-driver software, programs that supported the use of expanded memory could divide their data into 64KB sections, storing all the data within the EMS memory card. The programs would then allocate a 64KB memory region within the PC's reserved memory (the 384KB region above 640KB). When the program needed to access specific data, the EMS software would move the data from the EMS memory card into the 64KB region.

By swapping memory between conventional and EMS memory in this way, a program could access large amounts of data, such as a spreadsheet as large as several megabytes. Unfortunately, the swapping of data between expanded and conventional memory was quite time consuming, which decreased the system's performance. Eventually, therefore, expanded memory was replaced by extended memory.

NOTE: *Beginning with MS-DOS version 5, users running a 386 processor in a PC that did not have an expanded memory card could install the EMM386.EXE device driver to trick programs that required expanded memory into using extended memory as an expanded memory card.*

Understanding Extended Memory

When the IBM PC AT was released in 1984, it brought with it the 286 processor and a second memory technology called *extended memory*. Depending on the model, PCs can hold several hundred megabytes of extended memory. MS-DOS-based programs used extended memory to hold their data, such as a spreadsheet or large word processing document. MS-DOS-based programs could not store program instructions within the extended memory. The advantage of extended memory over expanded memory was that to access the data in extended memory the PC did not have to first swap the data to a region in the upper-memory area. As a result, extended memory was much faster than expanded memory.

Not all MS-DOS programs supported the use of extended memory. Often, users allocated a portion of extended memory for use as a disk cache.

To use extended memory, MS-DOS users had to install the *HIMEM.SYS* device driver within the *CONFIG.SYS* file using an entry similar to that shown here:

```
DEVICE=C:\DOS\HIMEM.SYS
```

Understanding High Memory

When the 386 processor was released in the late 1980s, MS-DOS users could take advantage of the first 64KB of extended memory, called the *high-memory area,* to hold MS-DOS. Normally, each time the system started, the PC would load MS-DOS into conventional memory. By directing MS-DOS to load into the high-memory area, users could free up the conventional-memory area MS-DOS previously consumed for use by other programs.

To load MS-DOS into the high-memory area, users had to first install the *HIMEM.SYS* device driver and then place the DOS=HIGH entry within the *CONFIG.SYS* file, as shown here:

```
DEVICE=C:\DOS\HIMEM.SYS
DOS=HIGH
```

Understanding Upper Memory

As discussed, the PC reserves the 384KB of memory above 640KB for use by the video display and other hardware devices. PC users refer to this memory region as the reserved-memory area or upper-memory area. Within the MS-DOS environment, part of the upper-memory area was not used. Beginning with MS-DOS version 5, users could allocate part of the upper-memory area to hold device drivers and memory-resident programs which would otherwise consume conventional memory. By moving device drivers and memory-resident programs to the upper-memory area, users freed up conventional memory for program use.

Before MS-DOS users could use the upper-memory area, they had to install the *EMM386.EXE* device driver within the *CONFIG.SYS* file, as shown here:

```
DEVICE=C:\DOS\EMM386.EXE    NOEMS
```

The *EMM386.EXE* device driver was designed to let users allocate extended memory for use as expanded memory. In this way, a user who did not have expanded memory installed in his or her PC could run programs that required expanded memory by using the device driver to trick the programs into using extended memory as if it were an expanded memory card. The most common use of the *EMM386.EXE* device driver, however, was to provide MS-DOS with the ability to use the upper-memory area.

In the previous DEVICE= entry, the NOEMS parameter told MS-DOS that the user did not want to use expanded memory, but rather the user is using the device driver to provide support for the upper-memory area. To use the upper-memory area, users also had to place a DOS= entry similar to the following within the *CONFIG.SYS* file:

```
DOS=HIGH,UMB
```

UMB is an abbreviation for *upper-memory block*. An upper-memory block is a section of memory within the upper-memory area. When users loaded a device driver or memory-resident program into the upper-memory area, MS-DOS would allocate an upper memory block to hold the program.

After a user installed support for the upper-memory area, the user could then install device drivers into the memory area using the DEVICEHIGH= entry (as opposed to the DEVICE= entry), as shown here:

```
DEVICEHIGH=C:\DOS\ANSI.SYS
```

When MS-DOS encountered a DEVICEHIGH entry within the *CONFIG.SYS* file, it would first try to load the device driver into the upper-memory area. If there was not enough memory in the upper-memory area to hold the driver, MS-DOS would load the driver into the 640KB conventional-memory region, just as if the user had used the DEVICE entry.

In addition to installing device drivers into the upper-memory area, users could also direct MS-DOS to load memory-resident programs (such as the MS-DOS Print command) into the upper-memory area using the LOAD-HIGH command. For example, the following LOADHIGH command directs MS-DOS to load the PRINT command into upper memory:

```
LOADHIGH=C:\DOS\PRINT.COM
```

To load the memory-resident programs they used on a regular basis, MS-DOS users would place one or more LOADHIGH commands within the *AUTOEXEC.BAT* file. Because of its frequency of use, MS-DOS let users abbreviate LOADHIGH as LH.

Viewing an MS-DOS System's Memory Use

To view an MS-DOS system's memory use, you can issue the MEM command, as shown here:

```
C:\> MEM   <Enter>
```

Memory Type	Total	Used	Free
Conventional	636K	44K	592K
Upper	0K	0K	0K
Reserved	0K	0K	0K
Extended (XMS)	65,468K	?	392,012K
Total memory	66,104K	?	392,604K
Total under 1 MB	636K	44K	592K

```
Largest executable
   program size              592K (606,576 bytes)

Largest free upper
   memory block       OK    (0 bytes)
MS-DOS is resident in the high memory area.
```

To view specifics about each program's (and device driver's) memory use, you can issue the /Classify switch (or simply /C) when you invoke the MEM command:

```
C:\> MEM   /Classify  <Enter>
```

Why You Still Must Care About These Older Memory Technologies

The memory technologies presented in this lesson existed to extend the capabilities of the MS-DOS operating system. The Windows operating system does not use these memory technologies. Instead, Windows uses a technique called virtual memory to allocate memory to programs. Lesson 25, "Understanding Virtual Memory," examines Windows memory management in detail.

Although the number of users running MS-DOS-based systems has thankfully become quite small, there may be times when you will encounter users who still run older MS-DOS-based programs within the Windows environment. Depending on the program, it may require the use of one or more of the memory technologies presented here. In such cases, you may need to place one or more of the entries discussed here into the user's *CONFIG.SYS* file or you may need to assign related settings to the program using the program file's Properties settings (that you can access within the Windows Explorer) as shown in Figure 24.1.

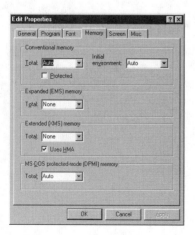

Figure 24.1 Using a file's Properties dialog box to set an MS-DOS program's memory requirements within Windows.

EXAM REVIEW

1. Users typically refer to a PC's first 640KB of RAM as _____ memory.

2. True or False
   The MS-DOS operating system loaded programs and their data into conventional memory.

3. Users refer to the 384KB memory region between 640KB and 1MB as _____ or _____.

4. To provide MS-DOS-based programs with the ability to access data beyond conventional memory, Lotus, Intel, and Microsoft developed the _____ memory specification.

5. True or False
   By swapping data between a special memory card and an area within the PC's reserved memory, EMS provided high-speed memory access.

6. The IBM PC AT introduced _____ memory that let programs access data beyond conventional memory without having to swap the data to and from the reserved-memory area.

7. True or False
   To use extended memory, MS-DOS users installed the *EMM386.EXE* device driver.

8. MS-DOS programs used expanded memory and extended memory to hold program _____ not program _____.

9. By taking loading device drivers and memory-resident programs into the _____ using the *CONFIG.SYS* file's DEVICEHIGH entry and LOADHIGH command, users could free up conventional memory for program use.

10. MS-DOS users referred to the first 64KB region above 1MB as the _____. To direct MS-DOS to load into this memory area (as opposed to using conventional memory), MS-DOS users had to place what entries within the *CONFIG.SYS* file?

Lesson 25

Understanding Virtual Memory

Before the CPU can execute a program's instructions, the instructions and the corresponding data must reside in the PC's memory. Within the Windows environment, users run multiple programs at the same time, which conceptually means that each program's instructions and data must reside in memory at the same time.

When two or more programs reside in memory at the same time, the operating system must provide a way to protect each program's instructions and data from other programs. Windows uses a memory-management technique called virtual-memory management to manage program instructions and data. Virtual memory is so named because it gives Windows and the programs running within Windows the illusion that they individually possess up to 4GB of RAM, far more RAM that the PC contains. Because the memory does not truly exist, users refer to it as virtual memory. In contrast, the memory chips you install in your PC comprise your PC's physical memory.

Virtual-memory management combines RAM with a special file on disk that users call the *swap file* to create the illusion of the large address space. For the CPU to execute an instruction or access a program's data, the instruction or data must reside within RAM. Depending on the amount of RAM the PC contains and the number of programs the PC is running, Windows may temporarily move one program's instructions or data from RAM to the swap file on disk to provide more space in RAM for a new program's instructions or data.

By continually moving programs (their instructions and data) between RAM and the swap file on disk, Windows virtual-memory management creates the illusion of a "virtually" unlimited memory address space.

F A C T S

- To manage the memory that contains program instructions and data, Windows uses a memory-management technique called virtual-memory management.

- Virtual-memory management combines RAM with a special file on disk called the swap file.

- Before the CPU can execute a program's instructions, the instructions, as well as the corresponding data, must reside in RAM.

- If Windows does not have enough available RAM to load a program's data or instructions into memory, Windows will temporarily move another program (its instructions, data, or both) from RAM to the swap file on disk. Later, when Windows must run a program that it previously swapped to disk, Windows will move the program back into RAM, possibly first swapping a different program from RAM to the swap file to make room in RAM for the incoming program.

- Because the disk drive is a mechanical device (with moving parts), the disk drive is much slower than the PC's electronic components. As the amount of swapping that Windows must perform increases, the system's performance will decrease due to the slow disk operations.

- By adding more RAM to a PC, you may improve your system's performance by reducing the amount of swapping Windows must perform.

- If Windows is not using your PC's current RAM, you will not improve your system performance by adding more RAM.

- Behind the scenes, Windows' virtual-memory management divides program instructions and data into fixed-size pieces called *pages*. To execute a program's instructions, Windows does not have to load the entire program into RAM. Rather, Windows must only load the page (or pages) containing the program's current instructions and data.

- When the page containing the instruction or data that the CPU requires does not exist in RAM, a page fault occurs that directs the operating system to load the page from disk into memory so the program can continue to run.

- By monitoring your system's page faults and available physical memory, you can determine whether adding more RAM would improve your system's performance.

- Windows' virtual memory is a combination of RAM and the disk space consumed by the swap file. The amount of virtual memory that Windows lets your system use will depend on the amount of RAM you have installed in your PC and the amount of available space on your disk.

- Although Windows lets you change some virtual-memory settings, the only setting you should consider changing is to move the swap file from drive C to another drive (in order to free up disk space on drive C or to take advantage of a faster disk drive).

Virtual-Memory Management Combines RAM and a Special Swap File

To manage the memory used by multiple programs at the same time, Windows employs a memory-management technique called virtual-memory management. Virtual memory is so named because it gives Windows, and the programs you run within Windows, the illusion of having much more available memory than the PC actually contains.

Before a CPU can execute a program's instructions or access a program's data, the instructions and data must reside within the RAM (the PC's physical memory). When you run multiple programs within Windows, there may be times when Windows no longer has space in RAM available to hold a new program's instructions and data. To make room, Windows will temporarily move one program from RAM to a special file on disk called a swap file, as shown in Figure 25.1. Users refer to the process of moving programs between RAM and the swap file as *swapping*.

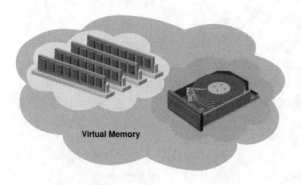

Virtual Memory

Figure 25.1 When Windows does not have sufficient RAM to load a new program and its data, Windows will swap an existing program's instruction and data to disk.

Later, when Windows must execute a program that it previously swapped to disk, Windows must move the program's instructions and data back from the swap file into RAM. Depending on its current use of RAM, Windows may first need to swap a different program (or possibly several programs) from RAM to the swap file in order to make room in RAM for the incoming program.

Over time, depending on the programs you are running and your system's available RAM, you may have several programs residing in RAM and several other programs swapped to disk.

Windows 98 names the swap file *Win386.swp.* Windows 2000 names the swap file *pagefile.sys.*

Program Swapping Decreases System Performance

To swap a program, Windows must move the program (its instructions, data, or both), from RAM to the swap file that resides on disk. Compared to the PC's fast electronic components, the mechanical disk drive, with its moving parts, is much slower. As the amount of swapping that Windows performs increases, the slow disk drive operations that move programs to and from the swap file will decrease system performance.

If a system performs excessive swapping, you may hear the disk drive operations as Windows moves programs between RAM and the swap file. You may also find that your programs seem to take longer to load or become active after you click your mouse in the program window.

When your system begins to perform excessive swapping, you should either run fewer programs at the same time or you should install more RAM.

Understanding Page Faults

To implement virtual memory, Windows divides a program's instructions and data into fixed-size sections called pages. As a program executes, Windows must place only the pages that contain the program's current instructions and data into RAM. When Windows needs an instruction or data that resides in a page that is not currently in RAM, a page fault occurs and Windows must load the page from disk into RAM. The more page faults Windows performs (and hence the more disk operations), the slower the system's performance will become.

By monitoring your system's page faults, you can get an indication as to whether your system has sufficient RAM. Normally, when you first run a program, Windows will immediately load many of pages that contain the program's instructions and data. Therefore, when you first run a program, the number of page faults should increase. Over time, however, Windows should have most of the pages it needs to run the program in RAM and the number of page faults should decrease. If your system consistently experiences numerous page faults, you may need to add more RAM in order to improve your system performance.

To monitor page faults within Windows 98, perform these steps:

1. Select the Start menu Programs option and choose Accessories. Windows will display the Accessories submenu.

2. Within the Accessories submenu, select System Tools and choose System Monitor. Windows will display the System Monitor window.

3. Within the System Monitor, select the Edit menu Add Item option. Windows will display the Add Item dialog box.

4. Within the Add Item dialog box, select Memory Manager and then choose Page Faults. The the System Monitor will then display specifics about your system's page-fault operations, as shown in Figure 25.2.

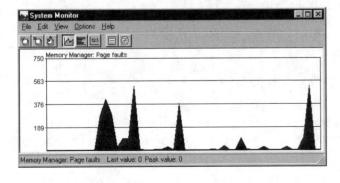

Figure 25.2 Monitoring page faults within the System Monitor.

To monitor page faults within Windows 2000, perform these steps:

1. Select the Start menu Settings option and choose Control Panel. Windows will display the Control Panel window.

2. Within the Control Panel, double-click on the Administrative Tools icon. Windows will display the Administrative Tools window.

3. Within the Administrative Tools window, double-click on the Performance icon. Windows will display the Performance window.

4. Within the Performance window, click the Add icon that appears as a plus sign. Windows will display the Add Counters dialog box.

5. Within the Add Counters dialog box Performance Object pull-down list, select the Memory. Then, within the Select counters from list, choose Page Faults/Sec. Click on the Add button to put your selection into effect.

To Improve System Performance, Add RAM

If you talk with other users regarding ways you can improve your system performance, someone will always immediately tell you that you should add more RAM. After all, by making more RAM available to Windows, you may reduce the amount of swapping that Windows must perform.

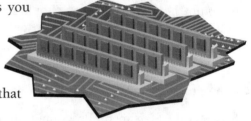

Before you run out and purchase more RAM, however, you should monitor your system's use of physical memory, which you can do using the System Monitor as previously discussed. Simply direct the System Monitor to monitor unused physical memory.

To monitor your system's available physical memory within Windows 2000, perform these steps:

1. Select the Start menu Settings option and choose Control Panel. Windows will display the Control Panel window.

2. Within the Control Panel, double-click on the Administrative Tools icon. Windows will display the Administrative Tools window.

3. Within the Administrative Tools window, double-click on the Performance icon. Windows will display the Performance window.

4. Within the Performance window, click the Add icon that appears as a plus sign. Windows will display the Add Counters dialog box.

5. Within the Add Counters dialog box Performance Object pull-down list, select Memory. Then, within the Select counters from list, choose Available Bytes, Available KBytes, or Available MBytes. Click on the Add button to put your selection into effect.

If you find that your system normally has unused physical memory available for Windows to use, you would not improve your system performance by adding more memory. Instead, Windows would simply have more unused physical memory. If, however, your PC continually runs low on unused physical memory, adding more memory would improve your system performance.

Changing Windows Virtual–Memory Management Settings

Normally, each time your system starts, Windows examines the amount of RAM your PC contains and the amount of free disk space on drive C to determine the amount of virtual memory it will support. Although Windows lets you change various virtual-memory management settings, as a rule you should not override the values Windows selects. The one exception is that you may want to change the disk drive that Windows stores the swap file on. If your system is running low on disk space on drive C, for example, you can move the swap file to a drive with more available disk space. Or, if you install a second drive that is faster than the swap file's current drive, you will improve your system performance by moving the swap file to the faster drive.

To change the drive used by Windows 98 to store the swap file, perform these steps:

1. Select the Start menu Settings option and choose Control Panel. Windows will display the Control Panel window.

2. Within the Control Panel, double-click on the System icon. Windows, in turn, will display the System Properties dialog box.

3. Within the System Properties dialog box, click on the Performance tab. Windows, in turn, will display the Performance sheet.

4. Within the Performance sheet, click on the Virtual Memory button. Windows, in turn, will display the Virtual Memory dialog box, as shown in Figure 25.3.

5. Within the Virtual Memory dialog box, click your mouse on the Let me specify my own virtual memory settings button. Then, within the hard disk field, precede the swap file name with the drive letter of the disk you desire.

6. Choose OK. You will then have to restart Windows for your change to take effect.

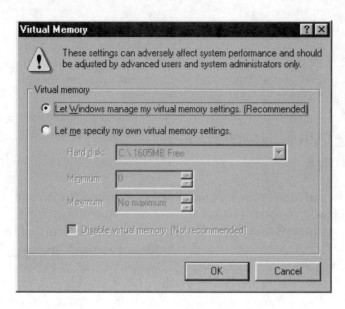

Figure 25.3 Using the Virtual Memory dialog box to change the swap file drive.

To change the drive used by Windows 2000 to store the swap file, perform these steps:

1. Select the Start menu Settings option and choose Control Panel. Windows will display the Control Panel window.

2. Within the Control Panel, double-click on System icon. Windows, in turn, will display the System Properties dialog box.

3. Within the System Properties dialog box, select the Advanced tab. Windows will display the Advanced sheet.

4. Within the Advanced sheet, select the Performance Options button. Windows will display the Performance Options dialog box.

5. Within the Performance Options dialog box, select the Change button. Windows will display the Virtual Memory dialog box.

6. Within the Virtual Memory dialog box Drive field, click on the drive letter of the disk you desire. Enter appropriate values in the Initial size (MB) and Maximum size (MB) fields. Click on the Set button and then the OK button to put your change into effect.

1. To manage the memory it uses as well as the memory it allocates to programs you run, Windows uses a memory-management technique called _____.

2. To implement virtual memory, Windows combines _____ and _____.

3. True or False
   By quickly moving programs between RAM and the swap file, Windows' virtual-memory management improves your system performance.

4. True or False
   By adding RAM to a PC, you will always improve your system performance.

5. Windows 98 names the swap file _____.

6. Windows 2000 uses a file named _____ as the swap file.

7. True or False
   To improve system performance you should increase the size of the Windows swap file.

8. Windows divides a program and its instructions into fixed-size pieces call _____.

9. A _____ occurs when Windows must load a page containing program instructions or data from disk to RAM.

Configuring the PC's CMOS Settings

ach time a PC starts, it retrieves information about key system settings from a special memory that users refer to as the CMOS memory. Within the PC's CMOS settings, the PC stores information such as:

- The order the BIOS will use to search disk drives for a bootable system disk.
- Specifics about the hard disk's geometry (the number of tracks, sectors per track, as well as low-level drive settings).
- Settings that can be used to select standard or enhanced parallel port operations.
- Entries used to enable or disable the PC's power management capabilities.
- Information about legacy (older non-plug-and-play) devices, such as the device's interrupt request (IRQ) line and I/O port settings.
- Information about the PC's use of RAM and cache memory.

CMOS memory is so named because the memory is made using Complementary Metal Oxide Semiconductor material. The advantage of the CMOS material is that it requires minimal voltage to retain the information it holds. When you power off your PC, the PC uses a small battery (typically 5 volts or less) that retain the CMOS settings.

This lesson examines ways you can use the CMOS settings to configure your PC. The lesson also presents the steps you must perform to replace the CMOS battery should the battery fail.

- CMOS is an acronym that stands for Complementary Metal Oxide Semiconductor. CMOS is a material from which chips can be produced.

- The advantage of the CMOS material is that CMOS-based memory chips require minimal voltage to retain their contents.

- The PC uses CMOS-based memory to store key system settings. Each time the PC starts, the PC uses the CMOS entries to configure various hardware devices.

- The PC powers the CMOS memory using a small battery that normally resides on the motherboard.

- Depending on your PC type, the steps you must perform to access the CMOS settings will differ. Normally, each time the system starts, before the system begins to load Windows, you can press a specific keyboard combination to run a program (the CMOS setup program) that lets you view and change CMOS settings.

- You should never change a CMOS setting's value without first recording the setting's current value. Should your change introduce a system error, you can restore the setting's previous value.

- You should never change the value of a CMOS setting whose purpose you do not understand. By assigning an errant value to a CMOS entry, you may prevent your system from starting.

- An easy way to record the values of each CMOS setting is to press the Shift-PrtSc keyboard combination as you view the CMOS settings within the CMOS setup program. When you press the Shift-PrtSc key combination, the PC will print the screen's current contents.

F A C T S

+ Several utility programs exist that let you save your PC's CMOS settings to a file on disk. Should you ever need to restore your CMOS settings, you can use these programs to restore the values you saved to the file.

+ Should your PC's CMOS battery fail, most CMOS setup programs provide a menu option you can select to restore the default settings. Normally, by selecting this entry, you can restore the PC to a bootable state. Then, you can individually change or fine-tune other settings.

+ Many CMOS setup programs let you assign a password which a user must enter before the PC will start and before the user can access the CMOS setup. Should the user forget the password, or should a disgruntled employee assign a password to his or her system on the day they leave the company, you will need to clear the current CMOS settings in order to discard the password.

+ To support plug-and-play operations, most CMOS setup programs let you reserve IRQ and I/O port settings for older non-plug-and-play (legacy) devices. The CMOS setup program will store the device information in a special area called the Extended System Configuration Data (ESCD) region.

Understanding the PC's CMOS Settings

Each time the PC starts, it examines a special memory that users refer to as the PC's CMOS to determine various hardware settings. Entries within the CMOS provide specifics about the PC's disk types, the order the PC will search drives for a bootable disk (meaning you can use a CMOS entry to direct the PC to boot your system from the hard drive without first searching the drives for a bootable floppy disk), information about the PC's RAM and cache use, and more.

CMOS is an acronym for Complementary Metal Oxide Semiconductor which describes a type of material designers can use to build chips. The advantage of the CMOS-based memory chip is that it requires minimal voltage to retain the information it contains. The disadvantage of the CMOS technology is speed—CMOS-based memory chips are considerably slower than traditional RAM chips.

To maintain the CMOS settings while the PC is not powered on, the PC uses a small 3-volt or 5-volt battery. If you examine your PC's motherboard, you can normally locate a small flat battery similar to that shown in Figure 26.1.

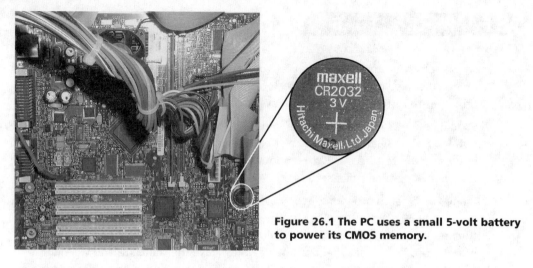

Figure 26.1 The PC uses a small 5-volt battery to power its CMOS memory.

Although CMOS batteries normally last several years, the battery will eventually fail. At that time, you must replace the battery as described later in this lesson. Then you must restore the CMOS setting values.

Viewing Your System's CMOS Settings

As discussed, the PC uses the CMOS entries each time your system starts to determine specifics about your various hardware devices and to configure key system settings. Depending on the PC's type, the steps you must perform to display the CMOS settings will differ. Normally, you will press one of the following keyboard combinations after your system completes its power on self-test and before the system begins to load Windows:

Del

F2

Esc

Ctrl-Esc

Ctrl -Alt-Esc

To let you view (and change) your PC's CMOS settings, your PC will run a program that users call the CMOS setup program. The information the CMOS setup program displays may differ based on the PC's type. Normally, as shown in Figure 26.2, the CMOS setup program will display settings that correspond to a user's menu-option selection, meaning, the program may separate disk, security, and memory settings, letting you display the specific settings you desire.

```
                    Dell Dimension 4100 SETUP
 Main   Advanced    Security      Boot     Exit
 BIOS Version          A05                        Enabling this option
                                                  enables the processor
                                                  serial number feature.
 Processor Type        Intel(R) Pentium(R)III     Disabling this option
 Processor Speed       1 GHz                       disables the
 System Bus Frequency  133 MHz                     processor serial
                                                   number feature.
 Cache RAM             256 KB
 Service Tag           ABC1234

 Total Memory          512 MB
 Memory Bank 0         256 MB (PC133)
 Memory Bank 1         256 MB (PC133)
                                                  <- -> Select Menu
 Processor Serial Number  [Disabled]             ↑  ↓  Select Item
                                                  Tab    Select Field
                                                  Enter  Select Sub-Menu
                                                  F9     Setup Defaults
 System Time           [18:52:16]                 F10    Save and Exit
 System Date           [Sun 08/19/2001]           ESC    Exit
```

Figure 26.2 Displaying CMOS settings within a CMOS setup program.

As discussed, the PC uses a small battery to power the CMOS memory. Should the battery fail, the contents of the CMOS memory will be lost. After you replace the battery, you must use the CMOS setup program to restore the system's previous setting values.

To simplify the process of restoring the previous CMOS settings in the event of a battery failure, most CMOS setup programs provide a menu option that lets you restore the default settings. Normally, by restoring the defaults, you can quickly bring a PC back to a bootable state. Then, you may need to individually change specific entries within the CMOS that you may have changed since you purchased your PC.

NOTE: *Several third-party software companies provide programs you can run to save your current CMOS settings to a floppy disk. Should your CMOS battery ever fail, you can use the third-party program to restore your saved entries.*

Changing the CMOS Entry's Value

As you perform PC upgrades, there may be times when you must change one or more of your CMOS entries. For example, to enable high-speed parallel port operations, you may need to change the CMOS parallel-port setting from standard to ECP (extended capabilities port) or EPP (enhanced parallel port) operations.

Before you change an entry within the CMOS, make sure you write down the entry's original value. Should your change introduce an error, you can easily restore the original setting. Further, because an errant CMOS entry can prevent your system from starting, you should never change the value of a CMOS entry that you do not fully understand.

After you make your changes within the CMOS setup program, you must direct the program to save your changes and to exit—at which time the BIOS will use the new settings to restart your system. Should you decide that you do not want to save your changes, most CMOS setup programs provide a menu option you can select to exit the program without saving your changes.

Should you make a change to a CMOS entry that prevents your system from starting and you do not recall the setting's original value, you should find a menu option within the CMOS setup program that you can use to restore the PC's default settings, as previously discussed. Depending on the severity of the error, you may need to first clear the current CMOS settings as discussed next.

Flushing (Discarding) the Current CMOS Settings

As discussed, before you change a CMOS setting, you should record the setting's current value. That said, should an errant CMOS setting prevent your system from starting, you may need to direct the CMOS to discard its current settings.

To increase security, many CMOS programs let a user assign a password to the PC that the user must later enter before the system will start and before the user can access the CMOS setup program. If the user cannot enter the correct password, the system will not load the operating system. Should the user forget his or her password, you will need to clear the PC's current CMOS settings.

One way to clear the CMOS settings is to remove the CMOS battery and then to wait for the chip to lose its contents. As discussed, the advantage of the CMOS technology is that it requires little voltage to maintain its contents. As such, after removing the battery, you may need to wait several hours before the chip loses its current settings.

To simplify the process of clearing the CMOS memory, most PCs provide a switch or jumper on the motherboard that you can use to drain the CMOS. For specifics on your PC's capabilities, visit your PC manufacturer's Web site.

After you clear the CMOS settings, you may need to update the entries you have changed from the PC's default settings.

Key CMOS Settings You May Need

Most users will never have to a need to change CMOS entries. That said, you should keep the following entries in mind as you begin to fine-tune PC operations:

Boot Device Order: By using the CMOS to select drive C as the first device the BIOS should search to find a bootable operating system disk, you can prevent a floppy disk that the user forgot to remove from drive A from preventing the system from starting. Also, there may be times following a hard-disk error that you must boot your PC from a floppy disk or CD-ROM drive. By changing the boot device order within the CMOS, you can start your PC from the device you desire.

Disk Type: For years, users identified their hard disk's geometry (number of tracks, sectors per track, and so on) using a special disk type number, such as a Type 1 drive, or a Type 2 drive. When you replaced a hard drive, you had to specify the new drive's type number within the CMOS. If you specified the incorrect drive type, your system could not read the drive's contents. Today, in contrast, most drives support an auto-configure option that lets the BIOS query the drive itself for its geometry information. Should you need to restore CMOS settings and you do not know your drive's type number (which should appear on the drive's case), you should try using the autoconfigure option.

Autoboot: If you work in an office where users shut down their PCs at the end of each day, you can take advantage of the CMOS autoboot entry to automatically power on the PCs at a specific time the following morning. You might, for example, direct the PC to power itself on at 7:30 AM so that when employees arrive at 8:00 AM, they will find their system up and running.

Password: To increase a PC's security (and to prevent other users from accessing CMOS settings), many CMOS setup programs let a user assign a password to the PC that the user must enter before the system will load the operating system. Should the user forget the password he or she assigns to the system, you must clear (discard) the PC's current CMOS settings.

Printer Port: Today, most PC parallel ports support bidirectional communication (so the printer can send information back to the operating system) as well as high-speed operations. Depending on your printer type, printer cable type, and parallel port, you may be able to improve your printer performance by enabling EPP or ECP parallel port operations.

Legacy Device Settings: To support plug-and-play operations, most CMOS setup programs let you reserve IRQ and I/O address settings for non-plug-and-play (legacy) devices. Later, when you install a new plug-and-play device in your PC, the BIOS will tell the device which resources you have reserved so that the new device does not try to use them.

Replacing the CMOS Battery

Over time, the PC's CMOS battery will eventually fail. At that time, you must replace the battery. When the CMOS battery fails, your system will normally display a message similar to the following when you power on your PC:

```
Invalid system settings — Run Setup
```

Most PCs use a small nickel-shaped battery to power the CMOS. Some PCs also support a battery pack that you can connect to the motherboard. To replace the CMOS battery, perform these steps:

1. Turn off and unplug your PC.

2. Gently remove your system-unit cover.

3. Locate the CMOS battery on the motherboard. If your system uses a battery pack, as shown in Figure 26.3, note the orientation of the wires before you unplug the battery from the motherboard.

4. Install the new battery.

5. Replace the system-unit cover.

6. Plug in and power on your PC. As your PC starts, run the CMOS setup program to restore the CMOS settings.

Figure 26.3 Using a battery pack to power the CMOS.

EXAM REVIEW

1. CMOS is an acronym for _____.

2. True or False
   CMOS memory is unique in that its contents can never be changed.

3. True or False
   To run the CMOS setup program, you select the Control Panel CMOS icon.

4. CMOS settings provide information about (select all that apply):

   ☐ The operating system version
   ☐ PC power management settings
   ☐ Hard drive geometry settings
   ☐ Legacy device resource use

5. If a user assigns a CMOS-based password to a PC and later forgets the password, you should _____.

6. When a CMOS battery fails, the system will normally display which of the following error messages:

   ☐ Operating system not found
   ☐ Invalid disk or disk error
   ☐ BIOS error – Run Setup
   ☐ Invalid system settings – Run Setup

7. To clear the CMOS settings you can _____.
   In addition, many PCs provide a _____ on the motherboard that you can use to flush the CMOS contents.

Understanding PC Bus Types

Within the PC, the electronic components communicate by sending and receiving signals across wires. A bus is a group of related wires. This lesson examines the various bus types that reside within the PC system unit.

Some of the key buses, such as the system bus (across which the CPU communicates with RAM), will not impact the decisions you must make when you install hardware devices—you will not connect devices directly to the system bus, for example.

Other buses, such as the PCI bus, across which the devices you install within the PC's expansion ports communicate, will impact your placement of hardware cards based on a card's type and your available expansion port slots.

By the time you finish this lesson, you will understand the evolution of the PC's buses from the original ISA bus to the PCI and AGP buses found in today's PCs.

F A C T S

✦ A bus is a group of related wires across which PC components send and receive electronic signals.

✦ The expansion slot inside the original IBM PC connected to an 8-bit bus called the Industry Standard Architecture (ISA) bus.

✦ Over time, the ISA bus evolved into a 16-bit bus with the release of the PC AT and later into a 32-bit bus with the release of the 80386. Users referred to the 32-bit bus as the Extended Industry Standard Architecture (EISA) bus.

✦ To remove the overhead of video data from the EISA bus, the Video Electronics Standards Association (VESA) introduced the local video bus that connected a video directly to the system bus (which the video card could use to access RAM).

✦ Today, the PC expansion slots connect to the Peripheral Component Interconnect (PCI) bus.

✦ To support older hardware cards, many motherboards will provide a 16-bit ISA slot or a 32-bit EISA slot in addition to PCI slots.

✦ The PCI bus connects to the system bus through an electronic interface users refer to as the North Bridge controller.

✦ To improve video performance, most video cards now connect to a special Accelerated Graphics Port (AGP) slot on the motherboard. The AGP port, like the PCI port, connects to the system bus via the North Bridge controller.

✦ The system bus is the primary motherboard bus that connects the CPU, RAM, and other key chips in the chip set.

A Bus is a Group of Wires

Within the PC system unit, devices communicate by exchanging signals across wires. A bus is simply a group of related wires. Table 27.1 briefly describes many of the common PC buses.

Bus	Description
System Bus	The primary motherboard bus that connects the CPU, RAM, and other key devices in the chip set.
Front Side Bus (FSB)	The wires that connect the CPU to RAM.
Back Side Bus (BSB)	The wires that connect the CPU to the L2 cache.
PCI Bus	The bus to which the PC's expansion slots connect.
AGP Bus	The bus to which a video card connects.

Table 27.1 Common PC buses.

Taking a Closer Look at the PC's Expansion Slots

Within the PC motherboard, expansion slots let users install hardware cards, such as a modem, SCSI adapter, or network interface card that "expand" the PC's capabilities. If you examine the expansion slots, you will find that the motherboard may provide different size slots. The different slot types exist to support different types of hardware cards that have emerged since the IBM PC was first released in 1981.

Taking a Closer Look at the ISA Bus

Within the original IBM PC, expansion slots connected to an 8-bit bus that could transfer data at 4.77MHz. The bus was called the Industry Standard Architecture (ISA) bus. The ISA bus consisted of 62 wires. ISA-based hardware cards had 31 connectors on each side, as shown in Figure 27.1.

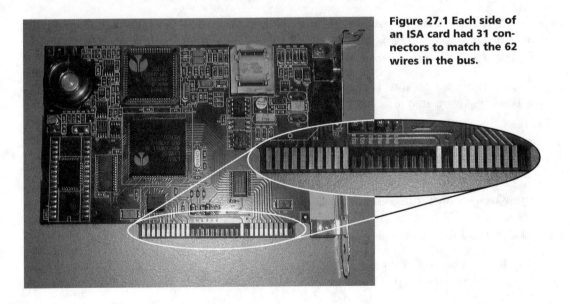

Figure 27.1 Each side of an ISA card had 31 connectors to match the 62 wires in the bus.

When the IBM PC AT was released in 1984, the expansion slots connected to a 16-bit ISA bus that operated at 6MHz. Over time, PC manufacturers increased the bus to 8MHz.

The 16-bit ISA bus changed the expansion slots by adding a second slot for each card. As shown in Figure 27.2, a 16-bit ISA card looked similar to an 8-bit card with the exception that it had a second connector.

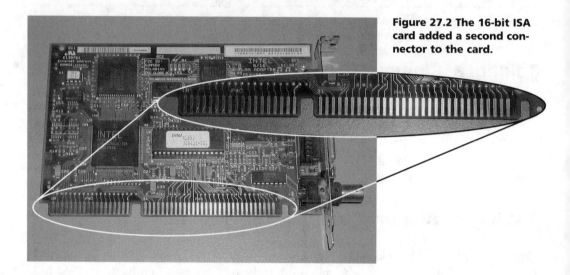

Figure 27.2 The 16-bit ISA card added a second connector to the card.

Because the front connector of a 16-bit ISA slot matched the original 8-bit slot, a user could plug an 8-bit ISA card into a 16-bit slot. The second slot would simply not be used.

When the was 80386 released in the mid-eighties, it introduced expansion slots that used a 32-bit Extended Industry Standard Architecture (EISA) bus that operated at 8.33MHz. By transferring four bytes with each clock tick, the EISA bus could transfer 33MBs.

The EISA expansion slots looked similar to the 16-bit slots. In fact, a user could install a 16-bit ISA card into a 32-bit EISA slot.

Taking a Closer Look at the VESA Local Bus

To display a video image, PCs rely on a video card that resides in an expansion slot. As the Windows operating system gained popularity in the early nineties, the data requirements of the Windows graphical user interface placed tremendous demands on the EISA bus, to the point where the bus became a system bottleneck.

To move video data from the EISA bus, the Video Electronics Standards Association (VESA) created a local bus that connected the video card directly to the system bus (the bus that provides access to RAM).

Although the VESA local bus improved system performance, many video cards encountered compatibility problems because the system bus speed could vary from one motherboard type to the next. To eliminate the timing issues between the video card and the system bus, hardware manufacturers created the PCI bus.

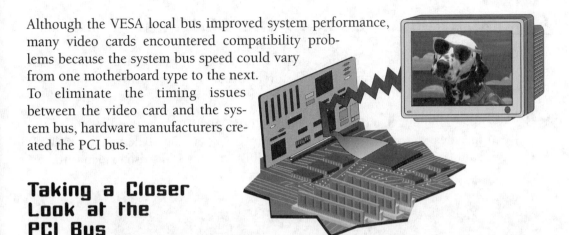

Taking a Closer Look at the PCI Bus

Today, PC expansion slots connect to the Peripheral Component Interconnect (PCI) bus. The original PCI bus was a 32-bit bus operating at 32MHz (132MBs). Today, many PCI buses are 64-bit buses that can operate at 66MHz (264MBs). Figure 27.3 illustrates a PCI-based card.

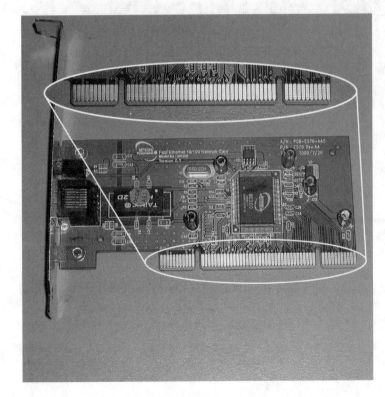

Figure 27.3 Most PC cards today are PCI-based cards.

Because the PCI slots are much different in size and shape from an ISA or EISA slot, most motherboards provide a 16-bit ISA or 32-bit EISA slot a user can use for an older hardware card. The slots connect to an ISA or EISA bus, which in turn, connects to the PCI bus through a special controller that users refer to as the South Bridge. The PCI bus, in turn, connects to the system bus through a controller called the North Bridge.

Taking a Closer Look at the AGP Bus

As the PC's video demands continued to grow (such as the need to display high-resolution images or video), hardware manufacturers created the Accelerated Graphics Port (AGP), a slot on the motherboard into which a user can install a video adapter card.

The AGP is a 32-bit bus that operates at 66MHz (264MBs). Devices that implement the AGP 2.0 specification can send data two or four times per clock tick, which produces a bandwidth of 528MBs or 1GBs. Figure 27.4 illustrates an AGP-based video card.

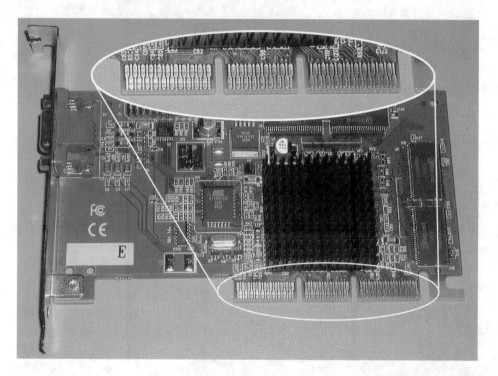

Figure 27.4 To improve system performance, most video cards connect to an AGP port.

The AGP, like the PCI bus, connects to the system bus via the North Bridge controller. The AGP provides video cards with access to RAM without placing overhead on the PCI bus. Because the AGP (unlike the VESA local bus) does not connect directly to the system bus (it connects to the North Bridge controller), AGP-based cards do not experience timing problems if you move the card between PCs that do not use the same system bus speeds.

Taking a Closer Look at the System Bus

Within the motherboard, the system bus is the primary bus. The system bus connects the CPU, RAM, and other key chips in the chip set. When the CPU sends or receives data to or from RAM, the transfer occurs across the system bus.

The speed of the system bus depends on the CPU speed. The system bus speed is normally a fraction of the CPU speed. A 2GHz CPU, for example, may use a 400MHz system bus. The system bus operates at a slower speed than the CPU because it must interact with slower devices, such as a memory controller, and it must send signals a greater distance than the signals travel within the CPU.

NOTE: *Within the system bus, users frequently refer to the wires that connect the CPU to RAM as the front side bus (FSB) and the wires that connect the CPU to the L2 cache as the back side bus (BSB).*

BEYOND A+ CERTIFICATION

Overclocking the System Bus

To improve performance, some users will speed up the clock that controls the CPU's operations. Users refer to the process of speeding up a clock as overclocking. By overclocking a 600MHz CPU, for example, a user may get the system to operate at 800MHz. As discussed in Lesson 22, "Understanding the CPU," PC manufacturers often slow down the CPU to ensure compatibility with other chips. Often, users can increase the CPU clock speed to improve their system performance.

In a similar way, for compatibility reasons, PC manufacturers often slow down the system bus speed. Again, by overclocking the system bus, users can improve their system performance. Depending on a user's PC type, the user may overclock the system bus by changing a CMOS setting or a jumper or switch that resides on the motherboard.

The problem with overclocking the system bus is that the faster speeds may introduce incompatibilities with slower devices that interact with the bus, or the increased number of signals may generate heat that leads to intermittent errors that are difficult to troubleshoot.

A+ CERTIFICATION — EXAM REVIEW

1. ISA is an acronym for _____.

2. True or False
   Expansion slots in the original IBM PC connected to an 8-bit ISA bus.

3. Today, the PC expansion slots connect to the _____ bus.

4. AGP is an acronym for _____.

5. The AGP and PCI buses connect to the system bus through special electronics called the _____.

6. PCI is an acronym for _____.

7. True or False
   The system bus is the primary motherboard bus that connects the CPU and RAM.

8. Users refer to the wires that connect the CPU to RAM as the _____ and the wires that connect the CPU and the L2 cache as the _____.

9. If a motherboard provides a 16-bit ISA or 32-bit EISA slot, the corresponding ISA or EISA bus will connect to the PCI bus through special electronics called the _____.

Understanding Interrupts and I/O Port Addresses

Within the PC, devices communicate by exchanging electronic signals. When you install a new hardware card into one of the PC's expansion slots, the device needs a way to interact with the CPU. There are two instances when the device needs to signal the CPU: when it needs the CPU to perform an operation on its behalf and when it needs to exchange data and status information with the CPU.

To signal the CPU that it requires the CPU to perform a specific operation, the device sends a signal to the CPU across a wire that users refer to as an interrupt request (IRQ) line. When the signal occurs, the CPU stops the processing it is currently performing in order to respond to the device. In other words, the device interrupts the CPU's current processing. After the CPU completes the operation for the device, the CPU resumes its previous task at the point it left off. In order for a device to be able to signal the CPU, it must be assigned a unique interrupt request line. Each device in the PC must use a unique IRQ line.

The CPU and the device must also have a way to exchange data and status information. For example, when a device interrupts the CPU, one of the first things the CPU must determine is what the device wants (which operation the device wants the CPU to perform). To exchange such information, devices allocate special memory locations called I/O ports. Each I/O port has a unique address. To prevent one device from overwriting information used by another device, each one must use unique I/O ports.

F A C T S

- When you install a device, such as a modem, network interface card, or video card into a PC expansion slot, the device must have a way to signal the CPU that it needs the CPU to perform specific processing on its behalf. The device also needs storage locations it can use to exchange data and status information with the CPU.

- To signal the CPU that it requires the CPU to perform specific processing, a device sends a signal across a special wire called an interrupt request (IRQ) line.

- Each device you install into the PC must have a unique IRQ. If two devices try to use the same IRQ line, one or both of the devices will not work.

- PCs support 16 IRQ lines.

- The PC uses two chips called interrupt controllers to manage the interrupt signals generated by the devices. The PC connects the second interrupt controller to the first in a cascaded fashion.

- The PC determines which controller is generating the interrupt by examining IRQ line 2. If the line contains a signal, the interrupt is from the second controller. Otherwise, if the line does not have a signal, the interrupt is from the first controller.

- For years, after a user determined which IRQ lines were available in the PC (not in use by other devices), the user assigned the number of an IRQ line to a new device using switches or jumpers that resided on the device card.

- To view a specific device's IRQ setting, you can use the Windows Device Manager. To view your system's current IRQ settings, you can run the Windows System Information utility.

F A C T S

- To exchange data and status information with the CPU, each device must have one or more unique storage locations, which users refer to as I/O ports. If two devices try to use the same I/O ports, one or both of the devices will not work.

- Just as users had to determine available IRQs within the system and then assign an IRQ value to the card, the same was true for I/O ports.

- To view a specific device's I/O port settings, you can use the Windows Device Manager. To view your system's current I/O port settings, you can run the Windows System Information utility.

- Sometimes, even though two devices erroneously use the same resources, you will not detect the problem until the user tries to use both devices at the same time. If a user, for example, complains that each time he or she moves the mouse his or her modem hangs up, the problem is a device conflict.

- Today, the plug-and-play devices alleviate the need for users to track and manually set IRQ and I/O port settings on newer devices.

Understanding Device Interrupts

To perform its processing, the CPU continually executes program instructions. The instructions, for example, might tell the CPU how to spell check a document or how to download and display a Web page. In addition, the instructions might tell the CPU how to respond to a mouse operation (such as a click), keyboard input, data arriving at a modem or network card, and so on.

Often, the devices you install in the PC require the CPU to perform specific operations on their behalf. For example, each time you press a keyboard key, the keyboard controller signals the CPU. The CPU, in turn, reads the key pressed. Likewise, each time you move the mouse, the mouse controller signals the CPU. In response, the CPU executes instructions that move the mouse pointer across the screen.

To signal the CPU that it needs the CPU to perform such operations on its behalf, a device sends a signal to the CPU across a special wire called an interrupt request (IRQ) line. When the CPU receives the interrupt request (the signal), the CPU temporarily suspends the operation it was performing in order to service the device. After the CPU completes the operation for the device (such as reading the keyboard key or moving the mouse pointer), the CPU resumes the task it was previously performing.

Device interrupts are so named because they direct the CPU to stop what it is doing in order to service the device. After the CPU handles the interruption, it resumes its previous task.

Each device you install into a PC expansion slot must have a unique IRQ line. If you assign the same IRQ to two devices, one or both of the devices will not work. In some cases, one of the devices will work until you try to use the other.

The PC supports 16 IRQ lines. Table 28.1 briefly describes common IRQ settings.

IRQ Line	Device Use
0	System timer
1	Keyboard controller
2	Cascaded to support the second interrupt controller
3	COM2
4	COM1
5	LPT2
6	Floppy disk controller
7	LPT1
8	Real-time clock
9	Redirected as interrupt 2
10	Available
11	Available
12	Default for PS/2 mouse
13	Math coprocessor
14	Hard disk controller
15	Default for a secondary IDE controller

Table 28.1 Common PC interrupt request (IRQ) line usage.

Behind the scenes, the CPU relies on two chips called interrupt controllers to process interrupts. The PC connects the two chips together in a cascaded fashion, as shown in Figure 28.1. As you can see, the wires from the second interrupt controller connect to the wires of the first.

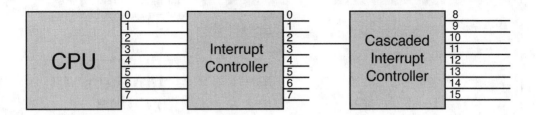

Figure 28.1 The PC cascades the two interrupt controllers.

Using the two interrupt controllers, devices that connect to the first controller can generate an interrupt the same as devices that connect to the second. The PC uses interrupt request line 2 to determine which controller is generating the interrupt. Each time an interrupt occurs, the CPU examines IRQ line 2. If the line does not have a signal, the CPU knows the interrupt is coming from the first interrupt controller (interrupts 0 through 7). If IRQ line 2 has a signal, the CPU knows the interrupt is coming from the second controller (interrupts 8 to 15).

The PC reserves IRQ 2 to "cascade" signals from the second controller. You should, therefore, never assign IRQ 2 to a device.

Viewing IRQ Settings

Years ago, before users installed a hardware card, they had to determine the IRQ settings currently being used by their system so they could then assign an unused interrupt to the new device. To view your system's interrupt settings, you can use the Windows System Information utility, as shown in Figure 28.2.

To view interrupt settings within the System Information utility, perform these steps:

1. Select the Start menu Programs option and choose Accessories. Windows, in turn, will display the Accessories submenu.

2. Within the Accessories submenu, select System Tools and choose System Information. Windows will display the System Information utility.

3. Within the System Information utility, click on the plus sign that precedes the Hardware Resources branch. The System Information utility will expand the branch's entry.

4. Within the Hardware Resources entries, click IRQs.

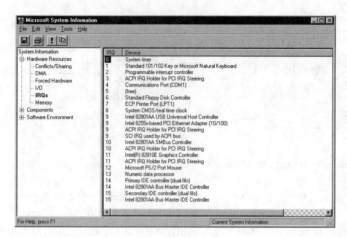

Figure 28.2 Viewing the system's interrupt settings.

Understanding a Device's I/O Port Use

After a device interrupts the CPU, the device must have a way to tell the CPU the operation it needs the CPU to perform. For example, when a user presses a keyboard key, the keyboard controller will send an interrupt request to the CPU. The keyboard controller needs a way to tell the CPU that the user pressed a key as well as which key.

To provide the CPU with such information, the device places data into special storage locations called I/O ports. Depending on the processing the device performs and the information the device must provide to the CPU, the number of ports the device requires will differ.

Each device you install within the PC must have unique I/O ports that it can use to exchange data and status values with the CPU. If you assign the same I/O port to two devices, one or both of the devices will not work. In some cases, the devices will work individually, but not at the same time. If, for example, a user's mouse stops working each time the user connects to the Internet, the problem is likely an I/O port conflict.

Viewing Your System's I/O Port Use

Just as you must assign a unique interrupt request (IRQ) line to each device, you must also assign unique port addresses. The documentation that accompanies your device will specify the number of ports the device requires and will specify the device's default settings. Using the Windows System Information utility, you can view your system's I/O port use, as shown in Figure 28.3.

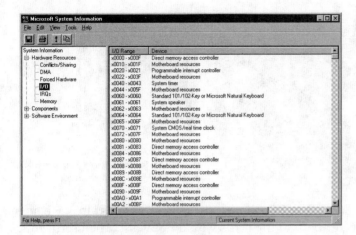

To view I/O settings within the System Information utility, perform these steps:

1. Select the Start menu Programs option and choose Accessories. Windows, in turn, will display the Accessories submenu.

2. Within the Accessories submenu, select System Tools and choose System Information. Windows will display the System Information utility.

3. Within the System Information utility, click on the plus sign that precedes the Hardware Resources branch. The System Information utility will expand the branch's entry.

4. Within the Hardware Resources entries, click I/O.

Assigning IRQ and I/O Port Settings the Old-Fashion Way (before Plug-and-Play)

For years, users had to determine and keep track of the IRQ line and I/O port assignments that the PC was using. Each time the user installed a new hardware device, the user had to assign an unused IRQ line to the device as well as unique I/O port settings. The user would assign such settings to the device by changing jumpers or switches that appeared on the card, as shown in Figure 28.4.

Figure 28.4 Using jumpers and switches to configure IRQ and I/O port settings for a device.

If the user accidently assigned an IRQ or I/O port to new device that was already being used by an existing device, one or both of the cards would not work. The user would then have to determine which devices were conflicting so the user could change settings on one of the two devices. Although some software programs existed to help the user view IRQ and I/O port use, often, to determine the conflicting cards, the user would remove one or more cards from the PC until the conflict went away. When the new device worked, the user knew that the last device that was removed from the PC was the conflicting device.

As you can imagine, resolving such conflicts was difficult at best for experienced technicians and nearly impossible for the average user.

Enter Plug-and-Play Devices

As you will learn in Lesson 33, "Taking Advantage of Plug-and-Play Devices," to simplify hardware installations, most PCs and cards today support a technology called plug-and-play. When a user installs a plug-and-play device, the device communicates with the other devices in the system to determine the resources (IRQs and I/O ports) that are available for use. Then the device simply configures itself. By coordinating operations in this way, plug-and-play devices eliminate most device conflicts making software upgrades much easier for users to perform.

EXAM REVIEW

① The two resources you must typically assign to a new device are an _____ and _____.

② IRQ is an acronym for _____.

③ True or False
The PC supports 12 IRQ lines.

④ Users often refer to IRQ line 2 as _____ because the PC uses the line to determine which controller is generating an interrupt.

⑤ To exchange data and status values with the CPU, devices use special memory locations called _____.

⑥ True or False
Plug-and-play devices do not use interrupts.

⑦ True or False
Devices can share I/O ports but not interrupts.

⑧ Devices use an IRQ signal to _____ the CPU and to request that the CPU perform an operation on the device's behalf.

Understanding Direct Memory Access (DMA)

Within the PC, the CPU is the workhorse that performs the instructions that direct the computer to accomplish specific tasks. A program, regardless of whether it is a word processor or Web browser, is simply a list of instructions that the CPU executes. In general, the speed at which the CPU can execute instructions dictates your PC's performance.

Before the CPU can execute instructions or manipulate data, the instructions or data must reside within the PC's random-access memory (RAM). Years ago, to load data from disk into memory, the CPU would oversee the transfer of the data. This means that to transfer 512 bytes of data (a disk sector), the CPU would have to execute instructions to move each byte of data into RAM. Although the CPU could transfer data between a device and RAM quite quickly, performing such operations temporarily prevented the CPU from performing other tasks.

To improve the PC's performance, hardware designers created a special chip (called a DMA controller), which the PC could use to transfer data between a device and RAM. DMA is an acronym for direct memory access. By using the DMA controller to perform data transfers between a device and RAM, the CPU was free to perform other tasks.

In general, when the operating system needed to read a disk sector into RAM, for example, the operating system would tell the DMA controller the sector to read and the starting address in RAM to place the data. After the DMA controller completed the transfer, it would notify the CPU (which had been free to perform other processing) that it could begin to use the data. This lesson examines direct memory access operations within the PC.

F A C T S

- DMA is an acronym for direct memory access.

- DMA processing involves the use of a special chip (a DMA controller) to oversee the transfer of data between a device and RAM.

- By using a DMA controller to transfer data between a device and RAM, the CPU is free to work on other tasks while the data transfer is in progress.

- Most newer PCs have two DMA controllers.

- To use a DMA controller to perform a data transfer, a device can request the controller's attention, much like a device can interrupt the CPU using an IRQ. To request that the DMA controller perform an operation on its behalf, a device will place a signal on a specific wire called a DMA request line.

- The original IBM PC used only one DMA controller, with channels 0 to 3. Beginning with the PC/AT, systems began using two DMA controllers, with channels 0 to 7. The PC cascades the second DMA controller to the first.

- You must assign a unique DMA channel to each device that performs DMA operations.

- Within the PC, the floppy disk drive typically reserves DMA channel 2. Likewise, printer ports that support DMA operations typically reserve channel 3. Channel 4 is reserved to cascade the DMA controllers together, in much the same way the PC cascades interrupt controllers.

F A C T S

- When you install a device that supports DMA operations, you may need to specify the DMA channel the device is to use. Depending on the device type, you may use a jumper or switch to select the DMA channel.

- Just as users use the term IRQ as an acronym for interrupt request, users often use the term DRQ for DMA request.

- Using the Windows System Information utility, you can view your PC's current DMA channel assignments.

- To transfer data between a device and RAM, the DMA controller on the original IBM PC would use the ISA bus to transfer 8 bits at a time. Later, using DMA channels 5-7, the device could perform 16-bit data transfers.

- Users refer to DMA operations that use a DMA controller to transfer data across an ISA bus as classic DMA.

- To improve performance over classic DMA, newer devices no longer use the DMA controller to perform data transfers. Instead, the device itself watches (monitors) the bus and transfers data when the bus is not in use. Users refer to devices that can take control of the bus in this way to perform a data transfer as bus-mastering devices.

- Users often refer to bus-mastering operations as ultra-DMA or UDMA.

Understanding Direct Memory Access

Before the CPU can execute a program's instructions or manipulate a program's data, the instructions or data must reside in RAM. Years ago, the CPU was responsible for moving data between a device (such as a disk drive) and RAM. If a program needed to read data from a file on disk, the CPU would interact with the disk, directing it to read the sector, and then the CPU would transfer the data into RAM.

To eliminate the CPU's need to oversee data transfers between a device and memory, chip designers created a special controller (a chip), called a direct memory access (DMA) controller, that could transfer data between a device and RAM. The controller was so named because it could place or retrieve data from memory itself (directly) without the need for the CPU's intervention.

To transfer data using a DMA controller, the operating system would tell the controller which device, whether it was moving data to or retrieving data from the device, and the starting memory location (the memory address) of the data and RAM, as well as the location on the device to place or retrieve the data (such as a disk sector number). The DMA controller, in turn, would then oversee the data transfer. To use the controller, you had to assign each device that supported DMA operations a unique channel (wire), which the device could use to signal the controller.

The original IBM PC had only one DMA controller, with channels 0 through 3. You might, for example, assign a sound card to use DMA channel 0, a tape drive to use channel 1, the floppy drive to use channel 2, and so on. Each DMA-based device had to have a unique channel.

With the release of the IBM PC/AT, PCs began using two DMA controllers, providing channels 0 through 7. The PC cascaded (connected) the second controller to the first, flowing the wires from the second controller directly to the first. The PC uses DMA channel 4 to determine which device is signaling the controller. If channel 4 is active (contains a signal), the device request is coming from the second controller. If channel 4 is not active, the request is coming from the first controller. Channel 4 is not available for device use.

You can think of DMA channels as being quite similar to the IRQ lines that devices use to interrupt the CPU. In the case of DMA, the devices do not use the channels to signal the CPU, but rather, to signal the DMA controller. Each device that performs DMA operations must have a unique channel. Users often refer to the signal that a device sends to the DMA controller as a DRQ (DMA request).

In the original IBM PC, the DMA controller performed data transfers across the ISA bus, one byte at a time. With the advent of the 16-bit bus in the PC/AT, the DMA controller could transfer two bytes of data at a time. Today, devices that require slower transfer rates (for which one byte at a time is sufficient) use channels 1 through 3 (DMA channel 0 is used for memory refresh operations), and devices that require faster data transfers (two bytes at a time) use channels 5, 6, or 7.

Users refer to such DMA operations as "classic DMA."

Understanding the Problem with Classic DMA Operations

The problem with classic DMA operations is that because they used the ISA bus, the operations were restricted to the bus's slow 8MHz speeds.

Today, few devices other than floppy disks, sound cards, and printers use classic DMA. Instead, to transfer data to or from memory, devices use a technique called bus mastering to monitor and then take control of the PCI bus that operates at 66MHz.

When a device determines that the bus is available, the device takes control of the bus (becomes the master of the bus) in order to perform the data transfer. After the device completes the data transfer, the device releases control of the bus.

Users often refer to such bus-mastering operations as ultra-DMA (or UDMA).

NOTE: *The PCI bus is not the only bus that supports bus-mastering operations. Some chip sets provide support for IDE bus mastering. In addition, the ISA bus provided some bus-mastering capabilities.*

Viewing Your System's Current DMA Settings

Each DMA-based device you use within your system must have a unique DMA channel. Depending on the device type, you might use a jumper or switch that appears on the device to assign the channel. To view your system's current DMA channel use, you can use the System Information utility, as shown in Figure 29.1.

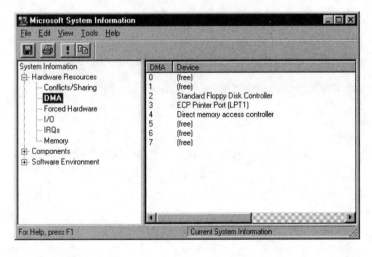

Figure 29.1 Displaying DMA channel assignments within the System Information utility.

To display DMA channel settings within the System Information utility, perform these steps:

1. Select the Start menu Programs option and choose Accessories. Windows will display the Accessories submenu.

2. Within the Accessories submenu, select System Tools and choose System Information. Windows will display the System Information utility.

3. Within the System Information utility, click on the plus sign that precedes the Hardware Resources entry. The System Information utility will expand the list of resources.

4. Within the resource list, click on the DMA entry.

EXAM REVIEW

① The acronym DMA stands for _____.

② DMA operations improve system performance by eliminating the need of the _____ to oversee data transfers between a device and memory.

③ To signal the DMA controller a device sends a signal across a wire (unique to the device) that users refer to as a

_____.

④ The acronym DRQ stands for _____.

⑤ True or False
Using the Control Panel DMA icon, you can view your system's DMA settings.

⑥ Today, few devices use "classical DMA" operations. Instead the devices use a technique called _____ that lets the device take control of the PCI bus to perform the data transfer.

⑦ The PC uses DMA channel _____ to determine which controller is generating the signal. The channel is not available for device use.

⑧ DMA channels _____ through _____ support 8-bit operations.

⑨ DMA channels _____ through _____ support 16-bit operations.

Connecting Devices to a SCSI Adapter

For years, computers used a special bus called the Small Computer Systems Interface (SCSI) to connect high-speed devices, such as a disk or CD-ROM drive to a PC. To connect a SCSI (pronounced "scuzzy") device to a PC, you must first install a special hardware card, called a SCSI adapter within the PC.

You connect the first SCSI device to the adapter card that resides in the PC. Then, you connect subsequent devices to one another to form a device chain. Depending on the adapter card's type, you can connect up to 7 or 15 devices to the chain.

The SCSI interface is ideal for high-speed external devices. However, there are some internal devices that connect to the SCSI device chain. This lesson examines the SCSI adapter and the steps you must perform to attach devices to the SCSI chain.

F A C T S

- SCSI is an acronym for Small Computer Systems Interface.

- Each SCSI device has two ports, one for an incoming cable and one for an outgoing cable that connects to a subsequent device. When you connect SCSI devices, you create a device chain, expanding the bus length with each device you attach.

- You must mark the end of the SCSI device chain by terminating the last device. If you do not terminate the chain, your system will not be able to use the SCSI devices.

- To terminate the SCSI device chain, you normally use a special connector called a terminator that you connect to the device's unused connector port.

- The devices you connect to the SCSI device chain can be external or internal devices. Each SCSI device requires its own power source.

- SCSI devices are not hot swappable. Before you remove a device from the SCSI chain, you must first shut down and power off your PC. Then, you must power off each device in the chain.

- Each device in the SCSI chain requires a unique id number. If the SCSI adapter supports seven devices, you will use id numbers 0 through 6. The card itself will normally use address 7. If the adapter supports 15 devices, you will use id numbers 0 to 14. The card, again, would normally use address 7.

- For SCSI cards that support 8 addresses, the device's id number specifies the device's priority within the SCSI chain. Should two devices try to use the SCSI bus at the same time, the bus will let the device with the highest id number (highest priority) access the bus first.

- For SCSI cards that support 16 addresses, the priority is as follows: 7, 6, 5, 4, 3, 2, 1, 0, 15, 14, 13, 12, 11, 10, 9, 8.

- The SCSI interface has evolved over time to support faster bus speeds and more devices. Users commonly refer to the original SCSI specification as SCSI-1. Today, systems make use of SCSI-1, SCSI-2, and SCSI-3 adapters and devices.

Understanding the Small Computer Systems Interface (SCSI)

For your computer to communicate with a hardware device, the device must be connected to the PC. A *SCSI adapter* provides a way for you to connect high-speed devices, often disk drives, to the PC. In short, the SCSI adapter creates a second bus to which you can attach devices. The devices you attach can be internal, residing within the system unit, or external.

You connect a SCSI-based device to a SCSI adapter, a hardware card that resides within your PC. As shown in Figure 30.1, most SCSI-based devices contain two connectors. You use the first connector to attach the device to the SCSI bus. If you only have one SCSI device, you would attach the device directly to the connector port on the SCSI adapter card. If you have multiple devices, you can connect one device to another, in a chain-like fashion. In other words, you use one of the connectors to attach the device to the device chain and the second connector to connect another device (to extend the chain of devices beyond the current device).

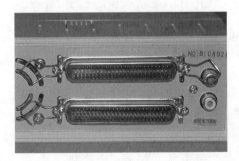

Figure 30.1 You use one of the SCSI's devices connectors to attach the device to the SCSI device chain. You can use the second connector to attach another SCSI-based device to the device chain.

You must terminate the last device in the device chain (to mark the end of the SCSI bus). To terminate a device, you normally attach a special terminator to the device's second connector. Some devices let you terminate the bus using special switches or even software settings. Figure 30.2 shows how you would use a terminator to mark the end of the SCSI device chain.

Figure 30.2 You must terminate the SCSI bus following the last device in the device chain.

Understanding SCSI-1, SCSI-2, and SCSI-3

Over the years, the SCSI standard has evolved to support faster data rates and more devices. The original SCSI interface, which users will sometimes refer to as SCSI-1, used a 50-pin (low-density) connector and an 8-bit data bus that operated at 5MHz. The original SCSI standard let users attach up to 7 devices to the SCSI bus. Today, users can attach up to 15 devices.

The SCSI-2 standard doubled the data rate to 10MHz for an 8-bit bus and 20MHz for a 16-bit bus. Early SCSI-2 adapters used either a 50-pin low-density or 50-pin high-density connector, similar to those shown in Figure 30.3. Using a special converter, you could change a low-density connector into a high-density connector and vice versa.

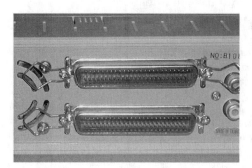

Figure 30.3 Early SCSI devices used 50-pin low-density or 50-pin high-density connectors.

Later, SCSI-2 devices and SCSI-3 devices begin to use a high-density 68-pin connector. The SCSI-3 interface can support data speeds of up to 160MHz. Many SCSI-3-based disks use an 80-pin connector. Because of its high speed, users sometimes refer to the SCSI-3 standard as "Ultra3 SCSI."

Installing a SCSI Adapter

A SCSI adapter is a hardware card that you install into one of the PC's expansion ports. If you are installing an older non-plug-and-play SCSI adapter card, you must specify a DMA channel, IRQ, and port address for the adapter. As you will learn in Lesson 33, "Taking Advantage of Plug-and-Play Devices," a plug-and-play SCSI adapter will configure itself.

To install the SCSI adapter card into your system, first power off and unplug your system unit. Then, remove the system unit cover and discharge all static from your body, by touching your system chassis. Select the expansion slot into which you will install the adapter. Remove the small metal slot cover and gently insert the adapter card. Replace the screw to hold the adapter securely in place.

If you are using one or more internal SCSI devices, cable and terminate the devices as necessary. Replace and secure the system unit cover. If you are using external SCSI devices, cable and terminate the last device in the chain. Plug in and power on your PC.

Depending on your adapter or the devices you are attaching, you normally must install device driver software before Windows can use the device.

NOTE: *If you are using a notebook PC, you can often use a PCMCIA-based SCSI adapter. Lesson 34, "Taking Advantage of PCMCIA Cards," examines the PCMCIA interface in detail.*

SCSI Devices Require On-Board Electronics and External Power

The devices you connect to a SCSI device chain must be SCSI devices. Each SCSI device contains controller electronics that lets the device interact with the bus. You could not, for example, connect an integrated drive electronics (IDE) hard drive to a SCSI device chain.

In addition to connecting the SCSI cable to the device, you must also provide power to the device. If you are installing an internal SCSI-based device, you will power the device using one of the power cables provided by the power supply. For external devices, you must plug the device into a power outlet. In contrast, in Lesson 31, "Using a Universal Serial Bus," you will learn that many of the devices you connect to the USB receive their power directly from the bus itself.

Understanding SCSI Device Numbers

When you connect devices to the SCSI device chain, you distinguish one device from another by assigning each device with an id number (called a *SCSI address*) that ranges from 0 to 7 or 0 to 15, depending on the type of SCSI adapter you are using. Normally, the SCSI adapter itself uses device number 7. Each device within the SCSI chain must have a unique id number. Many devices, as shown in Figure 30.4, provide a switch you can use to assign the device number. Some devices let you select an id number using dip switches or jumpers that reside on the device, while yet others let you select an id using software.

Figure 30.4 You must assign a unique id number to each device in the SCSI chain.

A common error that users make when connecting a device to a SCSI chain is to fail to assign the device an id number that is not in use. If your PC does not see a new SCSI device, after you restart your system following a SCSI device installation, make sure that you have assigned a unique id to the device. Then, make sure that you have not terminated the bus prior to the device (some devices let you terminate the bus using switches or jumpers on the device).

In addition to uniquely identifying each device in the SCSI chain, the id number also specifies the device's priority within the chain. When you connect multiple devices within a SCSI chain, there will be times when two or more devices try to use the bus at the same time. The device's priority dictates which device will get to use the bus first. Often, you will have a device, such as a disk drive, for which a fast response is critical to your system performance. By assigning the key device with a higher priority (a higher device id number), you ensure the device will get a faster response from the SCSI adapter. In contrast, if a scanner has to wait an instant before it could use the bus, your overall system performance would not suffer.

If you are using a SCSI adapter that supports 8 addresses, the id 7 will have the highest priority and the id 0 will have the lowest. If you are using a SCSI adapter that supports 16 addresses, the device priorities from highest to lowest are as follows: 7, 6, 5, 4, 3, 2, 1, 0, 15, 14, 13, 12, 11, 10, 9, 8.

Connecting a SCSI-Based Device

To connect a SCSI-based device to your PC, you must shut down your system and power off your PC. Then, you must power off the devices in the SCSI chain. Do not attach or remove a device to or from the SCSI chain while your system is running or the devices in the chain are powered on. Doing so may damage a device.

Next, assign a unique id number to the device that corresponds to the priority the device will require. You may, depending on the number of devices in the SCSI chain, need to change the id number on one or more existing devices in order to achieve the device priorities you desire.

Then, use a SCSI cable to connect the device to the device chain. If the device will be the last device in the chain, use a terminator or switches on the device to terminate the bus. Also, if the device to which you are attaching the new device was previously the last device in the chain, make sure the device is not using an internal switch or jumper to terminate the bus. Otherwise, the system will not be able to see your new device.

Finally, power on each of the devices in the SCSI chain and then power on and start your PC. After you restart your system, you may need to install a device driver for the device before Windows can use it.

Often, as your system starts, your monitor will display information about devices it encounters within the SCSI chain. If your system fails to see a device, consider the following items:

1. Is the device plugged in and powered on?

2. Is the device cabled correctly to the SCSI chain?

3. Does the device's id number conflict with another device in the chain? (Your system may have one or more internal devices in the SCSI chain that you do not see, such as an internal CD-ROM drive.)

4. If you move the device to a different location in the chain (by changing the chain's cabling), does the device appear? If so, one of your cables may be damaged.

Viewing a System's SCSI Devices

Using the Windows Device Manager, you can view information about your system's SCSI adapters, as well as the devices connected to the adapter, as shown in Figure 30.5.

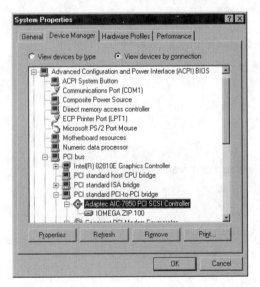

Figure 30.5 Using the Device Manager to list a system's SCSI devices.

To view SCSI devices within the Device Manager, perform these steps:

1. Select the Start menu Settings option and choose Control Panel. Windows will display the Control Panel window.

2. Within the Control Panel, double-click on the System icon. Windows will display the System Properties dialog box.

3. Within Windows 98, select the Device Manager tab. Within Windows 2000, select the Hardware tab and then choose the Device Manager button. Windows will display the Device Manager.

4. Within the Device Manager, select the View devices by connection option. The Device Manager will display a list of controllers to which you can connect devices.

5. Within the controller list, click on the plus sign that precedes the SCSI controller entry. The device manager will display a list of SCSI controllers on your system. To view the devices connected to a specific controller, click the plus sign that precedes the controller's entry.

EXAM REVIEW

① SCSI is an acronym for _____.

② True or False
SCSI devices are "hot swappable," meaning, you can connect devices to the device chain without shutting down and powering off your PC.

③ Depending on the SCSI adapter's type, you can connect either _____ or _____ devices to the SCSI device chain.

④ To mark the last device in the SCSI chain, you must _____ the last device.

⑤ For a SCSI adapter that supports 7 devices, the device ID with the highest priority is _____. Likewise, the device ID with the lowest priority is _____.

⑥ For a SCSI adapter that supports 15 devices, the device ID with the highest priority is _____ Likewise, the device ID with the lowest priority is _____.

⑦ Each device in the SCSI device chain requires a unique id number that corresponds to the device's _____ within the chain.

⑧ Normally, within the SCSI device chain, you should assign the highest device ID to the _____.

⑨ True or False
The SCSI bus provides power to the devices you attach to the device chain.

EXAM REVIEW

A+ CERTIFICATION

10. If your system does not see a SCSI-based device, you should (select all that apply):

- [ ] Ensure the device is plugged in and powered on
- [ ] Check that the device is properly cabled
- [ ] Move the device within the chain to determine if a cable problem or bus termination problem exists
- [ ] Ensure the device has a unique id number
- [ ] Make sure you have installed a device driver for the device
- [ ] Remove the bus terminator

11. True or False

Assume a user assigns id number 3 to a SCSI-based disk drive and then attaches the drive directly to the SCSI adapter. Then the user attaches a scanner to the disk drive and assigns the scanner the id number 4. Because the disk drive is closer to the adapter within the device chain, the driver will have higher priority than the scanner.

Lesson 31

Using a Universal Serial Bus (USB)

Over the past few years, the use of the Universal Serial Bus (USB) to connect devices to the PC has exploded. The USB is well suited for devices such as a mouse, printer, or scanner that does not have high-speed data requirements. A hard drive or CD-ROM drive that requires large data transfers would not be well suited to connect to a USB.

Most newer PCs provide two or more USB ports to which a USB-based device can be directly connected. If you require more than two USB devices, you can connect a USB hub to one (or both) of the USB ports. Then, you can connect multiple devices to each port. Further, many USB-based devices let you connect other devices in a daisy-chain-like fashion. Using hubs and direct connections between devices, you can connect up to 127 devices to a universal serial bus.

The USB is unique in that you can plug in or unplug devices "on the fly" without first having to shut down and power off your system. In addition, when you connect a device to a USB, you do not have to specify interrupt request (IRQ) and I/O port settings for the devices. USB-based devices do not use interrupts or I/O ports.

F A C T S

- The Universal Serial Bus lets you connect a myriad of devices to the PC. Most newer PCs provide one or two USB ports.

- If a PC does not have a USB port, for less than $50 you can install a USB adapter (a hardware card) within the PC that will provide you with ports to which you can connect USB-based devices.

- You can connect a USB-based device directly to a PC's USB port.

- If you require the use of several USB-based devices, you can connect a USB hub to the port on the PC and then connect multiple devices to the hub.

- By connecting one USB hub to another, you can connect up to 127 devices to the USB.

- Some USB-based devices provide a port to which you can connect another USB device in a daisy chain fashion.

- Older USB ports and devices support two speeds: 1.5Mbs and 12Mbs. The devices you connect to the USB must share the available bandwidth. Many newer devices and ports (that support USB 2.0) also support 480Mbs.

- The USB can provide power for devices you connect to the bus.

Understanding the Universal Serial Bus

The Universal Serial Bus (USB) lets users connect a wide range of devices to a PC. Most newer PCs provide one or two USB ports, to which you can directly connect a device or to which you can connect a USB hub that provides multiple device ports. Today, you can purchase of myriad of USB-based devices, including keyboards, mice, digital cameras, TV ports, Web cameras, and much more. As shown in Figure 31.1, USB devices use a cable with a small rectangular connector. Many USB-based devices provide a port into which you can plug in a second device in a daisy-chain-like fashion.

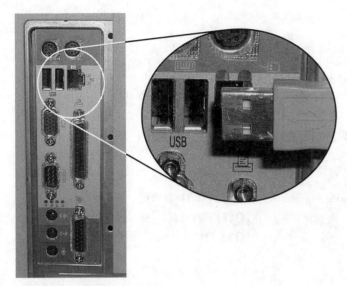

Figure 31.1 Connecting a USB device to a port on the PC.

If a PC does not have a USB port, you can install a USB adapter card into one of the PC's expansion ports that provides you with ports to which you can connect USB-based devices.

Determining the USB Controller's Bandwidth Use

Most USB connectors support two speeds: 1.5Mbs and 12Mbs. The devices that you connect to the USB share the available bandwidth. As you connect more devices to the USB, each device will have less bandwidth available for its use. Different devices will consume different amounts of bandwidth. In addition, normally the devices you connect to the USB will not all be in use at the same time.

That said, if you connect multiple devices to the USB (remember, you can connect up to 127 devices), there may be times when a specific device cannot operate because the device does not have sufficient available bandwidth. At that time, you may need to move the device to a different USB port or you may need to remove devices from the USB device chain.

To determine the USB controller's available bandwidth, perform these steps:

1. Select the Start menu Settings option and choose Control Panel. Windows will display the Control Panel window.
2. Within the Control Panel, double-click on the System icon. Windows will display the System Properties dialog box.
3. Within the System Properties dialog box, select the Device Manager tab. If you are using Windows 2000, select the Hardware tab and then click on the Device Manager button. Windows will display the Device Manager.
4. Within the Device Manager, click on the plus sign that precedes the Universal Serial Bus controllers entry. The Device Manager will expand its controller list.

5. Within the list of controllers, double-click on the Universal Host Controller entry. Windows will display the controller's Properties dialog box.

6. Within the Properties dialog box, click the Advanced tab. If you are using Windows 98, click the Bandwidth Usage button. Windows will display the amount of the available bandwidth your devices are currently using, as shown in Figure 31.2.

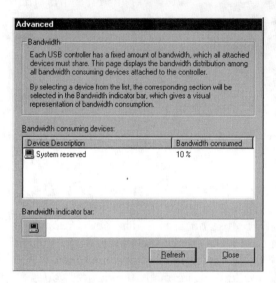

Figure 31.2 Displaying USB bandwidth information.

Determining a USB Controller's Available Power

Many smaller USB-based devices, such as a mouse or a network adapter, receive their power from the USB controller. Larger devices, such as a USB-based scanner, require a standard power connection. A USB hub can provide up to five volts of power to the devices you connect. Depending on the number of devices you connect to the USB, the hub may eventually run out of power. To display the amount of power a hub is currently providing, perform these steps:

1. Select the Start menu Settings option and choose Control Panel. Windows will display the Control Panel window.

2. Within the Control Panel, double-click on the System icon. Windows will display the System Properties dialog box.

3. Within the System Properties dialog box, select the Device Manager tab. If you are using Windows 2000, select the Hardware tab and then click on the Device Manager button. Windows will display the Device Manager.

4. Within the Device Manager, click on the plus sign that precedes the Universal Serial Bus controllers entry. The Device Manager will expand its controller list.

5. Within the list of controllers, double-click on the USB hub you desire. Windows will display the hub's Properties dialog box.

6. Within the Properties dialog box, click the Power tab. Next, if you are using Windows 98, click on the Power properties button. Windows will display the amount of power your devices are currently using, as shown in Figure 31.3.

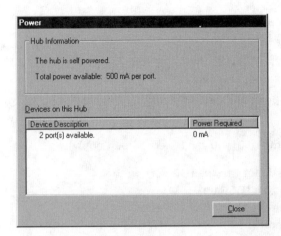

Figure 31.3 Displaying USB
power information.

Connecting a Device to a Universal Serial Bus

Using a Universal Serial Bus, you can connect up to 127 devices to your PC. If you have more USB-based devices than you have USB ports on your PC, you can buy a USB hub, which you connect to your PC's USB port and then to each device. To connect a device to a Universal Serial Bus, you simply plug in the device. You do not have to shut down and later restart your system as you do with a SCSI device.

In addition, you do not have to worry about configuring the device's IRQ and I/O port settings. Instead, you simply connect the device to the bus. If you are connecting a device to the USB for the first time, Windows may prompt you to install a device driver that it can use to interact with the device. When you purchase a USB-based device, you will receive a floppy disk or CD-ROM that contains the device driver you must install.

A unique aspect of the USB is that you can "hot swap" devices, which means you can plug in the device while the PC is running. If you must move a device from one PC to another, you can unplug the device from one PC's USB and then plug the device into the second PC's USB, while both systems are running!

Understanding How USB-Based Devices Communicate with the PC

The PC interacts with devices connected to the USB by exchanging message packets. When the PC must send a request to a device, the PC sends a packet down the bus to the device. As the message travels to the device, the packet may pass by other devices that are connected to the bus. However, only the device to which the PC sent the packet will respond to the packet.

In other words, to communicate with devices, the universal serial bus relies on software protocols and packets, in much the same way information moves across the Internet.

EXAM REVIEW

A+ CERTIFICATION

① USB is an acronym for _____.

② Older USB devices support two speeds: _____ and _____. Newer ports and devices support a third speed of _____.

③ To connect a device to the USB, you can (select all that apply):

☐ Connect the device directly to the USB port on the PC

☐ Connect the device to a USB hub

☐ Connect one USB device to another, provided one of the devices has a USB port

☐ Connect the device to the 9-pin serial port on the PC and use a CMOS setting to direct the PC to map the device to the USB

④ You can connect up to _____ devices to a USB.

⑤ True or False
Because of the USB's fast speed, the USB is well suited for connecting external hard drives and CD-ROMs.

⑥ True or False
The USB can provide power to all USB-based devices.

⑦ True or False
The USB allocates bandwidth to devices based on the order you attach the devices to the bus.

⑧ True or False
To view a USB hub's power usage, you select the Control Panel USB icon.

⑨ The USB supports hot swapping which means _____.

Using FireWire and InfraRed Devices

I n Lesson 31, "Using the Universal Serial Bus," you learned how to connect devices to the PC using the universal serial bus (USB). As you learned, the USB is well suited for devices that require a limited bandwidth, such as mouse, printer, and even a network interface card. The devices you connect to the universal serial bus share the USB's 12Mbs bandwidth. (USB 2.0 supports 400Mbs.)

To support higher speed devices, such as video cameras and disk drives, many newer PCs provide an IEEE 1394 port, which users commonly refer to as a "FireWire" port. Like the USB, you can connect devices directly to the FireWire port. You can also connect one FireWire-based device to another. In addition, you can connect multiple devices to a FireWire hub. The FireWire bus supports a bandwidth of up to 400Mbs. With the widespread use of handheld and notebook computers, many users now use InfraRed (IR) communication to exchange data between devices without the need for wires. Using an IR-based keyboard and mouse, for example, you can eliminate cables from your desk. Also, some users use IR-based communication to exchange files between a desktop and notebook PC (or other handheld device) and to print documents.

F A C T S

- The IEEE 1394 bus is more commonly known as the FireWire.

- The FireWire normally operates at 400Mbs. The devices you connect to the FireWire must share the available bandwidth.

- Using the FireWire bus, you can connect a myriad of devices (typically high-bandwidth devices) to the PC. Most newer PCs provide one FireWire port.

- You can connect a FireWire-based device directly to a PC's FireWire port.

- If a PC does not have a FireWire port, you can install a FireWire adapter for less than $50.

- If you require the use of several FireWire-based devices, you can connect a FireWire hub to the port on the PC and then connect multiple devices to the hub.

- By connecting one FireWire hub to another, you can connect up to 63 devices to the FireWire.

- The FireWire cable can provide power to devices (up to 40V). However, most devices rarely use the cable's power.

- Some FireWire-based devices provide a port to which you can connect another FireWire device in a daisy chain fashion (up to 16 hops).

- InfraRed devices communicate using a light wave, similar to a television's remote control. To communicate using IR, two devices must have a direct line of sight to one another.

- Today, you can find an IR-based mouse, keyboard, printer, and more.

- IR devices typically communicate at a bandwidth of 4Mbs to 16Mbs.

- Most newer notebook PCs and handheld devices have an IR port. If your PC does not contain an IR port, you can purchase and install an adapter card that provides IR support.

- Within Windows, two PCs can create a direct network connection using IR communication.

Understanding the IEEE 1394 FireWire Bus

The IEEE 1394 bus, or as it is more commonly known, the "FireWire," lets users connect a wide range of devices to a PC. Most newer PCs provide one FireWire port, to which you can directly connect a device or a FireWire hub that provides multiple device ports.

Because of its high bandwidth, 400Mbs, the FireWire is well suited for devices that send and receive large amounts of data, such as a video camera or an external disk drive.

FireWire devices use a cable with a small rectangular connector that looks quite similar to a USB connector. Some FireWire-based devices provide a port into which you can plug a second device in a daisy-chain-like fashion. If a PC does not have a FireWire port, you can install a FireWire adapter card into one of the PC's expansion ports that will provide you with ports to which you can connect FireWire-based devices (up to 16 hops). By connecting one FireWire hub to another, you can connect up to 63 devices to the FireWire bus.

Connecting a Device to the FireWire

Using a FireWire bus, you can connect up to 63 devices to your PC. If you have more FireWire-based devices than you have FireWire ports on your PC, you can buy a FireWire hub, which you connect to your PC's FireWire port and then to each device. To connect a device to a FireWire, you simply plug in the device. You do not have to shut down and later restart your system as you do with a SCSI device.

In addition, you do not have to worry about configuring the device's IRQ and I/O port settings. Instead, you simply connect the device to the bus. If you are connecting a device to the FireWire for the first time, Windows may prompt you to install a device driver that it can use to interact with the device. When you purchase a FireWire-based device, you will receive a floppy disk or CD-ROM that contains the device driver you must install.

A unique aspect of the FireWire is that you can "hot swap" devices; meaning, you can install the device while the PC is running. If you must move a device from one PC to the next, you can unplug the device from one PC's FireWire and then plug the device into the second PC's FireWire, while both systems are running!

Understanding How FireWire-Based Devices Communicate with the PC

The PC interacts with devices connected to the FireWire by exchanging message packets. When the device must send data to the PC, the device sends a packet down the bus to the device. Likewise, when the PC sends data or a request to a device, the PC will send a message packet down the bus to the device. As the message travels to the device, the packet may pass by other devices that are connected to the bus. However, only the device to which the PC sent the packet will respond to the packet. Conceptually, to communicate with devices, the FireWire relies on software protocols and packets, in much the same way information moves across the Internet.

Understanding the FireWire Controller's Bandwidth Use

The FireWire operates at 400Mbs. The devices that you connect to the FireWire share the available bandwidth. As you connect more devices to the FireWire, each device will have less bandwidth available for its use. Different devices will consume different amounts of bandwidth. In addition, normally the devices you connect to the FireWire will not all be in use at the same time.

That said, if you connect multiple devices to the FireWire (remember, you can connect up to 63 devices), there may be times when a specific device cannot operate because the device does not have sufficient available bandwidth. At that time, you may need to move the device to a different FireWire port or you may need to remove devices from the FireWire device chain.

Configuring a FireWire Controller's Power Settings

Some FireWire-based devices receive their power from the USB controller. Larger devices, such as a USB-based scanner, require a standard power connection. Depending on the number of devices you connect to the FireWire controller, the hub may eventually run out of power. To use the Device Manager to configure the bus's power settings, perform these steps:

1. Select the Start menu Settings option and choose Control Panel. Windows will display the Control Panel window.

2. Within the Control Panel, double-click on the System icon. Windows will display the System Properties dialog box.

3. Within the System Properties dialog box, select the Device Manager tab. If you are using Windows 2000, select the Hardware tab and then click on the Device Manager button. Windows will display the Device Manager.

4. Within the Device Manager, click on the plus sign that precedes the IEEE 1394 Bus controllers entry. The Device Manager will expand its controller list.

5. Within the list of controllers, double-click on the FireWire hub you desire. Windows will display the hub's Properties dialog box.

6. Within the Properties dialog box, click the Power tab. Windows will display the Power sheet within which you view and manage various power settings.

Viewing Specifics About InfraRed (IR) Devices

Today, most notebook PCs have an InfraRed (IR) communication port which the device can use to exchange data, messages, and files with another IR-based PC or printer. Using an IR port, two users might exchange business cards, and photographs, or a user may send output to a printer.

To communicate using the IR port, two devices must have a direct line of sight and must be within a few meters of one another. Unlike radio wave communication that can travel through walls, IR devices must be in the same room. Just as you cannot use your TV remote control's IR capabilities to change your TV's channels from a different room, devices that communicate using IR must be in close proximity to one another. IR devices communicate at 4Mbs to 16Mbs.

Infrared devices communicate by sending and receiving data using beams of light. The term *infrared* refers to the wavelength of the light beams, which falls into the infrared portion of the light spectrum, where light waves travel at terahertz frequencies.

If you are using a desktop PC and want to eliminate some of the cables that connect devices to your PC, you can purchase an IR-based keyboard and mouse. The devices will come with an IR receiver that you attach to your PC.

If you are running Windows 98 or later, you can use the Control Panel Infrared icon to configure the PC's IR ports, by performing these steps:

1. Select the Start menu Settings option and choose Control Panel. Windows will display the Control Panel window.

2. Within the Control Panel, double-click on the Infrared icon. Windows will display the InfraRed Monitor dialog box.

3. Using the sheets that appear within the InfraRed Monitor dialog box, you can customize IR communication settings, such as the maximum connection speed, your identification information, and more.

① The FireWire is also known as the _____.

② The FireWire supports a bandwidth of _____Mbs.

③ To connect a device to the FireWire you can (select all that apply):

☐ Connect the device directly to the FireWire port on the PC
☐ Connect the device to a FireWire hub
☐ Connect one FireWire device to another, provided one of the devices has a USB port
☐ Connect the device to a SCSI port on the PC and use a CMOS setting to direct the PC to map the device to the FireWire

④ You can connect up to _____ devices to the FireWire.

⑤ True or False
The FireWire cable can provide power to devices.

⑥ True or False
The FireWire allocates bandwidth to devices based on the order you attach the devices to the bus.

⑦ The FireWire supports hot swapping which means _____.

⑧ IR is an abbreviation for _____.

⑨ True or False
IR signals, like radio waves, can easily move through walls, making an IR communications well suited for a wireless network.

⑩ IR devices typically communicate at a bandwidth of _____ to _____ Mbs.

Lesson 33

Taking Advantage of Plug-and-Play Devices

For a PC to function properly, the CPU must be able to communicate with hardware devices. In general, that means a device needs a way to signal the PC that the device requires the CPU to perform operations on its behalf (meaning the device must be able to interrupt the CPU), and the device must have one or more storage locations the CPU and the device can use to exchange data and status information. Users refer to the storage locations the CPU and a device use to exchange such information as I/O ports. Each hardware device in a PC normally has the following unique device settings:

- An interrupt request (IRQ) number that corresponds to the wire that the device will use to signal the CPU that the device needs service

- One or more I/O ports that correspond to the special storage location the device and CPU will use to exchange values and status information

- Possibly a unique direct memory address (DMA) channel the device uses to transfer data directly into RAM

In the past, users had to manually assign these configuration settings to hardware devices using jumpers and switches on the device. Because each device required unique values for each setting, users had to keep track of the settings their PC devices were using. If the user assigned a setting value to a new card that conflicted with a setting in use by an existing card, one or both of the cards (and possibly the PC) would not work until the user resolved the error.

As you can imagine, having to manage and manually assign device settings was difficult at best for the experienced technician and nearly impossible for the typical user. To simplify device installations, card manufacturers, operating-system developers, and the BIOS chip producers established the plug-and-play specification. When you install a plug-and-play device into your PC, the device will communicate with other plug-and-play devices and the BIOS to determine the card settings (IRQ and I/O ports) that are in use. The card will then configure itself using available resources.

F A C T S

- Each device you install in a PC requires unique settings for an interrupt-request line, I/O ports, and possibly a DMA channel.

- A device uses its interrupt request (IRQ) line to signal the CPU that the device needs the CPU to perform an operation on its behalf.

- The CPU and the device use the device's unique I/O ports to exchange data and status values.

- Some devices use a DMA channel to communicate with the PC's DMA controller in order to transfer data directly to RAM, without the use of the CPU.

- In the past, before you installed a hardware card, you had to manually configure the card's settings using jumpers and switches on the card. Each card had to use unique settings. If the settings you assigned to one card conflicted with another card, one or both of the cards would not work.

- To eliminate the need for users to manually configure device settings, card manufacturers, operating-system developers, and BIOS chip producers defined the plug-and-play specification.

- The plug-and-play specification, in general, defines how a new plug-and-play device you install in a PC communicates with other devices to determine the available resource (IRQ and I/O port) settings. The device then automatically configures itself using available resources.

- Plug-and-play operations require the cooperation of the plug-and-play device, the BIOS, and the operating system.

- Users refer to non-plug-and-play devices, which the users must manually configure, as legacy devices.

- Today, if you are using a plug-and-play operating system, such as Windows, a plug-and-play BIOS, and use only plug-and-play devices, you will find device installations very easy.

- If, however, you still use one or more legacy devices (that do not participate in plug-and-play resource conversations), your installations can be more difficult.

- To reduce conflicts with legacy devices, many CMOS setup programs let you reserve settings for one or more legacy devices. Should you later install a plug-and-play device, the BIOS will tell the device about the settings you have reserved.

Understanding Key Device Settings

To communicate with the CPU, the devices you install in a PC require several key resource settings. In order for the PC and the devices to operate properly, each device must have its own unique values for these settings.

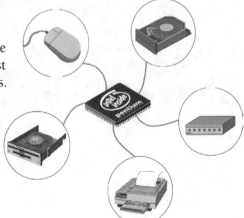

First, to request service from the CPU, the device will send a signal to the CPU across a special wire called an interrupt request (IRQ) line. By assigning a unique IRQ line to each device, the CPU can determine which device is requesting service.

Second, to exchange data and status information, the CPU and device use a set of storage locations that users refer to as I/O ports. Each of these storage locations has a unique address. As you examine system settings within programs such as the Windows Device Manager, you will often find the locations described as I/O ports, I/O port addresses, or I/O addresses.

Third, as discussed in Lesson 29, "Understanding Direct Memory Access," some devices use a special chip called a DMA controller to transfer data to and from RAM without the use of the CPU. By performing the data transfers using the DMA controller, the device frees the CPU to perform other tasks. Each device that performs DMA operations must use a unique wire to communicate with the DMA controller that users refer to as a DMA channel.

Assigning Device Resources

In the past, before a user installed a new hardware card, the user had to determine the settings that were already being used by other devices. Then, the user had to select unused resources to assign to the new card. To assign the resource settings to the card, the user would change jumpers or switches on the card, as shown in Figure 33.1.

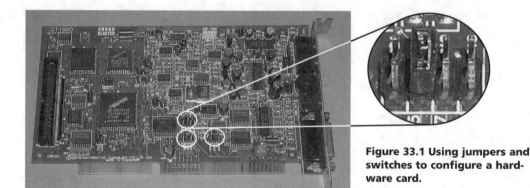

Figure 33.1 Using jumpers and switches to configure a hardware card.

If a user assigned settings to a card that were already in use by a different card, one or both of the cards would not work. To resolve device conflicts, users would remove one or more cards from their system to determine which two cards were causing the error. After the user determined the conflicting cards, the user setting could be changed on one of the cards (hoping that it wasn't a setting that was in use by yet another card). Because such conflicts were difficult to detect and resolve, it was nearly impossible for the average user to successfully install new hardware.

Enter Plug-and-Play Devices

To simplify device installations, card manufacturers got together with the programmers who were developing operating systems and the chip designers who were creating the BIOS chips and created the plug-and-play specification. In general, plug-and-play defines a way devices can communicate to determine available system resources. When you install a plug-and-play device, it will ask any other plug-and-play devices in the PC about the resources being used by each. The new device can then select unused resources and automatically configure itself.

To use a plug-and-play device, a PC must be running an operating system (such as Windows) that supports plug-and-play operations and the PC must be using a plug-and-play BIOS.

Dealing with Legacy Devices

Today, when a user installs a new plug-and-play device in a PC, the device will communicate with other plug-and-play devices to determine available resources and then will automatically configure itself. The term plug-and-play refers to the fact that a user should simply install the device (plug in the device) and the device will work (play).

The challenge to plug-and-play operations occurs when a PC is using an older device (such as an old sound card) that does not support plug-and-play operations. Users refer to such devices as legacy devices.

For a legacy device to operate, you must determine resource settings that are not currently in use and then you must assign those settings to the device, normally using jumpers or switches that appear on the device.

Unfortunately, should you later install another plug-and-play card, the new device may select the settings you assigned to the legacy device. That happens because when the new plug-and-play device asks the other devices what settings they are using, the legacy device does not participate in the plug-and-play device conversation. If the plug-and-play device uses one or more of the legacy-device settings, one or both of the devices will not work.

Enter CMOS Legacy Device Settings

If you are using a legacy device, you can normally use the CMOS entry similar to that shown in Figure 33.2 to reserve settings for the legacy device. Later, when you install a new plug-and-play device and the device asks the system about the resources that are in use, the BIOS will inform the device that you have reserved specific resources for a legacy device. As a result, the new plug-and-play device will not select a setting that conflicts with the legacy device.

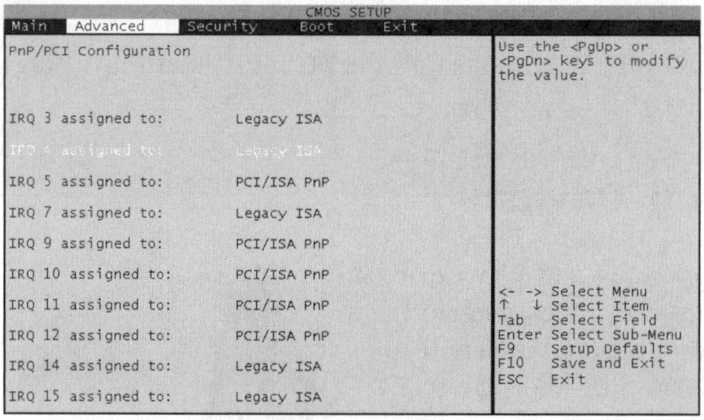

```
                            CMOS SETUP
 Main   Advanced    Security    Boot     Exit
 PnP/PCI Configuration                          Use the <PgUp> or
                                                <PgDn> keys to modify
                                                the value.

 IRQ 3 assigned to:      Legacy ISA

 IRQ 4 assigned to:      Legacy ISA

 IRQ 5 assigned to:      PCI/ISA PnP

 IRQ 7 assigned to:      Legacy ISA

 IRQ 9 assigned to:      PCI/ISA PnP

 IRQ 10 assigned to:     PCI/ISA PnP

 IRQ 11 assigned to:     PCI/ISA PnP     <- ->  Select Menu
                                         ↑   ↓  Select Item
 IRQ 12 assigned to:     PCI/ISA PnP     Tab     Select Field
                                         Enter  Select Sub-Menu
 IRQ 14 assigned to:     Legacy ISA      F9      Setup Defaults
                                         F10     Save and Exit
 IRQ 15 assigned to:     Legacy ISA      ESC     Exit
```

Figure 33.2 Using a CMOS entry to reserve settings for a legacy device.

Viewing Device Resource Use

Using the Windows System Information utility as shown in Figure 33.3, you can view the I/O port, interrupt, and DMA settings that the devices in your system are currently using. To view settings within the System Information utility, perform these steps:

1. Select the Start menu Programs option and choose Accessories. Windows will display the Accessories submenu.

2. Within the Accessories submenu, select System Tools and choose System Information. Windows will display the System Information utility.

3. Within the System Information utility, click on the plus sign that precedes the Hardware Resources branch. The System Information utility will display entries for specific resources. To view your system's I/O port use, for example, click on the I/O entry.

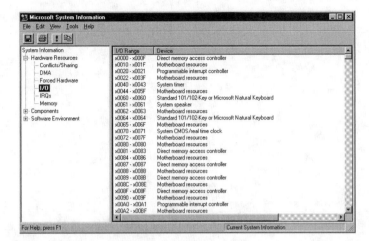

Figure 33.3 Viewing I/O port use within the System Information utility.

① The plug-and-play specification combines the use of
_____, _____, and _____.

② Users refer to devices that do not support plug-and-play
operations as _____ devices.

③ The two most common resource settings you must configure for
a device are _____ and _____.

④ True or False
Using the *config.sys* file, you can reserve settings for a non-
plug-and-play device.

⑤ Prior to plug-and-play devices, users assigned resource settings
to a device using _____ and _____ that resided on
the hardware card.

Taking Advantage of PCMCIA Cards

ithin a desktop PC, users expand the PC's capabilities by installing hardware cards into one of the PC's expansion slots. The hardware card that the user installs may correspond to a modem, network interface, SCSI adapter, and so on.

Because of their compact size, notebook computers do not use traditional expansion slots and cards. Instead, most notebook computers provide a special slot for a credit-card-sized hardware card called a PCMCIA card or simply a "PC card."

By installing one or more PCMCIA cards (most notebook PCs support two cards), users can add a modem, network card, USB port, or other common peripheral device to a notebook PC. PCMCIA cards are so named because the cards are based on a 68-pin standard defined by the Personal Computer Memory Card International Association.

FACTS

✛ Users commonly refer to PCMCIA cards as simply PC cards.

✛ The acronym PCMCIA corresponds to the association that defined the card's electronic standard: Personal Computer Memory Card International Association.

✛ PCMCIA cards use a 68-pin connector.

✛ There are three types of PCMCIA cards. Each card type uses the same 68-pin interface. The cards, which are simply called Type I, Type II, and Type III cards, differ only by the card's thickness.

✛ PCMCIA Type I cards are 3.3 mm thick.

✛ PCMCIA Type II cards are 5.0 mm thick.

✛ PCMCIA Type III cards are 10.5 mm thick.

✛ PCMCIA Type I, II, and III cards have the same length and width: 85.6 mm x 54.0 mm.

✛ Most notebook computers have two Type II PCMCIA slots, placed one on top of the other. Normally, the slot configuration lets the slot hold two Type I or II cards or one Type III card.

✛ PCMCIA cards are "hot swappable" which means you can remove one card and insert another without having to shut down your system and power off your PC. When you swap cards in this fashion, Windows will detect the card change and will immediately support the new device.

Expanding a Notebook PC

Today, notebook PCs offer users essentially the same capabilities as desktop PCs. Just as users can expand a desktop PC by inserting a card into one of the PC's expansion slots, notebook PC users can expand their PC's capabilities by inserting a special card called a PCMCIA card. Users commonly refer to PCMCIA cards as simply "PC cards."

PCMCIA cards are small credit-card-sized cards that contain the electronics for a specific device. Today, users can expand notebook PCs using PCMCIA-based modems, network adapters, USB ports, SCSI adapters, disk drives, and more.

On the side of most notebook PCs, you will typically find two slots for PCMCIA cards, as shown in Figure 34.1. To insert a PCMCIA card, you simply slide the card into the slot with the card label facing up and the end of the card that contains the connector inserted first. To remove a card from the slot, you press a small card-eject button.

Figure 34.1 Most notebook PCs provide slots for two PCMCIA cards.

Understanding PCMCIA Card Types

PCMCIA cards come in one of three types, which are simply named as Type I, Type II, and Type III cards. All three PCMCIA card types use the same 68-pin connector. The difference between the cards is the thickness. Table 34.1 lists the thickness of each PCMCIA card type, which you should know for the exam.

Card Type	Thickness
Type I	3.3 mm
Type II	5.0 mm
Type III	10.5 mm

Table 34.1 PCMCIA card types differ by the thickness of the card.

Depending on the complexity of the device or the operations the device performs, the size of the electronics required to implement the device (and hence the thickness of the PCMCIA card) will differ. A PCMCIA-based modem, for example, normally uses a Type I card. In contrast, a PCMCIA-based hard disk would use a thicker, Type III card.

Understanding Notebook PC PCMCIA Slots

Most notebook PCs provide two Type II PCMCIA slots that the notebook stacks one on top of the other to create a large slot. Because all three PCMCIA card types use the same 68-pin connector, you can install two Type I cards or two Type II cards within the PC's two PCMCIA slots, as shown in Figure 34.2. Because of the thickness of Type III cards, you can only use one Type III card at a time.

Hot Swapping PCMCIA Cards

PCMCIA cards are hot swappable which means you do not have to shut down your system to change cards. Instead, you could, for example, remove a PCMCIA-based modem card and replace it with a PCMCIA-based network card. Windows, in turn, will automatically detect the device change and will begin to support the new device (provided you have previously installed a device driver for the device).

Before you eject a PCMCIA card, you should first warn Windows that you are going to stop using the card. To notify Windows 98 that you are going to stop using the device, perform these steps:

1. Within Windows, select the Start menu Settings option and choose Control Panel. Windows, in turn, will open the Control Panel window.

2. Within the Control Panel, double-click on the PC Card icon. Windows will open the PC Card (PCMCIA) Properties dialog box.

3. Within the dialog box, click on the entry that corresponds to the card you are going to eject and then select Stop.

If you are using a Windows 2000 system, you can inform Windows that you are going to stop using a device by performing these steps:

1. In the Taskbar tray, double-click on the Unplug or Eject Hardware icon. Windows 2000, in turn, will display the Stop a Hardware Device dialog box.

2. Within the dialog box, select the device you plan to stop using and choose OK. Windows will display the Safe to Remove Hardware dialog box which states you can remove the device.

1. PCMCIA is an acronym that stands for _____.

2. Users frequently refer to PCMCIA cards as simply
   _____.

3. True or False
   PCMCIA card types differ by their connector type.

4. Notebook PCs normally provide slots for two PCMCIA Type
   _____ cards.

5. True or False
   Most notebook PCs will let you use two Type II or two Type III
   cards at the same time.

6. True or False
   Before you eject a PCMCIA card, you should first shut down
   Windows and then power off your PC.

Introduction to Networking

For years, businesses and universities have connected computers using networks to allow users to share resources such as files, printers, or a connection to the Internet. Users also rely on networks to exchange messages using e-mail. Today, many users are installing networks in their homes, by connecting PCs using cables or by taking advantage of wireless devices that exchange network messages across distances of up to several hundred feet, even through walls.

The next several lessons will examine network concepts that you must understand as you prepare for the A+ Certification exam. In this lesson, you will learn the "basics" of networking. Then, in the lessons that follow, you will take a closer look at the hardware, software, and protocols that networks use behind the scenes.

F A C T S

+ Computer networks let users share resources such as files or printers, and communicate using programs such as electronic-mail and instant messaging.

+ Users classify networks as either a local-area network or wide-area network, based on the distance that separates the computers in the network.

+ A local-area network normally connects computers that reside within the same office building.

+ A wide-area network connects computers that may reside across town, across the state, across the country, or even on the other side of the world.

+ Within a network, network administrators often select one or more computers to serve as a file or printer server. Users within the network (clients) can normally share such server resources.

+ Within a network, administrators must protect each user's files from other users. Network administrators combine hardware and software to implement various security policies.

+ The Internet is a network of networks that connects computer networks around the world.

+ To protect their network from hackers and computer viruses, network administrators often place a firewall between the network and the Internet to restrict the messages that pass into or out of the network. Firewalls combine hardware and software to implement a security policy.

+ To create a network, designers can connect computers to one another using a ring or bus framework, or they can connect each computer to a central hub.

+ Users refer to a network's shape as the network's topology. Each network topology offers advantages and disadvantages.

+ The three most common network topologies are the ring, star, and bus.

+ Windows provides support for numerous networks. Most local-area networks take advantage of TCP/IP (the protocol that drives the Internet). Likewise, users who connect to the Internet using a modem and dial-up connection use Windows dial-up networking.

+ Within Windows 98, you can view sharable files and printers using the Network Neighborhood folder. Within Windows 2000, you can use the My Network Places folder.

+ Before a remote user can access files or printers on your system, you must enable file and printer sharing within Windows.

F A C T S

✛ After you enable file or printer sharing, you can individually specify the files, folders, and printers on your system that you want to share. To designate which users can access specific resources, you can assign a password to each that a remote user must specify before accessing the resource.

Computer Networks Let Users Share Resources

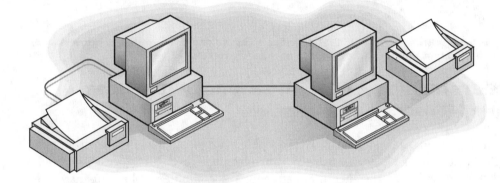

Computer networks exist to help users share resources such as files, printers, disk space, CD-ROM drives, and even Internet connections. The simplest computer network consists of only two computers. Users refer to simple networks, within which no computer plays the role of a server, as a peer-to-peer network; meaning, the computers within the network each have the same capabilities—they are peers.

Within a network, companies often select one computer to which they attach disks or printers that other users within the network can share. Users refer to such computers as *servers*, because when the user needs disk space or to print a file, the computer can provide the services. The user, in this case, becomes the server's client.

Figure 35.1 shows a print server within a network to which the network administrator has connected multiple printers that users within the network can share. In addition, Figure 35.1 shows a disk server that provides disk drives that users across the network can use to store and retrieve files. Using a disk server, users might access a remote database or store backup copies of their key files on a remote disk.

Within a network, network administrators use various software and hardware components to implement security policies that protect files from access by other users. In general, users can access only files and devices within the network to which the network administrator has given the user access.

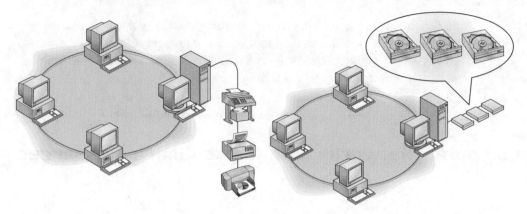

Figure 35.1 A print server is a PC that provides access to one or more shared printers. A disk server is a PC that provides access to one or more shared disk drives.

Understanding Local-Area and Wide-Area Networks

Computer networks exist to help users share resources, such as files or printers, or to communicate, using electronic mail. Within a business, users categorize computer networks based upon the distance that separates the computers. Most businesses use a local-area network, with the computers residing in the same office building, as shown in Figure 35.2. Users refer to a local-area network as a LAN.

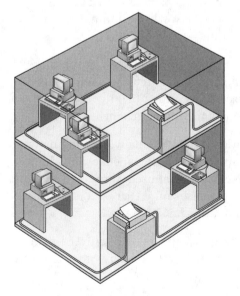

Figure 35.2 Computers in a local-area network reside in reasonably close proximity, such as in the same office building.

In contrast, as shown in Figure 35.3, in a wide-area network (which users refer to as a WAN), the computers may reside across town, the state, or even across the globe. Depending on the distance that separates computers in a wide-area network, the network may use phone cables, fiber-optic connections, or even satellite communications to connect the network computers.

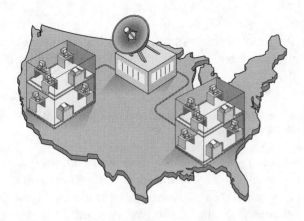

Figure 35.3 Computers in a wide-area network may reside in different cities, states, or countries.

Understanding How Users Connect Computers to Networks (the Network Topology)

To connect computers and other devices, such as printers, networks normally connect cables between each device. Depending on the network's design, a cable might run from one computer to the next, or the computers might all connect to a central network hub. Network designers refer to the network's layout as the network's topology. Figure 35.4 illustrates the three most common network topologies: the ring, bus, and star topologies.

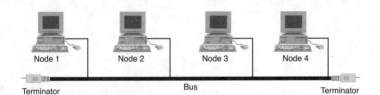

Figure 35.4 A network's topology is defined by the shape of the network.

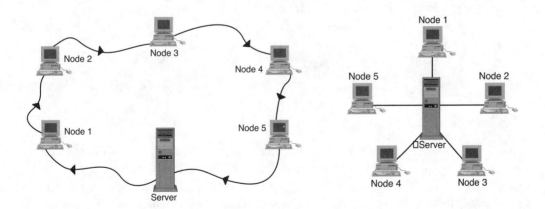

Within the ring and bus topologies, the network administrator connects PCs in a chain-like fashion, with each PC connecting to the next one. The disadvantage of connecting

PCs in this way is that should one network card, PC, or cable fail, the entire network will fail. The advantage of the bus and ring topology is its simplicity. Within a bus topology, the network administrator must terminate each end of the bus using a special terminator similar to that shown in Figure 35.5.

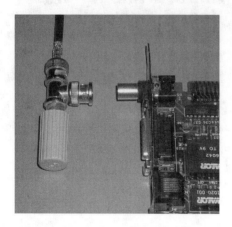

Figure 35.5 Using a terminator to mark one end of a bus-based network.

Within a star topology, the network administrator connects PCs to a central hub. Should one PC, network card, or cable fail, the rest of the network is unaffected. However, should the network hub fail, the entire network will fail.

Understanding the Internet—A Network of Networks

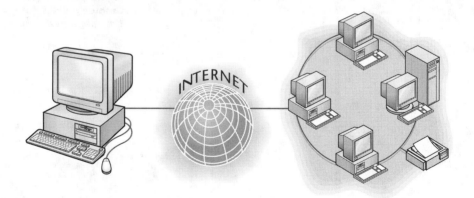

A network consists of two or more computers, connected to share resources, such as files or printers or to communicate using electronic mail. Today, hundreds of millions of users connect to the Internet—a network of networks. The Internet connects computer networks around the world. Across the Internet, users share files and devices and communicate using a variety of programs, one of which is electronic-mail.

To protect the networks they connect to the Internet from hackers and computer viruses, network administrators often place a hardware and software firewall between the network and the Internet. In general, the firewall acts a security guard, controlling the messages that can enter or leave the network.

Logging into a Network and Viewing Shared Resources

Depending on the network software you are running, the steps you must perform to access network resources will differ. In most Windows-based environments, you must specify a username and password before you can connect to the network. After you log into the network, you will access network disk drives using a disk drive letter, just as you would access the hard drive and floppy disk drives connected to your PC.

Within Windows, users make extensive use of the Explorer to view the contents of disks and file folders. After you log into a network, you can open the Network Neighborhood folder by double-clicking on the icon that appears on the Windows desktop. If you are using Windows 2000, double-click on the My Network Places icon. Within the Network Neighborhood folder, you can view information about the computers connected to your network, as shown in Figure 35.6.

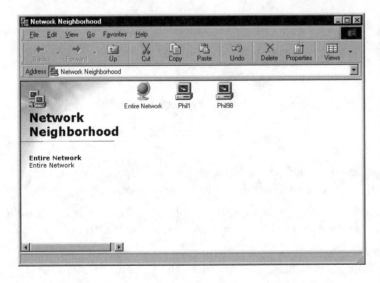

Figure 35.6 Using the Network Neighborhood to display information about the computers connected to a network.

If you double-click on the icon of a computer that appears within the network neighborhood, you can view the files and printers the PC is sharing. To prevent every network user from gaining access to a specific file, folder, or printer, users frequently assign security settings to each resource that specify which users are allowed to access the shared item.

Sharing Files, Folders, and Printers

Just because you are connected to a network does not mean that other users can access the files that reside on your system. Before a user can access files or a printer on your system, you must specifically enable file and printer sharing. To enable file and printer sharing within Windows 98, perform these steps:

1. Select the Start menu Settings option and choose Control Panel. Windows, in turn, will display the Control Panel window.

2. Within the Control Panel, double-click on the Network icon. Windows will display the Network Properties dialog box.

3. Within the Network Properties dialog box, click the File and Print Sharing button. Windows, in turn, will display the File and Print Sharing dialog box, as shown in Figure 35.7, which you can use to enable or disable sharing. Within the dialog box, select the settings you desire and then choose OK.

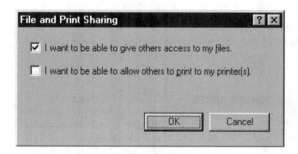

Figure 35.7 Before other users can access files or printers on your system, you must first enable file or printer sharing.

To enable file and printer sharing within Windows 2000, perform these steps:

1. Select the Start menu Settings option and choose Control Panel. Windows, in turn, will display the Control Panel window.

2. Within the Control Panel, double-click on the Network and Dial-Up Connections icon. Windows will display the Network and Dial-up Connections folder.

3. Within the Network and Dial-Up Connections folder, right-click on the connection that you desire and then choose Properties. Windows, in turn, will display the connection's Properties dialog box.

4. Within the Properties dialog box, place a checkmark in the File and Printer Sharing for Microsoft Networks checkbox and then choose OK.

After you enable file and printer sharing, you can specify which disks, files, folders, or printers you want to share. To share a disk, file, or folder, perform these steps:

1. Within the Windows Explorer, right-click on the item you desire. Windows will display a pop-up menu.

2. Within the pop-up menu, choose Sharing. Windows will display a dialog box similar to that shown in Figure 35.8, which you can use to control how and which users can access the item.

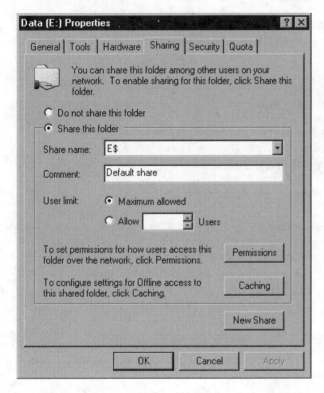

Figure 35.8 Windows lets you share a file, folder, or disk.

When you share a folder, remote users with access to the folder (those you have specified or those who know the required password) can access each of the files that the folder contains (regardless of whether or not the file is shared), as well as subfolders. Likewise, if you share a disk, users who can access the disk can access each and every folder the disk contains. As you share items, try to minimize the number of items you allow remote users to access. In other words, if a remote user only requires access to one file, share only that file as opposed to the folder within which the file resides.

EXAM REVIEW

(1) Networks exist to let users share resources, such as _____ and _____, and to communicate with other users.

(2) Users refer to a network's shape—how the computers connect to one another—as the network's _____.

(3) True or False
Within a local-area network, all users can view a listing of another user's files.

(4) Users who connect to the Internet using a modem and standard phone line make use of Windows _____ networking support.

(5) To protect networks that are connected to the Internet from hackers and viruses, network administrators place a _____ between the Internet and the network.

(6) The three most common network topologies are _____, _____, and _____.

(7) True or False
Before other users can access a shared file, folder, or printer, you must first enable file and printer sharing within the Shared Resources dialog box.

(8) True or False
A firewall may combine hardware and software to protect a network.

(9) True or False
The primary disadvantage of the ring topology is that a single failed PC, network interface card, or cable can prevent the entire network from working.

(10) For the entire network to fail within a star topology, the _____ must fail.

(11) True or False
To indicate the end of a bus-based network, you must place special connectors called terminators at each end of the network bus.

(12) True or False
Within Windows, you can share a file, folder, and even an entire disk with a remote user.

Understanding the ISO/OSI Network Model

A cross the Internet, computers use a wide range of operating systems and run a variety of network programs. To make it easier for different applications to communicate across networks, network programs follow a well-defined set of rules, called *protocols,* that define the data formats programs use to package data for transmission, as well as the rules the programs follow to coordinate sending and receiving of the data. Across the Internet, the Transport Control Protocol/Internet Protocol (TCP/IP) is the most widely used protocol. Similarly, to request HTML pages, graphics, and other files from a Web server, your browser makes extensive use of the Hypertext Transport Protocol (HTTP).

When programmers and network administrators discuss networks, they often group key network operations into functional layers that correspond to the ISO/OSI network model. The ISO/OSI network is just that—a model. It represents the functional operations a network performs. The model is so named because it was defined by the International Standards Organization (ISO) Open Systems Interconnection (OSI) committee. By understanding the operations suggested by the model that networks implement at each layer, you should find the discussion of TCP/IP in Lesson 37, "Understanding the Transport Control Protocol/Internet Protocol (TCP/IP)," quite straightforward.

F A C T S

+ Protocols define a set of rules that programs follow to communicate across a network, such as the Internet. Most protocols also define data formats that programs use to package information.

+ The International Standards Organization's Open Systems Interconnection (ISO/OSI) defined a seven-layer network model that network designers and programmers use to discuss and design network software.

+ Within the ISO/OSI model, each layer has a specific function to perform.

+ To send information across a network to a remote computer, network software breaks the information into smaller pieces called packets. The network software then sends the packets individually across the network.

+ After the destination computer receives the data packets, the network software reassembles the packets into the original data format.

+ At the lowest level of ISO/OSI model, the physical layer uses a communications channel, such as an Ethernet cable, to transmit data.

+ The data-link layer provides data in a format the physical layer can transmit. Within a PC, the network interface card provides the data-link layer.

+ When a computer sends a packet to a remote computer, the packet may travel through several computers or several networks. Within the ISO/OSI model, the network layer delivers data between two computers.

+ The transport layer delivers data between applications that are running on host computers.

+ The session layer lets a user establish a network session (log into the network).

+ The presentation layer provides application programs with services the programs can use to access network resources, such as remote disks and printers.

+ Within the ISO/OSI model, applications such as a Web browser, e-mail program, or a chat program reside in the application layer.

Understanding Network Protocols

Across the Internet, all computers use binary digits (ones and zeros) to represent data. Unfortunately, although all computers use binary internally, all computers are not alike. They run different operating systems and use different hardware, which, in turn, may cause two machines to store the same information differently. To help different types of computers exchange information, network developers built a set of rules (protocols) that define how computers communicate.

A *protocol* describes a set of data (message) formats and communication rules that network programs must follow in order to exchange information. The rules might define, for example, how fast the programs will send and receive data, the size of the messages, and how one program will notify the other when an error occurs. Before two programs can communicate across a network, the programs must agree on a protocol. Then, to send data to another program, the sending program must package the data in the format the protocol specifies. When the receiving program later gets the message, the program knows how to unpack the data by following the protocol.

Understanding the ISO/OSI Network Model

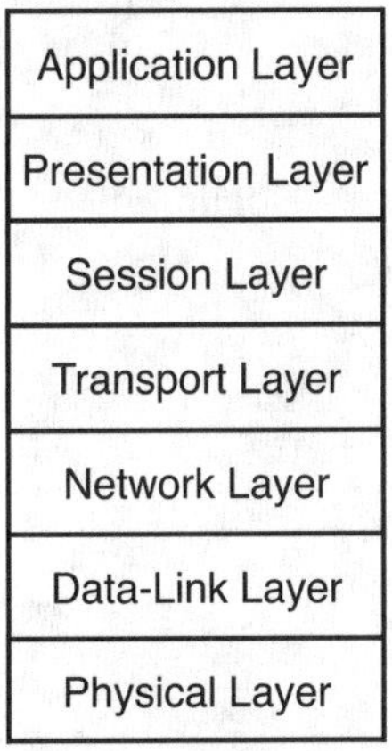

| Application Layer |
| Presentation Layer |
| Session Layer |
| Transport Layer |
| Network Layer |
| Data-Link Layer |
| Physical Layer |

The *ISO/OSI network model* provides a framework network developers can use to design networks. To define the operations a network performs, the ISO/OSI model stacks key network operations into layers. Each layer, in turn, performs a specific function in the process of sending or receiving data. As information flows up and down the network layers, the information cannot bypass a layer. As a result, each layer cares only about its adjacent layers. Figure 36.1 shows the layers in the ISO/OSI network model. The ISO/OSI network model provides seven layers. Within each of these layers, protocols exist to exchange data between adjacent layers.

Figure 36.1 Functional layers in the ISO/OSI network model.

When two computers communicate, the data transmission occurs across a communication channel defined by the physical layer. After a packet reaches its destination, the data will travel up through the layers to the application layer, where the network program can process it. If the program sends data to another network computer, the data will move down the layers and eventually pass back across the communication channel defined by the physical layer. Assuming that no errors occur, the data will travel across the channel and up through the network layers of the target computer. If errors occur, the network software will perform operations, as specified by the protocol, to resolve the error.

Networks Exchange Messages Using Packets

To exchange information, such as a file or e-mail message, network programs first break the information into smaller pieces called packets. The network software then transmits each of the packets individually to the receiving computer. Along with the data itself, each packet contains the destination computer's address as well as the address of the sender. You can think of a packet as an addressed envelope that contains a return address.

As packets progress across the network, the various packets that form the complete transmission may take different routes to their common destination. After the packets reach the destination, network software running on the computer reassembles the packets back into the original data format (such as a file or e-mail message).

As packets make their way across a network (or series of networks) to their target destinations, each computer along the path checks the packet to determine if the message is for that computer. If the computer is not the packet's destination, the computer passes the packet to another computer that resides within the packet's path. Figure 36.2 shows how a computer breaks information into packets and then passes the packets to another computer.

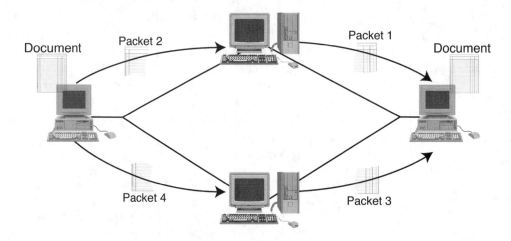

Figure 36.2 A computer separates information into packets and then transmits the packets.

Each computer running network software will route packets down the path that is most immediately available. The software does so through a switching process network professions call *packet switching*. Should one network path break down or otherwise become unavailable (the path may be quite busy), the network software will try to automatically route the packets to an alternate path. In its most basic form, packet switching works the same whether you are sending simple e-mail to a neighbor on your local-area network, or encrypted files over the Internet to someone a thousand miles away. In other words, regardless of your message size, network software breaks your message into small packets for transmission across the network.

Understanding the Physical Layer

Within a network, the physical layer transmits binary data (ones and zeros) across the network's communications channel. All messages that a network sends or receives travel through a communications channel defined by the physical layer.

The physical layer communicates with another network computer using binary data. The physical layer must, therefore, define how the network hardware will represent ones and zeros. Meaning, the physical layer must specify, for example, the analog-signal frequency or digital voltage the network will use to represent a one, versus that which it will use to represent a zero. Also, the physical layer must ensure that the destination computer receives the data correctly. Finally, the physical layer determines how the computers communicate, meaning, in one direction at a time (simplex), in both directions, but only one direction at a time (half-duplex), or in both directions at the same time (full-duplex).

Within the physical layer, you will also find the network's physical elements, such as its cables and connectors. The physical layer also defines the network's control signals, timing, and voltages. In other words, the physical layer determines the communications channel's physical and mechanical properties. For example, the physical layer specifies the number of electrical pins or wires within a network connection, the type of cable (coaxial or twisted pair) that connects systems, as well as other cable properties, such as bandwidth. The physical layer dictates the *network's technology*, such as Ethernet, Token Ring, or Fiber Distributed Data Interface (FDDI).

Understanding the Data-Link Layer

Above the physical layer, resides the data-link layer (or simply, the link layer). The function of the data-link layer is to transfer data (error free) between the physical layer and the network layer. As shown in Figure 36.3, the network interface card you install in your PC provides your network's data-link layer.

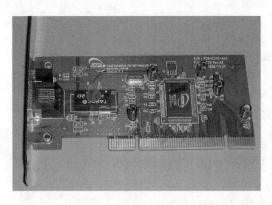

Figure 36.3 The network interface card defines the PC's data-link layer.

As discussed, the physical layer works with bits. The data-link layer, in turn, formats the bits into *frames* of data, which it then transfers to the network layer. Likewise, when the data-link layer receives data from the network layer, the data-link layer translates the data into the correct binary format for the physical layer.

The physical layer (the network technology, such as Ethernet) does not care how the network layer transmits data to the data-link layer. Likewise, the network layer does not care how the data-link layer packages the data for the physical layer. The network and physical layers are independent of one another.

Each physical network type requires a corresponding data-link layer. To connect your computer to a network, your computer must have a network interface card that matches the network's technology. As you shop for a network interface card, make sure the card matches your specific network technology and the network's speed. If your network card is not fully compatible with the physical network type, your network will not work. You could not, for example, connect a Token Ring network interface card to an Ethernet-based network.

To send information to the physical layer, the data-link layer packages the data into a frame, whose format is specific to the underlying network technology. For example, Figure 36.4 shows the data frame for an Ethernet-based network. As you can see, much of the Ethernet frame identifies and routes the frame. The 64-bit Preamble field, for example, helps receiving hosts synchronize the frames that arrive out of order. The destination address specifies the network location to which the network is sending the frame. Likewise, the source address specifies the location of the PC sending the message. Should an error occur during the message transmission, many network protocols require that the receiver notify the sender of the error. Finally, the Frame Type field identifies the type of data the frame contains.

Every network interface card has a unique 48-bit address called a Media Access Control (MAC) address. Normally, a card's MAC address is hard coded, which means you cannot change it. Part of the 48 bits describe the card's manufacturer. The remaining bits provide a number unique to the manufacturer. By combining the manufacturer information with a card number unique to the manufacturer, each network card's MAC address is unique.

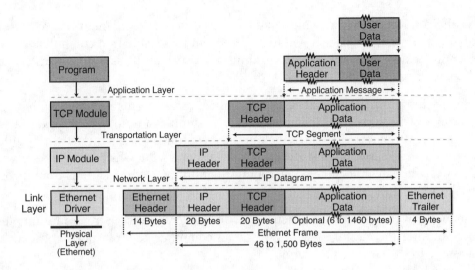

Figure 36.4 Packaging data into an Ethernet frame.

To detect errors that occur across the physical layer (which may be caused by a damaged cable or power surge), the sending and receiving data-link layers use a *cyclic redundancy check* (CRC) value. In general, a CRC is a 32-bit value the data-link layers calculate by performing a calculation on a frame's data. When a computer sends a packet, its data-link layer calculates the CRC value, which it then appends to the data frame. When the frame arrives at the receiving computer, that computer's data-link layer performs the same calculation on the data to determine the CRC. Then, the data-link layer compares its CRC value to the one stored in the data frame. If the two CRC values are the same, it is very likely no errors occurred in the transmission process (however, it is still possible, though unlikely, for an error to occur that the CRC algorithm did not detect). If the receiving data-link layer determines the CRCs differ, and therefore an error has occurred, the receiver can, based on the network protocol, discard the frame or notify the sender of the error.

Understanding the Network Layer

When computers communicate, it is seldom the case that the two computers are adjacent to one another, with no computers in between. Instead, the messages that one computer sends to another must often pass through other computers and other computer networks. If the two computers are connected to the same network, sending a message from one computer to the other simply requires that the sender transmit the message over the network cable. However, if the computers reside on different networks, the network software must determine how to route the message from one network to another, in order for the message to arrive at its correct destination. Within the ISO/OSI network model, the network layer determines the route that each message will travel.

Before the physical layer can send data across the network, the network layer must specify the path that the packet will follow to reach the destination computer. To perform its processing, the network layer examines network traffic as well as transfer rates across potential paths.

To route packets through a network, the network-layer software relies on a *routing table* to determine the best path for the packet. You can think of a routing table as a database which the network layer can use to look up the best routes (based on network traffic). Today, most large networks use dynamic routing tables for which network software automatically updates the table based on information the software gleans from incoming packets.

The network layer provides the functionality to deliver a message from one computer to another. After the message reaches the target computer, the transport layer delivers the message to the correct application.

Understanding the Transport Layer

Within the ISO/OSI model, the network layer delivers packets between computers. In a similar way, the transport layer delivers data from one application to another. After the network layer delivers data to the correct computer, the transport layer delivers data to the correct application within that computer.

Within a computer, a user may be running several different network applications, such as a Web browser and an e-mail program. Each network program will use the same underlying network software to send data across the network. When the PC receives incoming data from the network, the network software must determine which program should receive the data. Within the ISO/OSI model, the transport layer routes packets to the correct application.

As discussed, the network layer delivers data between network computers, handling network traffic and throughput concerns. Within a packet-switching network, such as the Internet, the transport layer, when sending a message, breaks apart (fragments) information it receives from the session layer, to put the data in a format the network layer requires. Likewise, when the transport layer receives a message, it reassembles the fragmented data that it gets from the network layer. Within a network computer, multiple programs may use the network at the same time and in different ways. The transport layer must receive data from, or send data to, the correct program. In other words, the transport layer must manage data for multiple network applications.

Understanding the Session Layer

The session layer provides a network application's interface to a network. Using the session layer, a network program negotiates a connection with an application that resides on a different host computer. To establish the connection, the session layer handles details such as account names, passwords, and user authorizations. For example, on many networks you must *log in* (enter your name or user identification and a password) before you can use any network services. Network programmers refer to each login as a *session*. Network designers often refer to the process of setting up a network session as a binding.

Before you can establish a network connection, both ends of the connection must negotiate options, such as data-transfer rates, error control, and the expected type of data transfer (simplex, half-duplex, or full-duplex). Either end of the connection can request modifications to these options. The session layer must manage requests for changes to a negotiated option.

In addition to authorizing user access, the session layer reconstructs data that is packaged for network transmissions (which the transport layer requires) into application data (that the presentation layer requires). Also, the session layer handles application requests for changes to data-flow rates and error control.

Network designers may eliminate the session layer if a network doesn't require application-to-application connection information. There is no session layer, for example, within TCP/IP which is widely used across the Internet. Most Internet-based programs that require session authorization place the required processing within the application layer. Additionally, the Internet transport-layer protocols include many functions the session layer normally handles.

Understanding the Presentation Layer

The presentation layer defines how the network software presents itself to the application developer. In other words, the presentation layer may provide services for remote-file management, encryption, data compression, and so on. Network designers build the presentation layer by creating libraries of functions that the user's applications can call to perform a specific task. Again, TCP/IP, the protocol that drives the Internet, does not contain an "official" presentation layer. Instead, the line between the transport layer and application layer is blurred.

Understanding the Application Layer

The application layer contains network-based programs, such as your browser or e-mail program. The programs, Active Server Pages, and Web services that programmers create for use across the Internet reside within the application layer.

EXAM REVIEW

① **True or False**
The ISO/OSI model is a set of operating-system-specific libraries that programmers use to build network programs.

② The ISO/OSI network model defines _____ functional network layers.

③ Within the ISO/OSI model, the _____ layer defines the network's technology.

④ Within the ISO/OSI model, the _____ layer routes packets between computers and the _____ layer manages packets for specific applications.

⑤ **True or False**
Within a packet switching network, it is possible that a computer may receive packets in an order that differs from the order the sending computer sent the packets.

⑥ TCP/IP, HTTP, and SNMP are examples of _____.

⑦ Within the ISO/OSI model, programs such as a Web browser and e-mail application reside within the _____ layer.

⑧ Based on the ISO/OSI model, network software would place program services such as encryption within the _____ layer.

⑨ To detect data-transmission errors, the data-link layer calculates and places a special value called a _____ or _____ within the frame it sends to the physical layer.

⑩ Every network interface card has a unique 48-bit address called the _____ or _____ address.

Understanding Network Technologies

In Lesson 35, "Understanding Computer Networks," you learned that network administrators can configure networks using a bus, star, or ring topology. In this lesson, you will examine network technologies. In general, a network technology describes the network's underlying hardware (cables, network interface cards, hubs, and so on) as well as very low-level communication protocols the network uses to exchange packets.

Today, most networks use the Ethernet technology. The A+ Certification exam will also include questions about the Token Ring and Fiber Data Distributed Interface (FDDI) networks. In the near future, many businesses and home networks will make extensive use of wireless networks, which are based on the 802.11 standard.

F A C T S

- A network's topology describes the network's shape (or configuration). The three most common network topologies are the ring, bus, and star.

- A network's technology describes the network's underlying hardware. The three most common network technologies are include: Ethernet, Token Ring, and Fiber Distributed Data Interface (FDDI).

- Ethernet networks support the bus and star technologies. Within a bus-based Ethernet network, you must attach a terminator to each end of the bus. To create a star-based Ethernet network, you must attach each network card to a hub.

- Ethernet uses the carrier sense multiple access/collision detection (CSMA/CD) to send one packet at a time across the network.

- The "carrier sense" in the term carrier sense multiple access/collision detection means that before a network interface card will place data onto the network, the card will listen to (sense) the network to determine if the network is currently transmitting data. If the network is in use, the card will wait a random period of time before it again senses the network. Then, if the network is not in use, the card will place its packet onto the network.

- The "multiple access" in the term carrier sense multiple access/collision detection means that more than one PC is connected to and can access the network.

- The "collection detection" in the term carrier sense multiple access/collision detection means that after a network card places data onto the network, the card will monitor the network to determine if the packet it placed on the network collided with another packet. If a collision has occurred, the network card will wait a random amount of time and then sense the network to determine when it can again try to send the packet.

- Users frequently describe Ethernet networks using terms such as 10BaseT or 100BaseF. The number that appears before the word Base in the description describes the network's speed. A 10BaseT Ethernet network, for example, communicates at 10MHz (10 million bits per second). The letter that follows the word "base" describes the cable type. A 10BaseT Ethernet network uses twisted-pair cables. A 100BaseF Ethernet network uses fiber-optic cables.

- To connect a network card to a bus-based Ethernet network, you normally use a BNC T-connector. To connect a network card to a star-based Ethernet, you normally use a cable with an RJ-45 connector to connect the card to a network hub.

F A C T S

- IBM developed the Token Ring network to provide a way to eliminate packet collisions. In a Token Ring network, only one network card can place a packet on the network at a time. Before a network card can place a packet on the network, the card must possess the network's token (which you can think of as a single permission slip that travels the network, giving the possessor the right to place data onto the network).

- To send a packet within a Token Ring network, a network card that possesses the token attaches the packet to the token and then sends the token on its way. As the token travels the network, each network interface card examines the token to see if it contains an attached packet. If a packet is attached to the token, the network interface card examines the packet's address to determine if the packet is targeted for the current PC. If the packet is for the current PC, the network card passes the packet up to the PC's network software. If the packet is addressed for a different PC, the network card sends the packet on its way. If the token does not have an attached packet, the network card can append a packet to the token.

- To connect a network card to a Token Ring network, you normally use a type 6 cable that is a shielded twisted-pair (STP) cable with stranded conductors to connect the card to a special hub called a multistation access unit (MAU).

- A Fiber Distributed Data Interface (FDDI) network is a dual-cabled ring network that directly connects network cards without the need of a central hub.

- Although the Fiber Distributed Data Interface network uses the term "fiber," you can create an FDDI network using cable types other than a fiber-optic cable.

- An FDDI network uses a token to control when devices can place packets onto the communication. Unlike a Token Ring network that lets a network interface card place only one packet onto the channel before the card must give up the token, an FDDI network lets a card send multiple packets before the card must place the token back onto the network for use by other cards.

- An FDDI network uses two cables to create a primary and secondary ring. Normally, devices communicate only across the primary ring. Should the primary ring fail, devices will then use the secondary ring.

Understanding Ethernet Networks

Today, Ethernet is the most widely used network technology. Over the years, the Ethernet technology has evolved to support faster speeds. Not long ago, Ethernet networks communicated at 1Mbs (one megabit per second). As cable and card technologies improved, Ethernet networks supported speeds of 10Mbs and later 100Mbs. Today, 1,000Mbs (1 Gbs or gigabit per second)) Ethernet networks exist.

Network administrators can configure an Ethernet network using a star or bus technology. To use a star topology to create an Ethernet network, you would connect each PC's network interface card to a special device called a network hub, as shown in Figure 37.1.

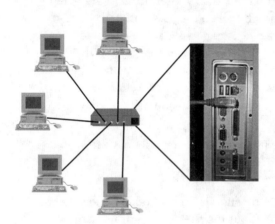

Figure 37.1 Connecting network interface cards to a hub.

Normally, to connect a network interface card to an Ethernet hub, you would use a Category 5 (Cat 5) cable with an RJ-45 cable, which looks similar to, but is larger than, a standard phone cable. Because of the widespread use of Ethernet networks, many PCs now ship with a built-in network port, much like a keyboard or mouse port.

To use a bus topology to build an Ethernet network, network administrators normally run a special coaxial cable from one PC in the network to the next. To connect the cable to the PC's network card, you would use a special BNC T-connector, as shown in Figure 37.2.

Figure 37.2 Using a BNC T-connector to connect a network interface card to a bus-based Ethernet.

At each end of the network bus, you must attach a special terminator to the T-connector. If you do not terminate both ends of the bus, the network will not operate.

Understanding Ethernet Speeds and Distances

As discussed, the speed of Ethernet devices has increased over time. For years, networks made extensive use of 10Mbs Ethernet cards, hubs, and cables. When 100Mbs Ethernet devices became available, network designers were faced with an upgrade challenge because the 10Mbs and the 100Mbs devices were not compatible.

If the network was small enough that the administrator could upgrade all the network hardware, the process was simple. Otherwise, the network administrator would often use a bridge to create two sub-networks, as shown in Figure 37.3, one that used 100Mbs devices and one that used the 10Mbs devices. To increase compatibility, network card manufacturers created cards and hubs that supported both speeds. Within the hubs, the electronics determines the speed of the corresponding cards and handles the flow of data across the network accordingly.

Today, with the introduction of 1,000Mbs (gigabit) Ethernet devices, network administrators face similar upgrade challenges.

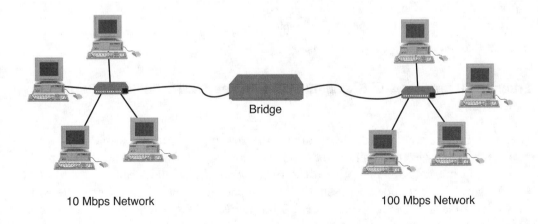

10 Mbps Network   100 Mbps Network

Figure 37.3 Using a bridge to create sub-networks that operate at different speeds.

As you learned in Lesson 35, "Introduction to Networking," as a signal travels across a cable, the signal eventually loses strength (the signal attenuates). To prevent the loss of data as signals travel extended distances, repeaters were placed in networks to amplify the signals. It used to be, within an Ethernet network, you should place a repeater every 100 meters. However, today the distance at which you should place a repeater depends on the network type. For a 10BaseT and 100BaseT Ethernet, for example, 100 meters is still a good distance. For a 10Base2 Ethernet, you should place a repeater after 185 meters. Many networks today have repeaters spaced as far as 1,000 meters apart.

Making Sense of Ethernet Descriptions

As you examine Ethernet hardware and when you discuss Ethernet networks with other users, you will encounter descriptions of the networks such as 10Base2, 10BaseT, 100BaseF, and so on. Network professionals describe Ethernet networks in terms of the cable types that connect the network devices. A 10Base2 network, for example, is a 10Mbs network that uses a coaxial cable. A 10BaseT network is a 10Mbs network that uses twisted-pair cable. Likewise, a 100BaseF network is a 100Mbs network that uses a fiber-optic cable. Table 37.1 briefly describes Ethernet types you will encounter on a regular basis and which you should know.

Description	Network Type
10Base2	10 MHz with thin coaxial cable
10BaseT	10 MHz with twisted-pair cable
100BaseTX	100 MHz with Category 5 cable or better
100BaseT4	100 MHz with Category 3 cable
100BaseF	100 MHz with a fiber-optic cable
1000BaseT	1 GHz with Category 5 cable

Table 37.1 Common Ethernet descriptions.

Ethernet Uses Carrier Sense Multiple Access with Collision Detection (CSMA/CD)

When computers are connected within an Ethernet network, it is possible that two or more computers will try to send data (packets) across the network at the same time. In such cases, the signals that represent the two packets will collide, causing the data to become garbled. To reduce the possibility of such packet collisions, an Ethernet network card that is ready to send a packet across the network first listens to the network to determine if the communication channel is currently in use. Network professionals refer to this listening process as a "carrier sense" operation. If the network is in use, the card will wait a random period of time to see if the network has become available. After the card detects the network is not in use, the card places its packet onto the network.

By waiting a random period of time (as opposed to a fixed interval), two network cards that "sense" the communication channel at the same time and find the network busy will not later sense the network again at the same time because each waited a different (random) time interval.

The process of sensing the communication channel for network activity before placing a packet onto the network reduces but does not eliminate the possibility of packet collisions. It is possible that two network cards may sense the network at same time, each finding the channel available. However, when both cards place their packets onto the network, the two packets will collide.

After an Ethernet card places a packet onto the network, the card then monitors the network to determine if the packet collided with another packet. When a packet collision occurs, the cards involved in the collision will wait a random period of time and repeat the process of sensing the channel to determine if it is in use. As you prepare for the A+ Certification exam, you must understand the CSMA/CD operations:

CS—Carrier Sense—Each Ethernet network card listens for the network's communication channel to become available before the card tries to send a packet.

MA—Multiple Access—Two or more network cards may access the network at the same time.

CD—Collision Detection—After a card places a packet onto the communication channel, the card must monitor the network for a packet collision and then respond accordingly.

Understanding the Token Ring Network Technology

IBM developed the Token Ring network technology to eliminate packet collisions that occur within and degrade the performance of an Ethernet network. Within a Token Ring network, a single "token" (a special packet that continually travels the network) controls when a network card can place data onto the network. If a network card does not possess the token, the card cannot place data onto the communication channel.

To send data, a network interface card attaches a packet to the token, which it then forwards along the communication channel to the next device in the network's ring. When a device receives the incoming token, the device examines the token's contents to determine if it contains a message addressed to the device. If so, the device sends the data to its network software. If the token contains a packet that is not addressed to the device, the device forwards the token to the next device in the ring. If the token does have a packet attached, and the device has a packet to send, the device attaches its packet and then forwards the token to the next device in the ring. If the token is empty and the device does not have a packet to send, the device forwards the empty token to the next device in the network ring.

Because only one device can attach data to the token at any one time, the Token Ring network eliminates packet collisions and, as such, is very efficient.

To build a Token Ring network, you connect each Token Ring network interface card to a hub called the multistation access unit (MAU), as shown in Figure 37.4. Depending on the network's size, the network may contain multiple MAUs. To connect a Token Ring network card to an MAU, you normally use a cable called type 6 that is a shielded twisted-pair (STP) cable that uses stranded conductors.

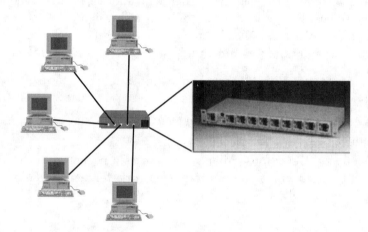

Figure 37.4 Connecting Token Ring network interface cards to a multistation access unit.

Understanding the Fiber Distributed Data Interface (FDDI) Network Technology

A Fiber Distributed Data Interface (FDDI) is a dual-ring topology that uses two cables to connect network devices as shown in Figure 37.5. Unlike a Token Ring network that uses a hub to connect devices, an FDDI-based network directly connects one network card to another to create the ring.

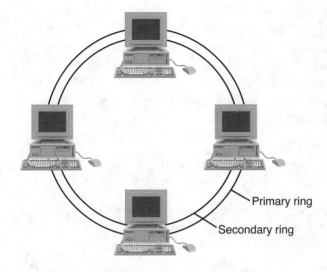

Figure 37.5 A Fiber Distributed Data Interface network uses a dual ring configuration.

To prevent packet collisions, FDDI networks use a token to control network transmissions. Unlike a Token Ring network that allows a sender to place only one packet onto the network before it must give up the token, an FDDI network lets a sender hold onto the token until it has completed its transmission, which means a network interface card can send several packets across the network before having to give up the token.

Although the FDDI network uses two rings, devices normally use only the primary ring to send and receive data. If the outer ring should fail, possibly due to a break in the cable or a failed network interface card, the FDDI network will begin to use the secondary ring.

To create a Fiber Distributed Data Interface network, you do not have to use a fiber-optic cable (although most FDDI networks do so). Network designers have created FDDI-based networks using other cable types, such as copper, which the designers refer to as a CDDI network. Because of its high-speed and efficient data transmissions, FDDI-based networks often provide a "backbone" that connects two networks.

EXAM REVIEW

CERTIFICATION

① **True or False**
The three most common network topologies are Ethernet, Token Ring, and FDDI networks.

② Network designers can create Ethernet networks using the _____ and _____ network topologies.

③ For a bus-based Ethernet to operate, you must attach special connectors to each end of the bus called _____.

EXAM REVIEW

A+ CERTIFICATION

④ The acronym FDDI stands for:
- ☐ Fiber-optic digital device interconnect
- ☐ Fast device data interface
- ☐ Fiber distributed data interface
- ☐ Fiber distributed data internet

⑤ True or False
Ethernet networks avoid packet collisions using a special packet called a token.

⑥ As a general rule, within a 100BaseT Ethernet network you should use a repeater every _____ meters in order to reduce lost data due to signal attenuation.

⑦ True or False
An FDDI-based network uses only fiber-optic cables.

⑧ True or False
The "10" in the description "10BaseT" Ethernet network implies that the network will support up to 10 devices.

⑨ The _____ network technology uses two cables to create a dual-ring network.

⑩ Token Ring networks use a special hub called a _____ or MAU.

⑪ True or False
An FDDI network lets a network card send multiple packets before the card must release the network token.

⑫ True or False
When a packet collision occurs within an Ethernet network, the network interface cards involved in the collision will wait 20 milliseconds before trying to resend their packets.

⑬ To connect an Ethernet-based network interface card to a hub, you normally use an _____ cable.

⑭ _____ designed the Token Ring network technology to eliminate packet collisions that occur within Ethernet networks.

⑮ To connect a network interface card to an MAU, you normally use a _____ cable.

Getting Started with TCP/IP High-Speed Internet Connections

A protocol defines a set of rules and procedures. A network protocol defines the rules and data formats that programs must follow to communicate across the network. The most common Internet protocol is the transmission control protocol/Internet protocol (TCP/IP). In fact, TCP/IP drives the Internet and programs users run to access Internet-based data.

This lesson examines several key TCP/IP and related concepts. You will learn how to view your TCP/IP settings within Windows and how to troubleshoot common problems. In Lesson 39, "Configuring a TCP/IP Network," you will learn how to change TCP/IP settings on your system.

F A C T S

- TCP/IP, the transmission control protocol/Internet protocol is the protocol that drives the Internet.

- In addition to TCP/IP, Internet-based programs use other protocols. A Web browser, for example, makes extensive use of HTTP. Likewise, an e-mail program uses POP and SMTP to receive and send messages.

- Each PC connected to the Internet must have a unique Internet protocol (IP) address.

- If you use a modem to dial into the Internet, your Internet service provider will assign an IP address to your PC each time you connect. If your PC is part of a local-area network that connects to the Internet, your network administrator or a special DHCP server will assign your IP address.

- To view your IP address and other key settings, you can run the WinIPCFG program.

- Users refer to Web addresses such as *www.onwordpress.com*, as a domain name.

- Internet programs do not send messages to sites using a domain name. Instead, the program must know the remote site's IP address.

- Programs use a special Internet-based server, called a domain name server (DNS), to convert a domain name into the site's corresponding IP address.

- Rather than manually configure the TCP/IP settings for each PC in a network, administrators often use a special server, called a dynamic host configuration protocol (DHCP) server, to configure network settings.

- Each time a system starts, it will send a message to the network requesting configuration settings. The DHCP server will respond by sending to the PC an IP address, gateway and subnet information, and the IP address the system should use for a domain name server.

- Within a network, a gateway routes messages to and from the Internet.

- To determine if a remote site is operating, you can use the ping command to send several network messages to the remote site. Normally, if the remote site is operational, it will respond to each ping message.

- As a message travels across the Internet to its destination, the message may move through a number of sites. To trace a message's path across the Internet, you can use the *tracert* command.

Taking a Quick Look at Key Internet Protocols

A protocol defines a set of rules and a set of data structures that programs will use to communicate across a network. Behind the scenes, programs make extensive use of the transmission control protocol/Internet protocol (TCP/IP) to send and receive messages across the Internet. TCP/IP, however, is not the only protocol programs use.

As you surf the World Wide Web, your browser makes extensive use of the hypertext transfer protocol (HTTP). When you have entered Web addresses in the past, you may have preceded an address with the characters *http://*, such as *http://www.ebay.com*. The letters *http://* tell the browser to connect to the remote site using the hypertext transfer protocol. However, because browsers will use HTTP by default, you can omit the letters *http://* from the start of the Web addresses you enter.

In a similar way, to send and receive electronic-mail messages, your e-mail software makes use of the post office protocol (POP) to download your incoming messages and the simple mail transfer protocol (SMTP) to send your outgoing mail. Likewise, many users download files from across the Internet using the file transfer protocol (FTP).

As users discuss protocols, keep in mind that a protocol simply specifies the rules a program must follow to perform network operations. In general, protocol specifics are only of importance to the programmers who must write network programs. Table 38.1 briefly summarizes the key Internet protocols.

Protocol	Description	Purpose
TCP/IP	Transmission control protocol/Internet protocol	The underlying protocol that drives messages sent across the Internet
HTTP	Hypertext transfer protocol	The protocol Web browsers follow to download text, graphics, and other objects from across the Web
POP	Post office protocol	The protocol e-mail programs use to download incoming e-mail messages
SMTP	Simple mail transfer protocol	The protocol e-mail programs use to send outgoing e-mail messages
DHCP	Dynamic host configuration protocol	The protocol network administrators use to automate the configuration of TCP/IP settings
FTP	File transfer protocol	The underlying protocol that programs can use to transfer files across the Internet.

Table 38.1 Key Internet protocols.

Understanding Internet Protocol (IP) Addresses

Across the Internet, every PC that connects to the Net must have a unique address. Users refer to the PC's address as its Internet Protocol (IP) address. Before you can perform any operations across the Internet, your PC must have an IP address.

If you connect your PC to a dial-up service, such as Earthlink, AOL, or a cable or DSL modem, your Internet service provider will assign a unique IP address to your PC each time you connect to the Net. The IP address you receive on one day may be quite different from the IP address you get on another.

If your PC is part of a local-area network that connects to the Internet, your network administrator will either assign a permanent IP address to your system or a dynamic host configuration protocol (DHCP) server on your network will assign a unique IP address to your PC each time your system starts.

To view your PC's IP address, you can run the WinIPCFG program as shown in Figure 38.1. The program will display your IP address, as well as information about your network gateway and submask, both of will be discussed in a later section.

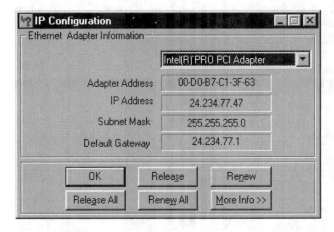

Figure 38.1 To display your PC's IP address, run WinIPCFG.

To run the WinIPCFG program, perform these steps:

1. Select the Start menu Run option. Windows will display the Run dialog box.

2. Within the Run dialog box Open field, type WinIPCFG and press Enter.

If Windows cannot find the WinIPCFG command on your system, you will need to install the program from your Windows distribution CDs.

Taking a Closer Look at IP Addresses

An IP address is a unique address that consists of four bytes. The IP address identifies both a network on the Internet and a computer within that network. In theory, the four-byte IP address provides for 4,294,967,296 (2^{32}) computers to be simultaneously connected to the Internet.

The IP address separates each byte with a period (such as 122.332.442.22), using a form that users refer to as a dotted-decimal address.

The high-order byte of the IP address was originally intended to hold the network ID. As a result, users could only connect to 256 networks. To overcome this address space limitation, Internet professionals created a simple but effective encoding scheme that created greater accessibility to networks. IP addresses no longer use the high-order byte for a network number. Instead, the high-order bits in the high-order byte identify what is called an *address class*. The address class specifies how many bytes the address uses for the network ID number. This sounds more complex than it actually is. Table 38.2 shows the basics of the address-class encoding scheme.

Class	High-Order Bits	Bytes Available for a Network ID
A	0 _ _ _ _	1
B	1 0 _ _ _	2
C	1 1 0 _ _	3
D	1 1 1 0 _	(Used for multicasting)
E	1 1 1 1 0	(Reserved for future use)

Table 38.2 The IP address-class encoding scheme.

A TCP/IP network requires that every network interface on the same physical network have the same network ID number but a unique host ID number. By looking at how classes expand Internet access space, you will understand better how the physical network determines a unique address.

Class A addresses have access to one byte for network addressing. Because the high bit of that byte indicates that class type, there are actually only 128 (2^7) different network IDs for Class A networks. However, the 7-bit address leaves room for 24 bits of network addressing, which means that up to 16,777,216 computers could be physically connected to a Class A network. In effect, the TCP/IP networking scheme uses Class A addressing only for those networks with more than 65,536 hosts physically connected to the network. Because the number of networks that might fall

within this category is extremely small, the fact that only 127 different networks are possible is not particularly important.

Class B addresses have access to two bytes for network addressing. Because the two high-order bits of those bytes are used to determine the address type, the Internet can connect 16,384 (2^{14}) networks with Class B addresses. Each network with a Class B address can connect up to 65,536 host computers. The Internet Engineering Task Force (IETF) reserves Class B addresses for those networks that require more than 256 host computers.

Class C addresses use up to three bytes for the class type and network ID, leaving one byte for host ID numbers. Because Class C addressing requires three high-order bits, 21 bits are available for Class C address encoding. As a result, an incredible 2,097,152 networks, each containing up to 256 host computers, can use Class C addresses.

IETF reserves Class D for multicast addresses, and Class E for future use.

Understanding Domain Names

As you surf the Web, you will often enter Web addresses such as *www.yahoo.com*, *www.ebay.com*, and others. Users refer to such site names as domain names.

Behind the scenes, Internet programs do not use domain names to send messages across the Internet. Instead, the programs must know the remote site's IP address.

In other words, when you enter a domain name such as *www.microsoft.com*, your browser must determine the remote site's corresponding IP address, which would be something like 207.46.230.220. As you can imagine, with hundreds of millions of sites on the Web, it would impossible for a program to keep track of each site's IP address.

Instead, when you use a domain name within a network program, the program uses a special server that resides on the Internet, called a domain name server (DNS), to look up the site's IP address.

You can think of a domain name server as a special site on the Internet that simply waits for programs to send it a domain name. Then, the domain name server looks up the corresponding domain name in its database and sends the corresponding IP address back to the requesting program.

Before the programs that you run can ask the domain name server to return an IP address for a specific domain name, you must specify which domain name server your system will use. Across the Internet, there are a myriad of domain-name servers.

To assign a specific domain name server to your system within Windows 2000, you can enter the server's IP address in the Internet Protocol (TCP/IP) Properties dialog box, as shown in Figure 38.2. If you are using Windows 9x, you will use the DNS sheet within the TCP/IP Properties dialog box. Normally, however, your network administrator will configure each PC to request the domain name server's IP address from the DHCP server that provides each system's IP address.

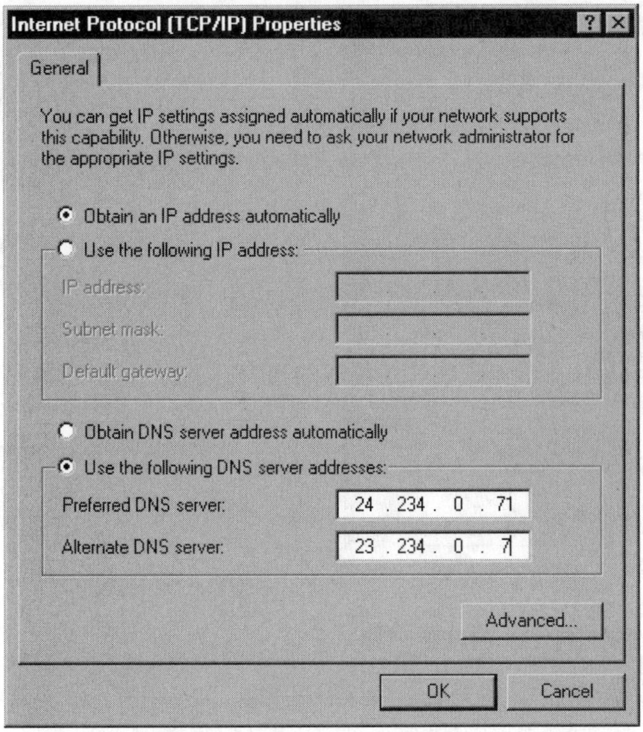

Figure 38.2 You must specify the domain name server your system will use to convert domain names into IP addresses.

If, when you surf the Web, your browser displays a message similar to that shown in Figure 38.3 that states the browser could not find a site, the problem may be that you are using an invalid address or that the site is down. Additionally, the problem may be with the domain name server your system is currently using. If the domain name server is down, your programs will not be able to convert domain names to IP addresses. In such cases, you will need to configure your system to use a different domain name server. To determine if the problem is a domain name server, try using your browser to connect to a site that you know exists, such as *www.yahoo.com*.

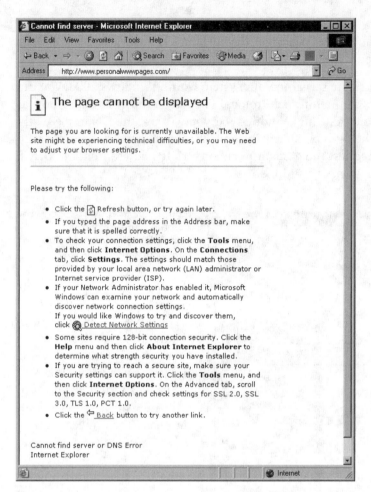

Figure 38.3 If a browser cannot find a valid site, the problem may be your domain name server.

Understanding Gateways and the Network Submask

If your computer is part of a local-area network that connects to the Internet, your network administrator will configure one system (probably the router) as a "gateway" to the Internet. In general, the gateway examines the messages that travel the network. If a message contains a target address that is outside of the network, the gateway will route the message onto the Internet for delivery to a remote system. If you cannot connect to a remote site, such as a Web site, run the WinIPCFG command as previously discussed to ensure your system has a gateway address assigned.

Within a network, every PC sees all the packets sent out onto the network. To control network traffic, network administrators will sometimes create subnetworks using routers or gateways. To identify PCs within a specific subnet, the network adminis-trator will use a submask value.

To assign a gateway address and subnet, you can use the Internet Protocol (TCP/IP) Properties dialog box within Windows 2000 or the TCP/IP Properties dialog box within Windows 9x. Normally, however, your network administrator will configure each PC to request the settings from the DHCP server that provides each system's IP address.

Pinging a Remote System

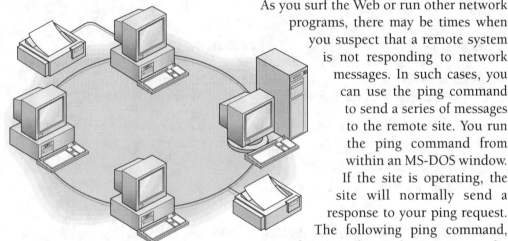

As you surf the Web or run other network programs, there may be times when you suspect that a remote system is not responding to network messages. In such cases, you can use the ping command to send a series of messages to the remote site. You run the ping command from within an MS-DOS window. If the site is operating, the site will normally send a response to your ping request. The following ping command, for example, sends messages to the site *www.yahoo.com*:

```
C:\>ping www.yahoo.com  <Enter>

Pinging www.yahoo.akadns.net [64.58.76.178] with 32 bytes
of data:

Reply from 64.58.76.178: bytes=32 time=90ms TTL=233
Reply from 64.58.76.178: bytes=32 time=80ms TTL=233
Reply from 64.58.76.178: bytes=32 time=90ms TTL=233
Reply from 64.58.76.178: bytes=32 time=90ms TTL=233

Ping statistics for 64.58.76.178:
    Packets: Sent = 4, Received = 4, Lost = 0 (0% loss),
Approximate round trip times in milli-seconds:
    Minimum = 80ms, Maximum =  90ms, Average =  87ms
```

However, if the site is not responding to network messages, ping will normally display a message telling you that your ping requests have timed out, as follows:

```
C:\>ping www.SomeSite.com  <Enter>

Pinging www.SomeSite.com [207.46.197.113] with 32 bytes of
data:

Request timed out.
Request timed out.
Request timed out.
Request timed out.

Ping statistics for 207.46.197.113:
    Packets: Sent = 4, Received = 0, Lost = 4 (100% loss),
Approximate round trip times in milli-seconds:
    Minimum = 0ms, Maximum =  0ms, Average =  0ms
```

If the ping command displays a message telling you that a site is unknown, you are either using an invalid address or you are experiencing a domain name server problem:

```
C:\>ping www.xxx.yyy.com <Enter>
Unknown host www.xxx.yyy.com.
```

Tracing a Packet's Route to a Remote Site

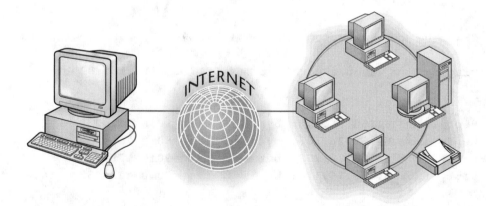

As network messages travel across the Internet to a remote site, the messages may have several intermediate stops at systems along the way. Using the *tracert* command, you can "trace the route" the messages are taking from your system to a remote site. There may be times, for example, when you cannot connect to a remote site that the problem is not the remote site itself, but rather a site along the message path. Using the *tracert* command, you can determine if your messages are arriving at their destination and if not, you may be able to determine the system along the message path that is causing the problem. The following command illustrates the message path from a PC to *www.yahoo.com*.

```
C:\>tracert www.yahoo.com    <Enter>
Tracing route to www.yahoo.akadns.net [64.58.76.176]
over a maximum of 30 hops:

 1 10ms 10ms 20ms ip68-98-84-1.ph.ph.cox.net [68.98.84.1]
 2 10ms 10ms 20ms chnddsrc02-gew0304.rd.ph.cox.net
[68.2.14.17]
 3 30ms 40ms 30ms dllsbbrc01-pos0102.rd.dl.cox.net
[68.1.0.146]
 4 30ms 30ms 40ms gbr6-p30.dlstx.ip.att.net [12.123.17.54]
 5 50ms 50ms 40ms ggr1-p380.attga.ip.att.net [12.122.12.50]
 6 40ms 50ms 50ms acr2-so-3-0-0-0.Atlanta.cw.net
[208.172.65.121]
 7 60ms 70ms 60ms agr4-loopback.Washington.cw.net
[206.24.226.104]
 8 60ms 70ms 60ms dcr1-so-6-3-0.Washington.cw.net
[206.24.238.61]
 9 60ms 70ms 70ms dcr04-g9-0.stng01.exodus.net
[216.33.96.146]
10 60ms 70ms 70ms csr21-ve241.stng01.exodus.net
[216.33.98.18]
11 60ms 70ms 70ms www7.dcx.yahoo.com [64.58.76.176]

Trace complete.
```

EXAM REVIEW

① TCP/IP is an acronym for _____.

② HTTP is an acronym for _____.

③ _____ is the protocol that drives the Internet. In a similar way, _____ is the protocol that drives the World Wide Web.

④ Users refer to Web addresses such as *www.microsoft.com* as a _____.

⑤ True or False
DNS is an acronym for domain naming service.

⑥ A _____ is a server that converts a domain name into the site's corresponding IP address.

⑦ True or False
To view IP and other TCP/IP settings within Windows, you can run the WinTCPIP command.

⑧ Within a network, a _____ routes messages to and from the Internet.

⑨ True or False
To determine if a remote site is operating, you can send messages to the site using the ping command.

⑩ To view the path a message follows to reach its destination, you can run the _____ command.

Configuring a TCP/IP Network

In most network environments, a network administrator will oversee network configurations and will assign the specific TCP/IP settings each system must use to access the network. That said, by having a general understanding of the key TCP/IP settings and the steps you must perform to change a setting, you can resolve many common network errors.

This lesson will examine the steps network administrators perform to manually assign TCP/IP settings and then how the network administrator can use a DHCP server to automate the configuration process. Although TCP/IP can seem quite intimidating at first glance, there are only a few key settings you must configure for a system to interact with a TCP/IP network such as the Internet.

F A C T S

- To configure a system to use the Internet, you must assign values to four key TCP/IP settings.

- Each system must have a unique IP address.

- Each system must know the IP address of the network's gateway that routes messages to and from the Internet.

- Each system must have a network submask value that identifies the system's subnetwork. Often network administrators will divide large networks into subnetworks using routers and gateways. The subnet masks identifies a subnetwork.

- Each system must have an IP address for a domain name server that converts domain names into a corresponding IP address.

- Rather than manually configure each system in the network, administrators normally use a DHCP server to configure the network systems.

- Within a Windows-based network, each system has a name, such as DataServer. If the network has a WINS server, users can use the Windows-based names within TCP/IP program, such as a browser. The WINS server will convert the name into the corresponding IP address.

Understanding the Four Key TCP/IP Settings

For a system to interact with a TCP/IP network, you must assign values for four key settings:

1. The PC's unique Internet Protocol (IP) address

2. The value of the subnet mask that identifies a subnetwork

3. The address of the domain name server which programs will use to convert domain names into IP addresses

4. The IP address of the network's gateway system that routes messages to and from the Internet

Your network administrator will tell you the values you should assign for each setting. To assign these key settings within Windows 2000, you use the Internet Protocol

(TCP/IP) Properties dialog box shown in Figure 39.1. To display the dialog box, perform these steps:

1. Select the Start menu Settings option and choose Control Panel. Windows will open the Control Panel window.

2. Within the Control Panel, double-click on the Network and Dial-up Connections icon. Windows will display the Network and Dial-up Connections folder.

3. Within the Network and Dial-up Connections folder, right click on the connection you desire and choose Properties.

4. Within the Local Area Connection Properties dialog box list of installed components, click on the Internet Protocol (TCP/IP) entry and then choose Properties.

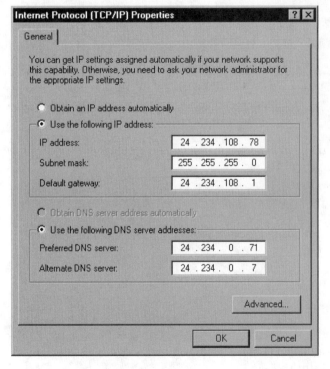

Figure 39.1 To configure a system for TCP/IP operations, you must assign an IP address, DNS server address, and gateway address.

If you are using Windows 9x, you will configure the settings using different sheets that appear within the TCP/IP Properties dialog box shown in Figure 39.2. To display the dialog box, perform these steps:

1. Select the Start menu Settings option and choose Control Panel. Windows will open the Control Panel window.

2. Within the Control Panel, double-click on the Network icon. Windows will display the Network Properties dialog box.

3. Within the Network Properties dialog box list of installed components, click on the TCP/IP entry and then choose Properties.

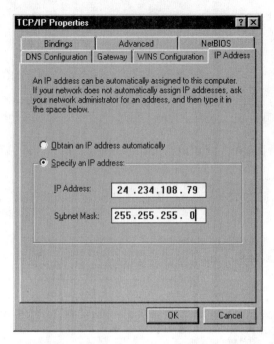

Figure 39.2 To configure TCP/IP settings within Windows 9x, you use the TCP/IP Properties dialog box.

Automating the TCP/IP Configuration Process

Within a small network of a dozen or fewer PCs, a network administrator could easily manually assign and manage each system's TCP/IP settings. However, as you can imagine, within a network of several hundred or several thousand PCs, the process of managing TCP/IP settings could become quite time consuming.

To simplify the process of configuring TCP/IP settings, most networks use a special server called a dynamic host configuration protocol (DHCP) server.

Within a DHCP-based network, each time a system starts, the system will send out a message asking for assistance in configuring its TCP/IP settings. The DHCP server, in turn, will respond to the message by sending the IP address to the PC that it should use, as well as the IP address for the domain name server and network gateway. The DHCP server will also send to the PC the value the PC should use for a network submask.

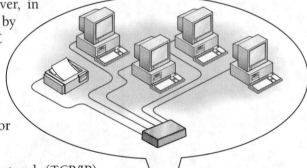

If you examine the Internet Protocol (TCP/IP) Properties dialog box for a system within a DHCP-based network, you will find that the dialog box settings direct the system to obtain the various settings automatically, as shown in Figure 39.3.

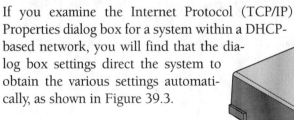

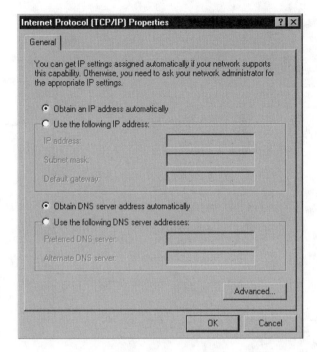

Figure 39.3 Using a DHCP server, network PCs can automatically configure key TCP/IP settings.

To configure the DHCP server, the network administrator will give the server a range of IP addresses that it can distribute to systems within the network. Administrators refer to the range of IP addresses as the IP address pool. When a system no longer needs its IP address (normally when the system shuts down), the DHCP server will return the system's IP address to the IP address pool. Administrators refer to the system's use of the IP address as a lease.

Understanding WINS, the Windows Internet Naming System

As you know, when you type in a domain name, such as *www.microsoft.com*, into an Internet program, the program will use a domain name server to determine the remote site's corresponding IP address. Within a Windows-based network, a WINS (Windows Internet Naming System) server performs similar operations, converting Windows-based network names to their corresponding IP addresses.

Within a Windows-based network, each PC can have a name such as Server1, DataSvr, Finance, and so on. When you view the contents of the Network Neighborhood folder, you can see the PC names, as shown in Figure 39.4.

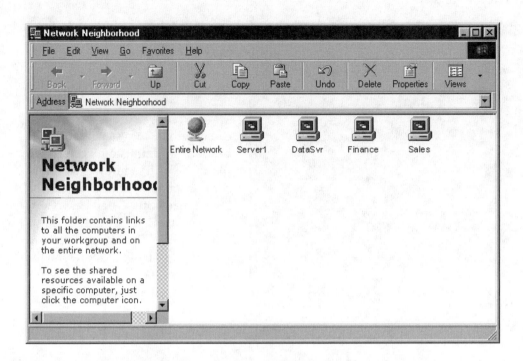

Figure 39.4 Viewing network names within a Windows-based network.

If your network provides a WINS server, you can use the Windows-based system names within TCP/IP-based programs. You might, for example, use your browser to connect to a server named Developer. Behind the scenes, the WINS server will convert the Windows-based system names into their corresponding IP addresses.

When you assign a system's TCP/IP settings, you can enable or disable support for WINS. You can also specify the IP address of the WINS server. In addition, you can also use the DHCP server to configure the WINS settings for each PC in the network.

① DHCP is an acronym for _____.

② True or False
A gateway routes network messages to and from the Internet.

③ True or False
Using a DHCP server, a network can automatically configure each PC's TCP/IP settings.

④ To configure a system to use the Internet, you must specify (select all that apply):

- ☐ A unique IP address
- ☐ The IP address of the network's gateway
- ☐ A network submask
- ☐ The IP address of a DNS
- ☐ The IP address of an FTP server

⑤ WINS is an acronym for _____.

⑥ True or False
A WINS server converts Windows-based network names into a corresponding IP address.

Using a Notebook Computer

Today, many users make extensive use of notebook PCs to take their PC operations on the road. Over the past few years, notebook PC capabilities have evolved so that users can easily run the same programs on a notebook as they would on a desktop PC.

This lesson examines a variety of notebook PC issues. For most operations, a notebook PC is identical to a desktop PC. The notebook PC, for example, has standard serial, parallel, and USB ports. In addition, many newer notebook PCs have a built-in network port. Further, most notebook PCs have a relatively fast CPU, several hundred megabytes of RAM, and a large disk drive.

F A C T S

- Notebook PCs contain most of the same electronic components as a desktop PC.

- A notebook PC has a motherboard that houses the CPU, RAM, the BIOS, and other key components.

- At the back of a notebook PC, you will normally find standard PC ports that include the serial, parallel, video, keyboard, and mouse ports.

- Most notebook PCs also provide USB, FireWire, and network interface ports.

- A notebook PC, unlike a desktop PC, does not have expansion slots into which a user can insert cards that expand the PC's capabilities. Instead, users expand notebook PCs using PCMCIA cards.

- The notebook PC's power adapter converts the wall outlet's 110V alternating current into low-voltage direct current required by the PC's electronic components.

- The notebook PC uses a liquid crystal display (LCD), so named because the screen uses particles with properties that are similar to crystals that float in a liquid. By aligning a red, green, and blue crystal for each pixel location, the screen can control the amount of red, green, and blue light that appears on the screen.

- LCD screens can be passive- or active-matrix.

- An active-matrix screen assigns a transistor to each crystal within the LCD to control the crystal's alignment. A passive-matrix screen assigns a transistor to each row and column. Because an active-matrix screen has finer control over the crystal orientation, it will produce a sharper image than its passive-matrix counterpart.

Taking a Closer Look at Notebook PC Ports

A notebook PC, like a desktop PC, provides parallel and serial ports as well as ports you can use to attach a monitor, mouse, and keyboard. Normally, as shown in Figure 40.1, the notebook's ports reside behind a small plastic cover on the back of the system unit.

Figure 40.1 Notebook PCs provide the same standard ports as a desktop PC.

In addition, most newer notebook PCs provide one or more USB ports, a network interface port, and possibly a FireWire port. To expand a notebook PC's capabilities, such as to add support for SCSI devices, users take advantage of the notebook's PCMCIA ports, as shown in Figure 40.2. Using a PCMCIA card, for example, a user may add support for a modem.

Figure 40.2 Users expand notebook PCs using PCMCIA cards.

Many notebook PCs are designed to support a docking station, that lets a user treat the notebook PC as the system unit for a desktop PC. When the user attaches the PC to a docking station, the user can utilize a larger monitor, keyboard, and mouse. The notebook PC will perform all the processing that occurs, and any files the user creates will reside on the notebook PC's hard drive.

Upgrading a Notebook PC's RAM

In Lesson 23, "Understanding Random Access Memory (RAM)," you learned that you may be able to increase your system performance by installing more RAM. To determine if your notebook PC would benefit from more RAM, monitor your system's available physical memory and page faults as discussed in Lesson 23. Depending on the notebook PC's type, installing more RAM can be much more difficult than adding RAM to a desktop PC. As shown in Figure 40.3, some notebook PCs require that you open the bottom of the system unit to add RAM, whereas others require that you open the notebook and remove the keyboard to gain access to the RAM slots. Many users will find it well worth the cost to have a PC technician who works with notebook PCs on a daily basis install their newly purchased RAM.

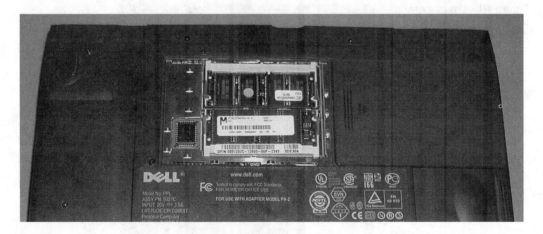

Figure 40.3 Adding RAM to a notebook PC.

Looking Closely at the Notebook PC's Power Adapter

Within a notebook PC, the CPU, RAM, and other electronic components work with low voltage and direct current (DC). The notebook PC's power adapter, shown in Figure 40.4, converts the wall outlet's high-voltage alternating current (AC) into the low-voltage direct current the PC requires. In other words, the power adapter serves the same purpose as a desktop PC's power supply.

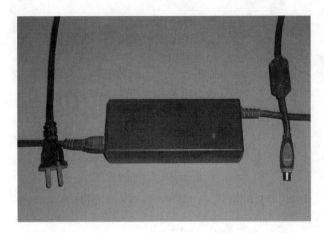

Figure 40.4 The power adapter converts high-voltage alternating current to low-voltage direct current.

In the United States, wall outlets provide power at 110V. In Europe, the wall outlets provide 220V. Many PCs provide a switch near the power supply that you can use to select a 110V or 220V input source. In contrast, most notebook PC power adapters simply perform the conversion.

Understanding Liquid Crystal Displays

To display an image, a traditional monitor heats red, green, and blue phosphors at different intensities, which causes the phosphors to glow. The combination of the red, green, and blue phosphor colors creates a pixel color on the screen. The flat nature of a notebook PC's screen, however, is not well suited for the electron gun that heats the pixels.

Notebook PCs use a liquid crystal display (LCD) screen. In general, within the LCD screen, particles that have properties similar to crystals float, suspended in a liquid. Each pixel has three corresponding crystals that control the amount of red, green, and blue light that reaches the screen. By changing each crystal's orientation, the screen can control the amount of light that illuminates for each pixel. The crystals themselves do not illuminate; they simply filter light.

LCD screens can use either an active- or passive-matrix of transistors that control the charge the screen applies to the corresponding pixels. An active-matrix screen assigns a transistor to each pixel. In contrast, a passive-matrix screen assigns a transistor to each row and column. Because the active-matrix screen has finer control over each pixel's orientation, it produces a much sharper image.

EXAM REVIEW

① True or False
Adding RAM to a notebook PC will always increase the PC's performance.

② True or False
Notebook PCs support small expansion slots on the mini-PCI bus.

③ LCD is an acronym for _____.

④ True or False
Because of its faster refresh rates, a passive-matrix screen creates a sharper image than its active-matrix counterpart.

⑤ Users expand a notebook PC's capabilities using _____.

Supporting Handheld Personal Digital Assistants

O ver the past two years, the use of handheld devices (once more commonly called Personal Digital Assistants or PDAs) has exploded. Today, users make extensive use of Palm OS devices as well as Windows-based handhelds to manage their appointments, "to do" lists, address information, memos, and even to send and receive electronic mail.

Admittedly, the A+ Certification may toss only one or two easy questions your way regarding PDAs. That said, you are likely to have to support PDA-related operations within most offices. This lesson will provide the general foundation you will need to support handheld devices.

F · A · C · T · S

- PDA is an acronym for Personal Digital Assistant.

- Because handheld devices have become much more powerful and the capabilities handhelds now provide far extend beyond simple schedule management, fewer users refer to the devices as PDAs and instead most users will use the term handheld.

- Today, users can use many handhelds to send and receive e-mail and to surf the Web using a wireless modem.

- The two most common handhelds are Palm OS devices and PocketPCs running Windows. Windows-based handhelds normally run a special (scaled down) version of Windows called Windows CE.

- Many newer handhelds provide a built-in wireless modem to connect the device to the Internet. Some handhelds let you attach a wireless modem and others support PCMCIA-based modems.

- Handhelds are battery-powered devices. Handheld devices do not have a hard drive upon which the user can store information. Instead, the handheld stores information within RAM. When the batteries fail, the data the user has stored on the handheld is lost.

- Handheld devices store the operating system in a read-only memory (ROM) that retains its contents even if the device's batteries fail.

- To prevent the loss of data, users back up files from the handheld to a PC by performing a "HotSync" operation.

- To perform a HotSync operation, the user normally places the handheld into a special device called a cradle that connects to the PC. Depending on the handheld's type, the cradle will normally connect to an RS232 serial port or to the universal serial bus (USB).

- Most handheld devices support InfraRed communication. Using IR, two handhelds can exchange information, a handheld can send data to a printer that supports IR operations, or the handheld can HotSync to a PC that supports IR.

Getting Started with Handheld Devices

The early personal digital assistants (PDAs) were quite simple handheld devices. In general, the early PDAs let users track appointments and "to do" lists, but not much more. Because the early PDAs were limited by the amount of RAM they could hold, the programs the PDAs could run were quite simplistic.

As shown in Figure 41.1, handhelds are battery-powered devices. Depending on the device's frequency and length of use, the amount of time the batteries will last will vary. Handheld devices, unlike PCs and notebook computers, do not have a hard drive. Instead, the handheld stores any files a user creates within RAM. Unfortunately, when the device's batteries fail, the contents of RAM are lost.

Figure 41.1 Powering handheld devices with batteries.

Unlike a PC that stores the operating system on a hard disk, the handheld (because it does not have a hard disk) loads the operating system from a read-only memory (ROM) chip. Because the ROM chip does not require constant power, the operating system is not lost when the handheld's batteries fail.

Many Handhelds Now Mimic PCs

Over the past year, the availability of low-cost RAM has greatly increased the capabilities of the programs a handheld device can run. Today, many handhelds support 64MB of RAM or more. Many Windows-based handhelds, for example, run Word, Excel, and Microsoft Outlook. Furthermore, most newer handhelds support full-color screen displays. Similarly, using a Palm OS device and a wireless modem, as shown in Figure 41.2, users can readily send and receive electronic mail and surf the wireless Web.

**Figure 41.2
Showing
that hand-
held devices
now run
many of the
programs a
user typically
runs on a PC.**

Understanding HotSync Operations

To prevent the loss of data when the handheld's batteries fail, users back up the files they create on a handheld to a PC by performing a "HotSync" operation. The HotSync operation is so named because it lets the user synchronize files that reside on both the handheld and the PC. Meaning, if the PC has a newer version of a file than the handheld, the HotSync operation will replace the file on the handheld with the newer version, and vice versa. By performing HotSync operations on a regular basis, the user can protect his or her data from loss due to a battery failure.

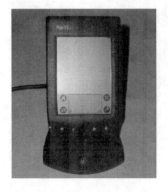

**Figure 41.3
Inserting a Palm
OS device into
a cradle for a
HotSync operation.**

To perform a HotSync operation, users normally place the handheld into a special cradle device, as shown in Figure 41.3. Depending on the handheld device type, the cradle will normally connect to the PC using an RS232 serial port or a USB port.

Taking Advantage of Wireless Handhelds

To extend their ability to mimic PC capabilities, many handheld devices support wireless modems that let the device connect to the Internet. Once connected to the Net, the device can send and receive e-mail, surf the Web, or participate in instant messaging. Many handheld devices have built-in wireless modems. Others support attachable or PCMCIA-based modems. To connect to the Internet, the user must have a wireless service (much like a PC must connect to the Net via AOL or another Internet service provider).

Finally, most handheld devices support InfraRed communication. IR enables handheld devices to perform a number of actions, such as allowing two devices to talk directly to one another, to send data to a printer that supports IR, or to HotSync to a PC that supports IR.

EXAM REVIEW

① PDA is an acronym for _____.

② Because handheld devices do not have a hard drive, the device stores the operating system in _____.

③ Handheld devices store the data a user creates (such as a memo or an address book entry) in _____.

④ True or False
When a handheld device's battery fails, the contents of the device's RAM is lost.

⑤ To back up a handheld device's RAM contents, users perform a special operation called a _____ by placing the device within a special "cradle" and running software that synchronizes data between the device and a PC.

⑥ True or False
Many handheld devices support wireless modems a user can use to surf the Web and send and receive electronic mail.

⑦ True or False
Because of their small size, handheld devices are limited to a black-and-white display.

⑧ Depending on a handheld device's type, the device's cradle will connect to a PC using a _____ or _____ cable.

Lesson 42

Understanding How Disks Store Data

One of the PC's primary purposes is let users store and retrieve information. Several of the lessons that follow will examine disk and file operations. This lesson examines how a disk stores and later retrieves information.

You will first learn how a disk uses partitions, tracks, and sectors to organize data. Then, you will learn how to partition a hard disk for use and why you must format each partition for use by the operating system.

Finally, we will take a brief look at RAID systems and how they provide users with very large storage capacities—in the terabyte capacity. The two primary advantages of RAID systems are high performance and fault tolerance.

F A C T S

- Disks store information by magnetizing data onto the surface of the disk.

- Within a disk drive, a mechanical read/write head records and later reads the data contained on a disk.

- Within the disk drive, the disk's platters spin rapidly past the read/write head at speeds up to 10,000RPM or more.

- An internal disk drive normally connects to the motherboard using an IDE (or EIDE) cable. IDE is an acronym for integrated drive electronics. An IDE disk has a built-in controller which the PC uses to interact with the disk.

- The information that is stored on the surface of disk drives is organized by dividing the disk surface into tracks and sectors.

- Depending on a disk's storage capacity, the number of platters the drive contains may vary. The disk can store data on both sides of the platter. To read and write data on the disk, each side of the disk platter must have its own read/write head.

- Before you can use a new hard disk, you must partition it. When you partition a disk, you can create one or more partitions. To the operating system, each partition will appear as a unique drive.

- The disk drive stores information about each partition within a master boot record.

- After you partition a drive, you must format the drive for use by the operating system.

- When you format a disk for use by the operating system, you essentially place the tables onto the disk that the operating system will use to track the files you later store on the disk.

- RAID is an acronym for redundant array of independent disks. You will also see RAID used as an acronym for redundant array of inexpensive disks.

- A RAID system combines multiple disk drives to produce a storage unit with very high capacity. Two other key advantages of RAID systems are high performance and fault tolerance.

Examining the Disk's Surface

Information is stored by magnetizing data onto the surface of a disk. The disk platter is made from high-precision aluminum or glass and is coated with a thin-film media to create a surface that can hold a magnetic charge.

Within a hard drive, a small read/write head records and later reads data on the disk's surface. The read/write head is a mechanical device (a device with moving parts). As the disk spins rapidly within the drive (at speeds greater than 10,000RPM), the read/write head moves in and out above the surface of the disk to the storage location it requires.

Figure 42.1 shows a read/write head and a disk platter within a hard drive. Never open a drive that you plan to use in the future. When you open the drive, you expose the surface of the disk to dust and other particles. The read/write head floats just above the surface of the disk. If a particle of dust or smoke were to fall on the disk's surface, the particle might collide with the read/write head causing a disk crash. This is where the head essentially scrapes the surface of the disk, which causes other particles to come loose that could further damage the disk surface.

Figure 42.1 A read/write head and disk platter within a hard drive.

NOTE: *To reduce the risk of a disk crash, you should never move a PC that is running. Instead, shut down and power off the PC before you move it—even if you are only moving the PC a few feet.*

Users refer to the disk's metal surface as a platter. A disk drive can store information on both sides of the platter. Each side of the platter has its own read/write head. Within a disk drive, there are normally several platters. The drive will provide a read/write head for both sides of each platter. When you read or talk about disks, you will often hear the term cylinder. Think of a cylinder as being similar to a track. Users use the term cylinder for disks that have multiple platters.

The disk drive, like each of the PC's components, represents data using ones and zeros. To store the value one, the disk drive magnetizes a storage location with a northern polarity. Likewise, to store a zero, the drive would magnetize the location with a southern polarity. Later, by reading a location's polarity, the read/write head can determine if the location is storing a one or a zero. Users refer to the actual storage locations on a disk as domains.

Because a disk stores information magnetically, you should never expose a disk to a magnet or electronic device (such as a vacuum) that can generate an electromagnetic flux strong enough to change the disk's magnetic properties. The X-ray portion of a security machine at an airport, for example, cannot damage a hard drive. However, the motor that drives the belt that moves your PC through the machine has the ability to generate a significant electromagnetic flux.

Connecting the Drive to the Motherboard

Within the PC system unit, a disk drive normally connects to the motherboard using an IDE or EIDE cable. Lesson 27, "Understanding PC Bus Types," examines the IDE bus in detail. IDE is an acronym for integrated drive electronics. Likewise, EIDE stands for enhanced integrated drive electronics. Internal drives can also connect to a SCSI adapter.

An IDE drive contains a built-in controller which the PC can use to interact with the device. Years ago, disk drives connected to controllers that resided on an expansion-slot card.

External hard drives normally connect to a SCSI adapter or FireWire port.

Using Tracks and Sectors to Organize Data on a Disk's Surface

To organize the information it records on the disk's surface, a disk drive divides the surface into tracks and sectors. Think of tracks as circles that increase in size from the center of the disk to the outer edge. A disk can have several hundred to over one thousand tracks.

Next, the disk divides each track into small storage locations called sectors. A disk sector normally holds 512 bytes of data. Users refer to the number of heads, tracks, and sectors contained on a disk as the disk's geometry.

Partitioning a Hard Drive

Years ago, disk capacities grew faster than operating systems could take advantage of the large drives. In some cases, the disks provided more storage capacity than the operating system could use. As a solution, users would use special software to divide a hard drive into multiple disks using partitions.

Using a 30MB drive, for example, a user might partition the drive into three 10MB drives, which the user would access using the drive letters C, D, and E. Or, the user might divide the disk into two 15MB partitions or a 20MB partition for drive C and a 10MB partition for drive D. Although the disk partitions reside on the same disk drive, each partition appears to the operating system as a separate drive.

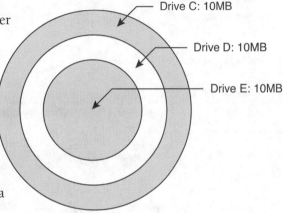

Before you can use a hard drive, you must create one or more partitions on the drive. If you are using Windows 9x, you partition a drive using the MS-DOS FDISK command shown in Figure 42.2.

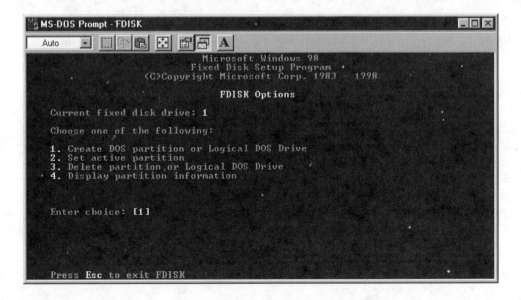

Figure 42.2 Within Windows 9x, you use the FDISK command to partition a disk.

To partition a disk within Windows 2000, you use the Disk Management tool within the Computer Management Administrative utility, as shown in Figure 42.3.

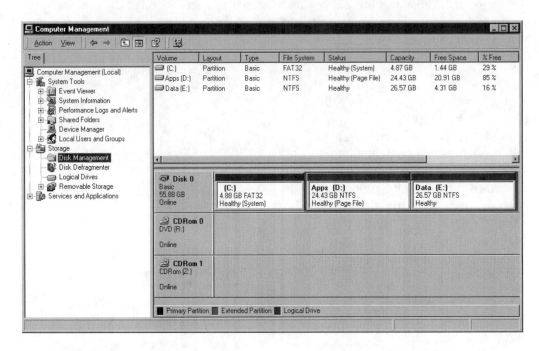

Figure 42.3 Within Windows 2000, you use the Disk Management tool to partition a disk.

WARNING: *Do not create a partition or change a partition on a disk that contains information that you need. The partitioning process will destroy the information the disk contains.*

Understanding the Master Boot Record (MBR)

When you partition a hard drive, the disk drive will store information about each of its partitions (such as the partition's size) within sectors on the drive that users refer to as the master boot record (MBR). Each time the PC starts, the BIOS first reads the contents of the master boot record to determine which partition it should use to load the operating system. Then, the BIOS will read the boot sector from the corresponding partition into RAM, which begins the operating system's startup process.

Understanding a Low-Level Disk Format Operation

As discussed, to organize the information that it stores on the disk's surface, the disk drive first divides the disk into tracks and then divides each track into sectors. To define the track and sector locations on the disk, the disk manufacturer performs a low-level format operation. After the low-level format divides the disk into tracks and sectors, it examines the disk's surface for sectors that, due to imperfections on the surface, are not be able to store data.

When users encounter severe disk errors, there are times when the user can perform a low-level format operation to correct the errors. In the process, however, the low-level format operation will destroy any information the disk contained. To perform a low-level format, you may be able to download a special program from the disk manufacturer's Web site. After the low-level format operation completes, you will need to partition and then format the disk for use by the operating system, just as if you were starting with a new disk.

Formatting a Disk for Use by the Operating System

Operating systems manage the files users store on disk using special software called a file system. As you will learn in the lessons that follow, the file system uses a table called the file allocation table (FAT) to track each file's location on disk. In general, each operating system uses its own file system. Windows 98, for example, supports the FAT16 and FAT32 file systems. While Windows 2000 supports the FAT32 file system, most Windows 2000 disks use the NTFS file system. The Linux operating system uses yet another file system.

After you partition a hard drive, you must then format each of the disk partitions for use by the operating system. Formatting a disk for use by the operating system is much different from a low-level disk format operation discussed in the previous section. When you format a disk for use by the operating system, you essentially create the tables the operating system will use to manage the files you store on disk.

To format a disk for use by Windows 9x, you use the MS-DOS format command. Within Windows 2000, you format a disk using the Disk Management tool. You can begin a format operation within Windows 9x or Windows 2000 by right-clicking on the drive in Windows Explorer and then selecting Format from the pop-up menu.

When you format a disk, you have the option of formatting it as a bootable operating system disk, which users refer to as a system disk. When you format a disk as a system disk, the format process will place the system files onto the disk that the operating system needs in order to start. Normally, you always format drive C as a system disk.

Because you would likely not boot your system from other drives, you would not need the format process to copy the system files to those disks.

Understanding RAID Systems

When the IBM PC XT was first released in the early 1980s (the PC XT added a hard drive to the original floppy-disk-based IBM PC), the XT came with a 5MB hard drive and later with a 10MB drive. When the IBM PC AT was released in 1984, users with a slightly larger budget could get a 20MB drive.

Over the past few years, disk drive storage capacities have increased tremendously. Today, most PCs ship with hard drives that range in capacity from 20GB to over 100GB.

Although PCs now support very large drives, users seem to always need more storage capacity. Many companies, for example, require terabyte (trillions of bytes) storage capacities. To implement these very large storage devices, hardware manufacturers frequently combine several very large disk drives using a redundant array of independent disks (RAID) system, similar to that shown in Figure 42.4. RAID systems were designed for fault tolerance and high performance.

Figure 42.4 A RAID system combines multiple drives to provide very large storage capacities.

In general, although the RAID system houses multiple drives, to the operating system, the RAID device appears as a single drive. What makes the RAID system very powerful is that the systems are designed to support the failure of a single drive, meaning that if one drive in the system fails, no information is lost and the system can continue to operate. To prevent the loss of data should a drive fail, the RAID system not only stores data, but also stores the information it needs to reconstruct the information stored on a failed drive. In other words, the drives use advanced software techniques to replicate data from each drive on the other drives in a very compact way, so the redundant data does not consume a considerable amount of disk space. Users refer to the process of distributing data across multiple drives as data striping. The level of a RAID system describes how the system implements its redundancy. RAID level 1, for example, simply maintains a complete "mirrored" copy of a disk's contents on another disk. RAID level 5, in contrast, uses data striping with distributed parity.

EXAM REVIEW

① A disk drive organizes data on the surface of the disk by dividing the disk into circular _____ that the drive then divides into 512-byte _____.

② Users refer to the individual storage locations on a disk's surface that store a single bit of information as a _____.

③ MBR is an acronym for _____.

④ To partition a hard disk within Windows 9x, you use _____. To partition a disk within Windows 2000, you use _____.

⑤ True or False
A low-level format operation prepares a disk for use by Windows.

⑥ True or False
The MBR contains information about the disk controller.

⑦ RAID is an acronym for _____ or _____.

⑧ True or False
By combining multiple disks into a single unit, a RAID system provides very large storage capacities, fault tolerance, and high performance.

⑨ True or False
If one disk within the RAID system fails, the entire system will fail.

Lesson 43

Using ScanDisk to Locate and Correct Disk Errors

Over the years, PC hard drives have become very reliable. Unless you work in a dusty or smoke-filled environment, or an office that is subject to extreme changes in temperature or periodic loss of power, you may seldom encounter disk errors.

To help you detect and possibly correct many hard-disk errors, Windows provides the ScanDisk utility. Often, a disk that is going bad due to a hardware failure will encounter minor errors before it fails completely. By running ScanDisk on a regular basis, you may detect disk problems before they result in a significant loss of data.

.FACTS

✦ The most common causes of disk errors include:

- Moving a PC that is powered on.
- Working in a smoke- or dust-filled environment.
- Working in a location that is subject to extreme changes in temperature.
- Intermittent loss of power.
- Turning off the PC without first shutting down the operating system.

✦ The ScanDisk utility supports two types of disk tests. The Standard test examines your disk's files and folders. The Thorough test also examines the surface area of your disk upon which the disk magnetizes the information it stores.

✦ Depending on the size of your disk, ScanDisk's Thorough test (which examines each disk location on the surface of your disk) can take several hours to complete.

✦ When a PC is turned off without first shutting Windows down, Windows will automatically run ScanDisk the next time the system starts, to examine the disk's files and folders for possible errors.

✦ ScanDisk will detect two types of errors: cross-linked files and lost file fragments.

✦ To store a file, the operating system allocates a cluster of disk space. A cluster is simply a set of consecutive sectors. Depending on the disk's size and file system, the number of sectors in a cluster will differ.

✦ The operating system stores a file's information within one or more clusters. The operating system keeps track of each file's clusters, using a special table called the file allocation table (FAT).

✦ When disk errors occur, the operating system may erroneously record information in the file allocation table, causing one file's clusters to appear lost or two files to appear to be sharing the same cluster.

✦ When ScanDisk encounters lost clusters (clusters in the file allocation table that the operating system has marked as "in use" but which do not correspond to a specific file), ScanDisk will create a root directory file named *file000n.chk,* such as *file0001.chk,* to which it assigns the lost clusters. In some cases, you can edit the file and recognize the lost data (such as information from a word-processing document). In most cases, however, the data will be meaningless and you will simply delete the file.

By default, when ScanDisk encounters cross-linked files (two files that appear to share the same cluster), ScanDisk will create two files so that each contains the data contained in the cross-linked clusters—the files will no longer be cross linked. One of the files will likely be correct and one will be incorrect. If both files are word-processing documents, for example, you can edit each file to determine which contains the correct content.

Understanding How Windows (and MS-DOS) Stores Files

When you format a disk, the format process divides the disk into circular regions called tracks. Next, the format process divides each track into fixed-length sectors (normally 512-byte sectors). When you store information on a disk, the disk drive magnetizes the data onto the sectors.

To improve performance and to make better use of disk space, most operating systems group multiple (consecutive) sectors into a unit of storage called a cluster. When the operating system later allocates space on the disk for a file, the operating system will allocate one cluster of disk space at a time. If the file is larger than one cluster, the operating system will allocate additional clusters to store the file's data.

Depending on your disk drive size and the file system you are using, the number of sectors the operating system assigns to each cluster will differ. To determine your disk's sector size and cluster size, you can run the *chkdsk* command or you can view the information within the ScanDisk results dialog box.

Remember that although the disk records information within sectors, the operating system tracks files using clusters (groups of sectors). The smallest unit of disk space that the operating system can allocate for storing a file is one cluster. If you create a file that contains only one byte of data, your disk's cluster size is 32,768 bytes (sixty-four 512-byte sectors), and 32,767 of the bytes within that cluster will be unused (and cannot be used to store other files).

Understanding How the Operating System Keeps Track of Each File's Clusters

When you store a file on disk, the file will reside, depending on its size, in one or more clusters. The operating system must keep track of which files on your disk reside in which clusters. Further, the operating system must track which clusters are available for use and which clusters are not usable due to a disk error in one of cluster's sectors (an error that prevents the disk drive from recording data in that sector).

To track clusters on a disk, the operating system uses a special table called the file allocation table (FAT). The operating system stores one or more copies of the file allocation table in specific locations near the start of each disk. In general, the file allocation table contains entries for every cluster on the disk. Using the file allocation table, the operating system essentially creates a chain of clusters that correspond to each file's data locations on disk.

Assume, for example, that a file resides on disk in clusters 100, 101, 103, and 107. As shown in Figure 43.1, within the file allocation table, the entry for cluster 100 would point to cluster 101. Likewise, the entry for cluster 101 would point to 103, which, in turn, would point to cluster 107. Because cluster 107 is the file's last cluster, the file allocation table would contain a special value that tells the operating system that it is the file's last cluster.

Entry	Next Cluster
⋮	⋮
100	101
101	103
102	Unused
103	107
104	Unused
105	Unused
106	Unused
107	Last
⋮	⋮

Figure 43.1 Tracking a file's clusters using the file allocation table.

To track a file's clusters using the file allocation table, the operating system must have a way to locate the file's first cluster. As it turns out, the file's directory entry, in addition to storing information such as the file's date and time stamps, size, and attributes, also tracks the file's starting cluster location.

Understanding File Allocation Table Errors

The operating system stores a disk's file allocation table on the corresponding disk. Each disk has its own file allocation table. Just as there may be times when a disk error may cause a drive to record a file's contents incorrectly, there may also be times when a disk error introduces an error into the file allocation table itself. Normally, such errors occur when the user turns off a PC without first shutting down Windows. The two most common file allocation table errors are cross-linked files and lost clusters.

As you have learned, the operating system locates a file's clusters by traversing a chain of cluster entries within the file allocation table. Cross-linked files occur when the operating system believes that two files use one or more of the same clusters. For example, assume file A uses clusters 101, 102, and 103 and that file B uses clusters 104, 105, and 106. Figure 43.2 shows the corresponding file allocation table entries.

Entry	Next Cluster
⋮	⋮
101	102
102	103
103	Last
104	105
105	106
106	Last
⋮	⋮

Figure 43.2 Tracking two file's clusters within the file allocation table.

Next, assume that because of an error during a disk operation, the operating system assigns entry 104 in the file allocation table to point to cluster 102 (instead of to 105). At that time, the operating system would believe that file A consists of clusters 101, 102, and 103 and that file B consists of clusters 104, 102, and 103. In other words, the files are cross-linked on cluster 102.

Because of the cross link, clusters 105 and 106 no longer correspond to a file. Users refer to such clusters as "lost clusters."

As discussed, if ScanDisk encounters cross-linked files, it will change the files so that each contains a copy of the data that resides in the clusters that were previously cross linked. Depending on the file's contents or purpose, you may then be able to edit or view each file's contents to determine which file contains the correct data. If ScanDisk encounters lost clusters, it will create a file for each lost cluster chain that it encounters. ScanDisk will place the files in the disk's root directory with the *.chk* extension. Using the ScanDisk Advanced Options dialog box, you can change these actions so that ScanDisk deletes or ignores files with cross-linked clusters and you can direct ScanDisk to delete lost clusters.

Analyzing the Surface of Your Disk

To store data, a disk drive magnetizes the data onto the surface of the disk. Although disk-surface errors have become quite rare, it is possible for locations on the disk's surface to become damaged, which prevents those sectors from successfully recording data. Using ScanDisk's Thorough test, you can direct ScanDisk to analyze each storage location on the surface of your disk. To perform its surface analysis, ScanDisk will read and write the data to each location on the disk (ScanDisk can perform this operation without damaging any data stored on your disk). Depending on the size of your disk, it may take ScanDisk several hours to complete its surface analysis.

Running the ScanDisk Utility

Before you run the ScanDisk utility, you should end and close all other programs that you have running. To perform its processing, ScanDisk makes extensive use of the file allocation table. Should a program create or change a file on disk, the operating system will change the file allocation table to reflect the new file's disk location. Each time the file allocation table changes, the ScanDisk program must restart. If you have other programs running when you run ScanDisk, it is possible that ScanDisk may not complete its processing.

To run the ScanDisk utility within Windows 98, select the Start menu Programs option and choose Accessories. Windows, in turn, will display the Accessories submenu. Within the Accessories submenu, select System Tools and choose ScanDisk. Windows, in turn, will display the ScanDisk window, as shown in Figure 43.3.

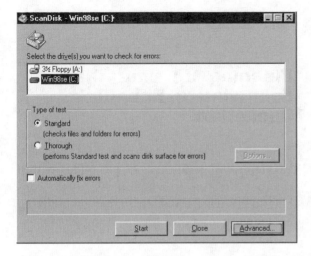

Figure 43.3 Selecting the drive you want ScanDisk to examine.

Within the ScanDisk window, select the disk drive you want to examine and the type of test (Standard or Thorough) that you want to run. Click Start to begin the operation. Normally, ScanDisk will display a screen similar to that shown in Figure 43.4, which tells you it did not encounter any errors. If ScanDisk encounters lost clusters, cross-linked files, or a damaged area on the surface of your disk, ScanDisk will display a dialog box asking you to specify how you want it to proceed.

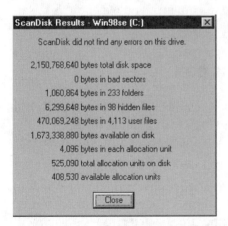

Figure 43.4 Displaying a successful ScanDisk operation dialog box.

To examine a disk within Windows 2000, perform the following steps:

1. Within the Windows Desktop, double-click on the My Computer icon. Windows will open the My Computer window.

2. Within the My Computer window, right-click on the drive you want to examine. Windows will display a pop-up menu.

3. Within the pop-up menu, select Properties. Windows will display the Properties dialog box.

4. Within the Properties dialog box, select the Tools tab. Windows will display the Tools sheet.

5. Within the Tools sheet, click the Check Now button. Windows will display the Check Disk dialog box as shown in Figure 43.5.

6. Within the Check Disk dialog box, select the options you desire and choose Start.

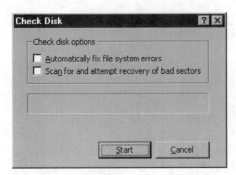

Figure 43.5 Displaying the Check Disk dialog box within Windows 2000.

Cleaning Up Your Disk Following a ScanDisk Operation

If ScanDisk encounters chains of lost clusters, ScanDisk will create one or more files within the root directory to which it assigns the contents that correspond to the lost chains. Should ScanDisk report that it has encountered such errors, you should examine your disk's root directory for files with the *.chk* extension, such as *file0001.chk*.

Normally, you will simply delete the files. Because the lost cluster chains will occur in the middle of a file, the information in the file that ScanDisk creates will usually be meaningless. If, however, you are able to recognize data (the file may, for example, contain text that you recognize from a word-processing document), you may be able to salvage part of your work.

Automating the ScanDisk Process

In general, you should run the ScanDisk utility on a regular basis (ideally weekly). If your disk has no errors, ScanDisk can complete its processing quite quickly. On the other hand, if ScanDisk encounters errors, you may want to make sure you have current backup copies of your key files.

In Lesson 19, "Automating Key Tasks Using the Task Scheduler," you learned how to schedule key tasks to run automatically at predefined times. Using the Task Scheduler, you may want to schedule ScanDisk to run at specific times when a user's system will not be in use, such as 6:00 PM on Friday night. By taking advantage of the Task Scheduler, you can ensure that your users run ScanDisk on a regular basis.

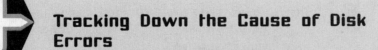

Tracking Down the Cause of Disk Errors

In general, disk failures have become quite rare. Should a user encounter errors on a regular basis while running ScanDisk, you should look for the cause of the error. Normally, disk errors occur when the user turns off the PC without first shutting down Windows. If the user is not doing this, you should examine the PC's source of power, to ensure the PC is not restarting on its own due to a periodic loss of power. Next, you should examine the PC's environment. If the PC is in a dust- or smoke-filled office, particles may have gotten into the disk drive. Also, you should make sure that the PC is not getting too hot or too cold. Finally, you should make sure that the user is not moving the PC (even a small distance) while it is powered on.

EXAM REVIEW

CERTIFICATION

① The disk formatting process first divides a disk's surface into concentric circles called _____, which it further divides into fixed-length areas called _____.

② True or False
The operating system allocates disk space in terms of sectors.

③ True or False
A one-byte file consumes only one byte of disk space.

④ The operating system tracks a file's storage locations using a special table users refer to as the FAT. The acronym FAT stands for _____.

⑤ The two most common errors the ScanDisk utility encounters are _____ and _____.

⑥ True or False
When the ScanDisk utility reports errors, the disk drive is probably bad and you should replace it.

⑦ True or False
One of the most common causes of disk errors is users turning off their PCs without first shutting down Windows.

⑧ True or False
It is not necessary to shut down a PC if you are only moving it a few feet.

Recovering Disk Space Using the Disk Cleanup Utility

I still remember when I questioned how I would ever fill the 5MB hard drive in my IBM PC/XT. Ok, so times have changed. Back then, I didn't download graphics files and MP3 files from the World Wide Web. Likewise, other users did not send e-mail messages to me that contained 1MB attachments.

So, despite the fact that very large gigabyte hard drives are now available, users still find a way to somehow fill them. As the amount of available disk space on a user's disk drive decreases, so too will the PC's system performance. That is because more files mean a greater chance of disk fragmentation, less disk space for Windows to use for swapping programs in and out of RAM, and less disk space for programs to use to create temporary files. Fortunately, using the Windows Disk Cleanup utility, you can often quickly recover space on a user's disk.

F A C T S

+ As users "surf" the Web, their browser creates temporary files on the user's disk to "cache" the contents of the sites visited. Should they later revisit the site, the browser can quickly retrieve the site's HTML and graphics files from the user's local disk as opposed to having to again download the files from across the Web. The contents of the cached files can consume considerable space on the user's disk.

+ When a user deletes a file, Windows does not actually remove the file from the user's disk. Instead, Windows moves the file into a special folder called the Recycle Bin. Should the user later want to "undelete" the file, it can be restored from the Recycle Bin folder to the file's original location. Therefore, until the user discards the contents of the Recycle Bin, the file will continue to consume space on the disk.

+ As many Windows-based programs perform their processing, the programs will create one or more temporary files on the user's disk. Normally, after the program completes its processing, it will delete these files. In some cases, however, perhaps due to a power loss or program error, the program will not delete the temporary files. Over time, such temporary files can consume considerable disk space.

+ Depending on the amount of space a user's disk contains, you may need to remove program files from the disk that correspond to applications the user no longer runs.

+ Windows and Windows applications normally store temporary files within the Windows\Temp folder (Winnt\Temp under Windows 2000). If a user is running low on disk space, you may be able to recover disk space by removing temporary files that applications failed to delete from the temporary folder.

+ The Windows Disk Cleanup utility makes it easy for you to quickly delete files contained in the user's Recycle Bin, files for Web sites the user's browser may have cached on the user's hard disk, and other temporary files.

Running the Windows Disk Cleanup Utility

To run the Windows Disk Cleanup utility, perform these steps:

1. Select the Start menu Programs option and choose Accessories. Windows will display the Accessories submenu.

2. Within the Accessories submenu, select the System Tools option and choose Disk Cleanup. Windows will open the Select Drive window.

3. Within the Select Drive window, choose the disk drive you desire and then select OK. Windows will display the Disk Cleanup window, as shown in Figure 44.1, that lets you choose the files you want to discard. It also displays a summary of the amount of disk space you will recover by discarding the files.

4. Within the Disk Cleanup window, place a checkmark in the checkboxes that correspond to the files you want to delete and then choose OK. The Disk Cleanup utility will delete the corresponding files.

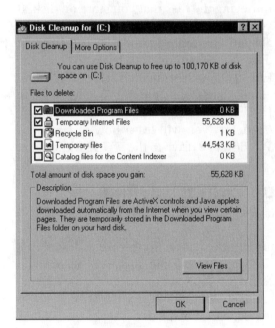

Figure 44.1 Selecting files for deletion within the Disk Cleanup window.

NOTE: *If you click on the a category within the Disk Cleanup window, such as Downloaded Program Files, the Disk Cleanup utility will display a message that describes the types of files that correspond to the entry. In the case of Downloaded Program Files, the utility will explain that the files correspond to ActiveX objects and Java applets the browser downloaded to let you view specific pages on the Internet.*

Using Disk Cleanup to Remove Unused Programs

After you remove temporary files and empty the Recycle Bin, if the user's disk is still running low on space, you may be able to free up additional space by removing program files that correspond to applications the user does not use. In Lesson 5, "Installing, Removing, and Troubleshooting Program Files," you learned how to use the Control Panel's Add/Remove Programs utility to remove program files from a user's disk. Within the Disk Cleanup utility, you can select the More Options tag to display a sheet that contains buttons, as shown in Figure 44.2, from which you can access the Add/Remove Programs dialog box.

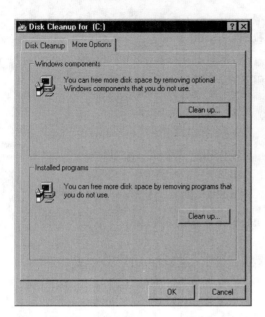

Figure 44.2 Freeing up disk space by removing unused programs.

Using Disk Cleanup to Select the FAT32 File System

Within an operating system, the file system is the software responsible for storing and retrieving the files that you store on disk. If you are using Windows 98, you may be able to free up additional space on your disk by directing Windows to use the FAT32 file system, which stores files more efficiently than the older FAT16 file system. In Lesson 45, "Increasing a Disk's Storage Capacity," you will learn how to convert a Windows 98 drive to the FAT32 file system.

Directing the Disk Cleanup Utility to Run Automatically

In general, users should use the Disk Cleanup utility to clean up their disk drives on a regular basis. In Lesson 19, "Automating Key Tasks Using the Task Scheduler," you learned how to direct Windows to automatically run programs at specific times. Using the Task Scheduler, you might, for example, direct Windows to run the Disk Cleanup utility every Friday evening, after the user leaves work for the day.

In addition to scheduling the Disk Cleanup utility to run at specific intervals, if you are using Windows 98, you can direct the program to run automatically each time the disk becomes low on space. To direct the Disk Utility to run automatically, select the Settings tag. The Disk Cleanup utility, in turn, will display the Settings sheet as shown in Figure 44.3 that you can use to direct the program to automatically run when disk space becomes low.

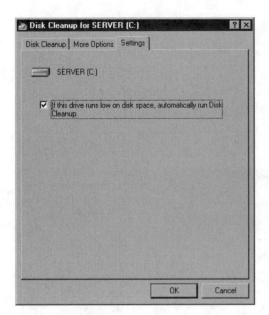

One of the biggest consumers of disk space is e-mail. Each time a user sends an e-mail message, most e-mail programs save a copy of the e-mail message in the Sent Items folder. Likewise, each time a user deletes an e-mail message, most e-mail programs do not remove the message, but rather, the programs move the message into the Deleted Items folder. Further, many users keep copies of e-mail messages that contain large file attachments (such as photos or large documents). If a user is running low on disk space, you should teach the user how to clean up the e-mail folders. For example, if a user deletes messages that appear in the Deleted Items folder, the e-mail program will discard the messages and will free up disk space the messages previously consumed.

Removing Unused Temporary Files

Within the Windows environment, many programs create temporary files. When you complete an operation (or end the program), the program will normally delete the temporary files. Periodically, due to a program error or possibly a power outage, the program will fail to remove its temporary files. Over time, the temporary files can accumulate and can consume considerable disk space.

To remove the unused temporary files from your disk, perform these steps:

1. Within Windows, close any applications you are currently running.

2. Next, start the Windows Explorer and select the Temp subfolder within the Windows (or Winnt folder for Windows 2000) folder. Explorer will display the temporary files that reside on your disk as shown in Figure 44.4.

3. Using the Windows Explorer, select and delete the temporary files.

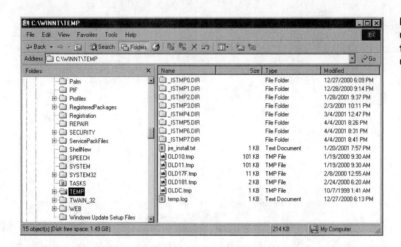

Figure 44.4 Deleting unused temporary files from your disk to free up disk space.

Increasing a Disk's Storage Capacity

In Lesson 44, "Recovering Disk Space Using the Disk Cleanup Utility," you learned how to free up space on disk that was consumed by temporary files, Internet files, and deleted files that remain in the Windows Recycle Bin. In this lesson, you will learn ways you can use disk and file compression to increase a disk's storage capacity.

The advantage of using compression is that you can squeeze more information onto an existing disk. The disadvantage of compression is that before Windows can access (read or write) a compressed file, Windows must first decompress the file, which introduces overhead that will slow your system performance.

Depending on the Windows version you are running, the steps you must perform to compress data on a disk will differ. Windows 9x, for example, provides software you can use to compress the entire disk. Under Windows 2000, you can compress a disk or compress specific files or folders.

F A C T S

- Within an operating system, special software called the file system stores and retrieves the information that you place within a file on disk.

- Windows 98 supports the FAT16 and FAT32 file systems. The FAT32 file system stores information more efficiently than the FAT16 file system. If a system is using the FAT16 file system, you can free up considerable space on the disk by simply converting the PC to the FAT32 file system.

- To convert a Windows 98 disk from the FAT16 to FAT32 file system, you use the Drive Converter (FAT32) utility.

- Windows 2000 supports the FAT32 and NTFS file systems. The NTFS file system extends the capabilities of the FAT32 system by providing better security, compression, and support for larger disk drives.

- Within Windows 9x, you can compress a FAT16 disk's contents by running the DriveSpace utility. You cannot use DriveSpace to compress a disk using the FAT32 file system.

- When you use DriveSpace to compress a drive's contents, Windows will create an uncompressed drive (which normally receives the drive letter H), that Windows uses to boot your system. After Windows starts, Windows will load special software that makes the compressed drive appear as drive C.

- Behind the scenes, the compressed drive is simply a large file that contains all the data the disk contains in a compressed format. Each time you access a file, special software running within Windows locates the file's contents within the large compressed file and then decompresses the contents.

- When you create a new file, the software simply allocates space for the new file within the large compressed file and then compresses the new file's contents, storing the data in the large compressed file. Users, however, are unaware of the large compressed file and the compression and decompression operations. Users simply perform normal file operations.

- Within Windows 2000, you can compress a disk drive, a file, or a folder that contains files and subfolders.

- To compress a disk, file, or folder, you simply right-click on the item within the Windows Explorer and then select the Properties option that directs Windows to display the Properties dialog box that you can use to compress the item. When you compress a disk within Windows 2000, Windows will not create the second uncompressed disk drive or the large compressed file (as was the case in Windows 9x). Instead, Windows 2000 will simply compress the drive's contents.

Converting a Windows 98 Disk from FAT16 to FAT32

Within an operating system, special software called the file system oversees the process of storing and retrieving files on disk. The file system is also responsible for managing the file folders you create. In Lesson 42, "Understanding How Disks Store Information," you learned that to track locations for each file on disk, the file system uses a table called the file allocation table (FAT).

Windows 98 supports two file systems, FAT16 and FAT32, whose names correspond to the number of bits the file allocation table uses to track the clusters on disk. The FAT16 file system uses 16-bit entries within the file allocation table, whereas the FAT32 file system uses 32-bit entries.

The FAT32 file system stores data more efficiently than the FAT16 system. By converting a disk that is using the FAT16 file system to FAT32, you can increase a disk's storage capacity.

To determine which file system a Windows 98 system is running, perform these steps:

1. Using the Windows Explorer right-click on the disk drive you desire. Windows will display a pop-up menu.

2. Within the pop-up menu, select the Properties option. Windows will display the drive's Properties dialog box that specifies the file system the drive is using, as shown in Figure 45.1.

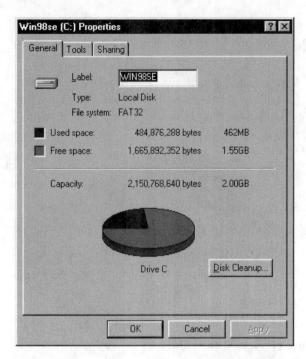

Figure 45.1 Displaying a drive's current file system.

To convert a Windows 98 system that is using the FAT16 file system to FAT32, perform these steps:

1. Select the Start menu Programs option and choose Accessories. Windows will display the Accessories submenu.

2. Within the Accessories submenu, select the System Tools option and choose Drive Converter (FAT32) entry.

3. Windows will start the Drive Converter Wizard, which will walk you through the steps you must perform to convert the disk's file system.

Converting a Windows 2000 File System to NTFS

Windows 2000 supports the FAT32 and the NTFS file systems. The NTFS file system improves upon FAT32 by providing better security, compression, and support for larger disk drives. You can select the file system you desire when you install Windows 2000 and when you format a disk.

To convert a FAT32 file system to NTFS, you must run the convert command from the system prompt. The following command, for example, directs Windows 2000 to convert drive C to the NTFS file system:

```
C:\> convert  C:  /fs:ntfs  <Enter>
```

Using DriveSpace to Compress a Windows 98 FAT16 Disk

If your disk uses the FAT16 file system within Windows 98, you can use the DriveSpace command to compress the disk's contents. You cannot use DriveSpace to compress a disk using the FAT32 file system.

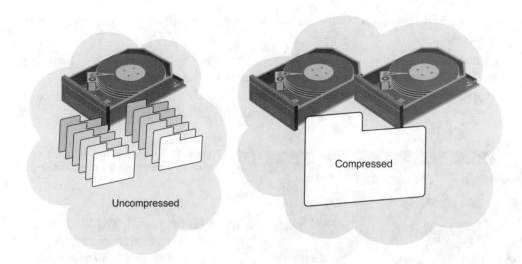

Uncompressed

Compressed

When you compress a Windows 98 disk using the DriveSpace utility, Widows will combine all the files on the disk into one large compressed file. As you create, store, and retrieve files, Windows will place, update, and retrieve the files from within the large compressed file.

If you use the Windows Explorer to view your disk drives, you will find that after you compress your hard drive, your system will show a new disk drive, which normally uses the drive letter H. When DriveSpace compresses a drive, DriveSpace renames the drive as drive H. Then, DriveSpace places the large compressed file (that contains your disk's contents) onto drive H.

Behind the scenes, Windows will map your file and disk operations that correspond to drive C (or the drive you compressed) to the large compressed file. In other words, you do not really have a compressed drive that corresponds to the drive letter C, but rather, Windows creates the illusion that the drive exists. Every time you perform a file or disk operation on drive C, Windows maps the operation to the large compressed file it has stored on drive H.

To compress a FAT16 disk using the Windows 98 DriveSpace utility, perform these steps:

1. Select the Start menu Programs option and choose Accessories. Windows will display the Accessories submenu.

2. Within the Accessories submenu, select System Tools and choose DriveSpace. Windows will display the DriveSpace window that you can use to select the drive you want to compress.

3. Within the DriveSpace window, click on the drive you desire and then select the File menu Compress option. DriveSpace, in turn, will display a dialog box as

shown in Figure 45.2 that summarizes the amount of disk space you will gain by compressing the drive.

4. Within the dialog box, select the Compress Now button. DriveSpace, in turn, will run the ScanDisk program to verify that the disk does not contain any errors. Then, DriveSpace will compress the disk's contents. After DriveSpace completes the compression, it will display a dialog box that summarizes the operation.

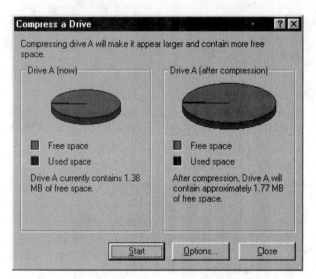

Figure 45.2 Viewing the amount of space you can gain by compressing a FAT16 disk.

NOTE: *Because the FAT32 file system stores information more efficiently on disk than does FAT16, most users will choose to regain disk space by converting a FAT16-based disk to FAT32. Although you cannot compress a FAT32-based disk using DriveSpace, you will also not incur the overhead introduced by compressing and decompressing files.*

Compressing Files, Folders, and Drives Under NTFS

Within Windows 2000, the NTFS file system lets you compress a file, folder, or an entire disk drive. To compress a file or folder using NTFS, perform these steps:

1. Within the Windows Explorer, right-click on the file or folder you desire. Windows will display a pop-up menu.

2. Within the pop-up menu, select Properties. Windows will display the item's Properties dialog box.

3. Within the Properties dialog box, click the Advanced button. Windows will display the Advanced Attributes dialog box, as shown in Figure 45.3.

4. Within the Advanced Attributes dialog box, place a checkmark within the Compress contents to save disk space checkbox and then choose OK.

Figure 45.3 Using the Advanced Attributes dialog box to compress a file or folder.

Should you want to uncompress the file or folder in the future, perform the same steps but remove the checkmark from the checkbox.

To compress a drive using NTFS, perform these steps:

1. Within the Windows Explorer, right-click on the drive you desire. Windows will display a pop-up menu.

2. Within the pop-up menu, select Properties. Windows will display the drive's Properties dialog box, as shown in Figure 45.4.

3. Within the Properties dialog box, place a checkmark within the Compress drive to save disk space checkbox and then choose OK.

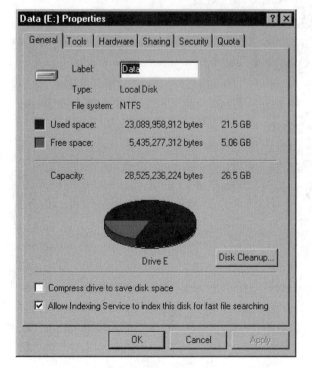

Figure 45.4 Using the Properties dialog box to compress a disk drive.

EXAM REVIEW

① True or False
Compressing a disk drive not only provides additional storage space on the drive, but it also increases system performance.

② Within the operating system, special software called the _____ oversees the files and folders you place on a disk.

③ To track the disk locations where a file resides on disk, the file system uses a special table called the _____ or _____.

④ Within the FAT16 and FAT32 file systems, the numbers 16 and 32 represent _____.

⑤ True for False
Because the FAT16 file system uses smaller entries in the file allocation table than the FAT32 file system, the FAT16 file system stores information on disk more efficiently.

⑥ Within Windows 98, you can use the _____ program to convert a FAT16 file system to FAT32.

⑦ True or False
Using the DriveSpace utility, you can compress FAT16- and FAT32-based drives under Windows 98 to increase the disk's storage capacity.

⑧ Within Windows 2000, the NTFS file system improves upon FAT32 by adding support for _____, _____, and _____.

⑨ To convert a disk using FAT32 to NTFS, you use the _____ command-line utility.

⑩ True or False
To compress a file using NTFS, you use the FileComp command-line utility.

Lesson 46

Replacing or Adding a Disk Drive

Several of the previous lessons have examined key disk operations in detail. Because a disk drive is a mechanical device (a device with moving parts), the drive may eventually fail and you will need to replace it. More likely, however, is that you will want to add a faster or higher-capacity disk to your system.

This lesson examines the steps you must perform to install a floppy, Zip, hard, or CD/DVD drive. As you will learn, the steps for installing each drive type are quite similar. In general, the only factor that will differ is the controller to which you attach the device, that lets the device and motherboard interact.

F A C T S

+ The steps to install a floppy, hard drive, or CD-ROM/DVD drive are quite similar.

+ If you are installing an internal drive, you will place the drive into one of the system unit's drive bays. Many systems hold it in place using drive rails within the drive bay onto which you slide the drive. If a drive bay does not contain drive rails, you must purchase and install the rails before you can secure a drive in place. Some drive bays provide mounting holes in a plate that you can use to secure the drive.

+ A Zip drive provides users with the ability to use removable disks that hold over 100MB.

+ Depending on the Zip drive's type, the drive will connect to a USB, SCSI, or bi-directional parallel port.

+ Floppy drives connect to the motherboard using a ribbon cable. The cable will contain two connectors, one that corresponds to drive A and one to drive B.

+ Hard drives can be internal or external devices. External hard drives normally connect to SCSI adapters; however, FireWire-based drives exist. An internal hard drive will normally connect to either a SCSI adapter or IDE cable.

+ IDE is an acronym for integrated drive electronics. An IDE drive contains a built-in controller that lets the device interact with the motherboard.

+ IDE drives connect to the motherboard using an IDE cable. Most IDE cables provide connectors for two devices.

+ When you connect two devices to an IDE cable, you must select one device to serve as the bus master and one as the bus slave. The bus master device determines when each device can use the cable to send and receive data.

+ CD-ROM/DVD drives can be internal or external devices. External drives normally connect to a SCSI or FireWire adapter. Internal drives normally connect to a SCSI or IDE cable.

Installing a Zip Drive

A Zip drive uses removable disks that look similar to a large floppy disk. That said, you cannot use a floppy disk within a Zip drive or vice versa. The removable Zip disk can store over 100MB of data, which makes the disk well suited for exchanging or backing up large files.

Although some PC manufacturers now ship systems with built-in Zip drives, most Zip drives are external devices. Depending on the drive's type, you may connect the drive to a USB port, bi-directional parallel port, IDE cable, or a SCSI adapter. An external Zip drive requires that you connect the drive to a power outlet. An internal Zip drive will use one of the power supply's power cables.

Before your system can access the Zip drive, you must install a device driver that lets Windows interact with the drive.

Installing a Floppy Drive

If you are using a notebook PC, you may have an external floppy drive that connects to a special port or PCMCIA card. Or, your PC may require that you swap the CD-ROM and floppy drives as your needs require.

Within a desktop PC, you will insert a floppy disk into one of the system unit's drive bays. Depending on your system unit type, the drive bays may or may not contain drive  rails onto which you slide the drive to hold it in place. If your system unit does not have drive rails, you may need to purchase and install the rails before you can install the drive.

After you secure the floppy drive in place, you must connect one of the power supply's power cables to the drive. Then, you must attach the ribbon cable that will connect the drive to the motherboard. Most older PCs were designed to support two floppy drives, drives A and B. The ribbon cable within such drives will contain two connectors. Depending on the connector to which you attach the drive, the drive will become either drive A or drive B. Often, the cable will label each connector with the corresponding drive letter.

Normally, after you restart your system, the PC will immediately recognize the newly installed drive. In some cases, however, you may need to specify the drive's type (such as a 1.44MB drive) within the CMOS Setup program, as shown in Figure 46.1.

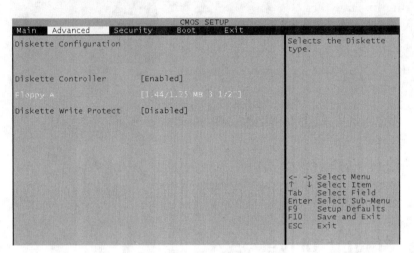

```
                        CMOS SETUP
 Main   Advanced    Security     Boot      Exit
Diskette Configuration                              Selects the Diskette
                                                    type.

Diskette Controller      [Enabled]

Floppy A                 [1.44/1.25 MB 3 1/2"]

Diskette Write Protect   [Disabled]




                                                  <- -> Select Menu
                                                   ↑  ↓ Select Item
                                                  Tab   Select Field
                                                  Enter Select Sub-Menu
                                                  F9    Setup Defaults
                                                  F10   Save and Exit
                                                  ESC   Exit
```

Figure 46.1 Some PCs will require that you specify floppy drive settings within the CMOS Setup program.

Installing a Hard Drive

Depending on your needs, you can purchase either an internal or external hard drive. Most external hard drives connect to a SCSI adapter within the PC; however, some newer drives support a FireWire interface. If you are installing an external drive, you will need to connect the drive to a power outlet.

Depending on the drive's type, an internal hard drive can connect to a SCSI or IDE controller. Again, before you can install an internal drive, your system unit's drive bays normally must contain drive rails.

IDE is an acronym for integrated drive electronics. IDE drives are so named because the drive itself contains the controller electronics which are used by the motherboard to interact with the drive. Years ago, hard drives required a separate disk controller which often resided on a card within one of the PC's expansion slots.

Using an IDE cable, you connect the drive to the motherboard. Most IDE cables provide connectors for two drives. To prevent both drives from trying to use the cable at the same time, one of the drives must serve as the "bus master" and one as the "bus slave." The bus master device will determine when each device can use the cable. Normally, you assign the master and slave settings using jumpers or cables that appear on the drive itself.

An internal SCSI drive will normally use a SCSI cable to connect to a special port on the SCSI adapter card. As discussed in Lesson 30, "Connecting Devices to a SCSI Adapter," you must assign a unique SCSI address to each device you connect to the SCSI device chain.

After you connect the drive to a SCSI or IDE bus, you must attach one of the power supply's power cables to the drive.

Normally, when you install an IDE drive, your system will not see the device, and you will need to configure the device within the CMOS Setup program.

Then, you must partition and format the drive for use by Windows.

Installing a CD-ROM or DVD Drive

As was the case with a hard drive, you can install an internal or external CD-ROM or DVD drive. Most external devices will connect to a SCSI adapter; however, FireWire-based devices do exist. An external drive will require that you connect the drive to a power outlet.

Normally, internal CD-ROM and DVD drives will connect to an IDE or SCSI adapter. Before you can install an internal drive, your drive bays must contain drive rails. The steps you must perform to attach a drive to either a SCSI or IDE bus are identical to those for a disk drive. Finally, you must connect one of the power supply's cables to the drive.

After you restart your system, you must install a device driver that Windows will use to interact with the device.

NOTE: *The steps you must perform to install a CD burner are identical to those presented here for a standard CD-ROM drive.*

EXAM REVIEW

① **Depending on the drive's type, a Zip drive may connect to a (select all that apply):**

☐ Bi-directional parallel port
☐ Universal serial bus
☐ SCSI adapter
☐ IDE cable connector

② **True or False**
The SCSI device chain will provide power to an external hard drive or CD-ROM drive.

③ **If your system has only one floppy drive and that drive appears to the system as drive B, what should you do to make the drive appear as drive A?**

④ **IDE is an acronym for _____.**

⑤ **If you connect two devices to an IDE cable, you must use switches on the devices to assign one device to serve as the _____ and one device to serve as the _____.**

⑥ **True or False**
In some cases, different PCs may require that you configure a drive within the CMOS Setup program before the system will recognize the device.

Improving Disk Performance by Defragmenting File Clusters

Within an operating system, special software called the file system oversees each file and folder you create on your disk. The file system stores each file's contents within one or more clusters (a group of consecutive disk sectors). To read a file's contents, the file system directs the disk drive to read the corresponding clusters from the drive. If the file's clusters reside in consecutive cluster locations, the drive can read the file's contents quickly. However, if the file's clusters are dispersed across the disk, the drive will take longer to read the file because it must wait for subsequent clusters to spin past the drive's read/write head or for the drive to move its read/write head from one track to another—a mechanical process which requires considerable time compared to the PC's fast electronic operations.

Unfortunately, files become fragmented through common operations as you create and later increase a file's size by adding more content. When many files on a disk become fragmented, the system's performance can suffer significantly.

This lesson examines the Windows Disk Defragmenter utility that you can run to eliminate file fragmentation. The Disk Defragmenter utility moves file clusters as necessary to place each file's clusters in consecutive locations on disk.

F A C T S

+ When a file resides on disk in consecutive sector locations, the disk drive can quickly retrieve the file's contents.

+ When a file's contents are dispersed (fragmented) across a disk, the disk drive requires more time to access the file, which decreases system performance.

+ Often, when many files on a disk become fragmented, you can actually hear the disk drive perform its operations (because the disk drive must move its read/write head in and out from one track to another).

+ File fragmentation occurs as a result of normal file operations. You cannot prevent file fragmentation; you can simply correct the fragmentation after it occurs.

+ Within Windows, you can run the Disk Defragmenter program to correct fragmented files. The utility moves file clusters on the disk so that each file's clusters reside in consecutive locations.

Reviewing How Disk Drives Read and Write Information

As you learned in Lesson 42, "Understanding How Disks Store Information," to store information, a disk drive records data in storage locations on the disk's surface, called *sectors*. The sectors reside within tracks on the disk surface that you can visualize as concentric circles. Normally, a sector stores 512 bytes.

To retrieve or write information within a sector, the disk drive contains special electronics in its read/write head that can read the information recorded (magnetized) in the sector or write (record) new information. Within the disk drive, the disk spins past the read/write head very quickly (from 3,600 to over 10,000 revolutions per minute (RPM) or more, depending on your disk drive type). To access a specific sector, the disk drive will move the read/write head in and out, to different tracks, as shown in Figure 47.1.

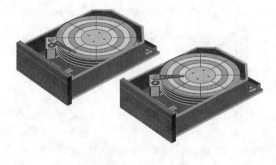

Figure 47.1 Moving the read/write head between tracks on the disk drive.

Because spinning the disk platters and moving the disk's read/write head between tracks requires mechanical operations (movement), the disk drive is much slower than the PC's electronic components. As a general rule, by decreasing the number disk operations your disk drive must perform, you will improve system performance.

Reading a Simple File

Assume, for example, that your disk contains a file named A+ Exam Review that resides in four consecutive sector locations on your disk, as shown in Figure 47.2. Users often refer to files whose data reside in consecutive sectors as *contiguous files*.

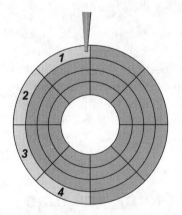

Figure 47.2 Residing in four consecutive sectors on a disk, this is called a contiguous file.

To read the file's contents, your disk drive will first locate the file's starting sector. The disk drive will then move its read/write head to the sector's track. As the sector spins past the read/write head, the drive can read the sector's contents. Then, because the file's contents reside in consecutive sectors, the drive can immediately begin reading the second sector, without having to first move its read/write head or wait for the sector to spin past. The disk drive, in this case, can read each of the file's four sectors very quickly.

Understanding How Fragmented Files Decrease System Performance

As just discussed, a disk drive can quickly read the contents of a contiguous file because the drive does not have to perform additional mechanical operations (such as moving the read/write head from one track to another or waiting for a subsequent sector to spin past the read/write head). In contrast, a fragmented file resides in sector locations dispersed across the disk. Assume, for example, that the file *NetworkExam.doc* just resides in four sectors that are dispersed across your disk, as shown in Figure 47.3. In other words, the file is fragmented.

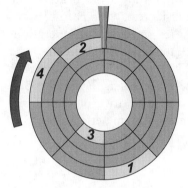

Figure 47.3 Showing fragmented files that reside in storage locations dispersed across a disk.

As before, to read the file's contents, the disk drive must first locate the file's starting sector. After reading the first sector, the disk drive must wait (over half a revolution) for the second sector to spin past the read/write head.

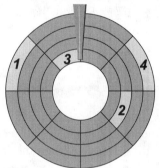

Next, to read the third sector, the disk drive must first move the read/write head to the correct track, then wait for that sector to spin past the head. Finally, to read the last sector, the disk drive must again move the read/write head, then wait for the sector to spin past.

To read the fragmented file, the disk drive had to repeatedly wait for the sector to spin past the read/write head. Such rotational delays add up, increasing the amount of time it takes to read a file that, in turn, decreases your system performance. An easy way to improve system performance is to reduce the number of slow disk operations your computer must perform. Correcting fragmented files does just that.

You Cannot Prevent Fragmented Files, You Can Only Correct Fragmentation After It Occurs

Fragmented files decrease your system performance by increasing the number of slow mechanical operations the disk drive must perform in order to access the file's contents. Unfortunately, files become fragmented naturally as you create, edit, and delete them. In other words, file fragmentation occurs as a result of normal operations. You cannot prevent files from becoming fragmented. Instead, you simply correct (eliminate) the fragmentation after it occurs.

Assume, for example, that you create the file *ExamNotes.doc*. When you save the file to disk, your disk drive records the information within a disk sector. Next, assume that you close the file and open a second file named *Resume.doc,* and begin typing your resume. After you save that file, your disk drive will store the file's contents into a sector on your disk, as shown in Figure 47.4.

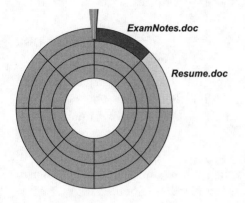

ExamNotes.doc

Resume.doc

Figure 47.4 Storing two files in two sectors on a disk.

Finally, assume that you resume entering A+ Exam notes into the file *ExamNotes.doc*. Because you have added content, the file now requires two disk sectors. Unfortunately, as shown in Figure 47.5, because the sectors that contain the file are not consecutive, the file has become fragmented. In this case, by simply creating and editing two files (by performing common file operations), the files on your disk became fragmented.

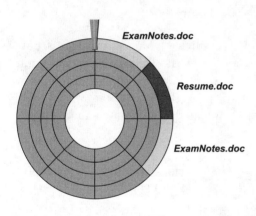

ExamNotes.doc

Resume.doc

ExamNotes.doc

Figure 47.5 Performing normal file operations results in file fragmentation.

Detecting Fragmented Files

Fragmented files decrease your system performance by increasing the amount of time it takes the disk drive to read the file on your disk. As you have learned, you cannot prevent file fragmentation. You can only correct the fragmentation after it occurs. Common symptoms that files on your disk may be fragmented include:

- Files or documents take longer to load.
- You can hear the disk drive as it reads and writes files on your disk (you actually hear the drive move its read/write head).

Correcting Fragmented Files

To correct fragmented files, you must run a special utility program that moves the data stored on your disk so that each file's sectors reside in consecutive storage locations. By defragmenting files, you do not free up additional disk space. Instead, you simply make better use of the disk space that has already been consumed. Within Windows, you can defragment your disk using the Disk Defragmenter program by performing these steps:

1. Select the Start menu Programs option and choose Accessories. Windows, in turn, will display the Accessories menu.

2. Within the Accessories menu, select the System Tools menu and choose Disk Defragmenter. Windows will display the Select Drive dialog box.

3. Within the Select Drive dialog box, use the Drives pull-down list to select the drive letter of the disk you want to defragment, and then select OK. The Disk Defragmenter program may display a dialog box that tells you how much of your disk is fragmented.

4. Within the dialog box, select Start. The Disk Defragmenter program, in turn, will begin defragmenting your disk, displaying a dialog box similar to that shown in Figure 47.6 that tells you how much of the disk it has defragmented.

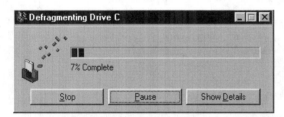

Figure 47.6 Viewing the Disk Defragmenter status information.

If you click on the Show Details button, the Disk Defragmenter program will display a screen similar to that shown in Figure 47.7 that lets you watch the program's processing. In other words, you can actually watch the program move data from one location on your disk to another.

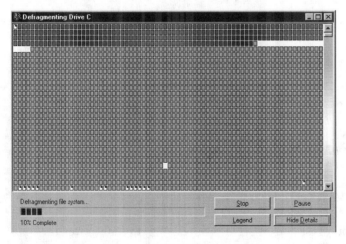

Figure 47.7 Viewing the Disk Defragmenter's processing.

Depending on the number of files your disk contains, defragmenting your disk can take a considerable amount of time. Often, users automate the process by directing Windows to run the Disk Defragmentation program at specific times. Lesson 19, "Automating Tasks on a User's System," discusses the steps you can perform under Windows 98 to automatically run Disk Defragmenter on a regular basis.

CERTIFICATION

1. When a file's data resides in sectors dispersed across a disk, users state that the file has become _____.

2. True or False
File fragmentation can be prevented by closely monitoring user operations.

3. Fragmented files decrease system performance by
_____.

4. True or False
Recently, advances in disk technology have increased disk performance so that disk drives are no longer a system bottleneck.

5. Common symptoms that a disk contains fragmented files include (select all that apply):

☐ Windows will display a warning regarding fragmented files when the system starts.
☐ Documents and programs take longer to load.
☐ You can hear the disk drive perform its operations.
☐ The ScanDisk utility reports cross-linked clusters.

Understanding PC Sound Cards

Today, PC users make extensive use of sound cards to play back music, multimedia sounds and audio, and even to talk with another user across the Internet. This lesson examines sound card operations in detail.

You will first learn how the sound card digitizes an analog sound wave for recording. Then, you will examine the sound card's various ports. Finally, you will look at settings Windows provides to help you fine-tune sound card settings.

F A C T S

- Sound travels in a wave-like fashion.

- Within a PC, a sound card can record and play back sounds.

- To record a sound, the sound card digitizes the analog sound wave by sampling the wave's amplitude (height) at fixed intervals. Depending on the sound card's type, the sound card will represent the wave's height using an 8-bit, 16-bit, or 32-bit value.

- Depending on the number of bites a sound card uses to represent a wave's amplitude and the number of samples the sound card takes per second, the size of the file that contains the digitized sound will vary.

- Sound cards normally provide ports to which you can connect speakers, a microphone, and an audio input line. Many sound cards also provide MIDI ports.

- MIDI is an acronym for musical instrument digital interface. Using a sound card's MIDI port, you can attach an electronic instrument, such as a guitar or keyboard.

- Sound cards contain a synthesizer that lets the card create the sounds that correspond to various music instruments.

- You can normally control your system's volume using a volume control on the speakers, the Windows Volume Control window, and possibly a volume control knob on the sound card itself.

Digitizing Sounds

Sound travels through the air, water, and other elements as a wave. A PC sound card records a sound wave and stores it in a digital format (using ones and zeros). Later, to play back a sound, the sound card converts the digital audio back into an analog format that the PC's speakers can process.

Users refer to the process of converting an analog sound wave into a digital format as digitizing the sound. In general, to digitize a sound, the sound card must sample the sound wave at fixed intervals of time, in order to measure the wave's amplitude (height), as shown in Figure 48.1.

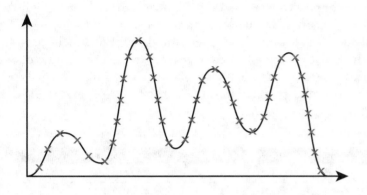

Figure 48.1 To digitize a sound wave, the sound card samples the wave's amplitude.

Older sound cards used 8 bits to represent the sound wave's amplitude, meaning the card represented the wave's highest peak with the value 255 and the lowest peak with the value 0, as shown in Figure 48.2.

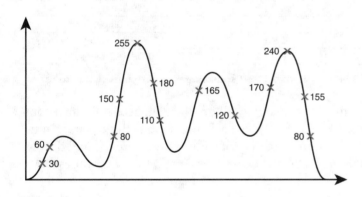

Figure 48.2 An 8-bit sound card represented a wave's amplitude using the values 0 to 255.

Today, sound cards use either 16 or 32 bits to represent the amplitude. A 16-bit sound card uses the values 0 to 65,536 to represent the wave's amplitude. Likewise, a 32-bit sound card can use values in the range 0 to 4,294,967,296. Because they could represent sounds more precisely, the 16-bit and 32-bit sound cards produce a much higher quality than their 8-bit counterpart.

Making Sense of Sampling Rates

To digitize a sound wave, the sound card must sample the wave's amplitude at fixed time intervals called the sampling rate. Table 48.1 briefly lists several common sampling rates.

Rate	Samples per Second
11KHz	11,000
22KHz	22,000
44KHz	44,000

Table 48.1 Common sound card sampling rates.

As the sound card samples the sound, it places its digitized result in a file. For high quality, you would obviously like to use a 32-bit sound card that sampled the wave at 44KHz. However, the size of such a digitized file can get quite large. With each sample, the 32-bit card must store 4 bytes (32 bits) of data. If you sample one minute of audio at 44KHz, the 32-bit card would produce a 10,560,000-byte file. Table 48.2 lists the file sizes a one-minute sound would produce for different sound cards and at different sampling rates.

Sound Card Type	Sampling Rate	File Size
8-bit	11KHz	660,000 bytes
8-bit	22KHz	1,320,000 bytes
8-bit	44KHz	2,640,000 bytes
16-bit	11KHz	1,320,000 bytes
16-bit	22KHz	2,640,000 bytes
16-bit	44KHz	5,280,000 bytes
32-bit	11KHz	2,640,000 bytes
32-bit	22KHz	5,280,000 bytes
32-bit	44KHz	10,560,000 bytes

Table 48.2 File sizes produced by 8-bit, 16-bit, and 32-bit sound cards at different sampling rates.

To reduce the size of the audio file, many programs store the digitized sound in a compressed format. Later, before the program plays back the sound, the program must decompress the audio. Programs can use a variety of software to compress and decompress audio. Users refer to such programs as codecs (for compressor/decompressor).

Taking a Closer Look at the Sound Card's Ports

If you examine the ports on a sound card, you will find, as shown in Figure 48.3, that most sound cards provide three similar ports to which you can connect speakers, an input audio source, and a microphone. Normally, the sound card will place small icons next to each port that indicate the port's use. In addition, most sound cards provide a MIDI connector to which you can connect a joystick or MIDI-based instrument.

Figure 48.3 Sound cards provide ports for speakers, an audio line in, a microphone, and MIDI devices.

MIDI is an acronym for musical instrument digital interface. MIDI defines a standard that electronic instruments, such as an electronic guitar or piano, use to interface with a sound card. When you connect a MIDI-based instrument to a sound card, you can often use the sound card to record the music generated by the instrument or to play back music using the device.

PC sound cards can also play back MIDI music through the PC's speakers. Within the sound card is a chip that synthesizes (creates) the sounds for various music instruments.

Connecting Speakers to a Sound Card

Depending on how a system is used, the type and cost of the speakers the user attaches to a sound card can differ significantly. Some music aficionados can purchase very high-end speakers, complete with tweeters and woofers that rival many home entertainment systems. Most users, however, will use small speakers similar to those shown in

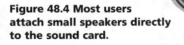

Figure 48.4. To power the small speakers, the user can use batteries or a small power supply.

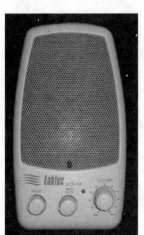

Figure 48.4 Most users attach small speakers directly to the sound card.

Controlling Speaker Volume

To control their speaker volume, users normally use the Windows Volume Control shown in Figure 48.5. Using the Volume Control, you can increase, decrease, or mute (turn off) the speaker volume.

Figure 48.5 Controlling speaker volume using the Windows Volume Control.

Many speakers also provide a volume control knob that you can use to increase or decrease the speaker's volume. Further, some sound cards provide a knob near its ports that you can use to adjust the card's output. Ideally, because the sound card may be hard to get to under your desk, you should set the sound card's volume control knob to a mid level and then later use either Windows or the speaker's volume control knob to control your system's volume.

Fine-Tuning Sound Card Settings within Windows

Depending on your sound card's type, the specific settings you can adjust for your sound card may vary. Most sound cards, however, will let you adjust the card's playback, recording, and MIDI settings within the Multimedia Properties dialog box, as shown in Figure 48.6. To display the Multimedia Properties dialog box within Windows 98, perform these steps:

1. Select the Start menu Settings option and choose Control Panel. Windows will display the Control Panel window.
2. Within the Control Panel, double-click on the Multimedia icon. Windows will display the Multimedia Properties dialog box.
3. Within the Multimedia Properties dialog box, select the Audio tab.

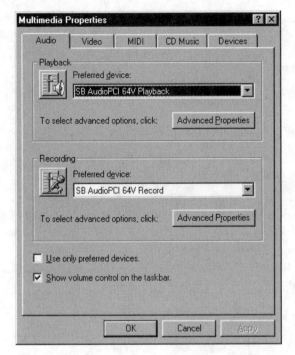

Figure 48.6 Adjusting sound card settings within Windows.

To display the Multimedia Properties dialog box within Windows 2000, perform these steps:

1. Select the Start menu Settings option and choose Control Panel. Windows will display the Control Panel window.

2. Within the Control Panel, double-click on the Sounds and Multimedia icon. Windows will display the Sounds and Multimedia Properties dialog box.

3. Within the Sounds and Multimedia Properties dialog box, select the Audio tab.

EXAM REVIEW

CERTIFICATION

① Codec is an acronym for _____.

② Users refer to the process of converting an analog sound to a digital format as _____ the sound.

③ MIDI is an acronym for _____.

④ A 30-second sound, digitized by a 32-bit sound card at 11KHz will generate a file of size _____.

⑤ If a user does not hear sounds from the system, you should (select all that apply):

☐ Check the speaker's volume control knob

☐ Check the sound card's volume control knob

☐ Ensure the speakers are plugged into the correct sound card port

☐ Check the Windows Volume Control

Performing Monitor Operations

Of all the PC components, the monitor is quite likely the most used device. Although the monitor is quite simple to use—normally you only have to power the monitor on—the A+ Certification exam can pose a myriad of questions regarding the monitor.

The monitor, like the power supply, contains a capacitor that holds enough voltage (even after the monitor is powered off and unplugged for an extended period of time) to kill you. Although the A+ Certification exam asks you questions regarding operations that you can perform inside the monitor's case, my suggestion is that most technicians should never open the monitor—especially those who are facing a promising career for having passed the A+ Certification exam. Even the boss' monitor is not worth dying for. If a monitor is not working, swap it out and take the monitor to a PC repair shop where either the technicians make the big bucks for taking such risks, or the technicians simply do not know better.

F A C T S

+ As a monitor operates, it generates a substantial amount of heat, which typically vents through openings on the top of the monitor's case. Make sure users do not cover the vents with books, papers, stuffed animals, or other items.

+ To display an image, a monitor illuminates red, green, and blue phosphors at different intensities. The three phosphors combine to create a picture element (pixel).

+ To illuminate the phosphors, a monitor uses electron guns that fire a precise charge which heats the red, green, and blue phosphors, causing the phosphors to glow. The combination of the red, green, and blue colors creates a pixel's screen color. Because of the use of red, green, and blue phosphors, users often refer to monitors as RGB devices.

+ To illuminate the entire screen, the electron guns scan across the screen from left to right, heating the corresponding phosphors. When the electron guns reach the rightmost edge of the screen, the guns move to the next line and continue to heat that row of phosphors. When the electron guns reach the lower-right edge of the screen, the guns resume their operation at the top row of the screen.

+ Users refer to the electron gun's movement from left to right across the screen as the horizontal refresh operation. To refresh a VGA monitor, for example, a monitor may refresh over 30,000 lines of pixels per second!

+ Users refer to the electron gun's process of refreshing all the lines of the screen as a vertical refresh operation. Monitors typically refresh the entire screen 60 to 80 times per second (depending on the monitor's frequency). Newer monitors can refresh the screen as often as 160 times per second.

+ Depending on a monitor's resolution and color use, and the video card type, the speed at which a monitor refreshes the screen may differ. A multisync monitor supports different refresh rates. You can normally connect a multisync monitor to a wide range of video cards.

+ To increase their "advertised refresh rate" some monitors will use a technique called interlacing which causes the monitor to refresh every other row of pixels when the monitor performs a screen refresh operation. By skipping a row of pixels, the monitor can perform the refresh operation in half the time. Unfortunately, the interlaced monitor often produces a wave-like display.

+ As you shop for monitors, you should avoid interlaced monitors.

F A C T S

- Monitors produce images by displaying picture elements (pixels) in different colors. The monitor's resolution describes the number of pixels the monitor can display across and down the screen, such as 800 x 600 (pronounced 800 by 600) or 1024 x 768. The higher a monitor's resolution, the sharper the screen image the monitor can display.

- Monitors use red, green, and blue phosphors to create each pixel that appears on the screen. A monitor's dot pitch describes the distance between successive phosphors of the same color (such as the distance between two successive green phosphors). The smaller the value of the monitor's dot pitch, the sharper the image the monitor will create.

- Users often refer to monitors that reduce the monitor's power consumption by implementing the Energy-Star services as "green" monitors, because the monitors support the environment.

- Over time, the electrons a monitor uses to illuminate phosphors can build up a magnetic interface that affects the appearance of images on the screen display. Many monitors provide a control (or menu option) you can select to perform a degauss operation that eliminates the magnetic buildup.

- To prevent a monitor from overheating, make sure a user does not cover the vents on the top of the monitor case.

Understanding How a Monitor Displays an Image

Regardless of whether a monitor is displaying text or a graphics image, the monitor represents the image by illuminating small dots on the screen, called picture elements (or pixels). Behind the screen, each pixel consists of a red, green, and blue phosphor. By heating the phosphor, the monitor causes the phosphor to glow at a specific intensity. The combination of the red, green, and blue phosphors produces the pixel's color. By changing the intensity at which each of phosphors glows, the monitor can change the pixel's color.

To heat the red, green, and blue phosphors, the monitor uses three electron guns that fire electrons precisely at each phosphor. The greater the intensity of the electrons, the hotter the phosphor's temperature and the brighter the phosphor glows. To display a white pixel, for example, the monitor heats each of the red, green, and blue phosphors to a level that causes the phosphors to glow brightly. To display a black pixel, the monitor would not heat the corresponding phosphors. Likewise, to display a pixel in red, green, or blue, the monitor would heat only the corresponding phosphor. By varying the intensity by which the monitor heats the phosphors, the monitor can represent colors across the color spectrum.

Making Sense of Monitor Frequencies

By heating the phosphors that represent a pixel, the monitor causes the phosphors to glow. In order for a monitor to be able to change a screen image, the phosphors must cool quickly so they can stop glowing. As the phosphor cools, it dims. To keep the screen image sharp, the monitor must continually reheat the phosphors—a process users refer to as refreshing the screen.

 Within the monitor, electron guns rapidly refresh one pixel's phosphors at a time, moving across the screen from left to right. When electron guns reach the right edge of the screen, the monitor turns the guns off briefly while it aims them at the start of the next row of phosphors.

Users refer to the process of updating a line (row) of pixels as a horizontal refresh operation. Within a monitor, horizontal refresh operations occur very fast. To refresh a VGA monitor, for example, the monitor may refresh over 30,000 rows of phosphors per second!

As you will recall from Lesson 4, "Getting a Handle on Kilo, Mega, Giga, and Tera," users refer to the number of events that occur in one second using the term hertz. The monitor, in this case, refreshes lines on the screen at a rate of 30,000 hertz (or 30KHz).

Each time the monitor's electron guns reach the bottom-right corner of the screen, the monitor again turns off the guns as it aims them back at the upper-left-most corner. Users refer to the process of refreshing the entire screen as a vertical refresh operation. Depending on the monitor's type, the screen settings (resolution and color), as well as the video card type, the monitor may refresh the entire screen 50 to 160 times per second. Often, as you shop for a monitor, you will see advertisements that express the monitor's speed using a value such as 72Hz. The speed value tells you the number of times per second that the monitor refreshes the screen.

To display an image, the monitor and video card must agree on the speed at which the monitor will perform its refresh operations. Today, most monitors sold are multisync monitors, which means the monitor can refresh the screen at various rates. The advantage of a multisync monitor is that you can attach the monitor to a wide range of video cards. Further, you can speed up or slow down the monitor's refresh rate to better match the user's video card settings, room lighting, and personal preferences.

Avoid the Use of Interlaced Monitors

 To increase their refresh frequency, some (typically less expensive) monitors use a technique called interlacing to refresh the screen phosphors. Rather than refreshing every row of phosphors with each screen refresh operation, interlaced monitors will refresh every other row. By skipping rows of pixels, the monitor can complete the screen refresh operation faster—which means the monitor can be advertised as having a faster frequency. However, because the interlaced monitor only refreshes every other row of pixels with each pass, it often creates a wavelike result, which can be very distracting. As you shop for monitors, you should look for *non-interlaced* frequencies, and you should avoid monitors that use interlacing.

Tweaking (Fine-Tuning) a Monitor's Display Settings

On the front of most monitors, you will find one or more controls similar to those shown in Figure 49.1 that you can use to fine-tune a monitor's display settings. Using the controls, you can increase the monitor's brightness and contrast, change the screen image's height and width, or center the image on screen.

Also, many monitors provide a control (or menu option) you can use to "degauss" the monitor (a process that removes the effects of magnetic interference that accumulates as a result of the electrons the monitor uses to heat the phosphor elements). By degaussing a monitor, you may eliminate ghost-like shadows that appear on the screen display. When you degauss the monitor, you will normally hear the monitor generate a tone as it uses a special coil to remove any magnetic buildup. Typically, the screen image will flicker for a few seconds following the degaussing.

Figure 49.1 Using the monitor controls to fine-tune monitor settings.

Make Sure a Monitor Can Vent the Heat It Generates

Often, users find that a monitor provides a convenient location to stack books, magazines, or incoming papers. Unfortunately, by placing objects on top of a monitor, users cover the vents that the monitor uses to discharge the heat its electronics generate to display images. If the monitor cannot vent heat, the heat may accumulate within the monitor's case and damage the monitor's electronics or cause a fire. Do not let users place any items over a monitor's vents. If a monitor's vents begin to collect dust, use an aerosol blower to remove the dust.

Cleaning the Monitor

I've never quite figured out why, but many users feel they need to touch the monitor's screen when they point at a graphic or text, leaving one or more fingerprints on the display. In addition, as the monitor's electron guns illuminate phosphors, the electronics also produce static on the screen that causes the display to attract dust.

Before you clean your screen display, always make sure that you first turn off your monitor and let the monitor sit unused for a few minutes. If you spray a cleaner onto the monitor's screen display while the monitor is in use, you run the risk of shock. If you do not electrocute yourself, you may generate sufficient static to damage your monitor or your PC.

Many computer stores sell cleaning chemicals made specifically for a cleaning monitors. Often, however, you should find that using a soft cloth with a little rubbing alcohol easily removes dust and finger prints from the display, as shown in Figure 49.2.

Figure 49.2 To clean a monitor's screen display, first turn off the monitor and then use a soft cloth.

Do Not Open the Monitor Case

As a rule, you should never open a power supply and you should never open your monitor's case. Both the power supply and monitor contain a capacitor that can retain sufficient voltage (even after the device has been powered off and unplugged for a period of time) to kill you!

The A+ Certification exam may present you with questions regarding operations that you can perform within the monitor case. Although you can perform these operations, you should not. If a monitor is not working, you should take the monitor to a PC repair shop.

That said, the A+ Certification exam may ask you questions regarding operations you can perform within the monitor case. In general, if you cannot fine-tune the shape or location of the image on the screen display using the monitor's external controls, you may be able to adjust the image using conversion controls and deflection magnet settings within the monitor case. Adjusting the convergence controls requires that you perform a set of internal calibrations. In addition, you may be able to adjust a "master" brightness control in order to give an older monitor a sharper display.

A Monitor's Dot Pitch Impacts the Monitor's Image Quality

To display an image, the monitor illuminates pixels, by heating red, green, and blue phosphors to a temperature that causes the phosphors to glow. A monitor's dot pitch is a measure of the distance between successive phosphors of the same color. The smaller the dot pitch value, the closer together the phosphors and the sharper the image the monitor can display. As you shop for a monitor, you should look for monitors with a dot pitch of 0.28mm or less.

A Monitor's Screen Resolution Also Impacts Image Sharpness

To produce an image, the monitor illuminates picture elements (pixels). The more pixels the monitor supports, the sharper the image display. As you will learn in Lesson 50, "Taking a Closer Look at PC Video Operations," the video card controls settings a monitor uses to display an image, such as the number of pixels or number of colors.

Users express a monitor's resolution in terms of the number of pixels across the screen by the number of pixels down the screen, such as 800x600. Figure 49.3 illustrates common monitor resolutions.

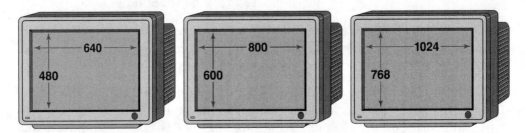

Figure 49.3 A monitor's resolution corresponds to the number of pixels the monitor can display across and down the screen.

Using Screen Savers to Prevent Phosphor "Burn In"

Years ago, when monitor quality was not as high as it is today, monitors would sometimes experience phosphor "burn in" when the same image remained on the monitor's screen for an extended period of time. An office PC, for example, might display the same main menu for several hours a day, every day. As a result of the same phosphors being continually illuminated, the monitor would develop a ghost-like display that would cause the main menu to always appear on the screen.

To prevent phosphor burn in, programmers created special programs called screen savers that after a period of PC inactivity become active to continually change the image that appears on the screen. When the user later moves the mouse or presses a keyboard key, the screen saver program ends and redisplays the screen's previous contents.

To assign a screen saver within Windows, perform these steps:

1. Right-click on an unused area on the Windows Desktop. Windows, in turn, will display a pop-up menu.

2. Within the pop-up menu, choose Properties. Windows will display the Display Properties dialog box.

3. Within the Display Properties dialog box, select the Screen Saver tab. Windows will display the Screen Saver sheet, as shown in Figure 49.4, which you can use to select and configure a screen saver.

4. After you select the screen saver and settings you desire. Choose OK.

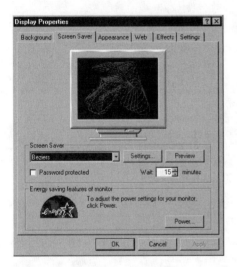

Figure 49.4 Assigning a screen saver within Windows.

NOTE: *Many users will password-protect their screen saver so that before the screen saver will end and display the screen's previous contents, the user must type in a password. By password-protecting a screen saver in this way, users can better secure their PCs should they step away from their office for a short period of time.*

Taking Advantage of Green (Energy Star Compliant) Monitors

A PC monitor consumes a large amount of power (up to 100 watts). To reduce the amount of power consumed by monitors that are not in use, Windows can turn off many monitors. Should the user later move the mouse or press a keyboard key, Windows can turn the monitor back on. Users refer to monitors that support such operations as "Energy Star Compliant" or "Green" monitors. To determine if you are using such a monitor, view the Display Properties dialog box Screen Saver sheet previously shown in Figure 49.4. If your monitor supports Energy Star operations, the dialog box will contain a Settings (or Power) button you can select to configure the amount of idle time you want Windows to wait before it turns off the monitor, as shown in Figure 49.5.

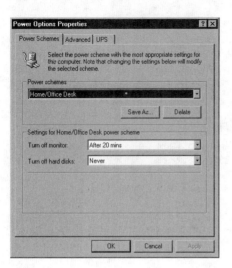

Figure 49.5 Configuring a monitor's power management settings within Windows.

EXAM REVIEW

CERTIFICATION

① The most common problem users introduce with respect to a monitor is _____.

② A monitor displays screen images by assigning colors to individual picture elements that users refer to as _____.

③ True or False
Each picture element consists of a red, green, and black phosphor.

④ The electron guns within the monitor heat the phosphors at different _____ which causes the phosphors to glow at different levels of brightness.

⑤ RGB is an abbreviation for _____.

⑥ Users refer to the monitor's refreshing of a row of pixels as a _____ refresh operation.

⑦ True or False
Using advanced technologies, interlaced monitors produce a high-quality image.

447

EXAM REVIEW

8 **True or False**
The monitor contains a high-voltage capacitor that can retain sufficient power to kill you, even after the monitor has been powered off and unplugged for a period of time.

9 The term _____ describes the distance between successive phosphors of the same color within a monitor.

10 **True or False**
When you no longer need a monitor, you can discard the monitor in the trash.

11 A monitor's frequency describes the number of times the monitor _____ per second.

12 Users refer to energy-efficient monitors that reduce the monitor's power consumption during idle times as _____.

13 Screen savers exist to prevent _____.

14 When shopping for a monitor, you should look for monitors with a dot pitch of _____ or less.

Lesson 50

Taking a Closer Look at Video Operations

n Lesson 49, "Performing Monitor Operations," you examined how the monitor displays images. The monitor connects to a video card within the PC system unit. The video card, in turn, controls the monitor's operations.

This lesson examines the video card and the factors that influence the quality of the images displayed by the monitor. You will examine the role of video memory (VRAM) and the accelerated graphics port (AGP) on the motherboard which you install the video card into. You will also examine how various graphics-related settings may affect your system performance.

F A C T S

✛ Within the system unit, the video card creates and stores the image which the monitor displays.

✛ The video card contains on-board RAM that stores the screen image. The video card maintains color information for each pixel within its RAM.

✛ Within the video card, special electronics called a digital-to-analog converter converts the screen image that resides within the card's RAM into the electronic signals the monitor requires.

✛ Video cards use a special dual-ported video RAM (VRAM) that lets the card's electronics read and write to the memory chips at the same time.

✛ The screen resolution and number of colors determines the amount of RAM a video card must provide. The higher the resolution or number of colors, the more RAM the card requires.

✛ Most newer video cards connect to the motherboard via the accelerated graphics port (AGP). If a PC does not provide an AGP slot, the video card will connect to a PCI slot.

Looking Closer at the Video Card

Within the PC system unit, the video card contains the electronics the PC uses to create and store the images that the monitor displays. As shown in Figure 50.1, when you attach a monitor to a PC, you connect the monitor to the video card.

The video card contains electronics, a digital-to-analog (D-to-A) converter, that converts the digital image (the image represented with ones and zeros) into the analog signals the monitor requires. In addition, the video card contains RAM that stores the image.

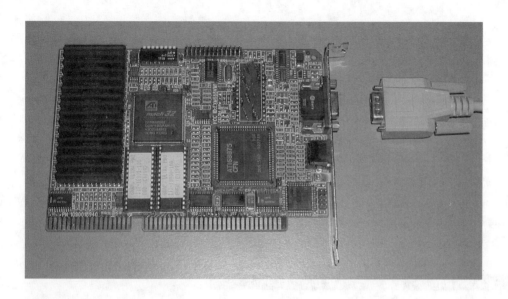

Figure 50.1 The monitor attaches to a video card within the PC system unit.

Understanding the Video Card's Use of RAM

A monitor displays an image by illuminating red, green, and blue phosphors that correspond to a picture element (pixel) on the screen display. What is shown on the PC's screen, be it text or a high-resolution image, is simply a collection of pixels.

The screen's resolution determines the number of pixels. A screen that displays a resolution of 800x600 uses 480,000 pixels. Likewise, a screen that displays a resolution of 1,600x1,200 uses 1,920,000 pixels.

The video card tells the monitor which colors to display for each pixel. The video card uses its onboard RAM to store color information for each pixel.

The number of colors each pixel can represent determines the amount of RAM a video card must hold. For simplicity, assume a screen only displays black and white images, meaning, each pixel is either on or off. The video card could represent each pixel's black or white color using a single bit. A black and white screen at 800x600 (480,000) pixels would require 60,000 bytes of memory:

RAM in bytes = Number of pixels x Bits per pixel / 8-bits per byte

= 800x600 pixels x 1 bit per pixel / 8-bits per byte

= 480,000 x 1 / 8

= 60,000 bytes

A byte (8 bits) can represent 256 different values. By assigning each pixel a byte of RAM, a video card can use 256 different colors for each pixel. Today, most video cards support 8-bit, 16-bit, and 24-bit colors. Table 50.1 describes the number of colors each setting can display.

Color Setting	Number of Colors
8-bit	256
16-bit	65,536
24-bit	16,777,216

Table 50.1 The number of colors a video card can display using different color settings.

To support 24-bit color, the video card uses three bytes to represent each pixel. To display an 800x600 image using 24-bit color, the video card will need 1,440,000 bytes of RAM:

RAM in bytes = Number of pixels x Bits per pixel / 8-bits per byte

= 800x600 pixels x 24 bits per pixel / 8-bits per byte

= 480,000 x 24 / 8

= 1,440,000 bytes

Similarly, to display an image at 1,600x1,200 using 24-bit color, the video card would need nearly 6MB of RAM:

RAM in bytes = Number of pixels x Bits per pixel / 8-bits per byte

= 1,600x1,200 pixels x 24 bits per pixel / 8-bits per byte

= 1,920,000 x 24 / 8

= 5,760,000 bytes

As you shop for video cards, you will find cards with 1MB, 2MB, 4MB, 8MB and so on. The amount of RAM on a video card determines the number of colors the video card can display at different resolutions. The more RAM, the more colors or the higher resolution the card will support.

Some newer video cards use 32 bits to represent each color. Normally, such cards use 24 of the bits to represent the pixel's color and 8 bits to represent the pixel's transparency (a setting programmers refer to as the pixel's alpha channel). Using the transparency value, a program can cause a pixel to appear similar to glass or the reflection off water.

Assigning Resolution and Color Settings

Within Windows, you can view and change the system's video resolution and color settings using the Display Properties dialog box shown in Figure 50.2. To open the Display Properties dialog box, perform these steps:

1. Right-click on the Windows Desktop. Windows will display a pop-up menu.

2. Within the pop-up menu, select Properties. Windows will display the Display Properties dialog box.

3. Within the Display Properties dialog box, select the Settings tab.

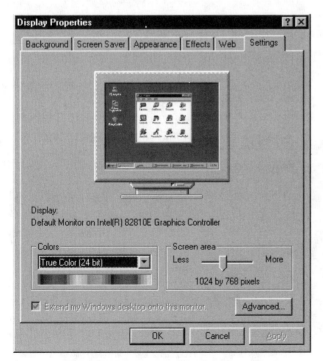

Figure 50.2 Using the Display Properties dialog box to view or change the video resolution or color use.

Depending on your video card type and the amount of RAM the card contains, the resolution and color settings you can select may vary. In some cases, if you select a high resolution, you can then only choose 16-bit or 8-bit color. That's because the higher resolution increases the number of pixels for which the video card must store color information. Likewise, selecting 24-bit color may limit the resolutions you can choose.

Understanding Video RAM

Lesson 23, "Understanding Random-Access Memory (RAM)," discusses the various types of random-access memory in detail. Video cards use a special video RAM (VRAM) that users sometimes refer to as "dual-ported RAM." The dual-ported nature of the VRAM chips lets electronics on the video card write to a chip (an example would be Windows updating a window's contents), while other electronics on the card is reading the chip's contents so that the card's digital-to-analog converter can create the signals the card sends to the monitor.

Improving Windows Video Performance

To maximize your system's performance, you should direct Windows to take advantage of any hardware accelerators the video card may provide. Within Windows 9x, you can use the Advanced Graphics Settings dialog box, shown in Figure 50.3, to control Windows' use of video accelerators. To display the Advanced Graphics Settings dialog box, perform these steps:

1. Select the Start menu Settings option and choose Control Panel. Windows will open the Control Panel window.

2. Within the Control Panel, double-click on the System icon. Windows will display the System Properties dialog box.

3. Within the System Properties dialog box, select the Performance tab. Windows will display the Performance sheet.

4. Within the Performance sheet, click on the Graphics button.

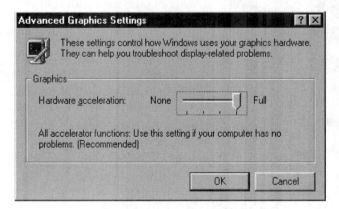

Figure 50.3 To improve perform-ance, direct Windows to use video accelerators.

If you experience problems with the video display after directing Windows to use the accelerator, restore the original accelerator settings. Then, try to locate a newer device driver for the card, which may support the accelerator use. To control Windows video per-formance within Windows 2000, perform these steps:

1. Right-click on the Desktop. Windows will display a pop-up menu.

2. Within the pop-up menu, select Properties. Windows will display the Display Properties dialog box.

3. Within the Display Properties dialog box select the Settings tab. Windows will display the Settings sheet.

4. Within the Settings sheet, click the Advanced button. Windows will open a new dialog box that lets you set various video settings.

5. Within the dialog box, select the Troubleshooting tab. Windows will display the Troubleshooting sheet where you can control Windows' use of video accelerators.

A+ CERTIFICATION — EXAM REVIEW

① Within the video card, special electronics called the _____ convert the image that resides in the card's RAM to the signals the monitor requires.

② To display 32-bit color at a resolution of 800x600 would require the video card to contain _____ bytes of video RAM.

③ Users often refer to VRAM as _____.

④ AGP is an acronym for _____.

⑤ Users refer to a screen's picture elements as _____.

Understanding PC Printer Operations

Regardless of how they use their PC, most users make extensive use of printers to print word processing documents, e-mail messages, spreadsheets, information displayed on a Web site, and more. This lesson presents key printer operations within Windows and the steps you must perform to accomplish them.

You will examine ways you can connect a printer to a PC and how your choice of connection type impacts your printer performance. You will also learn how to install printer software (the printer's device driver) for a local and network printer. Finally, you will examine how Windows' use of spooling improves printer operations.

F A C T S

+ Users can connect a printer to a PC using a variety of ports: serial, parallel, network, infrared, and USB. The connection type that you choose will impact your printer performance.

+ Years ago, users connected printers to PCs using a serial port. Because of the serial port's slow communication speed, you should no longer use serial ports for printer operations.

+ Today, most users connect printers to their PC using a parallel port.

+ Over time, the PC's parallel ports have evolved to support higher data throughput rates as well as bi-directional communication that lets a printer inform the PC of its operational status, such as being low on toner or paper.

+ Most newer PCs support an enhanced parallel port (EPP) or extended capabilities port (ECP) which can improve parallel-port performance by more than 10 times the speed of a standard port.

+ To use EPP and ECP port capabilities, your port and printer must support the operations and you must use an IEEE 1284 parallel cable. Further, you may need to change a setting in the PC's CMOS settings before the PC will enable EPP or ECP operations.

+ Many larger laser printers contain a network interface card you can use to directly connect the printer to a network. By connecting the printer directly to the network in this way, you not only make the printer available for all users on the network, but you also improve performance. Most networks support data transfer rates of 10Mbs to 100Mbs.

+ Within a network environment, users can also share printers connected directly to a user's PC.

+ After you connect a printer to a PC, you must install a device driver on the PC that lets Windows interact with the printer. The easiest way to install a printer device driver is to select the Control Panel Printers icon and then select the Add Printers icon in the Printers folder.

+ Before a user can print to a printer that connects directly to a network, the user must install a device driver for the printer on his or her PC.

+ To test whether or not a printer is working, you can print a test page using the printer's Properties dialog box.

+ If a user has multiple printers available, such as a local printer and one or more network printers, the user can select the printer to print to from a pull-down list that appears in the Print dialog box.

FACTS

➕ Using the Print dialog box Settings option, a user can change a variety of printer settings, such as the page orientation (portrait or landscape), the printer's resolution, and so on.

➕ Many laser printers provide a menu on their outside front panel that users can use to configure various settings.

➕ When you print within Windows, your program does not actually send data to the printer, but rather, the program sends the data to a special program called the spooler. The spooler, in turn, stores the program's printer output in a file on disk and then later prints the output. Should two or more programs try to print at the same time, the spooler will store each program's data on disk and print each program's output in the order it received the data, on a first-come, first-served basis.

Connecting a Printer to a PC

Users can connect a printer directly to a PC using a serial port, parallel port, network port, infrared connection, or USB port. Because the serial port is much slower than a parallel or USB port, you should avoid avoid using the serial port for printer operations.

The parallel port is the most common way that users connect printers to a PC. To attach a printer to a parallel port, connect a special cable, similar to that shown in Figure 51.1, that provides a 25-pin male connector which attaches to the PC and a Centronix connector which attaches to the printer.

 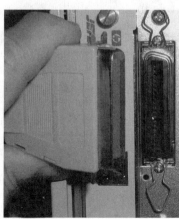

Figure 51.1 A parallel printer cable contains a 25-pin connector and a Centronix connector which attaches to the printer.

Although many newer printers support universal serial bus connections, few users actually use the USB to connect a printer. To support notebook

PCs and handheld devices, many printers now support infrared operations. Before a PC and printer can communicate using infrared communications, you must place the devices in a direct line of sight with each another.

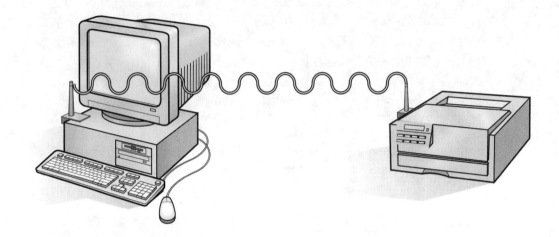

Exploiting Faster Parallel Ports

To improve data throughput between the parallel port and the printer beyond 150KB per second (the speed of a standard parallel port), hardware manufacturers released higher-performance parallel ports. The first parallel port enhancement, called the enhanced parallel port (EPP), provided improved communication technologies that increased data throughput to 2MB per second. The problem with EPP is that the CPU has to oversee communication between the port and printer.

Later, a second parallel port type called the extended capabilities port (ECP) improved upon the EPP's capabilities by introducing the use of direct memory access (DMA). This eliminated the CPU's role in the parallel port communication process.

A standard parallel port is an output device. In contrast, the EPP and ECP are bi-directional ports. Using the bi-directional communications, a printer, for example, can send status information back to the PC, such as that the printer is running low on toner or is out of paper. Further, a user can attach a device such as a Zip drive or hard drive to the bi-directional port.

To use an EPP or ECP port's bi-directional capabilities, you must use an IEEE 1284 cable. Then, you may need to use the PC's CMOS Setup program to enable EPP or ECP operations, as shown in Figure 51.2.

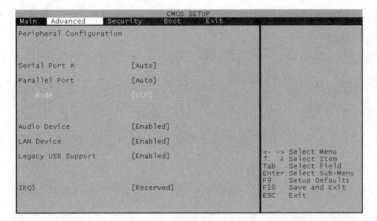

Figure 51.2 You may need to enable EPP or ECP operations using the CMOS Setup program.

To determine if your system supports EPP or ECP operations, select the Device Manager Ports option as shown in Figure 51.3. You must have an IEEE 1284 cable and you may also need to enable port operations on your printer (using the front panel menu).

Figure 51.3 Viewing a PC's parallel port type within the Windows Device Manager.

Connecting a Printer Directly to a Network

To allow network users to easily share a printer, many laser printers contain a network interface card as shown in Figure 51.4 that you can use to connect the printer directly to the network. Before a PC connected to the network can print to the printer, a device driver must be installed on the system. The advantages of connecting a printer directly to the network are ease of sharing and improved performance. Most networks support data transfer rates of 10Mbs to 100Mbs.

Figure 51.4 Many laser printers contain network interface cards that let the printer connect directly to the network.

In addition to sharing a printer that is connected directly to the network, users can also share printers that are connected to a remote PC, provided the remote user agrees to share the printer. To share a printer that connects directly to a PC, the user must first enable File and Printer Sharing as discussed in Lesson 35, "Introduction to Networking." Then, the user must direct Windows to share the printer by performing these steps:

1. Select the Start menu Settings option and choose Printers. Windows will display the Printers folder.

2. Within the Printers folder, right-click on the printer you want to share. Windows will display a pop-up menu.

3. Within the pop-up menu, select Sharing. Windows, in turn, will display the Sharing tab within the printer's Properties dialog box, as shown in Figure 51.5, that you can use to enable (and later disable) the device's sharing.

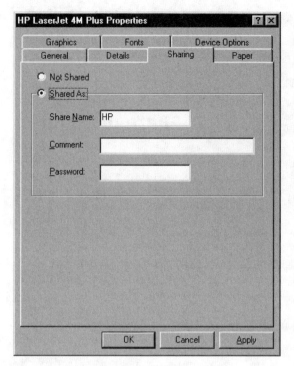

Remember, before the remote user can share the network printer, the user must install a device driver for the printer onto the system.

Installing Software Support for a New Printer

After you connect a printer to a PC, you must install a device driver that Windows can use to interact with the printer. Likewise, before you can print to a remote network printer, you must install a device driver for the printer on your system.

To install and configure a printer device driver, perform these steps:

1. Select the Start menu Settings option and choose Printers. Windows will display the Printers folder.

2. Within the Printers folder, double-click on the Add Printer icon. Windows, in turn, will launch the Add Printer wizard that will walk you through the steps of installing the device driver for a local or remote printer.

Selecting a Target Printer

When a user has multiple printers available (either local or network printers), the user can use a pull-down list that appears within the Print dialog box, as shown in Figure 51.6, to select a printer. To display the Print dialog box within a program, you normally select the File menu Print option.

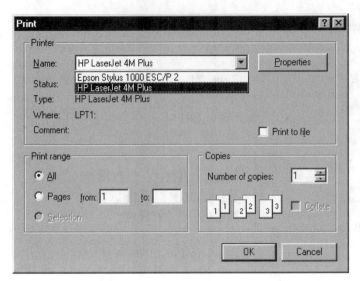

Figure 51.6 Using the Print dialog box, you can select the target printer you want to print to.

Selecting a Default Printer

If a user has multiple printers available, the user must select one printer to serve as the default, meaning, the printer to which Windows will print if the user does not select a different target printer. To change the default printer within Windows, perform these steps:

1. Select the Start menu Settings option and choose Printers. Windows will display the Printers folder.

2. Within the Printers folder, right-click on the printer you want to select as the default. Windows will display a pop-up menu.

3. Within the pop-up menu, select the Set as Default Printer option.

Understanding Print Spooling

Windows Spool File

The Windows operating system lets a user run multiple programs at the same time. Within Windows, it is not uncommon for a user to print a document from within one program, such as a word processor, and then to switch to a different program, such as a e-mail application, and to print a second document.

To prevent one program's printer output from interfering with another's, Windows uses a special program called the spooler to manage printer output. When a Windows program prints, the program does not send its data to the printer, but, rather, the program sends its data to the spooler. If the printer is not in use, the spooler will begin to print the data. Otherwise, the spooler will store the data in a file. Later, when the printer becomes available, the spooler will print the output it has filed (spooled), in the order the output was received. It is possible to disable spooling, so that a PC will send its data directly to the printer. However, within the Windows environment, spooling printer output will normally give you more flexibility.

To view the documents Windows has spooled for a specific printer, perform these steps:

1. Select the Start menu Settings option and choose Printers. Windows will display the Printers folder.

2. Within the Printers folder, double-click on the printer you desire. Windows, in turn, will display window similar to that shown in Figure 51.7 that lists the jobs the spooler is waiting to send to the printer, as well as information about the job that is currently printing.

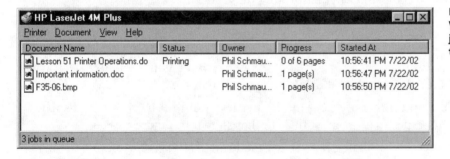

Figure 51.7 Viewing print jobs spooled to a printer.

Troubleshooting Printer Operations

If, after you connect a printer to a PC or network and you install a device driver for the printer on a user's PC, the user is unable to print to the printer, you must determine if the problem is:

- A problem with the printer itself
- A problem with the connection to the printer
- A PC-specific problem
- A Windows spooler problem
- An application-specific problem

If you have a second identical printer, you can swap the printers to determine if the problem is the printer itself. If the second printer prints, the problem is the first printer. If you have a nearby PC, connect the printer to the second PC and install the device driver on that PC. It is possible that the parallel port on the first PC is not functioning.

If you are connecting the printer to a parallel port and you have a second parallel cable available, try swapping the cables. If you are connecting the printer to a network hub, you might try using a different port on the hub or using a different network cable to connect the printer to the hub. In some cases, you must enable the printer's network support using the menu that appears on the printer's front panel.

Most printer problems correspond to device driver problems. You may need to reinstall the device driver and then restart the PC before the PC can use the printer. Then, you may want to try printing to the printer from more than one program to verify that the problem is not program specific. Finally, the problem may be due to the Windows spooler. Often, by restarting your system, you can correct most spooler errors.

To help you test whether or not a PC can print to a printer, you can direct Windows to send a test page to the printer by performing these steps:

1. Select the Start menu Settings option and choose Printers. Windows will display the Printers folder.
2. Within the Printers folder, right-click on the printer you want to select as the default printer. Windows will display a pop-up menu.
3. Within the pop-up menu, select the Properties option. Windows will display the printer's Properties dialog box similar to that shown in Figure 51.8.
4. Within the Properties dialog box, select the Print Test Page button.

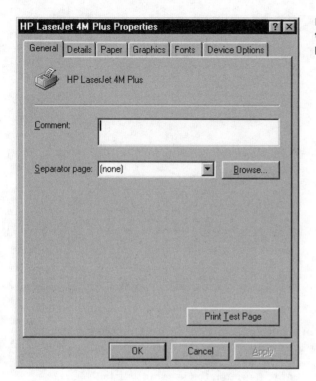

Figure 51.8 To test a printer connection, direct Windows to send a test page to the printer.

EXAM REVIEW

(1) Users can connect a printer to a PC using the following ports (select all that apply):

☐ Parallel port
☐ Serial port
☐ USB
☐ InfraRed connection
☐ Network connection
☐ PCI
☐ WRAM port

(2) EPP is an acronym for _____.

(3) ECP is an acronym for _____.

(4) A _____ port improves performance by adding DMA support.

(5) Two advantages of connecting a printer to a network are _____ and _____.

(6) Before a user can print to a printer, the user must install _____ onto the system.

(7) To exploit EPP or ECP operations, you must use a _____ cable.

(8) True or False
Because ECP and EPP ports support bi-directional communication, users can connect devices such as a Zip drive to the port.

(9) Windows applications normally do not send data directly to the printer. Instead, the applications send the data to a special program called the _____ that oversees printer operations.

Taking a Closer Look at Laser Printer Operations

In Lesson 51, "Understanding PC Printer Operations," you examined key printer operations within Windows. To prepare for the A+ Certification exam, you must take a closer look at laser printer operations.

This lesson examines the step-by-step operations a laser printer performs to print a page of output. Along the way, you will examine steps you can perform to maintain a laser printer and possibly to extend the life of a toner cartridge.

F A C T S

✚ The laser within a laser printer does not come into contact with the paper. Instead, the laser exists to draw the image onto the printer drum using an electrical charge that will later attract toner ink.

✚ The printer drum resides within the toner cartridge.

✚ To print a page, the laser printer first applies a charge to the entire printer drum. The charge will later attract toner so that the toner collects on the drum.

✚ The printer uses its primary corona wire to apply the charge to the printer drum.

✚ The printer then uses the laser to draw the page image onto the drum by discharging the areas that correspond to blank areas on the page. When the laser completes its processing, only those areas on the drum that correspond to text or graphics on the page will contain a charge.

✚ The drum will then pass by the toner which collects on the charged surface areas on the drum.

✚ The printer's transfer corona wire will then apply a charge to the sheet of paper. As the paper moves past the drum, the charge will attract the toner which will move from the drum onto the page.

✚ Finally, the printer will use heated rollers (fusers) to melt the toner onto the page.

How a Laser Printer Prints

As shown in Figure 52.1, a laser printer contains a toner cartridge that not only contains the ink the printer places onto a page, but also the printer drum, which is key to laser printer operations.

Many users incorrectly believe that a laser printer uses the laser to burn the toner onto a piece of paper. As you will learn in this lesson, that is not the case. Instead, the printer uses its laser to remove the charge from a printer drum so that the drum only attracts ink in the locations that correspond to the graphics or text that will appear on the printed page.

Figure 52.1 The toner cartridge contains ink and the printer drum.

In the printer, the laser itself never comes into contact with the paper. Periodically, a page may jam in the printer. When you remove the page, it will appear burned. The laser did not burn the paper. As the laser printer operates, its components become very hot (you need to take care when you work inside a laser printer to avoid burning yourself). The hot components are actually the cause of the burnt paper. Most likely, the burn occurred because the paper remained in contact with the printer's heated fuser rollers, which are discussed later in this lesson.

The key to understanding laser printer operations is the role of the printer drum. The drum is a cylindrical device that resides in the toner cartridge. Using the laser, the printer places a charge onto the surface of the drum that corresponds to the image that later attracts the toner. As the paper moves past the drum, the printer transfers the toner from the drum onto the page.

To print a page, the primary corona wire in the laser printer first applies a strong positive charge to the entire surface of the drum so that the drum will attract the laser toner.

Next—and here's where the laser actually comes into play—the printer will use its laser to discharge the areas on the printer drum that do not correspond to the image the printer is going to print. In other words, the printer draws the page contents onto the drum electronically by removing the positive charge previously assigned to the drum's surface area. The parts of the drum that correspond to the regions that will print will retain the positive charge to attract the toner.

The charged drum will then collect toner from the ink cartridge. The toner will collect on those areas of the drum that the printer previously charged.

Next, to transfer the toner onto the paper, a second corona wire, called the transfer corona, will assign a strong negative charge to the entire sheet of paper. As the paper moves past the drum, the printer will transfer the toner from the drum onto the paper (the toner will be attracted to the paper's charge).

Then, rollers inside the printer, which users often refer to as fusers, will melt the toner onto the page. The rollers essentially iron the toner onto the page.

After the page prints, wiper blades inside the printer will scrap any residue from the drum. In addition, an "eraser" lamp will expose the drum to a light that eliminates any remaining charge from the surface of the drum.

Understanding Laser Printer Problems

The laser printer contains powerful electronics. Never work inside the laser printer while it is plugged in. Further, as the laser printer performs its operations, the printer can generate considerable heat. Be very careful when you clean the printer or remove a piece of jammed paper. Many of the printer's components are very hot and can severely burn you.

Over time, the laser printer drum may become scratched or the surface may become damaged in a way that prevents the surface from effectively holding a charge. In some cases, your output may appear streaked. In such cases, you must simply replace the toner cartridge that contains the drum. Remember, you should not place a used toner cartridge in the trash. Instead, you should return the unused cartridge to either the cartridge manufacturer for recycling or to a facility that handles hazardous materials.

Eventually, the toner cartridge will become low on toner and you will need to replace it. Often, by gently shaking the cartridge from left to right, as shown in Figure 52.2, you can extend the cartridge's life for a few more printouts.

Figure 52.2 To extend the life a toner cartridge, gently shake the cartridge from left to right.

EXAM REVIEW

① **True or False**
The toner cartridge contains toner (ink) and the printer's drum.

② **The printer's primary corona wire applies a charge to the**
_____ whereas the transfer corona wire applies a charge to
the _____.

③ **The printer uses heated rollers that users often refer to as**
_____ to melt the toner ink onto the page.

Understanding CDs, DVDs, and Writable Media

Years ago, programs were shipped on one or more floppy disks. As programs became more powerful and complex, it was not uncommon for a program to require five or more floppies. In the mid-1980s, hard disks ranged in size from 10 to 20MB. At that time, it was common for users to back up their hard disks to floppies.

By the early 1990s, most new PCs were being shipped with CD-ROM drives included, and users made extensive use of multimedia upgrade kits to install CD-ROM drives and sound cards into older PCs. Software manufacturers quickly took advantage of the CD-ROM technology and began shipping their programs on CDs. Because the storage capacity of most hard drives now exceeded 100MB, many users migrated to tape drives to perform backups.

Today, many PCs ship with DVD-based drives that not only let PCs play moves, but which can also retrieve the programs and data stored on a traditional CD. To simplify the process of backing up large files, many users install drives that can record data onto a writable CD.

This lesson examines the evolution of CDs, DVDs, and writable media.

- CD-ROM is an acronym for compact disc read-only memory. A PC can read information (programs and data) from a CD-ROM, but a PC cannot record information on the disc.

- CD-ROM discs only store information on one side of the disc.

- A CD-ROM disc typically stores 700MB of data.

- To record data, the CD-ROM disc represents ones and zeros using the presence and absence of pits on the disc's surface. To read the disc's contents, the CD-ROM drive uses a laser to bounce a beam of light off the surface. The areas on the disc that do not contain pits reflect the beam. The areas on the surface that contain pits do not.

- The original single-speed CD-ROM drives (also called 1X drives) supported a transfer rate of 150KBs. Later, double-speed (2X) CD-ROM drives supported 300KBs.

- Today, CD-ROM drives support very high transfer rates. A 36-speed drive (also called a 36X drive), supports 5.4MBs (or 36 times the original 150KBs transfer rate). Likewise, a 48-speed (48X) drive supports 7.2MBs.

- CD-ROM discs, like hard and floppy disks, use a file system to organize the data that the disc contains. Users refer to the CD-ROM file system as CDFS as well as Joliet, ISO-9660, or the High Sierra format.

- CD-ROM discs that contain only data use the CDFS file system. Discs that contain audio (such as a music CD) use CD-DA (compact disc digital audio). A multimode CD supports CDFS and CD-DA.

- Today, many PCs support CD burners that can be used to create (burn) CDs. Using a CD burner (also called a CD writer), users can create a disc that contains data and programs or a disc that contains digital audio. Some CD burners provide software which users can use to create multimode discs that contain music and data.

- The original "writable" CD-ROM discs were CD-R discs (for compact disc recordable). Users refer to CD-R discs as write once read many (WORM) discs because the user could only record data onto the disc one time, but later, the contents of disc could be read an unlimited number of times.

- Today, most writable CDs are CD-RW (compact disc rewritable) discs. Using a CD-RW disc, you can record multiple sessions to the same disc. CD-RW discs provide a convenient way for users to back up large files.

Understanding CD-ROMs

In the early 1990s, as programs increased in size, it became infeasible for software manufacturers to distribute programs on floppy disk—the large programs simply would require too many floppies. Further, multimedia programs that integrated video, audio, and animations, required tremendous amounts of data.

To provide a way to better distribute programs and data, hardware manufacturers developed CD-ROM discs and drives. CD-ROM is an acronym for compact disc read only memory. Unlike a floppy, hard disk, or Zip disk, the contents of which a user can change by simply magnetizing data onto the disk's surface, a user cannot change or add to the contents of a CD-ROM disc—the disc can only be read.

A CD-ROM disc can store up to 700MB of data and programs. The disc stores data (and programs) by representing the data's ones and zeros through the presence or absence of microscopic pits that appear on the disc's surface. To read the disc's contents, the CD-ROM drive uses a laser to bounce light off the disc's surface (the disc only stores data on one side). The areas on the disc that contain pits do not reflect the light whereas the areas without pits do. Using the pitted and unpitted regions, the disc can represent zeros and ones.

Making Sense of CD-ROM Drive Speeds

When CD-ROM drives were first released, the drives could transfer data at a rate of 150KBs. Unfortunately, these initial CD-ROM drives were not fast enough for users to fully exploit multimedia. For example, assume that a program wanted to display a video within a 320x240 window at 30 frames per second. Assuming the video used only minimal colors (256 colors), the drive would need to support a data rate of over 2MBs as shown here:

320 x 240 = 76,800 pixels at one byte per pixel

30 frames per second x 76,800 bytes per frame = 2,304,000 bytes per second

To reduce data throughput demands, many early multimedia programs reduced the size of the data window as well as the frame rate.

Over time, hardware manufacturers released double-speed drives (2X drives) which were so named because the drives supported a 300KBs data transfer rate (or two times the rate of the 150KBs drive). Today, PCs commonly use 36-speed (36X) and 48-speed (48X) drives which are capable of data throughput rates of 5.4MBs and 7.2MBs.

Storing Data and Audio

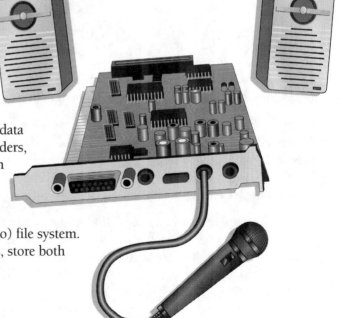

Users typically think of CD-ROM discs as storing only programs and data. However, the music industry makes extensive use of CDs to store and distribute music. To organize data on a CD-ROM within files and folders, CD-ROMs use a special file system called CDFS (compact disc file system). Likewise, to store music (or other audio), CDs use the CD-DA (compact disc digital audio) file system. Some CDs, called multimode CDs, store both data and audio.

Caring for and Maintaining CDs and DVDs

CDs only store data on one side of the disc. Some DVDs store data on both sides of the disc. To protect the disc from scratches, smudges, and spills, you should place discs that you are not using into a protective plastic cover, as shown in Figure 53.1.

Figure 53.1 Protect discs you are not using by storing them in a protective plastic case.

Should your CD-ROM drive experience problems when it tries to read a disc's contents, you may need to clean the disc's surface. If the disc is dusty, you can use an aerosol blower to remove the dust. If the disc contains smudges, you should use a soft cloth to clean the disc's surface, as shown in Figure 53.2. To clean the disc using a cloth, gently rub the disc's surface from the center of the disc outward. Do not rub the disc's surface in a circular fashion.

Figure 53.2 If a CD-ROM drive cannot read a disc's contents, try cleaning the disc's surface.

Recording Data on a CD

CD-ROMs are so named because they are read-only devices. You cannot record information onto a CD-ROM disc.

You can, however, store information (data and programs) onto CD-R and CD-RW discs using a special device that users call a CD burner or CD writer. The CD burner can read an existing disc's contents and can write data to a special disc. The surface of the CD-R and CD-RW discs contains a special reflective dye. To record data onto the disc, the burner changes the characteristics of the dye to create a pit-like region that will absorb (as opposed to reflecting) the drive's laser beam.

The original writable CDs were CD-R discs. CD-R stands for compact disc recordable. Using a CD-R disc, users could write data (files and folders) to a disc. Users refer to CD-R discs as WORM discs because users would write data to the disc one time (the WO stands for write once) and later read the disc many times (the RM stands for read many).

Today, most writable CDs are CD-RW discs. CD-RW stands for compact disk rewritable. Using software, a CD burner can overwrite the contents of a CD-RW disc thousands of times. In general, to reuse a CD-RW disc's contents, the software reformats the disc by restoring the dye on the disc's surface to its original reflective state.

Because of their large storage capacity, writable CDs are ideal for backing up large files. In less than an hour, a CD burner can easily back up 650MB of data.

Understanding Multiple Recording Sessions

Users refer to the process of recording data onto a CD-R or CD-RW disc as a session. Many CD burners allow you to place data onto a disc using multiple sessions. In other words, you might use the burner on Monday to copy that day's new files to a disc. Then, on Tuesday, you might place a second session onto the disc that contains that day's new files. By Friday, the disc would contain five sessions.

When you create a session, you do not overwrite the disc's previous contents. Instead, you simply append new data to that which you previously recorded onto the disc.

Many older CD-ROM drives do not support multisession discs. If one drive can read a disc that you have created and a second drive cannot, the problem is likely the multiple sessions. In some cases you can resolve the problem by directing the CD burner software to "close" the disc, which marks the disc's last session. After you close a disc, you cannot later add another session to the disc.

Understanding DVDs

Today, users typically think of DVDs in terms of movies. The DVD's tremendous storage capacity makes the discs very well suited to store several hours of full-motion video. The original DVDs were capable of storing 1.4GB of data. Newer DVDs can now store up to 17GB. In addition, depending on its type, a DVD drive can transfer data at rates ranging from 1.385MBs to over 22MBs.

DVDs can store data, programs, video, and audio. To organize the information they store, DVDs use the Universal Data Format (UDF) file system. Today, DVD burners exist that can be used to record data onto a special DVD-R or DVD-RW disc. However, the cost of the DVD burners is much higher than a CD burner.

EXAM REVIEW

1. Single speed CD-ROM drives can transfer data at _____ KBs.

2. True or False
   CD-ROMs normally store data on one side of the disc. A 2X CD-ROM drive, however, can read data from both sides of the disc.

3. CDs that can store both data and audio are called _____ discs.

4. True or False
   CDs organize data (files and folders) using the CFS file system.

5. CD-R is an acronym for _____.

6. True or False
   Users refer to CD-R discs as WORM discs because the user can record multiple sessions to the disc.

7. Users also refer to the CDFS file system as the _____, _____, or _____.

8. CD-RW is an acronym for _____.

9. A DVD drive can store up to _____ GB.

10. DVDs organize data, audio, and video using the _____ file system.

11. WORM is an acronym for _____.

12. A 24X CD-ROM drive can transfer data at a rate of _____MBs.

Lesson 54

Understanding Modem Operations

Users make extensive use of modems to connect PCs to the Internet. Although high-speed cable and DSL modems have become quite popular, most users still connect to the Net using a dial-up modem. Surprisingly, the speed and function of dial-up modems has not changed much over the years. As CPUs, disk drives, and networks have gotten much faster, dial-up modems have remained pretty much the same.

This lesson examines the basics of modem operations. We will look at how a modem sends and receives signals across a telephone line, and you will learn the fundamental concepts of data communication. Then, you will learn why dial-up modems do not support speeds beyond 56Kbs.

F A C T S

- Modem is an acronym for modulate/demodulate.

- Modems allow two computers to exchange information over standard phone lines.

- Across the Internet, most users connect to the Net using a dial-up modem connection.

- Modems are so named because to send data, the modem must modulate (convert) a digital value into an analog waveform for transmissions. Later, when the signal arrives at the receiving modem, that modem demodulates the analog wave, converting it back into a digital value.

- Before two modems can exchange data, the modems must agree on a communication speed and other settings such as the number of data bits and the use of parity and a stop bit.

- As modems send data across a phone line, transmission errors may change the data. Parity provides a way for modems to detect errors that change only the value of one bit.

- Modems can agree to use odd, even, or no parity. Even or odd parity corresponds to the number of bits in a message that are set to one. Using the parity bit, the sending modem can ensure the number of bits in the message are one or even as agreed. If the receiving modem finds an odd number of bits are one and the modems have agreed to use even parity, the receiver knows that a transmission error occurred.

- Because parity can only detect single-bit errors, modems often disable the use of parity and instead use error-correcting codes that not only can detect errors, but which can correct the errors.

- To help you monitor and troubleshoot modem operations, most external modems provide small LED lights that the modem illuminates as it performs different operations.

Modems Modulate and Demodulate Signals

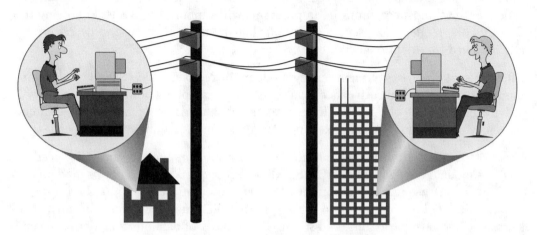

The term modem is an acronym for modulate/demodulate, two terms that describe how a modem sends and receives data across a standard telephone line.

Within a PC, information resides in a digital format, which the PC represents using ones and zeros. To send information across a phone line, a modem must convert the digital signals into an analog (wave) signal suitable for transmission. The term modulate describes the process of converting digital values into the corresponding analog wave.

When a modem receives an analog signal, the modem must covert the signal into the corresponding digital values. In other words, the modem must demodulate the signal. Within a modem, a UART (Universal Asynchronous Receiver Transmitter) chip oversees the sending and receiving of individual bits.

Understanding Low-Level Data Communication

Behind the scenes, before modems can communicate, they must agree on the communication speeds and the format of the messages they will exchange. Users frequently refer to the speed and data format as data communication settings. Modems normally communicate using full-duplex operations, which means data can travel to and from the modem at the same. In contrast, simplex communication occurs in only one direction and half-duplex communications can occur in both directions, but in only one direction at a time.

Modem communications occur asynchronously, which means that the sender and receiver do not synchronize when a transmission will start. Instead, each modem listens to the phone wire for incoming data. A sending modem will begin a communication by sending a start bit, which directs the receiver to wake up and prepare for the incoming data.

The number of bits a modem uses to represent data defines the message's data bits. Modems normally represent data using 8 bits. However, depending on the communication settings, most communication programs will support 4 to 8 bits. Following the data bits, the modem may send a parity bit that the modem can use to detect errors, and followed by an optional stop bit.

After the start bit arrives at the receiving modem, the receiver knows, based on the communication speed, when each data bit will arrive. For example, at 56Kbs, the data bits will arrive every 1/56,000 of a second. To receive the incoming data, the modem will examine the data communication wire at fixed intervals based on the communication speed.

Users often use the term baud rate to describe a modem's communication speed. A 28.8Kbs modem can send or receive 28.8Kb per second. Likewise, a 56Kbs modem can send 56Kb per second. It is important to understand that the baud rate does not correspond to data bits, but rather to total bits. To send a message, a modem must send start bits, stop bits, parity bits, and so on. The number of data bits a modem can send per second depends on the other bit settings. For example, if the modems are using 1 start bit, 8 data bits, 1 parity bit, and 1 stop bit, for a total of 11 bits, the maximum amount of data a 56Kbs connection can send per second would be 56Kb ÷ 11, or roughly 5KB per second.

Understanding Error-Correcting Codes (ECC)

As a signal travels across the phone line, errors may occur that change the corresponding data. To detect simple (single-bit) errors, modems often use a parity bit. Unfortunately, if an error changes two bit values, a parity bit will not detect the error.

Depending on the data communication settings, a parity bit will make the total number of bits whose value is 1 an even number or an odd number. For example, in the data bits 10110011, there are five bits that are one, resulting in an odd number of bits. If the data communication settings are using *odd parity*, the parity bit would be 0, so that when you count the number of bits set to 1, and add the parity bit (o), the total will remain odd. In contrast, if the data communication settings are using even parity, the parity bit would be set to 1, so when you add up the number of data bits that are set to 1 (five), and you add the parity bit, you would get an even value (six).

Assume that two modems are communicating using odd parity. The sender will send the data bits and parity setting that contains an odd number of bits, such as 00000011 and 1. If the receiver receives an even number of bits set to one, such as 00000001 and 1, the receiver knows that somewhere in the data a bit error occurred and the receiver should direct the sender to resend the data. However, if the errors result in an odd number of bits set to one, such as 00000000 and 1, the sender will assume the transmission is correct because the count of the number of bits set to 1 is odd.

Because of the parity bit's limited error-detection capabilities, modems will often disable parity and rely on more complex error-correction codes (ECCs) that not only detect errors, but also can determine which bit or bits have changed and then correct the data so the modems do not have to retransmit the incorrect data.

The use of error-correcting codes requires modems to send additional bits that they can use to detect and, if necessary, correct bit changes. These additional bits consume bandwidth that could otherwise have been used to send data. However, because they eliminate the need to retransmit incorrect data, most modems employ error-correcting codes during their transmissions.

Making Sense of Modem Lights

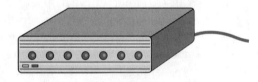

If you are using an external modem to connect to a standard phone line, your modem will normally have a series of LED lights you can use to understand your modem's current operations, and you can potentially troubleshoot modem problems. Table 54.1 briefly describes the lights that may appear on an external modem.

Light	Description	Meaning
AA	Auto Answer	The modem will answer an incoming call.
CD	Carrier Detect	Two modems have successfully established a connection.
HS	High Speed	The modem is transmitting at its highest possible speed.
MR	Modem Ready	The modem is on and operational.
OH	Off Hook	The modem has a dial tone and is ready for use.
RD	Receive Data	When flashing, the modem is receiving data.
SD	Send Data	When flashing, the modem is sending data.
TR	Terminal Ready	Normally indicates that a data communications program is running.

Table 54.1 Using modem lights to monitor modem operations.

Understanding AT Commands

To let users fine-tune modem operations, most modems support a set of "AT" commands, so named because the commands begin with the letters AT. In general, the letters AT ask the modem for its attention, because a command will follow. The AT command ATD800-555-1212 directs the modem to dial a specific number. Likewise, the AT command ATDT800-555-1212 also directs the modem to dial a number, but this time, using touch-tone dialing. Using AT commands, users can control a modem's volume, the initial connection speeds, and so on. Several sites on the Web provide a complete listing of the standard AT commands.

Installing a Modem

Modems can be either internal or external devices. External modems can connect to a USB, serial, or bi-directional parallel port. Internal modems will reside within one of the PC's expansion slots. Today, most internal modems are plug-and-play devices which greatly simplifies the device's installation (you normally do not have to worry about IRQ and I/O port settings).

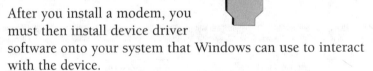

After you install a modem, you must then install device driver software onto your system that Windows can use to interact with the device.

As shown in Figure 54.1, modems normally provide two phone jacks, one labeled Line and one Phone. You connect the cable from the wall jack to the port labeled Line. If you want to share the phone line between your modem and a phone, you can plug the phone cable into the port labeled Phone. If your modem does not find a dial tone, make sure you have connected the phone jack to the modem port labeled Line and not the port labeled Phone.

Figure 54.1 Connect the phone jack on the wall to the modem port labeled Line.

Understanding Why Dial-Up Modems are Still Slow

In Lesson 55, you will examine high-speed DSL and cable modems. As briefly discussed, the speed of dial-up modems has not changed much over the years—at least not at the same rate as other PC devices such as CPU speeds.

As it turns out, the 56Kbs speed limitation is not due to modem technology, but rather, to phone companies and the Federal Communications Commission (FCC). Some older telephone equipment limits modem speeds to 35Kbs. If you are using an older, poorer-quality phone line, your speeds may become even slower. Further, because of noise on the line, phone companies with newer equipment may choose to limit speeds on analog lines to 35Kbs.

In the best case, if your connection travels only through fast-switching components, your dial-up connection will only achieve speeds of up to 53Kbs. That's because speeds beyond 53Kbs would consume more electricity. To eliminate the increased electrical use, the Federal Communication Commission (FCC) limits dial-up connections to a maximum of 53Kbs.

EXAM REVIEW

A+ CERTIFICATION

① Modem is an acronym for _____.

② Data communication operations that can send and receive data in both directions at the same time use _____ operations. In contrast, operations that send data in only one direction at a time use _____.

③ Within the modem, a special chip called the _____ oversees the sending and receiving of individual bits.

④ ECC is an acronym for _____.

⑤ True or False
Using parity, a modem can detect and correct data communication errors.

⑥ Assuming two modems are using 8-bit data and odd parity, what parity value would the sending modem use for the data 00001110?

⑦ True or False
The start bit directs the receiving modem to "wake up" because a data bit will follow shortly.

⑧ True or False
If a modem does not find a dial tone, it is possible that the user has connected the phone jack to the modem port labeled Phone as opposed to the port labeled Line.

Taking Advantage of High-Speed Internet Connections

n Lesson 54, "Understanding Modem Operations," you examined modem operations in detail. Today, most businesses connect computers that reside in a local-area network to high-speed Internet connections. While larger businesses use expensive and very fast leased lines, such as T1 and T3 connections, many smaller businesses take advantage of fast, yet cost-effective digital subscriber line (DSL) connections.

In addition, many users now connect their home PCs to DSL- and cable-based Internet connections. As you will learn in this lesson, such high-speed connections make use of the PC's network capabilities. In other words, to attach a PC to a high-speed connection, you connect a DSL or cable modem to a network interface card that resides within the PC.

By the time you finish this lesson, you will not only understand how to connect a PC to a high-speed Internet connection, you will also understand the various speeds different technologies offer. Further, you will learn how you can share a single Internet connection with multiple PCs in an office or your home.

F A C T S

+ Many small businesses and home-based PCs take advantage of high-speed cable and DSL Internet connections.

+ DSL is an acronym for digital subscriber line. In general, DSL is a technology that supports high-speed data connections over standard phone lines.

+ A cable modem is a modem that connects to a standard TV jack that you would normally use to receive television signals.

+ To connect a DSL or cable modem to a PC, the phone or cable company will install a DSL or cable modem that connects to a phone or cable outlet on the wall. Then, they will connect the modem to a network interface card that resides inside the PC.

+ To share a high-speed Internet connection in a home or office, you must simply connect the network cable that comes off the DSL or cable modem to a network hub (wired or wireless) that supports wide-area network (WAN) operations and which can act as a DHCP router to provide IP addresses for each PC.

+ For most users, faster download speeds is more important than upload speeds. Often, the phone or cable company may offer connection packages that provide fast download speeds and slower upload speeds.

+ When you surf the Web, your connection's download speed controls the rate at which your PC can retrieve (download) text and graphics. In contrast, your connection's upload speed controls the rate at which your PC can send data (which normally corresponds to keyboard input and mouse operations).

Connecting a PC to a High-Speed Internet Connection

Whether you connect a PC (or network) to a DSL or cable connection, the steps you will perform are quite similar. To begin, the phone or cable company will connect a DSL or cable modem (as appropriate) to a phone plug or cable jack. Then, the company will attach the modem to a network interface card (often an Ethernet card) that resides inside your PC. Figure 55.1, for example, shows a cable modem connected to a cable jack on the wall. The cable modem, in turn, connects to a network interface card inside the PC.

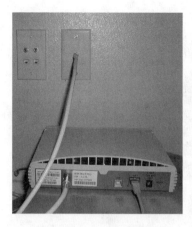

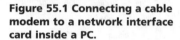

Figure 55.1 Connecting a cable modem to a network interface card inside a PC.

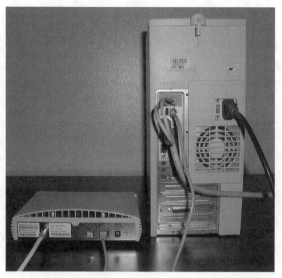

Recently, to simplify cable and DSL installations (and to simplify standard network connections), network manufacturers have released USB-based network interface devices. Using the USB-based network interface, you can easily connect a PC (such as a notebook) that does not have a built-in network interface card to a network.

Sharing a High-Speed Internet Connection

Because the DSL and cable modem connections use a network interface card, sharing a high-speed Internet connection in an office or home has become quite simple. If you are using "wired" network connections to attach PCs to a network hub, you simply connect the "network cable" that comes off the DSL or cable modem to the wide-area network (WAN) port on the network router that supports DSL or cable operations, as shown in Figure 55.2. Then, you must configure the PCs within the network to use the cable or DSL connection as their "gateway" to the Internet.

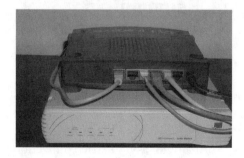

Figure 55.2 Sharing a cable or DSL modem connection using a network hub.

To share a high-speed connection in a home, where you likely do not want to run network cables, you can take advantage of a wireless network hub that supports a cable or DSL connection. Then, as shown in Figure 55.3, you can install a PCI-based or USB-based wireless network receiver/transmitter that lets the PC communicate with other wireless devices to a distance of up to 300 feet. The cost of sharing a high-speed connection using wireless hardware in this way is less than $100 per PC. In addition to sharing the Internet, the PCs that use the wireless hardware can perform standard network operations (such as sharing files and printers) across the wireless connection.

Figure 55.3 Using a wireless hub to connect PCs that use wireless receiver/transmitters.

BEYOND A+ CERTIFICATION

Leasing a High-Speed Connection

For years, to obtain a high-speed Internet connection, many businesses leased lines from the phone company. The most commonly used leased line was the T1 line, which provided businesses with speeds up to 1.5Mbs for less than $1,000 per month. Larger companies used T3 lines that, at a cost of nearly $10,000 per month, provided data rates of up to 45Mbs. The T1 and T3 lines are unique in that the lines provide the high-data speeds across two pair! For companies wanting yet faster speeds, the OC-1 and OC-3 fiber-optic technologies support data rates greater than a gigabit per second.

Understanding Symmetric and Asymmetric Data Rates

When you shop for DSL- and cable-modem connections, you will find that the cable and phone companies will offer various price plans that correspond to different data rates. Often, the company will describe a rate as being symmetric or asymmetric. In general, symmetric data rates provide the same upload (data from your PC to the Internet) and download (data from the Internet to your PC) rates. In contrast, asymmetric data rates have different upload and download speeds. Normally, an asymmetric connection will provide a higher download than upload data rate.

For most users, having a lower upload speed is not a problem. As you surf the Web, the data you upload often simply corresponds to the Web addresses that correspond to a hyperlink you select with your mouse or that you enter at the keyboard. In contrast, when you view a Web page, the remote server must download the page's text and graphics to your PC—which makes the download speed very significant.

If you have a Web site that receives tens of thousands of hits per day, having a faster upload speed from your server to the Internet could become important. Otherwise, as you shop for a high-speed Internet connection, select a package that provides a fast, cost-effective, download speed. Depending on the package you select, for example, you might receive download speeds of 1.5Mbs and an upload speed of 300Kbs.

Using a Satellite-Based Connection

Today, for many people who live outside of a major city, a satellite-based TV antennae provides the only way to receive a wide range of television stations. In a similar way, if you live beyond the cable- or DSL-modem services, you may want to use a satellite-based Internet connection.

For years, satellite connections provided users with relatively high-speed download capabilities. Meaning, the satellite antennae could receive data, but it could not send data back to the satellite. To use a satellite-based connection, a PC would receive data from the antennae and send data via a dial-up connection using a standard modem.

In other words, each time the user clicks on a hyperlink within a Web page, or the user typed data into a search engine, the PC would send the data across the Internet over a dial-up connection. To receive the selected Web page text and graphics, however, the PC would use the fast satellite connection.

Because the amount of data a user would normally send (keyboard and mouse operations) was quite small, the slow dial-up connection did not severely impact a user's ability to surf the Web without interruption.

Installing a High-Speed Internet Connection

As it turns out, installing a high-speed DSL- or cable-based Internet connection is actually quite simple. In fact, the phone or cable company will normally do all the work for you. In addition, the company will normally provide you with the DSL or cable modem as well as a network interface card for your PC.

EXAM REVIEW

CERTIFICATION

1. True or False
   To use a DSL- or cable-modem connection, you must install either a cable or DSL modem into your PC that Windows will use to access the Internet.

2. DSL is an acronym for _____.

3. A(n) _____ connection provides the same upload and download speeds.

4. True or False
   To share a high-speed Internet connection, you simply must connect the cable or DSL modem to a hub (wired or wireless) that supports a WAN connection and which can function as a DHCP server.

Lesson 56

Understanding File Attributes

Files provide users with long-term storage of information from one user session to another. Regardless of the type of information a file contains, such as a word processing document, spreadsheet, or graphics image, the operating system stores the file's contents on disk in the same way.

When you create a file, the operating system assigns several attributes to the file, such as the current date and time and the file's size in bytes. In addition, most operating systems will let you assign attributes that prevent the file from being inadvertently deleted, that mark the file as needing to be backed up, and so on.

This lesson examines the Windows file attributes and the steps you must perform to take advantage of the attributes.

F A C T S

✦ Each file on your disk has specific attributes, such as the file's size and the date and time you created the file or last changed the file's contents. In addition, Windows lets you set or clear a file's archive, hidden, read only, and system attributes.

✦ The archive attribute specifies whether a file has been created or changed since the last backup operation.

✦ The hidden attribute determines whether or not a file appears within a folder's file list.

✦ The read only attribute controls whether or not a user can change or delete a file's contents.

✦ The system attribute indicates that a file is a key operating system file.

✦ If you are using the NTFS file system under Windows 2000, you can also use the compress and encrypt file attributes.

Understanding the Windows File Attributes

Depending on the version of Windows that you are using, the file attributes you can set will differ slightly. Table 56.1 briefly describes the file attributes supported by all Windows versions.

Attribute	Purpose
Archive	Marks a file as requiring or not requiring a backup.
Hidden	Hides a file within a folder's file list.
Read only	Prevents a file's contents from being deleted or changed.
System	Indicates that the file is a key operating system file.

Table 56.1 File attributes supported by all Windows versions.

If you are using Windows 2000 (or Windows NT), you can also assign the attributes listed in Table 56.2.

Attribute	Purpose
Compress	Compresses a file's contents to reduce disk consumption.
Encrypt	Encrypts a file's contents for increased security.

Table 56.2 Additional file attributes supported by Windows 2000.

Viewing and Setting File Attributes

Using the Windows Explorer, you can view or set a file's attributes by right-clicking on the file and then selecting Properties from the pop-up menu. The Explorer, in turn, will display the file's Properties dialog box, as shown in Figure 56.1. Within the Properties dialog box, you set an attribute by placing a checkmark in the corresponding checkbox. To clear an attribute, you remove the checkmark.

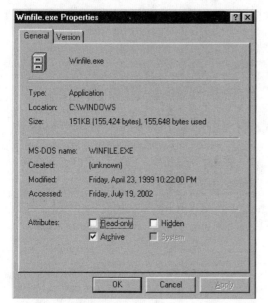

Figure 56.1 Using the Properties dialog box to set or clear file attributes.

If you are using Windows 2000 and the NTFS file system, you can select the Advanced button within the Properties dialog box to display the Advanced Attributes dialog box as shown in Figure 56.2. Within the Advanced Attributes dialog box, you can compress or encrypt a file's contents or change the file's archive attribute.

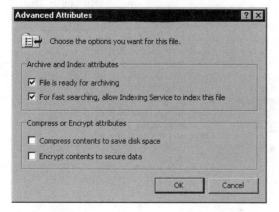

Figure 56.2 Using the Advanced Attributes dialog box in Windows 2000.

Taking Advantage of the Archive Attribute

Each time you create or change a file's contents, Windows sets the file's archive attribute, which indicates to a backup program that the file's contents are either new or have been changed and that the software should back up the file. After the backup program successfully backs up the file, the backup program will clear the archive attribute.

By taking advantage of the archive attribute, you can direct a backup program to back up only those files that are new or the contents of which have been changed since the previous backup. That way, you do not have to back up every file on your disk every time you perform a backup. By backing up only those files that have been created or changed since the last backup, you can complete a backup operation very quickly.

Normally, a user may back up all the files on his or her disk at the start of the month. Then, each day for the rest of the month, the user will back up only those files that are new or have been changed that day (actually since the previous backup operation the day before). The user must keep the tapes or disks for the complete backup operation as well as the daily backups. When the user successfully backs up the disk at the start of the next month, the user can recycle (overwrite) the previous tapes or disks.

Taking Advantage of the Read-Only Attribute

Using the Windows Explorer, you can quickly delete one or more files or folders. Likewise, by performing a file copy operation, you can overwrite one file's contents with that of another. To prevent an incorrect file operation from destroying (or deleting) the contents of a key file, many users take advantage of the read only file attribute.

When set, a file's read only attribute tells Windows that a user can view or print a file's contents (meaning a program can read the file's contents), but the user cannot delete or change the file.

Should you set the read only attribute for a file that contains a Microsoft Word document, you will later be able to open, view, and print the document, but you cannot save any changes that you make to the document to the same file. Likewise, should you try to delete a read only file within the Windows Explorer, the Explorer will display the Confirm File Delete dialog box similar to that shown in Figure 56.3 that states you are trying to delete a read only file and then forces you to select Yes to confirm that you truly want to delete the file.

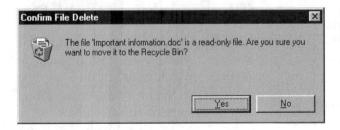

Figure 56.3 Windows will prompt you before deleting a read only file.

Taking Advantage of the Hidden Attribute

By default, when you create a file, programs such as the Windows Explorer will list the file within the corresponding folder's file list. Likewise, the file will appear within dialog boxes such as the Open and Save As dialog box.

Depending on the information that a file contains, there may be times when you do not want the programs to list the file. For example, if you are using your company's computer to create your resume, you may not want others to be able to readily view your file's contents. By directing programs not to include the file within the program's file list, you reduce the chance of another user locating the file.

Using the hidden file attribute, you can direct programs not to include a file within a folder's file list. In other words, the hidden attribute gives you the ability to hide a file from others.

If you are a system administrator or if you cannot remember the name you assigned to a file that you have hidden, there may be times when you want to view the hidden files that reside in a folder. To list hidden files within a folder's file list using the Windows Explorer, perform these steps:

Within Explorer, select the folder whose hidden files you want to view.

1. If you are using Windows 98, select the View menu Folder Options entry. If you are using Windows 2000, select the Tools menu Folder Options entry. Windows, in turn, will display the Folder Options dialog box.

2. Within the Folder Options dialog box, click on the View tab. Windows will display the View sheet as shown in Figure 56.4.

3. Within the View sheet, select the Show all files option and then choose OK.

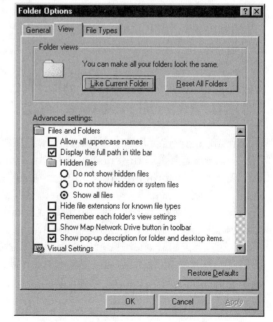

Figure 56.4 Directing Windows Explorer to list hidden files.

Taking Advantage of the System Attribute

The system attribute, like the hidden attribute, directs the system to not display the file within a folder's list of files. In addition, the system attribute marks the file as being necessary for the operating system. Windows, for example, might assign the system attribute to a key startup file or DLL file. In general, users should not set or clear a file's system attribute. In fact, Windows 2000 does not allow users to do so.

Taking Advantage of the Windows 2000 Encrypt Attribute

If you are using the NTFS file system under Windows 2000, you can direct Windows to encrypt a file's or folder's contents by setting the file's encrypt attribute. After you encrypt a file, you can use the file just as you normally would. In other words, if you encrypt a file that contains a Word document, you do not have to decrypt the file before you can use its contents. Instead, you would simply open the file within Word. Behind the scenes, Windows will decrypt the file as necessary. Should another user gain access to your folder, that user would not be able to use the file's content. Windows only decrypts the file for the user that created the file.

To reduce system overhead, you should only encrypt those files or folders with contents you do not want other users to access. Because Windows must decrypt a file before you can open it and then must again encrypt the file when you close it, encryption adds overhead to the file operations.

Taking Advantage of the Windows 2000 Compress Attribute

If you are using NTFS under Windows 2000, you can direct Windows to compress a file, folder, or disk's contents in order to save disk space. Unlike Windows 9x that used the DriveSpace program to compress a drive by creating a large file that contains a disk's contents within a compressed file, the NTFS file system can compress and decompress files on the fly. Although compressing files may save disk space, it also adds system overhead because Windows must decompress a file before you can use the file's contents and then later compress the file when you are done. That said, if you have files or folders that you do not use on a regular basis, you may want to free up disk space by compressing them.

EXAM REVIEW

(1) True or False
Setting a file's read only attribute prevents users from changing a file's contents.

(2) True or False
Setting a file's read only attribute prevents a user from deleting the file using the Windows Explorer.

(3) To prevent a file from appearing within a folder's file list, you should set the file's _____ attribute.

(4) True or False
If you are using the NTFS file system within Windows 2000, you can use file attributes to compress or to encrypt a file.

(5) The _____ file attribute specifies whether or not a file has been created or changed since the last backup operation.

Index

Notes